OUR NORTH AMERICA

The International Political Economy of New Regionalisms Series

The International Political Economy of New Regionalisms series presents innovative analyses of a range of novel regional relations and institutions. Going beyond established, formal, interstate economic organizations, this essential series provides informed interdisciplinary and international research and debate about myriad heterogeneous intermediate level interactions.

Reflective of its cosmopolitan and creative orientation, this series is developed by an international editorial team of established and emerging scholars in both the South and North. It reinforces ongoing networks of analysts in both academia and think-tanks as well as international agencies concerned with micro-, meso- and macro-level regionalisms.

Editorial Board

Timothy M. Shaw, Visiting Professor, University of Massachusetts, Boston, USA
Isidro Morales, Instituto Tecnológico de Estudios Superiores de Monterrey (ITESM), Mexico
Maria Nzomo, University of Nairobi, Kenya
Nicola Phillips, University of Manchester, UK
Johan Saravanamuttu, Institute of Southeast Asian Studies, Singapore
Fredrik Söderbaum, School of Global Studies, University of Gothenburg, Sweden and UNU-CRIS, Belgium

Recent titles in the series (continued at the back of the book)

Roads to Regionalism
Genesis, Design, and Effects of Regional Organizations
*Edited by Tanja A. Börzel, Lukas Goltermann,
Mathis Lohaus and Kai Striebinger*

New Regionalism or No Regionalism?
Emerging Regionalism in the Black Sea Area
Edited by Ruxandra Ivan

Community of Insecurity
SADC's Struggle for Peace and Security in Southern Africa
Laurie Nathan

Our North America
Social and Political Issues beyond NAFTA

Edited by
JULIÁN CASTRO-REA
University of Alberta, Canada

LONDON AND NEW YORK

First published 2012 by Ashgate Publishing

2 Park Square, Milton Park, Abingdon, Oxon OX14 4RN
711 Third Avenue, New York, NY 10017, USA

First issued in paperback 2016

Routledge is an imprint of the Taylor & Francis Group, an informa business

Copyright © Julián Castro-Rea 2012

Julián Castro-Rea has asserted his right under the Copyright, Designs and Patents Act, 1988, to be identified as the editor of this work.

All rights reserved. No part of this book may be reprinted or reproduced or utilised in any form or by any electronic, mechanical, or other means, now known or hereafter invented, including photocopying and recording, or in any information storage or retrieval system, without permission in writing from the publishers.

Notice:
Product or corporate names may be trademarks or registered trademarks, and are used only for identification and explanation without intent to infringe.

British Library Cataloguing in Publication Data
Our North America : social and political issues beyond
   NAFTA. -- (The international political economy of new
   regionalisms series)
   1. North America--Civilization. 2. North America--
   Population. 3. Civil society--North America.
   4. Intergovernmental cooperation--North America. 5. North
   America--Economic integration.
   I. Series II. Castro-Rea, Julián.
   970'.05412-dc23

Library of Congress Cataloging-in-Publication Data
Our North America : social and political issues beyond NAFTA / [edited] by Julián Castro-Rea.
   p. cm. -- (The international political economy of new regionalisms series)
   Includes bibliographical references and index.
   ISBN 978-1-4094-3873-1 (hardback) -- ISBN 978-1-4094-3874-8 (ebook)
 1. North America--Politics and government--20th century. 2. North
America--Politics and government--21st century. 3. Regionalism--North
America. 4. North America--Economic integration. I. Castro Rea, Julián.
   JJ1010.O87 2012
   327.7--dc23

2011036066

ISBN 13 : 978-1-4094-3873-1 (hbk)
ISBN 13: 978-1-138-26168-6 (pbk)

To Camilo, with love

Contents

List of Tables and Figures		ix
List of Abbreviations		xi
Notes on Contributors		xiii

1 Introduction   1
  Julián Castro-Rea

PART I   THE FIRST NORTH AMERICA, THEN AND NOW

2 Indigeneity and Transnational Routes and Roads in North America   27
  Isabel Altamirano-Jiménez

PART II   NORTH AMERICAN INTEGRATION: DEVELOPMENT AND CHALLENGES

3 The Uncertain Politics of North American Economic Integration   45
  Greg Anderson

4 The Security and Prosperity Partnership: Made in North America Integration or Co-operation?   67
  Jimena Jiménez

5 The Security and Prosperity Partnership: The Short History of a Strategic Bargain   85
  Janine Brodie

PART III   MIGRATION

6 A Dialectical Understanding of the Vulnerability of International Migrants   109
  Jorge A. Bustamante

PART IV   THE DEMOCRATIC DEFICIT

7 Canada and North American Integration – Bringing in Civil Society?   139
  Laura Macdonald

| 8 | Making Room for Democracy: Three Moments in the Struggle Against Trade and Investment Regimes in the Americas
John W. Foster | 151 |

PART V IDENTITIES IN FLUX

| 9 | Slippery Borders: Negotiating North American Hybrid Identities
Victoria Ruétalo | 171 |
| 10 | Our North America: A Continent of Cultural Change
James Lull | 183 |

PART VI INTERGOVERNMENTAL RELATIONS

11	Canada–US Relations: The Contemporary Imbalance *Tom Keating*	199
12	Saying 'NO' to North America: Canadian and Mexican Perspectives *Athanasios Hristoulas*	217
13	Critique of Mexico–US Relations: Beyond the Contemporary Impasse *Raymond A. Morrow*	231

PART VII CONCLUSIONS

| 14 | North America: A Trilateral, Bilateral, or Unilateral Space?
Stephen Clarkson | 255 |
| 15 | Our North America? From the Mexican Standpoint, Not Yet
Lorenzo Meyer | 271 |

| *Bibliography* | *283* |
| *Index* | *311* |

List of Tables and Figures

Tables

1.1	North America: Geographic and demographic facts	5
1.2	North America as world region	7
1.3	North America: Economic outlook	10
1.4	North America: Market integration	11
3.1	Trade within North America	48
5.1	Setting the agenda	93
5.2	Building consensus	93
5.3	Consolidating North America as a security community	94

Figures

6.1	Dialectic of migrants' vulnerability	129
9.1	*America* (1989), by Greg Curnoe. Printed with permission from Ms Sheila Curnoe and the Thielsen Gallery, London, Ontario Canada.	177
10.1	*Barrio Fino* album cover, Daddy Yankee (2004). Produced by the artist's own record label: EL CARTEL RECORDS. This album was a significant contribution in music industry.	184

List of Abbreviations

AFL-CIO	American Federation of Labor-Congress of Industrial Organizations
ASEAN	Association of Southeast Asian Nations
BITs	Bilateral investment treaty
CARICOM	Caribbean Community
CCCE	Canadian Council of Chief Executives
CEC	Commission for Environmental Cooperation
CFR	Council of Foreign Relations
CISEN	Centro de Investigación y Seguridad Nacional, Government of Mexico
CUFTA	Canada–US Free Trade Agreement
CUSP	Canada–US Partnership
DFAIT	Department of Foreign Affairs and International Trade, Government of Canada
DHS	Department of Homeland Security, Government of the United States
DI	Deep integration
DR–CAFTA	Dominican Republic–Central America Free Trade Agreement (DR / US / Central America)
EU	European Union
FDI	Foreign Direct Investment
FIOB	Frente Indígena Oaxaqueño Binacional (Binational Organisations Indigenous Front)
FTAA	Free Trade Area of the Americas
GATS	General Agreement on Trade and Services
GATT	General Agreement on Tariffs and Trade
HSA–ASC	Hemispheric Social Alliance – Alianza Social Continental
IBETS	Integrated Border Enforcement Teams (Canada–US)
ICC	International Criminal Court
IJC	International Joint Commission
ILO	International Labour Organisation, United Nations system
INS	Immigration and Naturalization Service (US)
ITF	Independent Task Force on the Future of North America
Mercosur	Mercado Común del Sur (Southern Common Market)
MI	Mérida Initiative (2007)
NAAEC	North American Agreement on Environmental Co-operation
NAALC	North American Agreement on Labour Co-operation

NACC	North American Competitiveness Council
NAFTA	North American Free Trade Agreement
NASPI	North American Security and Prosperity Initiative
NORAD	North American Aerospace Defence Command
NORTHCOM	Northern Command, US Department of Defense
OAS	Organization of American States (successor to the Pan American Union)
PAN	Partido Acción Nacional (Mexico)
PRI	Partido Revolucionario Institucional (Mexico)
PRD	Partido de la Revolución Democrática (Mexico)
PTA	Preferential Trading Agreement
RQIC	Réseau québécois sur l'intégration continentale (Quebec Network on Continental Integration)
SAGIT	Sectoral Advisory Group on International Trade
SLA	Softwood Lumber Agreement (2006)
SPP	Security and Prosperity Partnership of North America
TNC	Transnational corporation
WTO	World Trade Organization

Notes on Contributors

Isabel Altamirano-Jiménez (PhD, University of Alberta) is an assistant professor in the Department of Political Science and the Faculty of Native Studies at the University of Alberta. She wrote a dissertation entitled 'The Politics of Tradition: Aboriginal Self-Government and Women. Mexico and Canada in Comparative Perspective', currently under revision for publication with the University of British Columbia Press. In 2002, she joined the project Neo-Liberal Globalism and Its Challengers: Reclaiming the Commons in the Semi-Periphery – Canada, Australia, Mexico, and Norway. Among her recent publications are: 'Indigenous Political Autonomy and Self-government: Mexico and Canada in Comparative Perspective' in *Native Americas*, Summer 2003; and 'North American First Peoples: Slipping up into Market Citizenship?' in *Citizenship Studies*, December, 2004. Her research interests are: Aboriginal issues, citizenship, nationalism, gender issues, and Indigenous development.

Greg Anderson (PhD, Paul H. Nitze School of Advanced International Studies, Johns Hopkins University) is an assistant professor in the Department of Political Science, University of Alberta. He is also a Fellow of and Research Director for the Alberta Institute for American Studies at the same university. His research interests include Canadian–US relations, US foreign policy, and US foreign economic policy, with a particular emphasis on US trade policy and trade policy institutions. From 2000 to 2002, he worked in the Office of the United States Trade Representative as a policy analyst in the NAFTA office.

Janine Brodie (PhD, Carleton University) is a professor of political science at the University of Alberta. She served as department chair from 1997 to 2003. She was elected as a Fellow of the Royal Society of Canada in 2002, awarded a Canada Research Chair (Political Economy and Social Governance) in 2004, and a Trudeau Fellowship in 2010. Before joining the University of Alberta in 1996, she was Faculty Fellow of the Institute for Social Research at York University, Toronto and the first director of the York Centre for Feminist Research. Dr Brodie held the John Robarts Chair in Canadian Studies in 1994 at York University and the University of Western Ontario Visiting Chair in Public Policy in 1995. She has published over a dozen books and edited collections as well as numerous chapters and journal articles in the fields of Canadian political economy, gender politics, globalization, and social policy. She has also served as a consultant for, among others, the Royal Commission on Electoral Reform and Party Financing,

Status of Women Canada, the Attorney General of Ontario, and the Law Reform Commission of Canada.

Jorge Bustamante (PhD, University of Notre Dame) is Eugene Conley Professor of Sociology at the University of Notre Dame. He is founding president of El Colegio de la Frontera Norte, the prominent Mexican institute for the study of border issues. He is the author of numerous studies on the sociology of the US/Mexico border region and on Mexican-origin residents in the US. Dr Bustamante is a leading participant in international scholarly networks dealing with these themes and has played a major role in building and sustaining scholarly linkages between Mexico and the US. In 1988, Mexico's President awarded Dr Bustamante the Premio Nacional de Ciencias, the highest award granted to scholars by the Mexican government. He was also presented with the National Award on Demography for his research on Mexican migration to the US. In January 2001, Dr Bustamante was appointed to the advisory group on immigration and population policies by Mexico's Secretariat of Foreign Relations (SRE). On July 2005, he was appointed Special Rapporteur for the Rights of Migrants by the United Nations Commission on Human Rights. He was the recipient of the 2007 Cox–Johnson–Frazier Award, the highest award granted by the American Sociological Association.

Julián Castro-Rea (PhD, Université de Montréal) is an associate professor of political science at the University of Alberta. His broad research interest is North American politics from both comparative and trilateral perspectives, focused on particular issues such as federalism, nationalism, Aboriginal peoples, elections, and foreign policy, among others. He has written extensively on these issues. Among his recent publications are: 'After the PRI: Neo-Liberalism and Nationalism in Mexico', in *Against Orthodoxy: Studies in Nationalism*, edited by T. Harrison and S. Drakulic (University of British Columbia Press, 2011); 'Evolución, no revolución: la vía canadiense a la independencia', in *Historia comparada de las Américas. Sus procesos independentistas*, edited by P. Galeana (Mexico's Senate–Pan-American Institute of Geography and History, 2010); *Encyclopaedia of Case Study Research*, edited by A.J. Mills, G. Durepos, and E. Wiebe (Sage, 2009), s.v. 'Hypothesis'; 'Assessing North American Politics after September 11: Security, Democracy, and Sovereignty', in *Contentious Politics in North America: National Protest and Transnational Collaboration under Continental Integration*, edited by J. Ayres and L. Macdonald (Palgrave Macmillan, 2009). He is fully fluent in the three official languages of North America.

Stephen Clarkson (D. de Rech., Université de Paris) is Professor of Political Economy, University of Toronto where he specializes in North American integration. Among many other writings, he is the author of *Dependent America? How Canada and Mexico Construct US Power* (2011), *Does North America Exist? Governing the Continent After NAFTA and 9/11* (2008), and of the acclaimed

Uncle Sam and Us: Globalization, Neoconservatism and the Canadian State (2002); co-author of *Trudeau and Our Times, vol. 1: The Magnificent Obsession* (1990); *Trudeau and Our Times, vol. 2: The Heroic Delusion* (1994); and *A Perilous Imbalance: The Globalization of Canadian Law and Governance* (2009); and editor of *An Independent Foreign Policy for Canada?* (1968). He is a Fellow of the Royal Society of Canada and has been inducted into the Order of Canada.

John W. Foster (PhD, University of Toronto, D.D. (Hons), St. Andrew's College) is a lecturer in political science at Carleton University and at the University of Regina. He was principal researcher at the North–South Institute (Ottawa, 2000–2010), with a focus on civil society and global governance. Dr Foster has participated in a number of UN processes and conferences, including Financing for Development (Monterrey, 1992 and Doha, 2008). He has served as a member of Canadian delegations to the World Summit on Sustainable Development (Copenhagen, 1995 and Geneva, 2000). Dr Foster is well known as a speaker and writer, with an extensive bibliography of publications in such areas as human rights, globalization and health, AIDS and development, reform of international institutions, foreign policy, and social justice. He has twice been editor of the *Social Development Review* (International Council on Social Welfare), and a contributor to a number of events sponsored by the Montreal International Forum, the World Forum of Networks, the Worldwide Alliance for Citizen Participation, the Global Partnership for the Prevention of Armed Conflict, and the Stanley Foundation, among others. His recent publications include *Governing Globalization – Globalizing Governance: New Approaches to Global Problem Solving* (Finnish Ministry of Foreign Affairs, 2005); and 'NAFTA Beyond the Security and Prosperity Partnership', in *The USA and Canada 2011* (Routledge, 2010).

Athanasios Hristoulas (PhD, McGill University) is Professor of International Relations as well as the co-ordinator of the National Security Program at the Instituto Tecnológico Autónomo de México in Mexico City. He also regularly teaches at the Mexican Naval and Army Staff colleges. Before moving to Mexico from Canada, he was Military and Strategic Post-Doctoral Fellow at the Norman Paterson School of International Affairs, Carleton University. His research interests include civil–military relations, Mexican defence and national security policy, and Canada–Mexico–US relations. His most recent publications include two edited volumes, one on civil-military relations and the other on Canadian government and politics.

Jimena Jiménez (PhD, Carleton University) is a policy analyst/conseillère politique, North America Bureau/Direction générale de l'Amérique du Nord, Department of Foreign Affairs Canada/ministère des Affaires étrangères du Canada. Her PhD dissertation deals with the political implications of NAFTA.

Tom Keating (PhD, Dalhousie University) is a professor at, and former chair of, the Department of Political Science at the University of Alberta. He teaches in the areas of Canadian foreign policy and international relations. He is the author of *Canada and World Order. The Multilateralist Tradition in Canadian Foreign Policy* (Oxford University Press, 2002) and co-editor, with Andy Knight, of *Global Politics* (Oxford University Press, 2010).

James Lull is a professor emeritus of communication studies at San José State University, specializing in media and cultural studies. Prof. Lull has received two Fulbright scholarships, one that took him to Brazil in 1992, and another to Mexico in 1997. He was also granted a Leverhulme Trust Fellowship by England in 2002. Prof. Lull has taught courses at universities in Latin America, Asia, and Europe. He is author or editor of eleven books in English, subsequently translated into many languages. Fluent in Spanish, he has published many original articles in that language, and regularly teaches and conducts research in Mexico, South America, Central America, and Spain. Prof. Lull is also active in the popular media: he has worked for years as a professional journalist, media programmer, and radio announcer. Recently he has appeared as a cultural commentator on CNN, the BBC, National Public Radio, and many other radio and television stations in the US and abroad.

Laura Macdonald (PhD, York University) is a professor in the Department of Political Science and the Institute of Political Economy, and director of the Centre on North American Politics and Society at Carleton University. She is a former director of the Institute of Political Economy. She is the author of *Supporting Civil Society: The Political Impact of Non-Governmental Assistance to Central America* (Macmillan, 1997); and co-editor with Jeffrey Ayres, of *Contentious Politics in North America: National Protest and Transnational Collaboration under Continental Integration* (Palgrave Macmillan, 2009). Dr Macdonald has published numerous articles in journals and edited collections on such issues as the role of non-governmental organizations in development, global civil society, citizenship struggles in Latin America, Canadian development assistance, and the political impact of NAFTA on human rights and democracy in the three member states.

Lorenzo Meyer (Doctorado, El Colegio de México) has been a professor since 1970 at the Centre for International Studies at El Colegio de México in Mexico City, where he also directs the US–Mexican Studies Program. He has written eleven books on subjects ranging from domestic Mexican politics during the 1920s and '30s to contemporary Mexico and the US–Mexico relationship. He writes a weekly column in *Reforma*, one of Mexico's national newspapers, and hosts a weekly show on public television.

Raymond A. Morrow is a professor emeritus of sociology and an adjunct professor of educational policy studies at the University of Alberta. He taught and has published widely in the areas of social and political theory, methodology, cultural studies, and education. His current research includes work on Mexican intellectuals and democratic transition. His book *Critical Theory and Methodology* (Sage) was selected as a 1994 *Choice Magazine* Academic Book of the Year. In collaboration with Carlos Alberto Torres (UCLA), he has also published *Social Theory and Education: A Critique of Theories of Social and Cultural Reproduction* (SUNY Press, 1995) and *Reading Freire and Habermas: Critical Pedagogy and Transformative Change* (Columbia University Press, 2002).

Victoria Ruétalo (PhD, Tulane University) is an associate professor of Spanish and Latin American Studies in the Department of Modern Languages and Cultural Studies, University of Alberta. Her essays on Latin American film, popular culture, and cultural studies have been published, among other places, in *Studies in Latin American Popular Culture*, *Quarterly Review of Film and Video*, *Journal of Latin American Cultural Studies*, *Cultural Critique*, and in various anthologies. She has co-edited with Dolores Tierney *Latsploitation, Exploitation Cinemas, and Latin America* (Routledge, 2009). She is currently working on a manuscript about the work of Argentine sexploitation duo Armando Bó and Isabel Sarli.

Chapter 1
Introduction[1]

Julián Castro-Rea

'All animals are equal but some animals are more equal than others.'
George Orwell, *Animal Farm*, 1945.

Since 2005, once every year, the presidents of Mexico and the US and Canada's prime minister have met to discuss the future of North American integration. Despite some attempts at minimizing before the public opinion the importance of the issues under discussion, the meetings' agendas have in fact been quite ambitious. Until the April 2008 meeting, the agendas built on the Security and Prosperity Partnership (SPP) agreement that the North American leaders had adopted in their first Summit. SPP included broad areas of co-operation such as competitiveness, food safety, energy and environmental co-ordination, smart and secure borders, and emergency management and preparedness. In August 2009, however, the SPP was discreetly discontinued, under the pressure of the financial crisis and with new leadership in the White House. None the less, by holding uninterruptedly annual meetings, the three leaders are sending a message to the rest of the world about the existence of North America as an economic reality, and as a region that increasingly boasts a distinct global identity.

This book is about North America. This apparently simple, straightforward statement requires several clarifications:

First, North America comprises three, not two, sovereign states. Quite commonly, either in the media or even in general academic literature, people refer to 'North America' as a shorthand for 'Canada and the United States'. This book claims that this assumption is not only wrong but also ideologically loaded. The appropriation of the term North America by its two wealthier sovereign states means drawing a geopolitical line separating the global North from the South, the First from the Third World, and predominantly Anglo-Protestant cultures from a predominantly Ibero–Catholic one. Thus, restricting the term North America to the two northernmost countries builds on the old narrative of the 'Black Legend', according to which Britain stood on a moral high ground in its colonial enterprises because it was not a decadent and degenerate imperial power such as Spain.[2]

This ideological separation, moreover, obscures the deep undercurrents that explain not only present-day North America but also its centuries-old

---

1 I wish to thank Laura Way for her assistance in preparing this introduction. She compiled the statistical data and helped prepare the tables presented in this introduction.

2 See Isabel Altamirano-Jiménez's chapter in this book.

development process. Mexico has always been part of this joint process, either from the historical, economic, demographic, political, or cultural vantage points. Its presence has had consequences on the way the rest of the continent has evolved. It is easy to understand why the state-building processes in Canada and Mexico have been shaped by their constant concern with keeping the US' expansionism at bay – not always successfully. However, it is equally true that the US would not be what it is without the Mexican influence to the South and the Canadian presence in the North. Think of migration, labour, supply of natural resources, industrial production, expanded markets, social and family relations, cultural spill-over, and pollution, for example. Capillarity[3] of all kinds defines North America because it has occurred for centuries, affecting neighbouring populations and their cultures regardless of whether their governments have taken note of this influence.

Second, North America is about much more than trade and other economic transactions. Understandably, many analysts often see the region exclusively as an economic space, for North America's 'coming-out party' – its introduction to the world as a distinct region – was the North American Free Trade Agreement (NAFTA), launched in 1994. This perception, however, ignores the more complex realities that have shaped and still presently give form to the region. For example, to the extent that economic exchanges depend on government regulation, the policy apparatuses in the three NAFTA countries are now reciprocally influenced. The influence is compounded by the media presence of one country in the two others, which in turn creates patterns of emulation and encourages more economic exchanges.

For these reasons, this book does not focus primarily on economic issues such as trade and investment, which have been extensively studied from the moment NAFTA was first proposed in the early 1990s. Instead, the book aims at filling the gaps left by many previous studies about North America. It includes contributions from other disciplines of the social sciences besides economics, reflecting the belief that such eclecticism is the only sure way to make sense of the continent's complex realities. North America is indeed a tightly intertwined network of human relations, where power, wealth, ethnicity, gender, culture, family ties, and societal relations in general create a complex mix of interactions.

Third, the scope of this book is limited to societal realities in North America. Of course, other crucial commonalities bind the region together: think of the environment, migratory species, energy, transportation, and natural resources, for instance. This book, however, aims at contributing to the understanding of the

---

3   In physics, capillarity is 'the action by which the surface of a liquid where it is in contact with a solid is elevated or depressed depending on the relative attraction of the molecules of the liquid for each other and for those of the solid.' From "Capillarity" (2008). In *Merriam-Webster Online Dictionary*. Retrieved May 2011, from http://www.merriam-webster.com/dictionary/capillarity. Metaphorically, I refer here to the tendency of domestic societal issues to penetrate porous borders and affect the people within each of the three North American neighbours.

region by making use exclusively of the tools offered by the social sciences and, to a more limited extent, the humanities.

Fourth, most of the contributors to this book see North America as a single unit of analysis which has to be studied as a full entity, and not as either three countries or three separate bilateral relationships. Admittedly, some developments in the region are the result of the interactions between three distinct sovereign states. However, many realities make sense only if we look at them as unfolding in a single social space. For example, population movements within North America are not only a currently sensitive political issue between Mexico, the US and, more recently, Canada; they are also human realities that have shaped the very formation of the three national states. This human flow has in turn provoked shifts in relative regional political weight, the creation of new identities, and the emergence of new economic realities that keep shaping the North American region in an endlessly transformative way.

The title of this book is an invitation to the readers, likely inhabitants of the North American continent, to start thinking in different ways about the place they live in. North America is so much more than a collection of three countries casually located side by side, or than a marriage of convenience for business purposes, or than the large stretch of land sitting 'out there' in our global neighbourhood. It is, rather, a historically constructed human space, perceived from time immemorial as a unified whole which its original inhabitants called Turtle Island. Moreover, the reader is invited to realize that the North American architecture of today has an impact on virtually every aspect of the lives of the people residing there. Conversely, the shape that social structures and practices adopt is defined by the values and everyday actions (or lack thereof) of those people.

The title also pays homage to Cuban patriot José Martí's classic essay 'Our America'. Originally published in New York City in January 1891, this essay is an invitation to the peoples of the Americas to look beyond borders, and acknowledge similarities and common goals. 'Nations that do not know one another should quickly become acquainted', Martí wrote more than 120 years ago, a statement that also expresses, to a large extent, the purpose of this book.

Overall then, by calling this book *Our North America* we are inviting readers residing in North America to embrace their belonging to this continent, and to feel that everything happening within this part of the world is their concern and common responsibility. The future of North America depends not only on what the governments do, but on what all the people who live there decide to achieve.

Facts and Trends Defining North America Today

While we claim North America may be understood as a single and coherent reality, its complexity requires some breakdown for analytical purposes. Moreover, being a living reality, North America is constantly changing, so making absolute and definitive statements about its current state is quite difficult. Nonetheless, this observer has been able to identify several facts and trends that define its present form and will likely condition its immediate future.

North America occupies a large, easily identifiable chunk of land mass in the Northern Hemisphere, between the Atlantic, Pacific, and Arctic Oceans. It encompasses the second-, fourth-, and fourteenth-largest countries in the world, with a total land area of over 21.5 million km^2. Totalling close to half a billion people (451,911,120) as of July 2009, North America's population is considerable, although its demographic density and growth rate are relatively low by world standards. The region is also relatively well off in terms of average health and education indicators, even though Mexico lags slightly behind in those terms.

Table 1.1 provides more detail on North America's geographic and demographic realities.

Perhaps North America's most defining factor is asymmetry. More precisely, the fact that a world power – arguably today's undisputed world power – is part of the continent. This situation, unparalleled in other world regions, exerts a lasting influence over every aspect of regional dynamics. Internationally, it singles out North America as a peculiar region, not quite like any other. Internally, US predominance is a silently acknowledged fact, usually not mentioned in formal co-operative efforts in the region, but nonetheless implicitly accepted by all actors. Asymmetry is the main reason why North America is not a community of equals, will not become one in the foreseeable future and, as a global region, will never move in any direction where the US does not want to go.

Asymmetry is a reality not only among states, but also among sub-regions and human populations within the region, manifested in uneven regional development, socio-economic inequality, and skewed patterns of political influence. This situation has been a constant throughout North America's historical development; although the centres of population, wealth, and power have shifted over time, both outside and within present-day national state borders.[4] Rather than confront it head on, policy makers and other influential actors have accepted asymmetry as almost a natural feature, thus making room for the Orwellian paradox cited as an epigraph to this introduction: denizens of North America are supposed to be part of a community of equals, but deep real differences among them are regarded as inevitable.

Table 1.2 summarizes, from a global comparative perspective, North America's standing relative to other blocs and leading economies. Although in many respects North America's importance is overshadowed by the sum of all other world regions and major countries as an aggregate, its status is secure as one of the global poles of economic activity, with access to large territories and the resources found in them, sizeable population, and a high political standing in the UN.

In fact, in more than one respect, North America is the world's leading region. This fact, of course, has to do with the presence of the world's superpower within

---

4 For example, from at least the fourteenth to the seventeenth century, central Mexico was the most prosperous and influential region in North America.

Table 1.1 North America: Geographic and Demographic Facts

Attribute	Canada	Mexico	United States	Total or Avg. Selected Fields
Physical:				
Territorial area (sq km)[1]	9,984,670	1,972,550	9,826,630	21,783,850
World rank	2	15	3	
People:				
Population (2008 est.)[1]	33,487,208	111,211,789	307,212,123	451,911,120
World rank	36	11	3	
Growth rate (%)[1]	0.817	1.13	0.977	0.974
Population density (pop./km²)[7]	3.35	56.37	31.2	20.74
Birth rate (births/1,000 pop.)[1]	10.28	19.71	13.83	14.6
World rank	140	104	154	
Change 1998–2006 (yrs %)[2]	-5.34	*n/s	-3.15	
Fertility rate (children born/woman)[1]	1.58	2.34	2.05	1.99
Death rate (deaths/1,000 pop.)[1]	7.74	4.8	8.38	
World rank	113	192	107	
Change 1998–2006 (yrs %)[2]	8.33	n/s	-3.95	
Life expectancy[1]	81.3	76.06	78.11	78.49
World rank	7	71	49	
Change 1998–2006 (yrs %)[2]	3.57	n/s	1.57	
Health factors[4]				
Obesity (% of adult pop. with MMI>30 kg/m2)	22.4 (2004)	10.9 (2002)	30.6 (2002)	
Tobacco consumption (% of daily smokers among adult pop., 2004)	15.0	30.0	17.0	
Alcohol consumption (litres/person, age 15 plus, 2003)	7.9	4.6	8.4	
Number of people 15 and over who have HIV/AIDS/1,000 pop. (2005 est.)[5]	1.82	1.69	4.02	
		* n/s: not specified		

Table 1.1   Continued

Attribute	Canada	Mexico	United States	Total or Avg. Selected Fields
Healthcare expenditure:[3]				
Public spending on health in % of GDP	6.7	2.8	6.6	
Private spending on health in % of GDP	2.9	3.4	8.1	
Total (2002)	9.6	6.2	14.7	
Literacy rate:[1]				
Age 15+ who can read & write (%) (2003-04 est.)	99	91	99	96.33
Relative poverty:[3]				
Proportion of the population below 50% median income poverty threshold (2000)	10.30	20.30	17.10	
Family income inequality:[1]				
GINI Index (2008 est.)	32.1	48.2	45	41.76
Child poverty:[3]				
Share of children 17 years & under living in households with disposable income less than 50% of median income	13.60	24.80	21.70	
Net migration rate: migrants/1,000 pop.[1] (2007 est.)	5.63	-3.61	4.32	

Sources
1. CIA – *The World Fact Book*, online, July 2009 estimate.
2. Adapted from the CIA – *World Fact Book* and United Nations *Demographic Yearbook* 2002.
3. OECD 2005 Social Indicators.
4. OECD Health Data, 2006.
5. UNAIDS/WHO Epidemiological Focus on HIV/AIDS and STI, August 2006.
6. United Nations World Prospects Report (2004 revision).
7. Author's calculation.

Table 1.2   North America as World Region

Attribute	North America	EU	ASEAN	Mercosur**	Japan	China
Population:[3] (2006 est.)*	438,991,672	456,953,258	533,176,582	263,668,891	127,463,611	1,313,973,713
Territorial area:[3] (km²)*	21,588,640	3,976,372	4,493,629	11,861,825	377,835	9,596,960
UN membership: (2010)						
General Assembly	3	25	10	5	1	1
Security Council	2 (1 perm., 1 non-perm.)	2 (1 perm., 1 non-perm.)	0	1 (non-perm.)	1 (non-perm.)	1 (1 perm.)
Economic:						
GDP (trillion)[1,2] (2007 est.)*	16.165	13.31	0.79	0.93	4.664	2.225
Value of exports in millions of dollars (f.o.b/f.b.a.) (2004)	1,312,056	3,623,090	550,259	135,534	550,500***	752,200***
Value of imports in millions of dollars (c.i.f) (2004)	1,995,925	3,582,698	497,113	93,955	451,100***	631,800***

Sources and notes:
1. Official exchange rate.
2. The GDP for ASEAN does not include the amounts from Brunei and Myanmar, which were not available.
3. The data for Myanmar comes from the ASEAN website 2004 country statistics.
* CIA – The World Fact Book (North America, ASEAN, and Mercosur based on a compilation of individual member states)
** Only full members accounted for (not associate members)
*** 2005 est.

the region, but it goes beyond that. North America truly inaugurated a new phase of globalisation in the mid-1990s, consisting of a world defined by the interaction between major regional economic blocs. True, Europe had started its integrative process in the late 1950s, but it was mostly an inwards-looking integration, that is, more than anything else an attempt at creating an expanded European market. NAFTA, in contrast, was from the outset an outward-looking agreement, that is, one whose member countries created above all to enhance their international competitiveness. By implementing NAFTA, North America launched a competition with other economic blocs, starting with Europe, and followed mainly by Southeast Asia and South America. NAFTA was a decisive stepping stone for the creation of the World Trade Organization (WTO), in the process spearheading economic globalization as we know it. North America remains in a privileged position, acting as linchpin, sometimes even as ultimate referee, in this global struggle for influence (Katzenstein 2005).

Still, North America engages in fierce competition with other blocs and major economies. This competition clearly involves an effort to control markets, supplies, investment, and trade flows, but it is not about this attempt alone. Perhaps its most important aspect is political and ultimately ideological: the clash of contrasting economic models, or ways to manage economic activities with a specific mix of private and state intervention, regulation, and market liberalization. Different models generate different paradigms of regionalism. Presently, three main contenders vie for global predominance: North America, the European Union (EU), and the Asian network informally led by Japan and China. Other regional groupings have taken sides in this confrontation. Mercosur opted for the EU model, while the rest of Latin America and the Caribbean Community (CARICOM) are split between the European and North American paradigms (Cheng 2005; Cornejo 2008). While China aggressively participates in the competition for influence in Latin America (Heine 2008) and extends its activism to Africa, the Association of Southeast Asian Nations (ASEAN) countries follow the Asian leaders, Japan and China, perhaps not having much choice after all.

The three countries in the region are liberal democracies, showing none the less varied records in terms of pluralism, partisan competition, and citizen involvement. Until the election of Barack Obama as president of the United States in November 2008, all three countries were governed by leaders and parties from conservative/right-wing traditions, ideologies, and grass-roots support. This situation was quite unique in the continent, as bipartisan swings are a common occurrence in the US, and Mexico and Canada were ruled for most of the twentieth century by nationalist governments – the Partido Revolucionario Institucional (PRI) and the Liberal Party respectively – which frequently resorted to muscular economic state intervention. The current ideological landscape either may be expressing a structural ideological realignment of the citizenry in the three countries, or is probably a temporary occurrence, showing a projection of the influence that the Bush administrations and their security agenda had on the continent.

Whatever the answer, the three conservative governments clearly tightened the North American bonds as never before. At several meetings, the leaders offered each other mutual public support, thus granting enhanced ideological and diplomatic legitimacy to one another. On a more limited scale, the governments also helped each other more directly, mainly through informal consultation for policy decisions – especially for innovative matters such as reforming whole areas of state activity and for funding specific programs. This conservative co-operation has left an enduring imprint on the architecture of North America.

Government-to-government relations, although important, are only the most conspicuous expression of broader political co-operation in North America. Operating usually away from the media limelight, but publicly enough to be tracked down by interested observers, a network of civil society organizations engages in continuous cross-border collaboration. The existence of these transnational political networks has led to the emergence of what can arguably be seen as a common political space in North America (Castro-Rea 1996: 88–102), which, although working in an articulated way, is highly contentious (Macdonald and Ayres 2009). Civil society, of course, encompasses a wide array of political actors and organized interests, spanning from business to undocumented migrant workers, from feminist activists to evangelical religious advocates. These groups have realized the interconnectedness of politics in present-day North America and thus, in order to increase their effectiveness, engage in concerted activism and lobbying efforts in more than one country in the region at a time. Transnational collaboration occurs among groups such as labour, environmentalists, and women and gay rights advocates; but, arguably the most successful lobbying efforts are those of conservative organizations, who have been able to create a strong transnational right-wing movement supported by business, foundations, think tanks, advocacy groups, lobbies and, ultimately, governments (Castro-Rea 1996: 35–53; Castro-Rea 2009).

Accelerated market integration is also occurring in North America. Thanks to economic liberalization, North America has grown and reached a prominent position in world markets, although recently challenged by the financial crash. In fact, trade, investment, and production among the countries of North America have increased at a more dynamic pace than these countries' economic exchanges with the rest of the world.

Consider Tables 1.3 and 1.4, which offer a glimpse of North America's economic performance and regional market integration. Not only has the regional economy grown by around 60 per cent during the first ten years of NAFTA, but so has the relative importance of economic exchanges within North America. This development reveals that market integration did not significantly divert newly created trade outside the continent, for most trade created by NAFTA ended up inwards-oriented. This result is of concern especially for Mexico and Canada, whose dependence on foreign trade and import penetration have grown to dramatic levels (33 and 40 per cent respectively, as Table 1.3 reveals). Because

Table 1.3 North America: Economic outlook

Attribute	Canada	Mexico	United States
Gross domestic product: (US$ billion, 2009 est.)[1]			
Official exchange rate	1,319	866.3	14,270
PPP*[1]	1,287	1,473	14,250
% Growth, 1994–2004	60.20	59.69	66.43
GDP per capita: (US$, 2009)			
PPP*[1]	38,400	13,200	46,400
% Growth 1994–2004	45.41	37.19	49.17
Trade in goods and services as a %of GDP: (2004)	36.50	31.00	12.70
% Growth 1994–2004	7.99	61.46	16.51
Import penetration for goods and services as % of domestic demand: (2004)	40.70	33.70	15.20
% Growth 1994–2004	21.13	80.21	52.00
Current account balance of payments: (US$ billion)[1]	-36.32	-10.12	-380.1
Public debt as % of GDP	72.3	42.6	39.7
Unemployment rate: (%)[1]	8.5**	6.2**	9.4**
Change, 1996–2003 (%)	-21.65	-43.24	11.11

* Purchasing Power Parity.
** Does not reflect employment in the informal economy in Canada and the US (especially undocumented workers), or underemployment in Mexico (perhaps up to 25 per cent of the workforce)

Sources:
1. *CIA – The World Fact Book*, online, July 2009 estimate; all other data, *OECD Fact Book*, 2006.

of the intensity of North American exchanges, this dependence from international markets essentially means increased dependence from the US market.

Moreover, although market integration has promoted economic growth, its benefits have been very unevenly distributed. This statement applies mainly to individuals and households, but is also valid for economic sectors, sub-regions, and countries. At the household level, overall GDP per capita growth conceals widening disparities between the poorest and the richest in the continent. In the economic sectors, resource extraction, manufacturing, and retail have grown exponentially, whereas agriculture has experienced a profound restructuring, resulting in increased export-oriented production at the expense of small-scale

Table 1.4   North America: Market integration

Attribute	Canada	Mexico	United States	Total
Exports to other NA countries: (billion US$)				
1990	95.7	32.5	111.3	239.5
2004	270.1	170.4	299.9	740.4
% increase	182.2	424.3	169.4	209.4
% share of total exports, 2004				56
Exports ROW: (billion US$)				
1990	31.9	8.2	282.3	322.4
2004	46.4	18.7	518.9	584
% increase	45.4	128	83.8	81.1
% share of total exports, 2004				43.9

Source: WTO International Trade Statistics 2005.

farming operations and the people who live from them (Public Citizen). Moreover, pockets of accelerated growth coexist with neighbouring regions sidestepped by prosperity. Finally, gains from market expansion are clearer for the US, but more questionable for Canada and Mexico. More than fifteen years into NAFTA, Mexico still lags behind Canada and the US in average individual income, with a GDP per capita in purchasing power parity terms that is less than one-third that of Canada's and barely more than a fourth of the corresponding figure in the US (see Table 1.3). With a household Gini index of 50.9, Mexico also has the most economically unequal society of all three countries. Paradoxically, however, even though the US is the wealthiest country in North America and indeed in the world, household inequality is close to Mexico's in terms of Gini index, as well as in terms of both relative and child poverty (see Table 1.1).

This pattern of uneven growth and development has caused the informal economy in North America to swell to levels unimagined only a few years ago. Unaccounted-for and ill-registered – thus not contributing to the tax base – informal economic transactions do indeed explain the sheer survival of large sectors of North America's populations and even sustain the viability of some formal, open operations. For instance, remittances sent by Mexican undocumented workers in the US to their country of origin accounted for an estimated US$25 billion in 2007 (World Bank [2008]), thus surpassing the total flow of foreign direct investment (FDI) into the country for that year. The dollars sent are not only making possible the survival of families and entire communities in Mexico with scarce alternative sources of income, but are also helping to create up to 80 per cent of the new jobs in Mexico and to supply the country with the foreign currency necessary to maintain macroeconomic stability. Undocumented workers, in turn, make many agricultural and hospitality industry operations in southern US states economically viable, by providing abundant labour at rates under its legal market cost (Mize and Swords 2011). As an indication of the size of this labour pool, as of August 2008, 85 per cent of the farm workers and 56 per cent of the construction workers in the US were born in Mexico (Anon. 2008).

Informality has also led to the growth of transnational crime across North America, and the open borders that NAFTA was intended to promote are also helping illegitimate trade to thrive. Close interactions among the three countries in the region facilitate not only legal activities like trade and tourism, but also criminal activities like drug and gun smuggling. Of course, governments attempt to put an end to illegal activities but their actions are not always effective. Moreover, inter-governmental co-operation against crime is hampered by contrasting perceptions, different legal standards, and the unwillingness of governments to accept their full responsibility for the continuing existence of cross-border crime. The US government is not doing all it could to implement programs aimed at curbing domestic illegal drug consumption, and the Mexican government has not decisively tackled corruption among civilian and military public officials complicit with drug trafficking. Finally, the banking systems in all three countries launder drug money, thereby ensuring that the drug trade remains profitable.

Along with the markets, transportation systems across North America have also grown and improved their integration. Air, sea, and land (rail and road) transportation for goods and people has been subject to constantly increasing demand, and has sometimes not lived up to expectations. Disputes over the access of Mexican freight trucks to US territory pose an additional challenge to the system's ability to function effectively. North America's SuperCorridor Coalition, a tri-national alliance of business, local governments, and other stakeholders created in 1994, aims to eliminate the bottlenecks that transportation systems across North America encounter in their effort to cope with increasing demand (NASCO).

The concerns about sustainability are increasing in North America, as overexploitation of strategic resources such as water and non-renewable energy continues, and the environment is under increased strain. North America is one of the regions in the world where natural strategic resources are most intensively used and even wasted, particularly in the US, but Canada and Mexico also rank among the top consumers of strategic resources worldwide. Still, Mexico and Canada are subject to pressures from their water- and energy-thirsty common neighbour, who calls for pooling the continent's resources in an attempt to gain unlimited access to continental reserves.

The tri-lateral North American Agreement for Environmental Co-operation (NAAEC) is a NAFTA institutional by-product that was welcome by some environment advocates for allegedly providing the trade agreement with a 'green face'. However, its mandate is limited to overseeing the enforcement of domestic environmental law, and this has made the agreement ineffective at raising the overall continental standards for environmental protection (Carlsen and Nauman 2004).

North America also features relatively intense movements of people. Most movements are legal and occur within country boundaries, but a fair amount of them disregard regulations. The main factor propelling unauthorized migration is the stark individual, regional, and country-wide socio-economic disparities discussed above in section 6 (Faux 2003). The statistics in Tables 1.1 and 1.3 clearly reflect these disparities, and explain why Mexico is the only North American country with a negative migration balance.

Policy attempts to curb this flow have met with limited success, mainly because they are focused on policing rather than on addressing this problem's root causes. For instance, it is quite telling that whereas the cumulative value-added that Mexican workers created increased by 53 per cent from 1993 to 2002, real wages – minimum, contractual, and manufacturing – decreased by around 20 per cent during the same period of time (Salas 2001: 19; Canadian Auto Workers n.d.: 2). In other words, while over time Mexican workers have been contributing with more value to swelling corporate profits, every year they are less rewarded for that contribution.

Co-operation for security and military purposes also characterizes North America. The three countries in the region became allies in the Second World War, and then again during the Cold War. The level of co-operation between Canada and the US, starting with the 1940 Ogdensburg Agreement and consolidated with the creation of the North American Aerospace Defence Command (NORAD) in 1958, greatly surpassed the involvement of Mexico. In the aftermath of 11 September 2001 (9/11), this asymmetry widened, as the former countries enhanced their collaboration with the creation of the Northern Command (NORTHCOM) and joint participation in the war in Afghanistan. The February 2011 Canada–US joint declaration Beyond Borders: A Shared Vision for Perimeter Security and Economic Competitiveness seems to raise bilateral co-operation to new heights (Whitehouse 2011), thus marginalizing Mexico from North America's security architecture even further.

However, the enhanced Canada–US co-operation on defence matters hit at least two controversial limits, both originating in the US's resort to unilateralism in diplomatic and military matters: the building of a multi-billion dollar missile defence system and the war against Iraq. Both actions were perceived as beyond Canada's limits of collaboration with the US military.

Pervasive social problems plague North America, such as persisting gender disparities (Spieldoch 2004), deep socio-economic inequalities, systemic discrimination against Indigenous and other racialised people, increasing street and transnational crime, and uneven access to education and health care. No country has a monopoly on these problems, as even the wealthiest and most powerful state in the triad, the US, has alarming social deficiencies, particularly regarding relative and child poverty and the incidence of health problems (see Table 1.1). The existing institutions and policies in the three countries are vocal but barely effective at addressing those structurally entrenched problems.

The linguistic borders in the continent are blurred and do not correspond with national state borders. The US has *de facto* become an English–Spanish bilingual country, as shown in public signs in major cities, government services, product labelling and marketing campaigns (including country-wide political ads). Identities are equally ambiguous as migration spreads and electronic media reach every corner of the continent. Mixed cultures develop, blending US-made popular culture with regional identities and customs. In turn, local identities influence media messages, giving North America a distinct cultural flavour (Kirtz and Beran 2006: 119–35). Concerns about this process, perceived by some as a loss of national identity, provoke policy responses, such as declaring English the only official language in the US, the enforcement of 'Canadian content' in broadcasting, and restriction of foreign ownership of media outlets. Some ideological reactions are also noticeable, such as the debate that began in 2004 (sparked by Samuel Huntington's book, *Who Are We?* (2004)) pitching partisans of immigration control against a public in favour of borders friendlier to human flows, or the debate that began in 2007 about the 'reasonable accommodation' expected from migrants settling in Quebec.

Some observers consider that behind this cultural mix lies a gradual convergence of values encompassing North America as a whole. This convergence, these observers claim, motivated North American economic integration in the first place, and is propelling further co-operation (Inglehart *et al.* 1996). This interpretation, however, is contested by findings in the opposite direction, suggesting that core attitudes in the three countries are instead following divergent paths of transformation.[5] This mixed evidence at least suggests that a clear distinction must be made between the identities and prevailing values in any given country, and the contents of media messages and popular cultural expressions found in them.

As a corollary to all the facts and trends outlined above, some analysts argue that North America may well be experiencing a process of accelerated integration, prompted by market liberalization, which the governments would be well advised to acknowledge and support rather than attempt to reverse. Policy recommendations for 'deep integration', often presented as naturally flowing from objective academic studies, have been floated by diverse political actors and pressure groups in the three countries (Council on Foreign Relations 2005). These suggestions, however, raise the scenario of a harmonized North America led by US interests, priorities, and policies – a prospect whose benefits and liabilities are open to acrimonious debate.

---

5   See for instance Adams 2003.

Contents of this Book

The collection of chapters in this book aims at providing a portrait of the main social realities defining contemporary North America. Nevertheless, as history always has immediate contemporary relevance, historical references are unavoidable. Indeed, Tariq Ali's following observation clearly applies to North America:

> [H]istory has become subversive. The past has too much knowledge embedded in it, and therefore it's best to forget and start anew. But as everyone is discovering, you can't do this to history; it refuses to go away. If you try to suppress it, it re-emerges in a horrible fashion. (Ali and Barsamian 2005: 2)

In the following paragraphs, a summary of the contents of each chapter is presented, in the order and within the headings in which they appear in the book.

The First North America, Then and Now

Isabel Altamirano addresses the founding human realities in North America: the original Indigenous populations and the arrival of European settlers. In her chapter, she argues that, for centuries, interactions among Indigenous peoples were intense, complex, multi-layered and spatially located, through long-distance trade, warfare, marriage alliances, diplomacy, migration, and the exchange of information. However, colonialism distorted the existing links, and reconstructed North America as a racialized social space, producing different places of reference driven by colonial practices and narratives of exclusion and inclusion.

As racial formations shaped Indigenous spaces, European imperial competition influenced the transitions from colonies to national states and promoted the reproduction of racial categories and boundaries of citizenship. However, transnational Indigenous communities still challenge traditional meanings of citizenship, and remind us of the more complex interactions of the past.

North American Integration: Development and Challenges

Despite its millennia-long history, North America has been denied its very existence as a consistent geopolitical region because its space has been racially constructed. NAFTA reversed this historical denial and gave the continent a kind of birth certificate. Consequently, recent discussions about the continent and its future have usually developed within the framework of business opportunities – trade, investment, market expansion, etc. – and government-to-government diplomatic relations. Therefore, the definition of the region has been carried out mainly by government and business representatives. Greg Anderson, Jimena Jiménez, and Janine Brodie discuss this agreement's origins, implications, and spin-offs into other policy areas.

In his chapter, **Greg Anderson** discusses the future of North American integration and NAFTA as its main expression. Anderson's contribution focuses primarily on the fissures that have emerged within the agreement. To do so, the author studies a single bilateral dispute: the decades-long fight between Canada and the US over softwood lumber. This case illustrates how limited an agreement NAFTA actually is, to the extent that although the case is an outlier in terms of being an unresolved problem in NAFTA, it dramatically highlights both the limitations of the agreement itself and the obstacles to deeper forms of government-led North American integration. Indeed, this case shows that more grandiose integration projects, like the 'big idea' of deep integration[6] which has been promoted primarily by Canadian think tanks, remain limited by political realities in all three countries.

Jimena Jiménez pursues the discussion about the nature of North American integration and the development of North America as a distinct social, political, and economic entity. Critics of integration charge that the Security and Prosperity Partnership (SPP) and similar government-led initiatives represent secret schemes to form a 'North American Union' similar to the European Union, which may jeopardize the sovereignty of each member country. Others argue that SPP-like initiatives are merely ways for Canada, the US, and Mexico to co-operate and find solutions to common challenges. Jiménez's chapter asks what is really occurring in North America. Has 'political integration' – defined as the transference of political authority from the national to the supranational level – emerged in North America, or not? Is not 'co-operation' – defined as a process where countries work together to achieve common goals – a more precise description?

Jiménez argues that co-operation is increasing among the three countries, but it does not amount to integration – especially not in the way it has developed and been defined in Europe. North America's way, she argues, is pragmatic and incremental, negotiated among executives and bureaucracies away from public scrutiny, and can proceed through either trilateral or bilateral paths. Jiménez finds that, contrary to some of the theoretical formulations emerging from the European experience (such as neo-functionalism), the pressures for co-operation induced by the post-9/11 security environment, and competitive forces emanating from outside the region, did not force North America to create joint decision-making structures or supranational institutions. Jiménez concludes that major socio-political obstacles exist in the region that would prevent European-style integration from ever developing. Rather, as the North American case demonstrates, state actors can enter into a complex process of interagency co-operation in order to provide the necessary support systems needed to sustain high degrees of purely economic integration in a secure and protected North America.

After 9/11, as security became an overarching policy priority throughout North America, the US conditioned continental co-operation in any area on collaboration

---

6 'The Big Idea' is a proposal advanced by Canadian business professor Wendy Dobson in 2002, according to which Canada has to reconsider its relations with the US, embracing that country's concerns about security in exchange for improved trade relations.

on security matters. However, the measures arguably adopted to prevent the spread of terrorism have undermined people's privacy and civil liberties. Some categories of citizens such as Muslims and people of Arab descent have been especially targeted.

Janine Brodie further analyses the thorny implications of the security agenda; trying to determine to what extent 'security', very broadly defined, may still have a deeper impact on the continent. This analysis is of special relevance to Canada now that this country, under Conservative leadership, has engaged in a seemingly unstoppable wave of unprecedented co-operation with the US, even if the majority within the Canadian public has consistently opposed the idea of deeper continental integration.

Brodie argues that the SPP was the product of a relentless campaign directed largely by Canadian corporate leaders and their political allies to achieve deeper continental integration in the aftermath of 9/11. US borders were immediately closed on 9/11 and then made progressively more cumbersome as layers of security measures were imposed on borders both around and within North America. The SPP was crafted as a strategic bargain, fusing together the anxieties of Mexican and Canadian business about diminished access to the US market with Washington's preoccupations with national security. Consensus was shaped around this strategic bargain in the months following 9/11, but it ultimately failed to deliver on its twin agenda of security and prosperity for North America.

Migration

North America is a prosperous region by world standards but, as mentioned above, its wealth is distributed very unevenly. Poor farmers in Mexico, inner-city inhabitants in the US, and most Aboriginal persons in Canada have all been largely side-stepped by the prosperity created by economic growth and continental integration. Moreover, recent economic restructuring has created pockets of wealth within seas of poverty or, conversely, islands of poverty surrounded by affluence. Controls over migration within North America persisting despite increased mobility of investments, goods and services are an obstacle for the levelling of wages across borders, a situation that corporations readily make use of to maximize their profits. In all three countries, poverty strikes women more often than men, adding to other conditions of structural disadvantage for them. Poverty, ethnicity, labour, and gender intersect with one another, creating disadvantageous conditions for minorities, while policy actions have been unwilling or unable to address them and, thus, allow the informal economy to grow.

The solution that many Mexicans find to compensate for declining standards of living is international migration. The three countries of North America have been built mainly by migration throughout the centuries, and, to a large extent, still are. Migration has been, is, and will be an enduring continental issue, constantly shaping North America. Moreover, evidence indicates that, in the short term, NAFTA accelerated Mexican migration to the US (Martin 2003). Nevertheless, migration in all three countries has also always been controversial, at times even politically volatile. Debate constantly revolves around questions such as who is welcome and who is not, what are the acceptable quantities and features of newcomers, how they are going to blend into the host society, and so on.

Jorge A. Bustamante, from his expert viewpoint as a researcher of migration facts and policies for decades, discusses this complex topic. Bustamante focuses on Mexican migration to the US, providing this phenomenon's historical background to explain its transformations and political repercussions. Bustamante claims that the US government has consistently tried to solve this 'bilaterally-shaped' problem in a unilateral way, and blames the absence of a meeting of minds on the asymmetry of power between the two countries. He draws a parallel between this structural context and the corresponding asymmetry of power between Mexican farm workers and their employers in the US. Bustamante shows how various pieces of US government legislation have ignored the findings of a 1994 US Department of Labor study, which empirically defined the immigrant's labour function in agriculture as that of a 'subsidy' to the US economy.

On the other hand, the immigration of Mexican peasants to the US, he claims, represents an 'escape valve' that allows the Mexican government to deal with the increasing gap between the expectations of the Mexican peasants and its own interests. The indifference of the Mexican middle and upper classes to the problems of the migrant workers seems at odds with the national economy's dependence on the remittances of US dollars made by migrant workers. Bustamante notes that 'Only exports of Mexican oil have produced an income of US dollars per year for the Mexican economy higher than the close to US$20 billion that the Central Bank of Mexico has estimated as the total of remittances from the United States for the year 2005–2006.' This figure, we must add to underscore Bustamante's point, reached an estimated all-time high of US$25 billion in 2007.[7]

Immigrants are also politically important. Bustamante notes that the Latino vote is politically even more important in the US than NAFTA, and that Republican candidates could suffer by supporting anti-immigrant measures.[8] Both the elections of 1996 and, more clearly, of 1998, he writes, 'showed how the Latino vote of California punished the candidates of the Republican Party by giving the victory to Democrats'.

The author concludes his chapter by providing a theoretical framework – a Hegelian dialectical model, as he calls it – as an explanatory model of the vulnerability of international migrants. This framework explains how immigrants are vulnerable when they fall prey to the virtual contradiction between migration and human rights, a contradiction that has no justification in the legal realm.

---

7 Information available at http://siteresources.worldbank.org/NEWSSPANISH/Resources/remittances-LAC-SP.pdf, accessed Oct. 31, 2008.

8 As was dramatically shown by the defeat of Republican candidate John McCain in the November 2008 presidential elections in states with a high concentration of voters of Latin American descent, such as California and Florida.

The Democratic Deficit

Laura Macdonald and John Foster explore another permanent issue that has affected the development of North America: the practice of democracy in the definition of the economic integration agenda and the involvement of civil society in the process of its achievement. Critics of North American integration emphasize that all major continental initiatives have resulted from collaboration between governments and business, without significant input from ordinary citizens. This economic and political elite-driven process is not matched by any institutional or informal mechanisms that would allow for the meaningful involvement of the citizenry in the definition of present and future North America. This problem is, according to these critics, a major flaw in North American region-building. Is a democratic deficit developing in North America? What are civic organizations doing to overcome their alleged marginalization? Are they working together across borders? What are their strengths and their weaknesses?

In her chapter, **Laura Macdonald** argues that, despite Ottawa's relatively good record in attempting consultation for a wide range of trade agreements, civil society participation has been quite limited in decision-making about North American integration, probably because the stakes are highest for Canada in this domain. In order to do that, Macdonald contrasts the arguments that have been made for the inclusion of civil society in discussions of international trade agreements to an overview of actual civil society's engagement with the process of North American free trade.

As demonstrated in Canada's recent involvement in the (now discontinued) SPP, mechanisms for civil society participation in decision-making seem to be becoming increasingly rare, while big business involvement has become more institutionalised. While big business is an important actor with legitimate concerns that should be addressed, exclusion of other perspectives means that governments risk ignoring broader public concerns about a 'democratic deficit' in North America. In her conclusions, Macdonald wonders whether these trends indicate a shift to a more elitist 'club model' in future discussions of North American co-operation.

In turn, **John Foster** highlights, from his privileged position as an actor in the experiences he describes, three fairly distinct periods in approximately 15 years of civil society's engagement in issues of continental and hemispheric integration. The first of these periods is the initial engagement with the NAFTA negotiations, from roughly 1990 to mid-decade, in which the primary actors were nationally-based social coalitions allied in an informal tri-national alliance of civil society organizations and networks. The second period extends approximately from the Miami Summit of the Americas (1994), to the Mar del Plata Summit (2005), at which a hemisphere-wide association of coalitions developed the Hemispheric Social Alliance/*Alianza Social Continental* (HSA). The highlight of the third period, which Foster dates from 2001 through to the present day, has been opposition to the SPP. In this period, organizational responses involve, in part, a renovated tri-national civil society alliance.

Foster's chapter focuses on one locus within civil society: the social organizations, movements, and coalitions actively engaged and in tension with the dominant government-and corporate-sponsored generation of trade, investment, and intellectual property agreements. Foster contends that while civil society organizations have made considerable advances, these organizations' resources are scarce, and their political access is often limited, conditional, or non-existent. At the same time, those brought together by the Canadian Council of Chief Executives (CCCE) and the North American Competitiveness Council (NACC) have enjoyed much greater shares of both, and have experienced the satisfaction of seeing a good deal of their approach embodied in executive agreements at an international level. Foster points out that for civil society organizations, labour, and environmental movements, the essential issues are found not only in the details of trade, investment, and intellectual property agreements, although those are far-reaching, but also in the need to provide democratic governance.

Identities in Flux

Are specific cultures and identities threatened by continental integration? Is a common North American culture emerging? What are the impacts of technological change and cultural transformation on identities and state sovereignties? Are patterns of hybridity originally limited to border areas becoming widespread all over North America? These questions are among the many Victoria Ruétalo and James Lull address in their respective chapters.

By drawing on examples from Canadian, US, and Mexican culture, **Victoria Ruétalo** explores the use of the term 'hybrid identities' within the North American context. She argues that cultural hybridity, originally a subversive concept, has been stripped of its political value, notably by commoditisation. She therefore attempts to reformulate its use since NAFTA and post-9/11. She refers to Mexico/US border performance artist Guillermo Gómez-Peña's theorization of borders, which she believes can be useful for understanding the ever-changing reality of North America as a whole, with its constant flow of new immigrant groups. From this perspective, Ruétalo contends that the real concerns of people in the US about Mexican migration are the fear of the re-conquest of a once-lost territory and the conquest of US women by macho Mexicans. In both scenarios, fear can be overcome only by understanding and embracing the realities of racial and cultural hybrid identities.

Ruétalo concludes by suggesting a 'free idea zone' between Mexico, the US, and Canada, a zone of multi-lateral co-operation, cross-cultural dialogue, and artistic synthesis that would supplement NAFTA's economic space. She believes this 'third way' avoids the traps of nationalist chauvinism and homogenizing global consumerism. Moreover, this alternative cultural model extends NAFTA's cultural jurisdiction – limited to mass media industries and trade in fine art and antiquities – to include all other cultural expressions, not forgetting people in the process. Lastly, Ruétalo comments that with the ever-growing populations of immigrants, particularly from Latin America, Asia, and Africa in both Canada and the US, Gómez-Peña's vision of hybridity reminds us that, despite the borders that will always exist, North American hybrid identities have been forming both inside and out for a very long time and will continue to do so.

James Lull, in turn, appeals to the recent musical phenomenon *reggaetón* as a starting point for a reflection on the meaning of hybridity. He examines various phenomena related to globalization and their influence on the cultures of the Americas. As Lull points out, the confusions and contradictions of cultural hybridization, the emergence of new cultural forms (such as *reggaetón*), and the role of mass media and the cultural industries in the creation and spread of these forms brings about a vibrant cultural mix at the global level, often with a Latin American inflection. Furthermore, Lull contends that globalization will not necessarily result in some universal, technology-based super society which covers the globe and destroys local social systems and cultures. He contests the widespread thesis of US-led global cultural homogenization, claiming instead that the new global culture is a mix of multiple reciprocal influences. However, Lull does acknowledge that potent homogenizing forces such as English, Chinese, Spanish, Arabic, and other dominant languages, military weaponry, advertising techniques, internet protocol, media formats, international airports, and fashion trends undeniably affect consciousness and culture in every corner of the world.

However, Lull concludes that, despite all the effects of globalization and related phenomena, local and regional ways of thinking and living do not disappear in the face of imported cultural influences. Lull contends that delivering culturally-rich symbolic resources, television, the internet, and all other mass and micro media would open up and extend the possibilities of cultural work in every direction, resulting in, for instance, invention, creolisation, and retrenchment. While globalization is irreversible, Lull believes the global has not destroyed or replaced the local. As he points out, the very concept of culture presumes difference.

Intergovernmental Relations

The chapters in this section discuss the contemporary government-to-government relations in North America. **Tom Keating** discusses Canada–US relations, undoubtedly the most crucial global relationship from Canada's perspective and the largest bilateral trade relationship in the world. The installation of a Conservative government in Ottawa in January 2006 increased the possibility of collaboration with the powerful neighbour to the south. How real is this possibility? Is it positive or negative from a Canadian point of view, or partially both? Are there any limits to co-operation that Canada should not exceed? In whose interest is this co-operation?

Keating argues that changes in the US's domestic and foreign policies have altered domestic policy, creating an environment that is less conducive to the sort of senior level management of Canada–US relations that was used in the past. Bilateral issues are now less amenable to executive-level management, and foreign policy activities of the two countries are more likely to come into conflict in the global arena. One of the significant reasons for the deterioration in bilateral relations has been the significant changes that have occurred in the US. Equally important have been policy shifts in the way in which the US and Canada engage with the rest of the world. These policy shifts have put Canadian and US foreign policies more significantly out of synch than has traditionally been the case. To suggest that Canada should adapt in response to these changes because of the overwhelming importance of the US to Canada and especially the Canadian economy, as the current Conservative government does, is to overlook the fact that such changes would force an alignment on Canada's part to converge its foreign policy with that of the US.

The Obama election also raises the question of which policies to adapt as US policies undergo their own transition. Therefore, trying to devise a convergence of policies or to appeal to the US by supporting its most urgent security or foreign policy concerns may do little to alter the less hospitable domestic environment which confront Canadian interests in the US and generate little of real value in resolving bilateral differences. However, these changes risk affecting Canada's global standing in negative ways.

In his chapter, **Athanasios Hristoulas** discusses Canada–Mexico relations. Some analysts believe that the only relationship that matters for Canada in North America is the one with the US, because Canada and Mexico are not immediate neighbours and have little in common. This interpretation is being challenged by those who think Canada and Mexico are becoming strategic partners in North America, bound by similar approaches to foreign relations in their dealings with their common neighbour. Which interpretation is closer to reality? To what extent have Canada and Mexico been able to solidify their bilateral relationship, in a way anticipated by NAFTA, in order to avoid the 'hub and spokes' model whereby co-operation in North America is only possible when mediated by the US?

Focusing on regional security, Hristoulas perceives that the North American agenda has changed. The SPP has failed and nobody talks about deep integration any more. His chapter aims at answering why this is so, by looking at Canada-Mexico relations after 9/11 and within the context of North America. According to Hristoulas, both Canada and Mexico had resoundingly said 'NO' to further North American integration. Finally, his chapter provides a discussion of what the future might bring in Mexico–Canada relations. The central conclusion of the chapter is that very little has changed in the nature of bilateral Mexico–Canada relations. This is partly because Canada does not see Mexico as a partner in North America and partly because Mexico's attention is almost wholly absorbed by internal problems, mostly the war against drug cartels.

Finally, **Raymond A. Morrow** analyses contemporary Mexico–US relations. The relationship is complicated because it involves two countries who share a 3,000-km border. Along that border, a developing country meets the most powerful country in the world. Naturally, the least powerful one fears its neighbour, but also wishes to reap the benefits from proximity. However, in fact, influence works both ways. The mix of anxiety and opportunity found in Mexico is matched in the US: the biggest economy in the world takes advantage of Mexico's abundant supply of inexpensive workers and strategic resources, but the biggest exporter of popular culture in the world is paradoxically wary of Mexican cultural influence over US society.

Morrow discusses what he perceives as being a standoff in Mexico–US relations, fuelled by defensive nationalisms and associated feelings of mutual rejection. The stand-off between the US and Mexico on a complex set of disputes, he argues, cannot be dealt with or resolved within the presuppositions and policies maintained by the existing political elites. On both sides of the border, defensive nationalisms, political contradictions, and self-serving platitudes have fuelled hatred and anxieties that only reinforce the difficulties of the current situation. He claims that accepted theories of international relations, be they realism or neo-liberal globalization approaches, provide no alternatives to overcoming this impasse and have, in fact, only worsened the confrontation.

Instead, a critical social theory of globalization and international relations may help overcome the deadlock. Such a model, Morrow believes, results in a balanced perspective, one that remains engaged in the name of the interests of the victims on both sides of the border, irrespective of their national or ethnic origins. It provides potential alternatives to 'the bad and the ugly' paradigm, allowing longer-term emergent possibilities and transformative outcomes. Otherwise, Morrow concludes, without fundamental changes, these relations will tend to reproduce their inhumane and unjust consequences over time – even with a change of governing parties in the US.

Conclusions

Building on the discussions in the chapters, senior scholars Stephen Clarkson and Lorenzo Meyer draw the general conclusions of this collection, asking themselves what is North America's real nature, and whether it is mostly a trilateral, bilateral, or unilateral space.

Trying to grasp what North America is really about, **Stephen Clarkson** confronts its manifold realities: simultaneously a formal scheme of economic integration, a network of transnational governance agreements, a drive toward harmonization in several policy areas, and an unclear commitment to common security. North America, he finds, adopts any among these multiple shapes at the same time, depending on the issue under consideration and the observer's standpoint, being a unique reality that simultaneously is more, less, and only what meets the eye.

In turn, **Lorenzo Meyer** wonders whether the very idea of 'Our North America' is applicable to Mexico. In his view, North America as a common historical enterprise merging convergent interests under a common political arrangement is,

15 years into economic integration, still more a theoretical prospect than a reality. The gaps between Mexico on the one hand and Canada and the US on the other are not negligible and are not shrinking but widening. Nevertheless, many Mexicans, especially the poorer, resort to migration as if borders did not exist, thus making North America a *de facto* unified reality.

— o —

As a final note, I, together with all authors in this book, wish to express our hope that this volume will advance the discussion of contemporary issues in North America. We expect that this collection will contribute to providing solid grounds for the world-wide conversation now underway, and also to establishing North American studies as distinct interdisciplinary area studies.

PART I
The First North America, Then and Now

Chapter 2
Indigeneity and Transnational Routes and Roads in North America

Isabel Altamirano-Jiménez

This chapter critically and historically maps the processes, contexts, and relationships shaping the articulation of indigeneity and contemporary Indigenous politics in North America. The chapter argues that the racialized formation of North America as a social space has produced different places of reference driven by European imperial competition, complex racial categories, and boundaries of citizenship. Different systems of domination and dispossession are crucial in understanding the articulation of indigeneity, and transnational actions challenging Eurocentric geographic understandings of the region. I understand articulation as the process of producing meanings, creating practices and political possibilities. In using the concept of articulation I underline how discourse and practices are embedded in specific locations, and economic, political, and cultural processes. By exploring two Indigenous North American experiences, the Binational Organisations Indigenous Front (FIOB in Spanish) and the struggle of the transborder Tohono O'odham nation, I attempt to illustrate how these cases challenge imposed understandings of borders, sovereignty, history, and otherness.

This chapter first discusses a view of Indigenous North America. Second, the chapter attempts to analytically distinguish between settler and extractive colonialism and show how different systems of domination and subjugation have been crucial in constructing difference. Third, this chapter analyses how different colonial projects shaped the construction of an Anglo-American narrative of the region as a White, orderly space. Finally, this chapter explores Indigenous transnationalism as way to reclaim North American Indigenous roads and routes.

The Diversity of Turtle Island

Turtle Island is the Indigenous name for the continent that includes Canada, the US, and Mexico. Many Indigenous creation stories speak of Indigenous peoples coming from the unseen world to settle on the back of a huge turtle. Turtle Island is North America, a continent of difference, and of diverse cultural roads and routes. Although limited to Canada and the US, Winona LaDuke's idea of Indigenous North America can be extended to include Mexico and represent the region as an archipelago, where each island represents an Indigenous people and their territory (LaDuke 1995). Some of them were larger than others, and some were more powerful and stratified than others. This archipelago was extremely diverse and had its own social, cultural, political, and economic dynamics. Indigenous interactions occurred in different ways through trade relationships, diplomacy, cultural exchanges, and alliances. In making this argument, I am not interested in replicating a fixed or essentialized geographic understanding of Turtle Island, for it was a dynamic and contested geopolitical landscape. My intention is rather to highlight centuries of Indigenous history – economic, military, and cultural conflict and negotiation – and that history did not start with European colonization and that North America did not come into existence because of NAFTA.

One of the issues that has received a great deal of attention from archaeologists and anthropologists has been the exchanges and influences that developed between Meso-American and northern Indigenous societies. Platform mounds surmounted with temples, standard community layouts with plazas, and certain artefacts and decorative motifs have for several decades induced scholars to speculate about the cultural connections among diverse peoples (Hudson 1982; Ortiz 1983; Foster 1986). Although the connections between what is now the US southwest and Meso-America are now widely accepted, their specific influence on local development is still the subject of dispute. What is relevant for the purposes of this chapter is that in most Indigenous North American societies, trade and exchange were deeply embedded in social institutions, principles, and practices. The long-distance trade identified by archaeologists was one of the components of the wider processes that included warfare, marriage alliances, diplomacy, peoples' migration, and the exchange of information. Thus, Indigenous peoples' interactions were complex, multilayered, and spatially located.

Oral history remains an important source for tracing Indigenous interconnections. For instance, the famous myth of the origins of the Mexicas, or Aztecs, speaks of an ancient homeland, Aztlán, located somewhere north of Mexico, although not all sources agree on how far north. Influenced by the nationalist discourses of the nineteenth and early twentieth centuries, Mexican archaeologists argued that if Aztlán existed, it would have been in Colima or Chicomostoc, within Mexico's contemporary borders (Krickeberg 1971; León-Portilla 1961). Regardless of the precise location, the important issue here is that the story of Aztlán, like other similar oral accounts, remains as an example of Indigenous peoples inhabiting and travelling through Turtle Island.

Geographies of Land and Labour

The colonization of the Americas by different European empires such as the British, Spanish, and French Crowns initiated gigantic transformations in Turtle Island. Although generally speaking colonialism remapped the discursive and physical spaces and places of Indigenous peoples through a variety of mechanisms, not all empires wanted the same thing from their colonies, nor were all colonized spaces constituted evenly. British and Spanish imperial enterprises differed in important ways. In this section I attempt to analytically distinguish between settler and extractive colonialism, and I show that competing systems of domination and subjugation have been crucial in constructing an Anglo-American narrative of North America. I am aware that colonialism involved more than the English and the Spaniards; however, for analytical purposes in this section I specifically distinguish between their respective colonial projects.

Patricia Seed contends that while the English conquered land and property, the Spaniards colonized people, allowing them to retain their lands in exchange for labour, resources, and social humiliation. These different approaches did not result simply from ecological accidents and historical encounters, but rather from different traditions about valuing, transferring, and allocating wealth that emerged in Europe before colonial quests (Seed 2001: 2). Conquering land presupposed that the land was symbolically emptied (*terra nullius*) or inhabited by *homo nullius* (non-humans). Seed contents that because land was at the very foundation of the British legal system and economic transactions, the central objective of English colonization was to own land and to separate people from their lands. The English used different means for land ownership. Until the seventeenth century, England did not require written documents for land ownership. Land could be acquired by exchanging goods, paying money, and/ or developing vacant land. Labour allowed the English settlers to legitimize dispossession and value themselves in opposition to 'the savage', the 'lazy Indian'. In the-so-called New World, settlers' actions such as building a house or a fence were considered actions that counted for acquiring land. Transforming the land by bringing slaves to work on Indigenous land and/or paying money were other means to acquire land. Treaties also figured as a way of acquiring land. However, Seed notes, treaties were not agreements between nations. In the sixteenth century, English and, to some extent, French traders used treaties as a way to acquire everything from fur to sugar from Indigenous peoples.

Indigenous territories were deeply imprinted by human actions and their inhabitants were governed by complex systems of land use and ownership. However, as the British Empire expanded through northern North America, tensions between settlers and Indigenous peoples became common and the notion of forest primeval became increasingly used to designate Indigenous lands. One effective attitude that abetted the practice of reducing the presence of Indigenous peoples was to simply disavow the reality of who they were, instead constructing them as 'hunters/gatherers' and their lands as being waste or 'wilderness' (Seed 2001: 50).

In this regard, Patrick Wolfe notes that settler colonialism has manifested in a tendency that he calls the 'logic of elimination', which can be inherently eliminatory but not always genocidal. Indigenous peoples were dispossessed, driven away, fenced in, their ancestry regulated in an attempt to reduce numbers, and their children abducted and re-socialized in residential schools. From this perspective, Wolfe continues, where Indigenous peoples were and not who they were was the primary motive of elimination (Wolfe 2006: 387–409). In the logic of eliminating Indigenous peoples, settlers were characterized as being settled by creating permanent replicas of the places they left. In contrast, Indigenous peoples were deemed fragile and in the process of disappearing (Veraccini 2011: 1–12). By the late nineteenth century, colonial policy had shifted to other practices of elimination of the Indigenous 'Other'. Jennifer Brown and Theresa Scheck argue that through this shift cultural difference became political deviance and cultural representation ideological domination (Brown and Schenck 2002). The invocation of the idea of progress, the analogy between barbarians and civilisers, turned logical distinctions into moral hierarchies that targeted the existence of Indigenous persons, law, and governance systems by colonizers who never left. In resisting the logic of elimination, Indigenous peoples engaged in unequal labour relations for the purpose of surviving as distinctive peoples and fulfilling their collective obligations.

However, English colonialism was often represented as an orderly business carried out through treaty and trade relationships with Indigenous peoples, punctuated by a few regrettable 'accidental' episodes. In contrast, the 'Black Legend', or the story about Spanish atrocities in the New World, became a way for English imperialists to distinguish their benign project from the Spaniards' destructive one. According to Butcher, the distinction between the two colonial projects and the idea of two separate worlds would later be used for the normalization of interracial marriage taboos, racial segregation, and the creation of reservations, all characteristics of English colonial enterprises in North America (Butcher 1990: 18–20).

Unlike English settler colonialism, Spanish colonization relied on the extraction of wealth and conquering people. While Indigenous peoples were recognized as being peoples, they were subjugated for the purpose of exploiting labour. Rather than obstructing access to land, Indigenous peoples provided access to wealth: the more subjugated people, the greater the access to wealth. As such, labour was a colonial imposition and a form of discipline that involved everyday life and was embedded in social and power relations producing relations of domination. As a set of practices, labour not only involved the modes of implementation, but also peoples' everyday negotiation, appropriation, suffering, and living in a specific labour regime. Thus, labour can also be considered as a locus of social agency (Silliman 2006: 147–65). While colonizers used labour to extract wealth, Indigenous peoples maintained some degree of social agency to maintain continuity, exercise circumscribed autonomy, and reconstruct their identities.

To exploit the rich sources of gold and silver, Indigenous people were enslaved in silver mines under conditions that shortened their lives to a few months. Only in the second half of the sixteenth century did this exterminatory slavery practice started to erode. From then on, and once control had been established and Indigenous leaders had accepted Spanish presence, a *modus vivendi* based on relations of domination was institutionalized. Indigenous communities were allowed to retain their lands in exchange for paying tax, or 'tribute'. In Spanish, the word 'tribute' is more than simply paying taxes. Rendering tribute or *rendir tributo* is also about deference and recognizing someone's social superiority. Certainly the practice of paying taxes was very familiar to the many Indigenous peoples in Mexico where extractive institutions were already in place when the Spaniards arrived. The Mexica or Aztec Empire had managed to subjugate different Indigenous regions in Meso-America.

Because extractive colonialism is driven by a determination to sustain subordination rather than elimination, Spanish colonizers allowed Indigenous communities, which were based on the Aztec notion of *altepetl* or autonomous communities, to reproduce themselves. They could maintain their own normative systems, including the rules for transmitting property and assigning lands within the *República de Indios* (in English this concept could be better understood as Indigenous subjugated communities) in return for tribute and acceptance of colonial rule (Florescano 1998: 186). The making of the colonial space rested on parallel spaces, the *República de Españoles* (Spaniards' Republic) and the *República de Indios* (Indian Republic) distinguishing between conquerors and colonized people. The Indian Republic maintained different types of land including lands for community celebrations and lands for communal and individual use. These communities rested upon a moral economy of reciprocity, which can be defined as a set of social practices and relations based on a moral code aimed at fostering reciprocity and networks of security in the form of community work or *tequio*, among equal kin and hierarchical neighbours. Based on this moral logic of reciprocity, what is taken and what is given (service, gifts, resources, goods) must be returned in 'similar value'. These networks of support constitute a local mechanism to resist exploitation and domination. Moreover, the community and the communal provided Indigenous peoples institutional organization and a strategy of resistance.

Although the *Leyes de Indias* (Laws of the Indies) gave Indigenous peoples local political and legal independence and title over surface lands, not everywhere did the Spanish colonizers follow such legislations, particularly in the midst of the introduction of the *repartimiento* or forced labour and consumption system. Even when they did, the Indian Republic became the space associated with 'inferior peoples' but also the space of survival and resistance to domination. The Indian Republic shaped Indigenous peoples' social practices, relations, and political actions. The denial of the dignity of the Indigenous Other, in some contexts, became the cause for the perpetration of physical violence and the violation of personhood and rights.

Because extractive colonialism maintains the difference between metropolis and colony, in New Spain, Creoles, did not enjoy the same benefit as Peninsular Spaniards.[1] The latter's wealth and loyalty to the metropolis displaced Creoles

---

1 Creole were descendants of Spaniards born in the colonies; Mestizos were persons of Indigenous and Spanish ancestry; Afromestizos were persons of African, Indigenous, and Spanish ancestry. (Editor's note)

from institutions and municipal levels of government. Over time, this distinction fuelled Creoles' resentment and desire for independence from the metropolis. Because Creoles were a minority, they had to include Mestizos in their nationalist movement (Wimmer 2002: 122). In addition, Creoles attempted to indigenize themselves by reclaiming the great Indigenous past in order to distinguish themselves from the metropolis and to appeal to the Indigenous population. At the outset of Mexico's transition from colonial rule to independence, legal pluralism, Indigenous land tenure systems, and enclosed communities existed in most of the country. In an effort to draw clear-cut distinctions with the colonial past, the newly independent government looked to France and the US as models to construct the new nation.

Drawing on these examples, a republic based on the notion of one people, one culture, and private property emerged. Creoles, Mestizos, Afromestizos, and all 'pacified' Indigenous peoples were transformed into citizens. But while this legal uniformity facilitated the construction of a homogeneous national identity out of the regional, ethnic, and linguistic diversity that dominated the landscape, it erased Indigenous subjectivities. Although the independence movement formally replaced the exogenous relation of domination, decolonization had important limits. Seizure of political power only transferred control to a different social group that, although it conceived of decolonization as progress, did not include Indigenous peoples. In this context, liberation brought a new form of post-colonial authoritarianism in which the political elite secured privileges for itself and turned the State into an instrument of control.

Although settler and extractive colonialism are characterized by specific modes of governance, both depend on knowledge production, the creation of a system of signification and values and spatialized strategies that are simultaneously international, continental, national, regional, and local (Lyon 1990: 284). Thus, scale may be used as a tool to inscribe difference at various levels and is important to the internal geopolitics of race and racism, particularly where national state building and 'national identities' are constructed and the fate of increasingly dependent Indigenous peoples unfold. Terms such as 'Indigenous', 'Métis', 'First Nations', and 'Native Americans', while positioning Indigenous peoples within and in relation to colonial frames of reference, also reduce them to minority groups within the national state scale, overriding significant differences among these peoples and also obscuring some of their commonalities (Delaney 2002: 8). According to Robert Young, reifications of race and somatic characteristics are used to police borders of countries, persons, and collectivities (Young 1995: 54). Moreover, like whiteness in Canada and the US, *métissage* is celebrated in the Mexican context and is embedded in imperialist obsessions, which are translated into social differences and skin-colour undertones that obsessively distinguish between Indigenous peoples and Mestizos.

Space, Borders, and the Peoples In-between

Post-colonial theory and critical geography have been concerned with how power and knowledge served to create territories, norms, and subjectivities within processes of colonization. However, these concerns are not merely historical, for the legacies of colonialism continue to shape the boundaries of contemporary identities and social and cultural formations. Post-colonial and critical geography have included attempts to contribute to an understanding of how colonial knowledge and power have shaped the conditions of possibility for particular practices both in the past and present, and how these conditions are to be contested (Harris 2001; Young 1995). In colonial contexts, difference was not only a way of making and appropriating spaces but was also a way to manage the interpellation of particular subjects. As Ann Stoler observes, colonial practices were not imported directly from European societies and then planted in the colonies. Rather colonial projects emerged from new constructions of Europeanness that were geographically and demographically distinct (Stoler 1989: 134–61). Thus, distinctions between colonizers and their multiple Others did not pre-exist colonialism but emerged in response to specific colonial political, social, economic, demographic, and cultural circumstances.

In North America, the gigantic transformations produced by colonial processes and structures created the colonizer and colonized internal spaces of reference and imperial competition. In particular, the rivalry between Spain and England shaped the creation of additional spaces of difference that continue to haunt present-day North America. As shown in the previous section, the distinction between the English 'colonial orderly business' and the 'Black Legend' demonizing the Spanish resulted from European imperial competition. Since the interests of England and France in the North American region were circumscribed by the context of ferocious competition with Spain and Portugal, which had firmly established their possessions in the New World, northern European Protestants attempted to discredit the Spanish colonizers by constructing them as the European savages. However, as Eliga H. Gould observes, the colonization of North America is based on entangled histories that reveal the extent to which these empires influenced each other as well as these asymmetric perceptions in the process of constituting each other (Gould 2007: 766).

The asymmetric relationship between Spain and Great Britain touched every aspect of England's overseas enterprise. As Gould observes, this influence was particularly notorious in the arguments with which the British sought to legitimate their possessions in North America (Gould 2007: 771). While the British emulated some key elements of Spanish colonial enterprise, they consciously rejected others, particularly the claim to sovereignty over American lands and waters based on papal bull. Rather, the British justified their possession with the terra nullius doctrine, in which the Americas were constructed as 'empty things' existing in the world. Since Indigenous peoples in northern North America cultivated only a small portion of the land, the British were supposedly free to purchase and settle on any 'unoccupied' land, for property rights and sovereignty did not exist as they did in Europe. In this way, the British distinguished themselves from the Spaniards, who had subjugated more populated and 'civilized' Indigenous societies (Gould 2007).

According to Gedges Gonzalez, in their attempts to discredit Spain, English colonizers omitted scenes of violence and decadence from representations of their colonizing project (Gonzáles 1999: 35). Instead, they viewed their own colonial enterprises as business carried out through treaty and trade relationships with Indigenous peoples. However, as Adelman and Aron have observed, British North Americans embraced Indigenous allies not because of their commitment to embrace diversity, but rather because of their contingent necessity (Adelman and Aron 1999: 823). At different times and in different contexts neither the Spanish, nor the French and the British would have survived their rivalries without Indigenous allies (*Ibid.*: 839). Where European competition developed, Indigenous peoples fashioned economic, diplomatic, and personal relations that rested to a large extent on Indigenous ground.

The Black Legend, the story about Spanish atrocities in the New World, was an English construct to distinguish how their own project to impose racial segregation was (comparatively) benign. Certainly Spaniards and English perceived miscegenation very dissimilarly. While this difference resulted from the latter's attempt to distinguish themselves from the former, both the English and the Spanish confronted very different contexts. Spain faced very large Indigenous populations, and its colonial system rested on the feudal exploitation of a Native labour force (Axtell 1992: 206). Unlike the métissage that occurred in British North America, the Iberian North American one eventually resulted in a single society with class distinctions and racial undertones, where Mestizos became mainstream and differentiated from the Indigenous population, and only instrumentally drew on the substantial Indigenous past (Esteva-Fabrigat 1995: 57).

Although New Spain was not colour-blind, by the end of the seventeenth century, the Ibero-American population was large enough to continue the Spanish colonization to the southeast of what today is the US. Mestizos (women in particular) were instrumental in the process as they played a central role in pacifying 'rebellious' Indigenous peoples. When English colonists arrived in this area, they encountered a society deeply rooted in cultural and racial assimilation (Brown and Schenck 2002). The practice of intermarriage that occurred between Indigenous women and English men at the borderland was undermined by moral discourses of civilization and English superiority once the costs of ethnic alliances had surpassed their benefits and when European empires decayed (Barman1999: 14–20; Nelson 2003; Van Kirk 2002: 1–11). As Bahbha observes, colonial discourses turn on the recognition and disavowal of racial/cultural/historical differences and function to create specific space for 'subject peoples' (Bhabha 2004). This function suggests that in North America the frontier also existed as a moral frontier (Nelson 2003: 24).

By the end of the nineteenth century, competition in trade, rather than territorial expansion, became crucial to the transition from colonial enterprises to national state building. Although borders were formalized, they did not prevent the flow of people, capital, and goods. Thus, migration, dispossession, resettlement, the expansion of markets, the coexistence of labour systems, and metropolitan growth were part of the new bordered lands. The national states of North America became the centre for conferring or denying rights to peoples within their borders. The borders legally divided original North American peoples, and also embodied exclusivist notions of citizenship under which newly trans-border Indigenous peoples became particularly vulnerable.

As Adelman and Aron argue, the colonial conflict over land shaped the peculiar and contingent configuration of the North American national states' international relations (1999: 816). Similarly, David J. Weber notes that Anglo North American meta-narratives inherited the colonial view that the Spaniards were cruel, fanatical, superstitious, corrupt, and decadent. In the nineteenth century, this view extended and constructed miscegenation as physical and moral degeneration (Weber 1992: 4–24). As Mexico became an independent country, it also became the target of Anglo-America's 'civilization project' while Mestizos, as a social group, inherited the qualities attributed to colonial Spain. Thus, the Anglo-American war against Mexico was elevated to a clash of moral influences and principles that conveniently served to keep Mexicans 'in their place', while constructing Anglo North America as a 'white space' that conveniently erased the presence of Indigenous peoples and racialized minorities. I would argue that this view has undermined the extent to which fluid borders, colonial imperial rivalries, geographic perceptions, and identity constructions have influenced the history of this region and the contemporary images that North American countries have of each other.

In the context of national state building, treaties redefining borders dramatically disrupted Indigenous-European arrangements and unleashed a model of land property and liberal state-building hungry for land. For example, the Treaty of Oregon (1846) between the US and Great Britain set the boundary between the US and Canada. The result divided previously unified Indigenous peoples into those who lived south of the border and came under the jurisdiction of the US, and those who lived north and came under the control of Canada. The Treaty of Amity, or Jay Treaty, (1794) between the US and Great Britain had granted Indigenous peoples the right to move back and forth across the border. However, their cultures have been affected because separate governments and policies unevenly regulated the way of life of culturally similar peoples.

Another example is the Treaty of Guadalupe Hidalgo (1848), which ended the war between the US and Mexico. Prior to the end of Mexico's independence, in 1816 Spain had fixed the Nueces River as the northern Mexican border, and the US ratified that in 1819, when it purchased Florida and renounced claims to Texas. Nevertheless, according to the terms of the 1848 treaty, Mexico ceded 55 per cent of its territory to the US including parts of California, New Mexico, Texas, Colorado, Nevada, and Utah. The treaty terms protected the property and civil rights of the Mexican nationals living within the new US boundaries (Arce 1997).

The annexation of the ceded territories to the US had severe consequences for Indigenous peoples' interactions. First, the US failed to treat all citizens living in its territory equally. Second, the right of the Californians and South Westerners to use Spanish as a lingua franca was never respected. Third, Indigenous peoples were adversely affected by the re-definition of North American countries' boundaries. While Canada and the US protected the rights of Indigenous peoples and trans-border peoples whose lands were bisected in similar treaties, no explicit protection was granted to Indigenous peoples such as the Kumeyaay and Tohono O'odham, who lived on both sides of the Mexican/US border.

Unlike the policies for the Canada/US border, those for the US/Mexico border resulted in restrictive immigration, racial segregation, and limited citizenship – all factors which harmed peoples such as the Yaquis, Tohono O'odham, and historical Mexicans, who became 'border citizens', or people living on the margins of the US society and whose rights of belonging have been questionable (Meeks 2008). For over a hundred years, informal agreements allowed trans-border Indigenous peoples to cross the US/Mexican border. However, as more restrictive crossing procedures have been implemented since 9/11, trans-border Indigenous peoples' integrity, way of life, and kin relationships have become increasingly threatened (Luna-Firebaugh 2002: 159–81).

Although an extensive literature on international migration, relocation and removal exists, Indigenous migration and border-crossing rights have not been widely studied. Border-crossing populations exist at the edge of current transformations of concepts of sovereignty, national identity, and citizenship. The broad scope of contemporary international Indigenous migration raises new questions about Indigenous peoples' rights in their places of origins, transit, and destination, as well as trans-border peoples' rights and citizenship, which current migration theories based on the modern understanding of national state boundaries do not clearly address.

Indigenous Transnationalism and Trans-border Peoples

Like other terms such as 'globalization', 'transnationalism' serves as an inclusive category for multiple interactions taking place across boundaries. This concept encompasses varieties of social and political activism occurring simultaneously in multiple places. As an overarching term, transnationalism includes new communities of people who belong to different countries and helps in rethinking social issues such as place and identity in light of people's multiple affiliations and experiences. In the 1990s, the term transnationalism became very important for re-conceptualizing people's mobility and their incorporation into adopting societies. The concept became particularly relevant in the work of scholars such as Portes and Pries among others (Portes 2003: 814–92; Pries 2001). Later contributions made by geographers linked ethno-national conflict and economic globalization and suggested that transnationalism is the theme of social boundary formation and change (Ley and Kobayashi 2002: 111–27). Globalization not only transcends but also reconfigures state and ethno-national boundaries.

Since the late 1980s, movements by marginalized groups, including Indigenous peoples and migrants, have relied on international alliances to broaden their political reach and later challenge the destructive effects of economic globalization including the emergence of quasi-constitutional forms of economic integration such as NAFTA, which has fuelled new conflicts over the control of strategic natural resources located within Indigenous territories (Brysk 2000; Ramos 1998). Local economic activities and resources are used less for the benefit and development of communities and more for the enjoyment of international consumers. While not all Indigenous peoples are equally victims of economic integration, many Indigenous communities have been negatively affected by it.

Thus, transnationalism is strongly connected to economic globalization, takes place within and across borders, and includes resistance, contestation, hybridity, networks, and a sense of self and community that transcend the limits of the national state to respond to increasingly transnational social problems (Cleaver 1998). While it has been argued that the transnational empowers ethnic minority groups to mobilize from the 'local' against the supranational and the State, border studies have asked rather, where do the borders start and end (Madsen and Van Naerssen 2003: 61–75)? Furthermore, definitions of transnationality highlight Eurocentric geographies that tend to conceal agency and other routes and roads that have long existed on Turtle Island. These overlapping histories are part of the contradictions and the entangled history of North American history and its Indigenous geographies.

In this section I explore two North American Indigenous experiences: the Binational Organisations Indigenous Front (FIOB in Spanish) and the struggle of the trans-border Tohono O'odham Nation fighting for its right to exist as a cohesive whole. These examples of transnationalism are not the only ones in North America. However, the complexity of the FIOB mission deserves attention while the fact that the Tohono O'odhams' crossing rights were never protected presents significant challenges to the Mexican/US border in the context of increasing homeland security actions. Both cases are relevant in examining the social and spatial formations made and remade through transnational connections and political practices and discourses. As expressed by Indigenous peoples and organizations, one of the most important qualifications for claiming indigeneity is self-identification. In this analysis, self-identification is particularly relevant in relation to transnational or trans-border Indigenous communities, whose location and migratory status may not always be clearly distinguished.

The FIOB and 'Oaxacalifornia'

Human migration is an important feature of economic globalization. At the same time, this phenomenon underscores the tensions between state sovereignty and cross-border flows. People leave to search for a better life, for political and family reasons, and to flee genocide. Indigenous migration is increasingly part of these migrant flows. Indigenous migrants do not only move to distant places, but they also create communities all along their migrant routes to counteract border control and racism, and to provide social security networks in the absence of citizenship rights. How is Indigenous migration changing Indigenous communities? How do they remain Indigenous yet foreign? I argue that borders provide important insights into understanding contested regions, state sovereignty, dynamic identities, and Indigenous people's unique experiences.

Mexican migration to the US is a major contention in US–Mexico relations. Despite periods of shared interests in promoting migratory flows, contemporary US immigration legislation has become more restrictive even though Mexico continues to be one of the most important countries of origin for migrant workers to enter legally and illegally into the US. While some migration has occurred previously, the first wave of Indigenous migration did not start until the 1940s, when Purépecha workers took advantage of the Bracero Program. However, it was during the 1990s that the Mixtec and Zapotec set a different trend for widespread international migration in North America. The proportion of predominantly Indigenous migrants from Oaxaca, Mexico on California farms almost doubled during the 1990s (Valdez 1995).

Indigenous migrants arrive in the US with many disadvantages. Many are monolingual or speak Spanish poorly and face racism by both Mexicans and Americans (Zabin *et al*. 1993). In all three North American countries, Indigenous migrants are subordinated as both Indigenous and migrants. They work in ethnically defined labour markets, confront racist attitudes and systemic language discrimination. Indigenous migrants have experienced some form of self-consciousness, which has been a stimulus to re-assert their Indigenous identities as Mixtec or Zapotecs and reorganize along these lines. Indigeneity, long-term settlement and Indigenous geographic concentration in California have been central to developing distinctive forms of transnational social organization and cultural reproduction. Indigenous migrant collective initiatives draw on Indigenous principles such as reciprocity and responsibility in building organizations in their place of destiny. These Indigenous principles are expressed in cultural practices that range from civic-political organizing, to the celebration of religious fiestas, basketball tournaments, bi-national newspapers, Indigenous-Spanish radio programs, translation services, and traditional festivals such as the Guelaguetza. These activities and practices not only serve to connect migrant families but also serve to foster connections between homeland and place of destiny through the practice of family-scale package services moving food and remittances from north to south to north. Beyond the economic dimension, these practices have an impact on migrants ties to home and life in California. The term 'Oaxacalifornia' has been widely used to signify this transnational connection.

Among Oaxacan migrant organizations, the most consolidated coalition is the FIOB. This well-studied organization represents six distinct Indigenous peoples, including the Mixtecs and Zapotecs now living in the Mexican state of

Baja California and the US State of California. The FIOB maintains three offices providing interpretation services in Indigenous languages, health clinics, and other community services for migrants. The FIOB transnational social experience challenges traditional conceptions of cultural identity as exclusively linked to a geographical location or territory. Described as transnational because of its ability to maintain and reaffirm social ties between the Indigenous homelands and diasporas, this organization has been organized in the place of destination to reclaim and maintain its members' unique identities (Fox and Rivera-Salgado 2004). Moreover, FIOB grassroots networks are also closely knitted with the politics of their place of origin. During the social uprising and dissolution of state power in Oaxaca in 2006, the *Asamblea Popular de los Pueblos de Oaxaca* (Popular Assembly of the Peoples of Oaxaca) was created as a horizontal and decentralized governing body. The FIOB immediately united with other bi-national grassroots organizations to form a branch of the *Asamblea* in Los Angeles to support the struggle of their sister communities south of the border.

Indigenous bi-national politics surpasses the local and national circumscription of state laws and transcends borders. The FIOB was also instrumental in electoral politics in Oaxaca in 2010, when through an interactive radio program migrants engaged in conversations with their sister communities to support Indigenous normative systems, and discuss the meaning of political autonomy and the role of Indigenous migrants in bringing about change in Oaxaca (www.oaxacalifornia. com). While to most Indigenous communities, migration is a matter of survival, most recently at the tri-annual assembly of FIOB Indigenous communities in both Oaxaca and California started to be engaged in what they call "the right to stay home." In asserting this right, these communities are challenging the inequalities and exploitation facing migrants, the reasons forcing people to migrate in the first place and emphasizing the need for social change (Bacon 2008).

Glick Schiller observes that as homeland politics have been the most visible transnational involvement of migrants, policy makers are increasingly paying attention to this type of transnational connection and its implication for migrant integration in their places of destiny (2005). Security policies accentuated after 9/11 occasioned a lively debate questioning the right of migrants and their descendants to organize their everyday activities and preserve their languages and collective identities through principles and practices closely linked to their ancestral homeland. In my view, a missing piece in this debate is what drives Indigenous communities to leave in the first place. Indigenous diasporas raise questions about what it means to be an Indigenous migrant and how long-distance membership in their home communities is maintained. More specifically, Indigenous transnational political action is useful for re-thinking the relationship between territory, sovereignty, and the selective character of border control.

The Tohono Oo'dham: The Border Crossed Us

Narratives of a 'broken border' that encourages brown invasion from south of the border have long been part of popular culture and the media in the US (Chavez 2001; De Genova 2004). Calls for taking control of the border reassert these narratives by refusing access to illegal transnational actors, namely those who operate across borders and challenge state laws and sovereignty. Issues of state sovereignty would seem to suggest there is a clear distinction between what or who is within and who is not. The question is, how do borders and securitization operate in light of entangled colonial and national histories for peoples who have been simultaneously constructed as being at home and far from home? I would argue that borders both reiterate state power and erase long-established distinctions between external and internal others. Muller observes that while border securitization seems to limit the space of what is politically visible, it can also serve to open the door to a politics of resistance that challenges border constructions as existing a priori (Muller 2009: 67–78, 80). An example of Indigenous transnationalism that calls for the re-evaluation of conceptions of sovereignty and otherness in North America is that of the trans-border communities living at the borderlands, such as the Tohono O'odham nation.

Historically, this people inhabited an enormous area in the US southwest extending south to Sonora, Mexico, north to central Arizona, west to the Gulf of California, and east to the San Pedro River. Indigenous peoples moved freely to engage in social, economic, religious, and cultural interactions. Since the eighteenth century, their land has been occupied and ruled by different governments. When Mexico became an independent country in 1810, the O'odham fell under Mexican rule. Later with the Guadalupe Hidalgo Treaty and the Gadsen Purchase in 1853, their land was divided in half between the US and Mexico. The US agreed to honour the land rights held by Mexican citizens including the Tohono O'odham, and to grant them the same citizen rights of any US citizen. However, the Treaty of Guadalupe Hidalgo consolidated Anglo-American occupation of the area. Over time colonial history, racialized processes, and identity constructions led to the use of terms such as 'Hispanic' and 'Latino', which conveniently blur distinctions between Indigenous peoples, historical Mexicans, and migrants. Despite these developments, for decades these Indigenous communities continued to move freely across borders for livelihood, religious, cultural, and family purposes. In recent years, the US homeland security and the militarization of the borders have been placing great pressures on these communities and creating major barriers to their intertribal communication. Confusion over who is an 'immigrant' Indigenous person and who is a federally recognized tribal member in the US has contributed to the criminalization of trans-border Indigenous communities.

In October 2006, President George W. Bush held a White House press conference as he signed into law the Secure Fence Act. In his statements, the president acknowledged, '[O]urs is a nation of immigrants.' He went on to highlight some of the new law's provisions, including 'construction of hundreds of miles of additional fencing', 'more vehicles barriers, checkpoints, and lighting'. With the passage of the Secure Fence Act, the US has planned an estimated 700-mile double-layered fence and a greater US military presence from San Diego, California, to the Gulf of Mexico border region. In the US/Mexico borderlands, the national immigration emergency has had a polarizing effect not only in national politics but also at the rural level. While many people continue to be relatively indifferent to this phenomenon, others have formed vigilante groups to defend what they consider their national norms with little concern about how trans-border communities are been affected and their lands taken over.

Historically, trans-border communities have challenged the US's efforts to reinforce a 'homogeneous national culture' and territorial and racial boundaries, and have insisted on defining the terms of their relationship to both their own nation and the national State (Meeks 2008). As citizenship precludes trans-border peoples from enjoying the same rights and benefits reserved for US nationals, Indigenous traditional travelling patterns converge with wider issues of illegal migration to the US. US immigration authorities often question the authenticity of the Tohono living in Mexican territory, because the Tohono O'odham nation is territorially and legally based in the US. This situation has serious implications for them (Madsen and Van Naerssen 2003). The differential treatment of the O'odham living in the US and in Mexico is founded only on citizenship rights and disregards their belonging to an Indigenous nation, which has been bisected by modern state borders (Luna-Firebaugh 2002: 164). Thus it is relevant to ask, where do Indigenous peoples living in the borderlands belong? Moreover, how can these peoples maintain and make sense of their identity in the current circumstances? Transnational politics and protest against the US policies have been at the centre of Tohono O'odham activism. They have demanded the extension of US citizenship to the Tohono O'odham living in Sonora, Mexico and have secured funding for ten-year visas and money to lobby Congress to recognize the dual citizenship of 1,200 tribal members living south of the border.

In addition, the Tohono O'odham hosted the Indigenous Border Summit of the Americas organized by the International Indian Treaty Council and the American Indian Movement in 2006. At the Summit, Indigenous peoples raised concerns over the desecration of sacred and burial sites, the violation of environmental laws, and the failure to consult with tribal nations as new border policies are developed affecting Indigenous lands (Eagle Woman 2008). The participants, representing communities from both sides of the border, put forward a new vision of Indigenous border solidarity and approved the Declaration of San Xavier calling for the recognition of 'Indigenous peoples' traditional migration routes' and requesting governments to 'establish policies to put an end to the death of all Indigenous peoples and immigrant populations crossing their lands'. The Summit opposed the Secure Fence Act because it will divide the ancestral lands of several Indigenous nations. In January 2008, Native American community leaders and private owners announced their intention to fight the Department of Homeland Security's attempt to use its powers to illegally seize private lands and build the controversial border security wall. Indigenous peoples, whose lands have been bisected by the US/Mexico border, shared historical and current stories of their experiences.

Like the case of the FIOB, the Tohono O'odham activism challenges conceptions of state sovereignty and borders. The configuration of the modern State and the reconfiguration of state powers through processes that both deterritorialize and disembody migrants and trans-border communities continue to naturalize colonial geographies and othering, defining which subjects are allowed in and which are not. The framing of political spaces as the lines that divide in from out serve the purpose of managing identities and their access to particular spaces. It is not only about who is authorized to access certain sites, but also about who you are and where you should be.

Conclusions

Turtle Island was an archipelago of diversity with its own interactions, trade and cultural exchanges, military conflicts, and negotiations. The radical changes brought about by colonial enterprises in North America informed the representation and construction of Indigenous difference and Others. Variations in representations and discourse are contingent and contradictory, and depend on the contexts in which they are deployed. The historical construction of difference and borders in North America has subsumed the complex interactions, entangled histories, and the Other's human agency in an attempt to maintain an Anglo narrative of the North American space. Therefore, notions of history and alterity continued to be exercised with power for the purpose of maintaining asymmetric and selective economic understandings of what the region is and is not.

Indigenous transnationalism challenges Eurocentric conceptions of borders, identities, and state sovereignty and citizenship as membership in a clearly defined national territory. Transnational and trans-border narratives provide an understanding of how Indigenous peoples maintain ties with distant and 'foreign' relatives across present-day North American borders. As such, the concept of transnationalism is useful to question the ways in which reified understandings of history, nation, and indigeneity are constituted in relation to walls and borders.

Part II
North American Integration: Development and Challenges

Chapter 3
The Uncertain Politics of North American Economic Integration

Greg Anderson

The Salience of the Border

In Chapter 9 of *Here: A Biography of the New American Continent* (2001), *New York Times* correspondent Anthony DePalma recounts the experience of being reassigned from covering Mexico from Mexico City, to covering Canada from Toronto. While in Mexico, there was no shortage of signals reminding DePalma that he was in a foreign country; language, culture, politics, and among the most salient of them all, the US/Mexican border. Although the border between the US and Mexico is long, and in most places extremely porous, the vicinity around major crossing points is anything but. Large fences, long lines, and grumpy customs and immigration officials from both countries always stood in the way of simple entry and exit; parts of the US/Mexican border resemble a kind of militarized zone between the two countries complete with heavily armed border patrol staff, aircraft surveillance, sniffer dogs, and motion detectors.

In stark contrast, DePalma's arrival in Toronto featured just a few questions from a customs inspector and a very short wait while comparatively friendly immigration authorities examined entry papers. Much more extensive checks just for visitors – to say nothing of those seeking residence – are routine along the US/Mexican border. So, for DePalma, it was as if he had returned to the US even though he was in Toronto. In fact, several months later when he checked in at Toronto's Pearson Airport for a quick business trip to the home office in New York, he had completely neglected to bring along his passport and missed several flights as a result – a pre-trip item that would have been at the top of his 'to do' list had he been preparing for the same trip from Mexico City. DePalma had quickly assimilated to Canadian society because the differences between English Canadians and Americans are comparatively subtle. It was a point that was driven home even further several months later when he and his family tried to arrange for their housekeeper in Mexico City to join them in Canada. Unlike the experience of the DePalma family itself, the bureaucratic hurdles and restrictions placed upon their housekeeper were arduous – so much so that their domestic helper, feeling alienated and unwelcome, stayed a mere six months.

This story could be used as part of a critique of Canadian immigration officials (the apparent differential treatment given DePalma compared to that of his housekeeper) or to tritely suggest that there are few differences between English Canadians and Americans. Yet, this story is much more telling in terms of highlighting the relative salience of the border for Mexicans, Americans, and Canadians. DePalma's experience at Pearson Airport brought this point into sharp relief. While he had more or less forgotten that he was in a foreign country, he was in one and the 49th parallel still meant something. As he notes:

> That was my first lesson in understanding the line separating Canada and the United States. In time, I came to appreciate that the northern border is so complex because of its ubiquitously dual nature. For Americans, the border is almost invisible, whereas Canadians are painfully conscious of it all the time. We [Americans] see the border as joining Canada to the United States. For Canadians it is the last frontier separating us from them. (DePalma 2001: 186)

Without question, North America's two internal borders are at once similar, and yet vastly different in terms of how they shape imaginations and affect the lives of the people they separate. While the struggle and debate over the meaning, impact, and utility of North America's borders has been raging for more than two centuries, the past two decades have witnessed some of the most dramatic reconsiderations of our shared borders in the form of the debates over the Canada–US Free Trade Agreement (CUFTA) and then NAFTA. When President Carlos Salinas proposed in February 1990 that Mexico and the US enter into a free trade agreement (Salinas de Gortari 2002: 48), President Salinas was initiating the formal reconsideration of not just of the US/Mexican border, but also of all of North America's borders at the same time. In so doing, Salinas initiated an awkward three-way marriage in what had been, and still largely is, a tale of two bilateral relationships.

This chapter aims to discuss the future of North American integration and that of NAFTA as its principal anchor. For all of the popular and scholarly rhetoric about the many ways in which NAFTA transformed North America, elements within the agreement itself are suggestive of both NAFTA's limitations and the future pathways the North American economic space may take. After stipulating a few basics on the economics of NAFTA, this chapter will focus primarily on the fissures that have emerged within the agreement by looking rather narrowly at the merits and weaknesses of NAFTA's major dispute-settlement mechanisms, Chapters 19 and 11. In the first instance, Chapter 19, a single dispute, the decades-long softwood lumber dispute, is indicative of NAFTA's limitations and of the possibilities for deeper institutionalization in North America. Similarly, the controversy surrounding the aftermath of the Chapter 11 investor–state dispute resolution mechanisms, and the three governments' efforts to address their shortcomings, have also laid down important markers about where integration of the North American economic space may (or may not) be headed. More clearly stated, the operation of the dispute settlement mechanisms of NAFTA dramatically highlights both the limitations of the agreement itself and prospects for future, government-led integration projects in North America. While NAFTA went some distance toward eliminating the economic, and to some degree political, significance of North America's borders; these bright lines separating Canadians, Americans, and Mexicans from one another are as salient as ever. Hence, the experiences of the DePalma family will be replicated again and again for the foreseeable future.

A Note About Security

In this chapter I deliberately skirt some of the deep linkages between security and economics in North America flowing from the 9/11 terrorist attacks on the US. I do so because the evolution of this nexus of issues and some of their broad societal implications are dealt with more thoroughly elsewhere in this volume.[1] However, the impact of the awkward linkage of economics and security on the North American agenda cannot be overstated. In fact, the imperatives of security have complicated the increasingly poisonous politics of the economic relationship that I describe below to the point of being the primary impetus animating the trilateral relationship.

In Search of the One-Armed Economist

President Truman famously grew tired of his economic advisors scattering their policy advice with phrases such as 'on the one hand…' or 'on the other hand…' and eventually asked if someone could simply find him a one armed economist. Were Truman alive today, he might apply his complaint about economists to those debating the impact and merits of NAFTA. After more than a decade in operation, about the only thing that can be agreed upon with respect to the 'impact' of NAFTA is that it has generated plenty of debate. One's view of how NAFTA has worked depends mightily on what you thought the agreement was actually designed to do. A middle-of-the-road summary of this debate suggests the following: NAFTA has not lived up to the lofty hype put forward by its most ardent proponents, such as the US Business Round Table, the Council of the Americas, or the Canadian Council of Chief Executives. At the same time, NAFTA has not been the abject disaster predicted by opponents of the deal such as Ross Perot or Maude Barlow. Part of the problem with assessing NAFTA's impact has been one of simple statistical measurement (World Bank 2003: iv; Hufbauer and Schott 2005: 18–19; Weintraub 2004a: 3–20). Moreover, trade liberalization inherently generates 'winners' and 'losers'. For those who want to point to NAFTA's benefits, heralding the winners is challenging since the benefits

---

[1] In this volume, see Jimena Jiménez's and Janine Brodie's chapters (4 and 5). See also Anderson and Sands 2007.

of liberalization are broadly felt in the form of less expensive consumables, longer domestic production runs, and newly expanded export markets. By contrast, identifying the losers from trade liberalization is relatively easy since painful adjustment from trade liberalization and the attendant increase in foreign competition tends to be highly concentrated in particular economic sectors. Consumers enjoying the benefits of lower-cost goods or factory workers putting in longer shifts to service new foreign markets do not make the evening news. Those in sectors displaced by trade liberalization often do.

We could quibble over how many of those jobs supposedly lost because of NAFTA might now be in China or other low-cost labour zones had there never been a NAFTA. More challenging still are the critiques of NAFTA that assign it responsibility for a range of social, economic, and political ills. Are such problems really rooted in a shallow integration agreement (NAFTA), or are they part of broader macro- and micro-economic influences?

Given this debate, the following are a few standard measures of what has been happening economically in the NAFTA area since the agreement's inception. As much as they describe the depth and significance of the North American economic space, they are also measures of what continues to be, after more than a decade of free trade in North America, a tale of two bilateral relationships.

A Few Statistics

Trade

We can draw several conclusions about NAFTA from these descriptive statistics, the most readily apparent of which is the relative dependence of Canada and Mexico on the US economically. Whereas both Canada and Mexico are highly dependent on US market access for a significant proportion of their respective

Table 3.1   Trade within North America

2004	% GDP from Exports	%GDP from Imports	% Exports to Other NAFTA Partners	% Exports to Other Major Trading Partners
Canada (GDP $905.6 billion)	46.1	40.3	85 (to US)	2.1 (to Japan) 1.6 (to UK)
US (GDP $12.2 trillion)	11.2	15.1	23 (to Canada) 13.6 (to Mexico)	6.7 (to Japan) 4.4 (to UK) 4.3 (to China)
Mexico (GDP $701.1 billion)	31	32.9	81 (to US) 5.9 (to Canada)	1.1 (to Japan)

GDPs, the US is both less dependent on trade as a share of its GDP, owing mainly to its vast domestic consumer marketplace, and more diversified in terms of its trading partners, although Canada and Mexico are key. However, in the period 1994–2004, the NAFTA area experienced a dramatic increase in trade volumes with each other that outstripped trade growth with each country's non-NAFTA partners. US trade volumes with Mexico in this period rose more than 225 per cent whereas US trade volumes with its non-NAFTA partners were up only 127 per cent. US exports to and imports from Canada in this same period were up 140 and 190 per cent respectively. As important, under NAFTA, Canadian and Mexican dependence on the US for its trade has increased, whereas US rates of growth in trade with Canada and Mexico have paralleled US trade growth with the rest of the world (Hufbauer and Schott 2005: 18).

Foreign Direct Investment

Between 1980 and 1993, foreign direct investment (FDI) into Mexico was steady at between US$3 billion and US$5 billion per year. However, after it was apparent that NAFTA was going to come into existence, the average from 1994 through 2002 shot up to more than US$13 billion per year (Weintraub 2004a: 13; Hufbauer and Schott 2005: 30–35). Like Mexico in the early 1990s, Canada in the late 1980s hoped that CUFTA would act as a stimulant to foreign investment. 'Two-way FDI stocks between Canada and the US increased from $104 billion in 1989 to $289 billion by year-end 2003, a gain of 187 percent.' However, 'US two-way FDI with non-NAFTA countries increased by 333 percent between 1989 and 2003' (Hufbauer and Scott 2005: 35). In other words, the lack of more substantial growth in FDI flows into Canada under free trade has been a bit of a mystery (Sancak and Rao 2000).

The Fissures Within

As impressive as these statistics are, they hide an underlying debate about NAFTA that has raged since the agreement's completion in 1994. In many ways, NAFTA has become symbolic of a broader re-assessment of the merits of trade liberalization and economic policy that ensnared other proposed agreements, such as the Free Trade Area of the Americas (FTAA), or organizations like the World Trade Organization (WTO), the International Monetary Fund, the World Bank, and the G8 into a noisy debate about the merits of economic openness – the anti-globalization movement. Wherever leaders met to discuss economic policy throughout the 1990s, violent protests ensued. By the late 1990s, free trade had become a dirty word, 'contagion', the unwanted consequence of global economic interdependence, and 'outsourcing' a major political problem for the leadership of many industrialized countries.

What was a rapid expansion of regional and multilateral trade liberalization activity, typified by NAFTA, the conclusion of the Uruguay Round of the General Agreement on Tariffs and Trade (GATT), and the initiation of new arrangements like the FTAA has given way to a prolonged period of stagnation in the pursuit of new trade and investment liberalization (see Anderson 2005: 79–93). The indicators of this malaise are numerous, but one stands out: after expending enormous political capital to win congressional support of NAFTA in 1994, President Clinton rarely mentioned NAFTA again during the remainder of his two terms in office (Studer 2007: 64–65; Destler 1997). Moreover, after a period of relative activity by the administration of George W. Bush on US trade policy, NAFTA again became a political hot potato during the 2008 presidential campaign. As Senators Barack Obama and Hillary Clinton competed fiercely for the Democratic presidential nomination in Ohio in early 2008, NAFTA was vilified as the source of many economic problems throughout the US mid-west. While both candidates talked tough on trade, Senator Obama went so far as to call for a re-opening of the agreement if elected president (*Newsweek* 2008). NAFTA's supporters cried foul, alleging that the presidential campaign had fallen victim to the shrill populist rhetoric about NAFTA that tagged the agreement with failures in policy areas the agreement was never designed to address.

It is against this poisonous backdrop of trade politics in the years following NAFTA's completion that the agreement itself has generated criticism. Some have called for North America's leaders to dramatically build upon the foundation established by NAFTA and pursue ever-deeper stages of economic integration among the three countries (Pastor 2008, 2001; Dobson 2002; Goldfarb 2003; Robson and Laidler 2002; Conference Board 2003). Others have called for incremental fixes to the existing text.[2]

As noted above, post-9/11 security concerns have re-invigorated, and driven, a public debate about the North American agenda. However, from the moment the ink on NAFTA was dry, scholars and public policy practitioners have been speculating and arguing about 'next steps'. In the context of a badly deteriorating political climate and a weak public stomach for such debates, they were largely restricted to academia and think tanks. These discussions coincided with the lengthy implementation and phase-in of NAFTA in some areas such as agriculture over the course of fifteen years. In that time, NAFTA has both done what it was designed to do and revealed some shortcomings that were unanticipated by negotiators.

---

2 For example, Chapter 16 of the NAFTA covering temporary entry of business professionals actually created a whole new category of visa, the TN Visa; a rarity for such a politically sensitive policy area. However, the "positive" list of professionals qualifying for the new visas has proven inflexible since it did not include categories such as IT workers that not even emerged in the early 1990s. Moreover, Americans and Canadians can typically apply for TN Visas at ports of entry while Mexican nationals are still required to apply in advance through consular offices.

Hence, the balance of this chapter will focus on the operation of NAFTA itself, and two variants of dispute settlement mechanisms within, Chapters 19 and 11. The most well-known of the dispute settlement mechanisms, Chapter 19, was designed to deal with a range of domestic anti-dumping and countervailing duty laws as they could be applied to the exports of each NAFTA country. Chapter 11 was designed to insert a legal process into a vague area of international law covering private investment. Each of these NAFTA dispute settlement mechanisms is revelatory of the limitations of NAFTA itself, the broader political, economic, and social cleavages poisoning debates over globalization, and the limited near-term prospects for significantly altering the status quo in North American economic relations through a major government-led process aimed at deeper integration.

The Dispute that Broke NAFTA?

There are certainly issues in the US-Mexico context that merit discussion in the context of dispute settlement, including long-festering disputes over trade in cement, sweeteners such as high-fructose corn syrup, and Mexican trucks operating in the US (Kotschwar 2009; World Trade Organization n.d.).

However, none has reached the status of the Canada–US softwood lumber dispute in terms of its longevity or bitterness. Nor has any other dispute become such an immediate threat to NAFTA itself. The softwood lumber dispute is also useful for examining the operation of dispute settlement mechanisms, because it is the only dispute to have been litigated in four separate dispute-settlement mechanisms: Chapter 19 of the FTA, Chapter 19 of NAFTA, and dispute settlement mechanisms of the WTO and of its predecessor, GATT. One key to understanding the vociferous debate over both softwood and NAFTA is to appreciate just how limited an agreement NAFTA actually is.

The Canada–US softwood lumber dispute is one dispute no one seems to be able to resolve. Everyone, in Canada at least, has an opinion about it, yet few are able to readily discern the details of this fourth iteration of this dispute (known as Lumber IV),[3] in part, because the details are so arcane and specific as to defy simple understanding of who is winning or losing. As such, the popular press, academics (myself included), and even some of those directly involved, should be forgiven for misconstruing this case. However, one misconception about this case does need correction. We often read that NAFTA and its negotiators failed to fix the softwood lumber problem. This is patently untrue. NAFTA and its

---

3 The rough dates for each of the four major rounds of this dispute are as follows: Lumber I, October 1982–April 1986; Lumber II, May 1986–December 1986; Lumber III, October 1991–April 1996; Lumber IV, April 2001–Present. For an overview of Lumber I, II, and III, see Gagne 2003: 335–368.

dispute settlement mechanisms are working as designed and have successfully, and satisfactorily, been applied to many disputes, including softwood lumber (Macrory 2003). Unfortunately, that dispute never seems to go away. Moreover, the news of a new softwood lumber agreement that emerged in the spring of 2006 seemed only to confirm the futility of NAFTA as a viable arbiter of disputes. At the same time, the details of the new softwood deal came as no surprise since they resembled each of the previous truces agreed to over the past thirty years.

Lumber IV began in April 2001, when the last negotiated truce, the 1996 Softwood Lumber Agreement (SLA), expired. The 1996 SLA itself was the product of several years of litigation under Lumber III that commenced in 1992 with Canada's cancellation of the 1986 Memorandum of Understanding. This issue nearly derailed the CUFTA talks in 1986, continues to play havoc with the NAFTA process, and could well be an issue for many years to come (Hart et al. 1994: 144–146, 160–163).

The essence of the softwood battle is a dispute over different systems of land management. In the US, logs are harvested mainly off of private land at prevailing market prices. In contrast, Canadian lumber is harvested off of Crown lands, the fees for which are set by the province with jurisdiction over that land (Anderson 2004: 661–669). Neither CUFTA nor NAFTA were ever intended to resolve such basic differences in governance between Canada and the US. However, the dispute settlement mechanisms of both agreements *were* designed as a forum for litigating commercial disputes arising from those differences. Prior to the May 2006 truce, there were no fewer than *fourteen* separate cases winding their way through either NAFTA's or the WTO's dispute settlement mechanisms (Anderson 2006b: 585–610). Sorting out who has won or lost each of these cases is not as straightforward as the popular press often depicts, although recent NAFTA panel decisions (Summer and Fall 2005) have tended to favour Canada's position.[4] Yet, it is the furore over the US reaction to each of these decisions that looms large for both NAFTA in and of itself and trilateral relations as rooted in the agreement, because the softwood dispute has highlighted some of the central differences in how both countries fundamentally view NAFTA, and suggests that major hurdles would need to be overcome for a new deep integration project in North America to take flight.

---

4 See Certain Softwood Lumber Products from Canada. Final Affirmative Countervailing Duty Determination File USA-CDA-2002-1904-03, Decision of the Panel on the Fourth Remand Determination, 5 October 2005; Decision of the Panel on the Fifth Remand Determination, 17 March 2006.

Degrees of Integration and Separation

When Canada first broached the subject of free trade with the US in 1985, one of Canada's principal goals was to achieve immunity from US trade remedy laws (anti-dumping and countervailing duty). Canada did not get exactly what it was after, nor did Mexico when it sought, with Canada's support, a similar kind of immunity during the NAFTA negotiations. Between 1985 and 1987, Canada's pursuit of major changes to the application of trade remedy laws in the Canada–US context several times threatened to scuttle the talks altogether, but eventually gave way to the now-famous Chapter 19 dispute settlement mechanisms.[5] In the NAFTA negotiations, even the combined efforts of Canada and Mexico were unable to persuade the US to go any further toward reigning in trade remedy laws, and Chapter 19 became enshrined in NAFTA.

The important thing about all of this is that NAFTA itself, as well as the structure and operation of the dispute settlement mechanisms, are highly revealing as to how each country views the purpose of Chapter 19, and more broadly, NAFTA itself. First of all, recall from first year international trade textbooks that a preferential trading arrangement (PTA) like NAFTA is the shallowest form of economic integration, followed by free trade areas,[6] customs unions, common markets, and monetary unions. Preferential trade agreements entail the fewest commitments and obligations on the part of their members. While a range of border measures, such as tariffs, and behind-the-border measures, such as customs procedures, might be harmonized under PTAs, the vast majority of a country's policy autonomy remains, including domestic trade remedy law.[7]

The consequences of the fact that NAFTA is a shallow PTA should be well known to students of economics or international relations theory, and provides some immediate insight into the course that Lumber IV has taken since April 2001. Simply put, strong countries like to preserve their policy autonomy and eschew the restrictions and obligations that come with membership in binding international bodies. In contrast, weaker countries tend to be the great joiners of international

---

5 See Hart *et al.*, 1994: 318–42. In fact, the details of Chapter 19 were hotly contested throughout the negotiations and were the final item on which agreement was reached as the US legislative clock for completing the CUFTA ticked in early October 1987.

6 The NAFTA, like most preferential trading arrangements, is sanctioned under the GATT 1947 (now incorporated within the WTO) Article 24 (8(b)) which allows trade preferences arrangements so long as "duties and other restrictive regulations of commerce are eliminated on substantially all the trade between the constituent territories they liberalize more trade than they restrict."

7 It is worth noting here that the shallowness of the NAFTA might also be cast in terms of each state's interest in preserving elements of the Compromise of Embedded Liberalism, made famous by John Ruggie. As integration deepens, policy latitude in addressing the social dislocations arising from greater openness is inherently more restricted. The relative shallowness of the NAFTA preserves most of these elements, even including trade remedy measures. See Anderson 2003: 87–108.

bodies and prefer institutional settings that can augment their influence in a manner disproportionate to their power in the international system. In short, smaller and weaker countries tend to favour institutions that can restrain and limit the arbitrary actions of larger countries by subjecting such actions to rules.[8] This is precisely what Canada and Mexico sought in NAFTA, and in particular the dispute settlement mechanisms, and also exactly what the US sought to limit. Beyond the shallowness of NAFTA itself in terms of the degree of integration it contemplates, this same clash of interests, in terms of the strong party wanting to preserve its sovereignty and the weaker parties wanting to restrain it, is also reflected in the very structure of the Chapter 19 process.

Chapter 19 of NAFTA allowed all three countries to maintain their respective legal regimes governing the application of anti-dumping and countervailing duty investigations, but shifted review of administrative investigations away from domestic judicial review and to a bi-national panel system. However, Chapter 19 panel reviews of administrative decisions could, as in CUFTA, only examine the rather narrow question of whether investigating agencies had correctly applied national laws to the investigation. In other words, panels could only rule on whether the law, as written and as interpreted through legislative histories, had been correctly applied. If a panel ruled that national statutes had not been applied correctly in a particular case, panels were authorized only to 'remand' cases back to administrative agencies for 'action not inconsistent with the panel's decision' (Article 1904.8) – essentially, further investigation and clarification. This, in effect, represents a major caveat to the idea that Chapter 19 is binding in the manner that Canada and Mexico hoped.[9] This situation still reflects to some extent the relative power of each country. The limitations of Chapter 19 are part of the explanation for why these mechanisms have, thus far, failed to resolve the softwood lumber dispute to anyone's satisfaction and why, in two of Canada's six NAFTA challenges in softwood, there have been four (NAFTA 2002) and five (NAFTA 2005) remands back to US administrative agencies.

As much as Canadians would love for a NAFTA panel to at some point determine who is right and who is wrong in the softwood dispute, panels in the Chapter 19 process are not really in the business of playing referee to a dispute. Again, they rule only on the narrow question of whether a domestic agency properly applied its law to the investigation of an allegation of dumping or subsidy. They do not rule on whether one side or the other is wrong. An important limitation of the dispute settlement mechanisms is that Chapter 19 panels will never address head-on which country's land management system allows the harvest of trees in a manner that reflects their value as a scarce, but renewable, resource. The reason is that once

---

8   For more on this particular topic, see Anderson 2009.

9   For accounts of Canadian and Mexican efforts to win immunity from US trade remedy law under the CUFTA and NAFTA negotiations, see Hart *et al.* 1994: 170–72, 207-10; Cameron and Tomlin 2000: 88–89, 117; Gotlieb 1998: 522–538; Hufbauer and Schott 2005: 210–11.

the Chapter 19 process has been engaged, it becomes an essentially commercial dispute in which the interests of third-party stakeholders are unheard. This is an especially important consideration in softwood because of the environmental implications of this industry. In fact, in the early stages of Lumber IV, environmental organizations, many of them Canadian, lobbied the US government to consider lax enforcement of Canadian environmental regulations (endangered species protections, riparian zone limitations, control of excess erosion from clear-cuts into fish-bearing streams, etc.) as a major subsidy conferred to Canadian timber companies. More importantly, these same groups argued that the arbitrary setting of provincial cutting fees encouraged over-harvesting at rates that effectively subsidized production at levels that did not reflect the true value of the resource. Unfortunately, these issues fell off the agenda as soon as the litigation process took over. Aside from the question of whether US actions in softwood are justified, the Chapter 19 process has more or less immunized Canadians from having to ask themselves whether provincial stumpage systems are providing them with a reasonable return on a public resource (see Anderson 2004: 661–699).

As circumscribed as the Chapter 19 process is, as a commercial dispute settlement mechanism it was a significant step toward reigning in the arbitrary use of trade remedy laws. Rather than the uncertainty of litigating disputes in domestic administrative and legal systems, such investigations became subject to review by a panel made up of individuals from the countries involved. According to Patrick Macrory, the Chapter 19 process has been an effective alternative means of appeal of trade remedy litigation for all three NAFTA countries. Since NAFTA came into force on 1 January 1994, Canadian and Mexican exports to the US have been subject to far fewer trade remedy investigations (Macrory 2003: 2, 15; Gagne 2000: 77–91; Gagne 2003: 335–368; Audley, Papademetriou, Polaski, and Vaughn 2003). Chapter 19 has proven very successful, and is, for several reasons, overwhelmingly preferred by Canada over the pre-CUFTA system of challenging US agency investigations domestically through the United States Court of International Trade.

Back to Square One?

Softwood represents an anomaly within the NAFTA, but one that is becoming more and more dangerous for the legitimacy of the agreement itself. Not only is softwood sorely testing the limits of the Chapter 19 process with successive panel remands and re-determinations by US agencies, it is testing the many Canadians' confidence in NAFTA itself and possibly undermining the validity of the Chapter 19 process as an alternative dispute settlement process. As this chapter has already suggested, each of the NAFTA parties holds different views of what NAFTA is and what the Chapter 19 process is supposed to do. For Canada, NAFTA is about adherence to the rule of law as found in both the language and spirit of the agreement. This means not only adhering just to the narrow rulings of Chapter

19 panels, but also honouring the spirit of such rulings as well. Yet, as we have seen evidenced in recent NAFTA rulings, the US has viewed these mechanisms as binding, but only through a narrow reading of the agreement's provisions, which means re-interpretation of panel rulings and further delay, not finality. In a sense, while Canada and Mexico might view the panel process with some hope of final resolution, dispute settlement for the US seems to have more utility as a means of keeping the prospect of a negotiated settlement alive, which is precisely what seems to have materialized in Lumber IV.

The End Game in Softwood?

In late April 2006, US and Canadian negotiators agreed to a truce to the latest iteration of the long-running softwood lumber dispute. Details were not finalized until September 2006, but this should not have been a surprise to anyone who has followed this dispute, since the broad outlines of a new agreement function much like those in previous truces: a Canadian-managed graduated export tax on Canadian lumber, and a fixed US market share of between 30 and 35 per cent distributed among the four major timber-producing provinces (BC, Alberta, Ontario, and Quebec), all with a duration of seven to nine years and a promise by Canada to cease current litigation.[10] Moreover, the fact that the 2006 truce has been fraught with enforcement and oversight problems and on the verge of collapse from its inception suggests Lumber V will ensue when the current truce collapses.[11]

Yet, this agreement is only a temporary truce and will essentially defer having to tackle three important issues leftover from Lumber IV:

First, Lumber IV featured another challenge to the constitutionality of the Chapter 19 process when US lumber interests filed suit with the DC Court of Appeals.[12] It was not the first time a constitutional challenge to the legitimacy of NAFTA has been launched within the US (United Steelworkers of America 2001), nor, because of the truce, will it be the last. Past cases have challenged the

---

10 See text of 2006 SLA at http://www.international.gc.ca/controls-controles/softwood-bois_oeuvre/other-autres/agreement-accord.aspx.

11 For a long list of disputes under 2006 SLA, see http://www.international.gc.ca/controls-controles/softwood-bois_oeuvre/other-autres/agreement-accord.aspx. See also *United States of America v. Canada, Request for Arbitration*, January 18, 2008, pursuant to Article XIV of the 2006 Softwood Lumber Agreement, accessed at www.ustr.gov, February 4, 2010; See United States Trade Representative, Press Release, "Tribunal Finds Canada Failed to Cure Breach of Softwood Lumber Agreement," September 2009.

12 *Coalition for Fair Lumber Imports Executive Committee v. United States of America, et al.*, United States Court of Appeals for the District of Columbia, September 2005. In December 2006, the DC Court of Appeal said that it lacked jurisdiction to rule on the Coalition's arguments as a result of the 2006 Softwood Lumber Agreement having rendered the case "moot."

president's executive power to conclude executive agreements such as NAFTA under Article II of the US Constitution and argued that NAFTA should have been put through the Senate treaty ratification process as called for under Article I, Section 3. This particular line of reasoning failed in front of the US Supreme Court. However, the line of argument advanced because of Lumber IV by US interests argued that NAFTA's Chapter 19 process unconstitutionally denies due process of law to litigants as provided for under the 5th and 14th Amendments, and entirely circumvents the process of judicial review as provided for under Article III of the US Constitution (Coalition for Fair Lumber Imports 2005). It is unclear how big a threat this new line of reasoning would have been to NAFTA in the US context, and because of the truce we will have to wait to find out.[13] However, US courts have historically held that Congressional power over foreign commerce (Article I, Section 8), and the delegation of that power to the executive branch, are constitutional. In other words, presidential authority to adhere to NAFTA, including rulings by its dispute settlement mechanisms, is likely to remain intact.

Second, the US used an obscure provision in the Uruguay Round Agreements Implementation Act (Section 129 (a)(4)) to keep collecting cash deposits on Canadian softwood so long as the dispute continued to be played out, in effect leaving in legal limbo the millions of dollars in bonds posted by Canadian firms to US Customs and Border Protection authorities. The awkward phrasing of the US statute makes it unclear whether panel (NAFTA/WTO) or court decisions should apply to duties already collected, even when the panel ruling affects the validity of the underlying ruling. The March 2006 truce postponed resolution of this issue, most probably until after the new agreement expires and Lumber V begins.

However, it is in a third, but related realm in which Lumber IV pushed NAFTA to a potentially critical point of challenge. Part of the rationale for Chapter 19 was to pull challenges to trade remedy action out of domestic court systems and give them to bi-national panels where it was hoped that outcomes would be less biased toward domestic interests. Yet, the most important fight in Lumber IV had begun in precisely the venue that Canada wanted to avoid by proposing dispute settlement in the first place: the US Court of International Trade.

Between August 2001 and the May 2006 truce, the US had collected bonds on imported Canadian softwood equivalent to the rate of subsidy and dumping found by the US Department of Commerce. By early 2006, those bonds amounted to roughly Can$5 billion, money that Canada wants refunded as a result of successive NAFTA rulings that seem to have favoured the Canadian position. The issue is again over the wording of US NAFTA-implementing

---

13 Because of the 2006 Softwood Lumber Agreement, the DC Court of Appeals lacked jurisdiction to rule on constitutional questions and dismissed the case. See next footnote.

legislation and the simple question of whether collected duties ought to be refunded after a Department of Commerce redetermination, or retroactive to the original Commerce determination: essentially, a question of timing. This fight was about to move out of the NAFTA process altogether because under the NAFTA implementing legislation, only the US Court of International Trade can issue such a ruling on the retroactive return of duties. In short, we were about to enter uncharted waters under Chapter 19 as we were about to again be litigating aspects of softwood in a domestic court setting.[14]

This could have been a serious subversion of the NAFTA process, since the dispute effectively moved beyond NAFTA and was being fought in a domestic setting, just as these kinds of cases were prior to NAFTA or CUFTA. Here, Canada might have won the battle, in terms of collecting some Can$5 billion in posted duties, but ultimately lost the war because of the additional damage this suit could have done to the already tattered credibility of NAFTA.

For some, the April 2006 truce might be viewed as stopping irreparable damage from being done. For Prime Minister Harper, the temporary truce pulled softwood lumber from the front pages of the Canadian press and reduced its importance in Canada–US relations. For Canadians, in particular, pushing NAFTA to the brink is a double edged sword since the Chapter 19 process has essentially worked, giving Canada a mechanism it did not otherwise have, and providing a way for Canada to gain leverage in these kinds of disputes that it previously did not have. Yet, the 2006 truce also postponed an important opportunity to deal with many of the very questions about NAFTA and the Chapter 19 process itself that the softwood dispute was bringing to the fore.

As a result of the April 2006 truce, Lumber IV will, unfortunately, likely turn into Lumber V sometime after 2013,[15] in part, because critical issues in Lumber IV were not allowed to play themselves out. The only long-term solution to the softwood lumber dispute is continued cross-border integration of the entire North American forest sector. Such integration will change the coalitions of stakeholders in each country, in that it will be increasingly difficult to differentiate and identify firms with particular nations; hence, the incentives to protect your own industry and market will shift and make additional litigation less and less likely. For some, this sounds like inevitable Americanization of Canada's softwood production. However, since Canada's softwood sector has become a world leader in efficiency, it could just as easily mean the Canadianization of US softwood production.

---

14 See *TEMBEC* n.d. Similar to the constitutional challenge in the DC Court of Appeals, the Court of International Trade case was rendered "moot" by the 2006 Softwood Lumber Agreement, but the United States Court of International Trade did rule in Canada's favour.

15 The 2006 Agreement's duration was set at seven to nine years. However, as noted above, a series of compliance disputes have shaken the truce and could result in its collapse prior to the 2013–2015 window.

Because NAFTA never set out to resolve differences in alternative systems of governance (as in private land holdings vs. Crown lands in forest management), the NAFTA dispute settlement mechanism, unlike firm-level cross-border integration, is ill-equipped to deal with this dispute in a way that will bring closure.

The Chapter 11 Surprise

A very different set of dispute settlement mechanisms contained in NAFTA have also threatened to undermine public confidence in the entire agreement: the so-called 'investor-state' provisions of Chapter 11. The incorporation of alternative dispute settlement mechanisms in NAFTA was expected by negotiators to herald a shift toward more predictable economic relations by shifting disputes from the realm of impassioned politics to quasi-judicial, and impartial, panels of experts. Much as Chapter 19 did this for politically charged domestic trade remedy laws, Chapter 11 was supposed to have plugged gaps in international private investment law. However, unlike Chapter 19, which generated some controversy in the Canada–US free trade negotiations in the late 1980s, the investment provisions of Chapter 11 generated comparatively little in either the bilateral (CUFTA) or trilateral (NAFTA) talks. However, for reasons not anticipated at the time of negotiation, Chapter 11 has become NAFTA's most controversial set of provisions, further undermining prospects for deepening North American integration (Hufbauer and Schott 2005: 204).

Long History, Little Controversy

Since the early 1980s, the US has employed bilateral investment treaties (BITs) as a means of dealing with private commercial law issues in the context of international law between states.[16] A series of investment disputes between Canada and the US in the early 1980s led to the incorporation of Chapter 16 into the CUFTA covering investment (Fry 1983: 80–89). Chapter 16 is essentially a US-style BIT, one of the first ever concluded between two developed countries and the first incorporated into a US trade agreement (Salacuse 2002: 10).

Chapter 16 of CUFTA guaranteed that investments made in the host country by each other's nationals would be accorded treatment no less favourable than that accorded to firms in the domestic market (national treatment). Such treatment included securing rights of establishment, acquisition, sale, and conduct of enterprises in each other's territory (Article 1602). In addition, the threat of the imposition of performance requirements, such as minimum export levels or local

---

16 See Salacuse 1990: 664–673. Salacuse points out that the United States was slow compared to Europe in employing the BIT as a means of managing its investment relations (656–57). See also Bergsten and Graham 1992: 15–44.

content rules, as a condition of investment would no longer be permitted under CUFTA (Article 1603). And, of course, both parties agreed to a prohibition on measures that directly or indirectly nationalized or expropriated investments of the other party in its territory, and would not impose any measures that would be tantamount to expropriation, such as those that intentionally depressed foreign asset prices (Article 1605).

Chapter 16 of CUFTA was relatively uncontroversial, and remained so when the same provisions were replicated in NAFTA a few years later as Chapter 11. Yet, members of Congress began to have doubts about Chapter 11 when Raymond Loewen, chairman of The Loewen Group, filed a Chapter 11 case in 1998 claiming that an unfavourable 1996 Mississippi jury decision against The Loewen Group denied the firm national treatment, expropriated the firm's private property, and limited its future earnings (Loewen Group 1998). While this case was eventually dismissed in its entirety in June 2003, five years of litigation, and the apparent mechanism provided by Chapter 11 for circumventing the decision of a Mississippi jury, suggested that the BIT-like investor protections in US trade agreements were not being used as intended. Indeed, as of the fall of 2010, 40 separate Chapter 11 arbitration cases had been filed: 12 against Canada, 12 against Mexico, and 16 against the US. The distribution of cases by itself has alarmed critics of NAFTA and members of Congress alike since, given its history of expropriation, the presumptive target of Chapter 11 investor protections was actually Mexico (Hufbauer and Schott 2005: 201–203; Cameron and Tomlin 2000: 40–42). However, critiques of the case distribution were merely indicative of a broader and growing set of concerns unforeseen when *fast track* was renewed or extended between 1984 and 1991.

Both the case distribution and the apparent abuse of the provisions to challenge domestic legal regimes, in spite of explicit language within NAFTA to the contrary (Articles 1101 and 1114), have alarmed public interest advocates, environmentalists, and a growing number in Congress. Several cases have drawn the ire of environmentalists,[17] but none more so than *Methanex Corp. vs. United States of America*. Methanex Corporation, a Canadian marketer and distributor of methanol, claimed damages of close to US$1 billion for alleged injuries resulting from a California ban on the use or sale of the gasoline additive MTBE that contains methanol as a key ingredient. Methanex contended that a California executive order banning MTBE was a discriminatory act tantamount to expropriation of its property under several provisions of NAFTA Chapter 11 (Methanex 1999).

Unfortunately, Chapter 11 of NAFTA was given no clear definitions or criteria for determining which measures rise to the level of expropriation, no body of jurisprudence to draw upon, and a clause in the agreement (Article 1136 (1)) explicitly separating the cases from one another, thus limiting the scope

---

17 For instance, *Ethyl vs. Government of Canada*, *S.D. Myers vs. Government of Canada*, or *Metalclad vs. United Mexican States*.

for creating precedent. In partial response to critics, and in light of several worrisome cases such as *Methanex*, in July 2001 the NAFTA Commission issued a definitional 'interpretation' concerning the 'minimum' and 'fair and equitable' standards of treatment private investment could expect under NAFTA's rules.[18] The interpretation laid down an important political marker for future arbitral panels regarding the standard by which foreign investment was to be judged (NAFTA Free Trade Commission 2001). More importantly, the interpretation came at a time when the George W. Bush administration was trying to build support for his trade initiatives in Congress. The July 2001 NAFTA interpretation not only outlined how Chapter 11's provisions should be read, but directly altered US negotiating positions in trade agreements thereafter, notably those with Chile, Singapore, five Central American states (Costa Rica, Honduras, Nicaragua, Guatemala, and El Salvador) and the Dominican Republic (DR–CAFTA). The investment chapters of each of these agreements go to great lengths, much further than NAFTA, to more precisely define terms such as 'fair and equitable' and 'full protection and security'.[19] Yet, the language contained in 2002's Trade Promotion Authority, the Congressional legislation granting presidential negotiating authority, goes much further than the NAFTA Commission's interpretation, by mandating that new US trade agreements contain greater specificity on what expropriation is – something NAFTA did not do.

Chapter 11 Beyond NAFTA?

Perceived weaknesses with the language and operation of NAFTA Chapter 11 have led to much greater specificity in subsequent US trade agreements in those areas where creative lawyers and ill-definition had threatened NAFTA. For instance, unlike NAFTA, which leaves customary international law undefined, each of the new agreements does so explicitly by confirming 'their shared understanding that "customary international law" generally and as specifically referenced ... from a general and consistent practice of States that they follow from a sense of legal obligation'[20] In 2001, the three NAFTA countries could

---

18 Recall that Customary International Law, like international law generally is difficult to define since it all it really refers to is the ever changing customary practice of states.

19 See Article 10.4 of the United States-Chile Free Trade Agreement, Article 10.5 of the US–Central American FTA, and Article 15.5 of the US–Singapore FTA, all available at Each of these agreements also contains a provision regarding the Parties shared understanding regarding the definition of the "minimum standard of treatment" under customary international law which reads: 'the customary international law minimum standard of treatment of aliens refers to all customary international law principles that protect the economic rights and interests of aliens.'

20 See US–Central American FTA, Annex 10-B and US–Chile FTA, Annex 10-A. See also, *Inside U.S. Trade* 2002a, 2002b.

not reach an agreement on how best to limit or define the limits of expropriation under Chapter 11. However, in 2002 when considering President Bush's request for trade promotion authority, the US Congress offered important limitations to expropriation that have been incorporated into the text of every post-NAFTA US trade agreement (US Congress 2002). In a clear response to the perceived threat posed by cases like *Methanex*, the Chile FTA is more explicit than NAFTA in saying that national legislation aimed at public welfare objectives, such as public health, safety, and the environment, do not constitute indirect expropriations.[21]

While it was never the intention of NAFTA negotiators that frivolous lawsuits challenging the State's power to legislate in the public interest be a consequence of Chapter 11, the case history suggested the potential for abuse and required language in subsequent agreements that possibly limited the future application of investment protections to future situations.[22] In response to critiques regarding process transparency, Congress also mandated that new investment provisions provide for third-party amicus submissions, appellate mechanisms, and more accurate wording to prevent the launch of frivolous claims.[23] While augmented transparency might be desirable, these new provisions do significantly alter the original intent behind Chapter 11 and its BIT antecedents by introducing a range of potential new actors to the process. Whereas the US BIT program was designed to help manage the narrow relationships between firms and hosts, negotiating US investment provisions now contemplates the inclusion of a much broader range of interests with increasing Congressional oversight and an uncertain utility in resolving investment disputes.

Renaissance or Façade?

Early in the administration of George W. Bush, Fred Bergsten of the Institute for International Economics referred to a new vigour in US trade policy as a 'renaissance' (Bergsten 2002: 86–98). In many ways, Bergsten was correct, particularly when activity by the Bush administration was contrasted with that of the Clinton years. Whereas the Clinton administration failed in three separate

---

21 "Except in rare circumstances, non-discriminatory regulatory actions by a Party which are designed and applied to protect legitimate public welfare objectives, such as public health, safety, and the environment, do not constitute indirect expropriations." US–Chile FTA, Annex 10-D, 4(b).

22 The US Department of State, which litigates Chapter 11 cases on behalf of the US Government, does point out that it has successfully litigated every case that has been brought against it by a private interest under Chapter 11.

23 *Ibid.*

efforts between 1994 and 2000 to obtain congressional negotiating authority,[24] and was the first US administration to have had such authority expire, the Bush team managed to stickhandle their way to approval by Congress in the spring of 2002 (US Congress (2002).

However, while optimists looked at fast-track renewal as evidence that the US was poised to reassume leadership for additional liberalization of the global trade regime, particularly in the newly launched (November 2001) Doha Development Round of the WTO, and push for conclusion of the FTAA agreement by January 2005, the political landscape was hardly rosy enough to justify calling it a renaissance. In fact, the politics of US trade policy have in many ways become more, not less, complicated since the infamous 'Battle in Seattle' at the November 1999 WTO ministerial meetings in Seattle, Washington.

The source of growing US discontent and reconsideration of trade liberalization can actually be traced to the debate over NAFTA itself. After endorsing NAFTA during the 1992 presidential election campaign, Bill Clinton used much of the political capital he won during the election fighting to win passage of NAFTA-implementing legislation in late 1993.[25] The battle badly fractured the Democratic Party and bitterly alienated many of the party's most ardent supporters in US labour unions. In a sense, much of the political momentum that seemed to have been building for additional trade liberalization with the advent of CUFTA, NAFTA, and then the completion of the Uruguay Round of the WTO in 1994, seemed to be lost just as quickly in the bitterness of the fight.

With the advent of the administration of George W. Bush, the subsequent launch of the Doha Development Round, and passage of US fast-track legislation, the US seemed to be poised to be a much more serious participant in leading the global trade regime. And, looking back, there is perhaps some justification for calling this period a renaissance. However, the flurry of activity masked deep divisions that were not bridged simply because of the launch of the Doha Round or the success in winning trade promotion authority. In fact, trade promotion authority made it through the US House of Representatives by only the slimmest of margins (215:212) with a larger margin in the Senate (61:38).

The FTAA has long since passed its original January 2005 deadline for completion, but was effectively stalled long before then because of US insistence that agricultural issues be dealt with in the multi-lateral Doha negotiations rather than regionally as Brazil and others have wanted (see Weintraub 2004b). However, had the FTAA come to fruition as planned, it would have had an uphill ratification

---

24 For an explanation of fast track as an institution in US trade policy, see Destler 1997: 5–10, 16–19.

25 "To Implement the North American Free Trade Agreement," introduced as House Resolution 311, November 1993 and became Public Law 103-182 on December 8, 1993. Passed the House 234-200 and Senate 61–38.

battle within the US – a battle that DR–CAFTA recently fought and barely won in the summer of 2005.

Not since the NAFTA debate has trade animated so many voices in opposition to an agreement. Business groups, trade unions, Latino associations, environmental advocates, and narrow protectionist organizations such as Idaho sugar-beet growers, all chose sides and nearly killed the agreement. As it was, the DR–CAFTA implementing legislation narrowly won approval in the US House by just two votes (217:215), and only then after heavy pressure on legislators by the administration to approve the agreement.

Agreements like DR–CAFTA are of negligible significance for the US economy and are instead more heavily influenced by broader US foreign policy objectives (see Zoellick 2001; Eckes 1995; Pollard 1985). Yet, the fight over DR–CAFTA is indicative of the long-standing, post-NAFTA malaise in the US about major new integration projects.

A Closing US Window?

Since the expiration of trade promotion authority in mid-2007, the Bush administration adopted a more *ad hoc* approach to winning Congressional acquiescence on trade policy, which includes the semantic sleight-of-hand that has shifted the labelling of agreements from 'free trade agreements' to 'trade promotion agreements'.[26] In the absence of blanket grants of negotiating authority, the administration has had to engage in closer consultations and bargaining with members of Congress to win assent. It is increasingly likely that the administration will have to do likewise if the Doha Round is to come to fruition. The stakes could not be higher for the success of the Doha Round, a round that was supposed to be focused on enhancing trade benefits for the WTO's least developed members (Elliot 2006). The failure of the Doha Round could deal a significant blow to the multilateral trading system. Several setbacks in the Doha Round are indicative of the emergent tensions between the developed and developing worlds over economic policy, particularly agriculture (Anderson 2005: 3–9; Bhagwati 2004). Yet, as indicative of the difficulties for the global trading regime as Doha has become, these same challenges are equally indicative of the political atmosphere on trade policy in the US that inevitably spills over into considerations of North American integration.

Some Canadian observers have pointed to US frustrations over Doha as a potential window of opportunity, similar to that which existed in the late 1980s in the midst of the Uruguay Round, and seemingly led the US to be more receptive to an FTA with Canada (Hart *et al.* 1994: 36–53; Dobson 2002; Haynal 2004).

---

26 For instance, the US–Colombia *Trade Promotion* Agreement (signed 2006), or the US–Peru *Trade Promotion* Agreement (2006) in contrast to the US–Chile *Free Trade* Agreement (2004), (emphasis mine).

Debates about the 'big idea' or a 're-bilateralization' of North America in recent years, many of which emanate from Canada, have more or less neglected an analysis of the US (Carleton 2009; Dark et al. 2009; Castro-Rea 2009). The assumption has been that if Canadians could merely pitch the right big idea to Washington, the US would respond and get on board with the project. This line of reasoning holds that the US understands Canadian political sensitivities (and Mexican for that matter) and merely needs the junior partner to make the first move forward with a proposal.[27] This entire line of reasoning fails to consider US politics and institutions and does not even consider the likely prospect that the US itself would balk at such a proposal, given its experience with NAFTA and the deterioration of the politics of trade since.

America's foreign and domestic policy agendas are full already (healthcare, financial reform, immigration, two overseas wars) and hardly have room for a major integration project like the big idea. Further, the security agenda has focused itself on existing borders as major lines of defence against terrorism. There is undoubtedly greater co-operation among government agencies in all three NAFTA countries, but the focus of attention is on the borders, thereby making them more salient, not less so. The politics of trade in the US are complicated enough with respect to agreements of little substance, such as DR–CAFTA, that any remaining political capital in the near term is going to be spent supporting completion of the Doha Round, not a new project here in North America.

The prevailing malaise over trade liberalization in the US has been compounded by the anti-NAFTA rhetoric of the 2008 presidential campaign and, of course, the onset of the financial crisis rooted in the US housing market. As others in this volume detail, all of this has been further complicated by the insertion of security atop the North American agenda. More subtly perhaps is the lack of consensus among the US public and, interestingly, the US business community about what the North American agenda ought to be or how to move it forward. In 2006, the North American Competitiveness Council (NACC) formed out of a collection of business interests in all three countries trying to plug themselves into the North American Security and Prosperity Partnership (SPP) launched the year before at Waco, Texas (Anderson and Sands 2007: 19–25). Three things about the NACC's contribution to the SPP process are of significance for the future of the North American agenda: First, the NACC itself came together spontaneously in response to the SPP. Business interests had not, until then, been a significant part of the original agenda-setting process for the SPP (Anderson and Sands 2007). Second, the NACC's recommendations were a shopping list of issues, all of which were important for competitiveness but challenging to tackle politically. Third, and most significantly, the NACC has largely faded from view since its recommendations were presented to leaders at the 2006 North American Leaders' Summit in Cancun, Mexico.

---

27 See Haynal 2004: 2. As Haynal adroitly points out, arguments by Canadian advocates of deeper integration in North America fail to consider the US domestic context.

Whither NAFTA?

NAFTA is a 'mature' trade agreement in that the phase-in of all its provisions is now complete. The big idea in North America is not dead. After all, in the years immediately preceding the start of Canada–US free trade talks in 1985, most observers would have said such an agreement was preposterous. But prospects for a new integration project on the scale of NAFTA are as weak as they have ever been. Frustrations with parts of NAFTA itself have generated some reconsideration of its virtues (Chapter 19) and its unintended consequences (Chapter 11). In the end, NAFTA has, by and large, done what it was designed to do: liberalize the North American trade and investment regime. As evidenced by the impressive growth in trade and investment flows, this goal has been achieved.

Yet, for those who emphasize NAFTA's shortcomings including its lack of supranational institutions, the absence of a mandate for addressing a range of social ills, or the weakness of its labour and environmental side agreements, the goal of a deeper, more robust kind of North American governance remains in the variants of the big idea. Economic integration will continue to advance as local and regional interests continue strengthening their cross-border ties to one another.

Critics of NAFTA's weaknesses worry about the implications of a deeper integration project in North America such as a customs or monetary union. Yet, the more immediate problem is that the hardening of borders as a result of security becoming the dominant paradigm for thinking about North America is challenging our ability to maintain the economic openness that fuels our prosperity. NAFTA remains an important factor in maintaining that openness, but it may not be enough, and the weaknesses outlined above suggest areas in need of some changes.

For the time being, North America's borders have become more, not less significant; less, not more, porous; and more, not less, prominent in our economic, social, and political lives. As a result, the passport Anthony DePalma forgot while living in Toronto several years ago is as necessary as ever.

Chapter 4
The Security and Prosperity Partnership: Made in North America Integration or Co-operation?

Jimena Jiménez

The Security and Prosperity Partnership of North America (SPP) is dead, states a left-leaning Canadian website; it died at the trilateral leaders' summit that took place in Guadalajara in August 2009 (Trew 2009). Indeed, the SPP was not at all mentioned, not even a whisper, at the most recent North American Guadalajara Leaders' Summit in Guadalajara, in 2009, at least not explicitly (White House 2009). As if to further prove the point, the US government's SPP website states the following: 'The Security and Prosperity Partnership of North America (SPP) is no longer an active initiative and as such this website will act as an archive for SPP documents. There will not be any updates to this site' (SPP, US government site, 2010). Is the SPP really dead, like some speculate? What happened to the SPP? Why have officials been so silent on it?

The supposed death of the SPP is good news for its many critics and detractors. The SPP, a trilateral initiative announced in 2005 to facilitate co-operation between Canada, the US and Mexico on common challenges, became feared and vilified by particular sectors of the North American public. The SPP faced real legitimacy and credibility problems revolving around the way it was implemented (without public consultation) and who was included at the table (the private sector) (Pastor 2008: 93). The SPP, and initiatives that came before it, like the 2001 Canada–US Smart Border Declaration and the 2002 US–Mexico Border Partnership, became entangled in a broader debate about what some observers viewed as the process of integration in the region and about the development of North America as a distinct social, political, and economic entity. At one end of the spectrum were critics who charged that the SPP and similar government-led initiatives represented a secret scheme to 'integrate' the continent and form a 'North American union' *à la Européenne* that jeopardized the sovereignty of each country. At the other end, others argued that SPP-like initiatives are merely ways for Canada, the US and Mexico to co-operate and find solutions to common challenges.

In this chapter, I argue that it is the latter rather than the former process that most accurately characterizes what is taking place in North America – at least at a government level. There is co-operation (defined as a process where countries work together to achieve common goals) between the three countries, and it is increasing, but it does not amount to integration (defined as the transference of political authority from the national to the supranational level) – especially not in the way it has developed and been defined in Europe. Major socio-political obstacles exist in the region that would prevent European-style integration from ever developing. Rather, as the North American case demonstrates, state actors can enter into a complex process of interagency co-operation in order to provide the necessary support systems needed to sustain high degrees of economic integration in a secure and protected North America. The result is a particular brand of North American co-operation that at times encounters problems that raise some important questions for the future of governance in North America.

Indeed, the SPP is a case in point of the challenges facing the region. At best, it can be characterized as an instrument that enables co-operation and communication on key areas of concern. Its announcement in 2005, and some of the work that has progressed under it over the years, had signalled, to a certain extent, the existence of a North American agenda. However, in the face of public discontent over the initiative, the three governments have chosen to relay the SPP to the background, as if it doesn't exist. In fact, North American officials responsible for it have purposefully and cautiously attempted to delink the SPP from the broader North America Leaders' Summit agenda, and away from the public light. So, the SPP is not dead; it may have changed in shape and form, but it still continues to operate on its own. More importantly though, the way in which North American officials have handled the SPP is a barometer of the current state of politics in North America. Rather than putting it on the back burner, they could have chosen instead to directly engage the public in a dialogue on the importance of North America and its future, and made a case for the SPP, thereby demonstrating some leadership and vision – something the North American project badly needs.

In this chapter, I explore the SPP and its Smart Border predecessors in the context of both functional theories of international relations, and fears exposed in each country that the SPP is serving as a Trojan horse for further political integration. I maintain that, contrary to some of the core theoretical formulations emerging from the European experience such as neo-functionalism, pressures for co-operation induced by the post-September 11 security environment, and competitive forces emanating from outside the region do not require the creation of joint decision-making structures or supranational institutions. Nor are they ever likely to. I argue these points by first entering into a brief discussion about the central theoretical postulations put forth by neo-functionalism, the core integration theory deriving from Europe. I maintain that although one could make the case that the process of 'bureaucratic integration' demonstrated by the SPP and Smart Borders policies is in line with some of the tenets of functionalism, it is not entirely useful in explaining the absence of supranational institutions in North America. Next, I analyse the SPP and, to a lesser extent, Smart Border policies, by focusing on three features: bureaucratic-led policymaking, systematic incrementalism, and dual bilateralism. I contend that these traits explain why it is precisely co-operation rather than integration that has evolved in North America. Finally, I discuss some of the governance implications raised by the SPP and the particular brand of co-operation that it represents.

Neo-functionalism and the Concept of Integration

Much of the academic and political debate that has surfaced in recent years around the nature of social, political, and economic processes underway in North America has been influenced to a large extent by the European experience and some of the theoretical formulations originating from that context. Indeed, many scholars who study the region base their analyses and conclusions on socio-political processes underway in North America on the European model.

Perhaps the theoretical body that has most dominated the study of integration in Europe is neo-functionalism. This body of literature set the initial parameters and context for the academic and political debate that frames the concept of integration in North America. Neo-functionalism is based on some of the work produced by early functionalists such as David Mitrany. Viewed by many as the father of functionalism, Mitrany maintained that economic and social co-operation between states would become increasingly important and take over the place held by the territorial state (Eastby 1985: 2–3).

Mitrany focused on task-oriented international institutions that could efficiently address human issues. According to his world views, political actors would for practical reasons choose to create functional institutions that would be organized according to the specific nature of the function, 'the conditions under which it has to operate, and ... the needs of the moment' (Mitrany in Rosamond 2000: 3).

Over time, these task-oriented organizations would eventually give rise to attitudinal changes among those who were involved in the organization. The 'practical experience of functionalism in action' would generate the production of other similar functional agencies, eventually forming an intricate web of organizations that would encourage and reinforce dependency and discourage conflict among the political actors involved (Rosamond 2000: 36).

This early functionalist work by Mitrany was the foundation for neo-functionalism. His emphasis on moving beyond the nation state, the sectoral logic of functionalism, and in general his conception of the post-Westphalian order, all resonate in neo-functional principles.

One of neo-functionalism's central concepts is that of 'spill-over': the idea that integration in one sector will lead to integration in other sectors. The logic here is that there exist within industrial economies some sectors that are so interdependent that it is counterproductive to treat them separately. Thus, attempts to integrate some functional sectors will lead to the integration of other interrelated sectors (O'Brien 1995: 697).

Neo-functionalism, as described by Lindberg and Haas, also contains an explicitly political element, or what was referred to as 'political spill-over'. In this view, political actors such as interest groups, parties, and governments will undergo a learning process during which it will be realized that their interests are better served by seeking supranational instead of national solutions. As such, they will refocus their activities to the new centre, a process that will lead to political integration (Mikkelson 1991: 5).

The functionalist literature implies a particular definition of 'integration' that I argue does not lend itself easily to an analysis of the North American case study. The concept of integration is difficult to define. At its most basic level, one can define integration as constructing a whole out of separate parts, or joining together independent units into a new entity, but this definition often leaves the concept open to ambiguity. For instance, integration is often confused with and used interchangeably with intergovernmental co-operation, political unification, and political community (Nye 1968: 856). For some, integration appears to signify consultation over foreign policy issues. For federalists, it has meant the establishment of new federal institutions. Others equate integration with ad hoc bargaining between sovereign states, a definition more akin to intergovernmental co-operation than to integration per se (Smith 1999: 5). Functionalists suppose integration to demand the reordering of national authority into a new supranational area of political activity. Political integration in this sense is defined as the process whereby political actors in separate national settings create a new type of political centre with a centralized co-ordinated decision-making authority that overrides the sovereignty of national jurisdictions (Mikkelson 1991: 4).

However in North America, there really has been no move on the part of political actors in the three countries to create a political union. To be sure, the NAFTA governments have engaged in a process of narrow bureaucratic and administrative co-operation that is much in line with functionalists tenets. Clearly, the past success of NAFTA in both increasing and solidifying economic ties between all three partners has in turn generated associated pressures. For example, the enhanced movement of goods, services, and people across North American borders has produced pressures to ameliorate and amplify transportation systems. Indeed, both the Canada–US and US–Mexico Smart Border policies include sections on 'Secure Infrastructure'. Under the Canada–US plan, parties pledge to 'coordinate physical and technological improvements to key border points and trade corridors aimed at overcoming traffic management and growth challenges' (Canada, DFAIT 2001). The US–Mexico plan seeks to identify priority infrastructure projects to avoid bottlenecks (Gabriel, Jimenez and Macdonald 2003: 31).

Nevertheless, although responding to spill-over pressures, these initiatives, and an extensive list of similar ones developed through the SPP and Smart Border frameworks, do not inevitably result in the erection of a new supranational structure similar to the European Union (EU) as neo-functionalists predict. Rather, a number of different socio-political variables particular to the region will mediate any emergent processes. Models that merely export European generalizations miss this important point.

Indeed, North America is not the EU. In terms of origin and founding purpose, for instance, the EU and NAFTA are significantly different. The EU's origin had to do with the devastating effects of two wars that consequently prompted the European leaders to construct a deliberately united Europe. As the European preamble to the Treaty Establishing the European Coal and Steel Community notes, the European establishment of a community or union would replace 'age old rivalries' and bring together 'peoples long divided by bloody conflict' (cited in Pastor 2001: 28). Second, the Europeans have constructed a complex institutional infrastructure to support the political integration project. Institutions like the European Commission, the European Parliament, and the European Court all function as supranational entities that direct EU policies and uphold the end goal of uniting member countries into an integrated Europe (Pastor 2001: 29). Third, notwithstanding economic and social differences, the European member countries are more balanced and equal in terms of power. EU structural aid policies help to achieve relative social and economic parity in an effort to reduce the gap between rich and poor members (Pastor 2001: 29). Indeed, this is one of the most important goals of the EU. In contrast, NAFTA was created in response to purely economic interests, with goals designed to eliminate barriers to trade and create a secure market that increased the competition of firms (Pastor 2001: 96). Moreover, North American leaders intentionally avoided creating an institutional structure to channel the integration project. In fact, the North American region is practically devoid of supranational institutions. The institutions that do exist, like the NAFTA Free Trade Commission or the Commission for Environmental Cooperation (CEC), are minimalist in composition and possess limited powers (McKinney 2000: 243).

Perhaps the most important differentiation between the North American region and Europe is the imbalanced and asymmetrical nature of the trilateral relationship between the region's three countries. The sheer political and economic magnitude of the US puts Mexico and Canada at a considerable disadvantage when dealing with the US, resulting in power asymmetries between Canada, the US, and Mexico (Canada, Parliament 2002: 180). The co-existence of a political heavy-weight with two much smaller, much weaker, powers and the asymmetries generated by their interaction, to a large extent structures the North American complex.[1] Associated with this is the fact that although each country is an equal partner in NAFTA, the

---

1   The EU is also characterized by asymmetries, however, they are not as pronounced or as overwhelming as those that define North America. Jennifer Welsh explains that no country in modern history has come even remotely close to the United States' current hegemony in the world system, whether viewed through an economic, military, or political lens. Even Germany, the largest power in the enlarged EU, has much more limited powers than the US (see Welsh 2004: 35). Moreover, the EU has a "built-in counter-asymmetric" system that through various institutional mechanisms and a qualified majority voting system in the Council of Ministers mitigates the potential power of any one state from controlling the whole system (see Clarkson 2002: 26). Compare this to NAFTA's purposefully-weak institutional structure accompanied by a superpower that is highly skeptical and suspicious of institutions that might diminish its sovereignty.

North American economic landscape is, in reality, constituted by two separate bilateral relationships: Canada–US and Mexico–US.[2] Integration in North America is also shaped by much more pronounced disintegrative pressures than is the EU, such as loss-of-sovereignty claims, domestic issues, and unilateral attitudes due to US hegemony. These features preclude the creation of shared, top-down, formal institutions that limit state sovereignty.

Instead, what has developed is a particular brand of co-operation that is conditioned by the socio-political realities that define North America. The NAFTA governments have found ways to collaborate on common issues of importance without creating an overarching governance superstructure. Smart Border policies and the SPP are a case in point.

Smart Borders and the SPP: North American Style Co-operation

For much of the pre-9/11 era, the contours of North America as a socio-political entity, as more than just a geographic region, were only just gradually beginning to emerge. NAFTA, of course, has been the cornerstone of continental co-operation. NAFTA, through both government actions and market-driven forces reflecting the independent choices of businesses and consumers independently from governments, has led to an increasingly linked North American economic zone of activity. Indeed, for all intents and purposes, the economies of Canada, the US, and Mexico operate as a single continental North American market. Much of the trade between the three countries is intra-regional trade – between usually US parent firms and their Canadian or Mexican subsidiary (McDougall 2004: 14). However, beyond NAFTA, for various historical reasons, the government-led North American agenda has lacked an explicit socio-political dimension and can be described as ambiguous at best.

---

2 There are of course multiple and even bilateral relationships operating in the EU context. Subgroups of member states co-operate on special issues that are of particular interest to them. For instance, in 1985, West Germany, France and Benelux countries co-operated outside the framework of the EU to create what eventually was referred to as Schengen co-operation, in order to facilitate passport-free travel across national boundaries. In the European literature this concept is referred to as 'close co-operation', or the idea that member states can engage in certain European projects that do not involve all member states. However, as stipulated in the 1997 Treaty of Amsterdam, the expectation is that 'close co-operation' be aimed at furthering or contributing to the goals of the Union. Additionally, 'close co-operation' is open to all member states who wish to participate in the project. Indeed, in the case of Schengen co-operation most EU member states eventually joined the agreement (see Donnelly and Hawes 2004). By contrast, in the North American case, the lack of a common North American trilateral space in which to co-operate means that bilateral relationships tend to dominate.

The events of September 11 propelled the North American agenda forward, injecting it with a heavy dose of political will as all three countries reordered their existing conceptual and infrastructure frameworks. For the US, the systemic shocks of 9/11 affected how it thought about the world and its role within it. The events of 9/11 enabled the US to legitimately construct a new identity and role for itself. This novel identity was based on an understanding of a new enemy defined broadly as 'terrorism' and consequent new practices associated with defining this elusive enemy (Croucher 2004: 4). A redefinition of the US self-identity also included a re-conceptualization of how the US saw its neighbours and allies. As bordering states, Canada and Mexico fell into the 'us versus them' category. By virtue of their geopolitical position and the fact that US officials recognized that to improve security the co-operation of its two neighbours was paramount, Canada and Mexico would effectively have to comprise the 'us'. They would have to be located within the North American security perimeter.

For Canada and Mexico, the actual and anticipated response to 9/11 constituted a clear and present threat to their economic wellbeing. For both countries, given the depth of their economic integration with the US, the key question revolved around security of market access. The US's unilateral imposition of a security-one level alert at its borders demonstrated very effectively the consequences of a disruption in cross-border relations. Consequently, both countries, albeit at times reluctantly, moved to assuage US fears and their own by calling for Smart Border plans and later agreeing to the US call for an SPP.

In December of 2001, Canada and the US signed the Canada-US Smart Border Declaration. The Declaration included a 30-point action plan based on four pillars: (1) the secure flow of people; (2) the secure flow of goods; (3) secure infrastructure, and (4) co-ordination and information sharing (Canada. Parliament 2002: 93). The US and Mexico also signed a parallel agreement, the US-Mexico Border Partnership, a few months later in 2002. Although the latter version included fewer sections than its Canada–US counterpart, and encompassed only 22 action points, both border accords have as their objective creating a Smart Border by focusing on high-risk targets and managing them without impeding the flow of legitimate people and goods (Canada. Parliament 2002: 167).

The SPP was born just a few years later in March 2005, in Waco, Texas. It is a trilateral initiative meant to induce co-operation on common issues of concern faced by all three countries. Specifically, the SPP obligates the North American partners to address what government officials view as two complementary agendas: security and prosperity.

On the security side, the SPP advances three mutually reinforcing goals: (1) securing and protecting North America from external threats; (2) preventing and responding to internal threats from within North America; and (3) streamlining the safe and speedy movement of legal traffic across North America (SPP, Canadian Government Website, 2005: 28).

On the prosperity front, the objective is to encourage transformation in key sectors of the economy in order to harness competitiveness and deal with the growing economic strength of emerging countries like China and India. Initiatives include (1) implementing a trilateral regulatory co-operation framework to ameliorate productivity; (2) further building on NAFTA by expanding duty-free treatment through rules of origin liberalization; and (3) focusing on 'enabling' sectors like transportation and energy. The prosperity agenda also includes a quality-of-life component that has as its goal ensuring high quality of life for the citizens of North America through measures aimed at the environmental, food safety management, and the disease control domains (Ackelson and Kastner 2005: 3).

In its initial iteration, the SPP included the creation of various security and prosperity working groups. Since 2005, these working groups have provided annual reports to leaders on their progress and key accomplishments at each North American leaders' summit (except for the August 2009 Summit in Guadalajara). The 2005 report set out the initial proposals of how to accomplish SPP objectives and specified some high-priority initiatives for work (including electronic commerce, rules of origin, developing higher safety and health standards, and dealing with environmental challenges) (Lake and Villareal 2009: 1). In August 2007, Prime Minister Harper, President Bush, and President Fox met in Montebello, Quebec for a third North America leaders' summit. The Summit followed a second meeting that took place in Cancún, Mexico in March 2006 where leaders focused their attention on five areas of co-operation: (1) creation of a North American Competitiveness Council; (2) advancing co-operation on avian and pandemic influenza; (3) a North American Energy Security Initiative; (4) North American energy management; and (5) smart and secure borders (White House 2006).

Aside from taking stock of progress on the SPP agenda since Cancún, the Montebello Summit (as it was commonly referred to by the media) attempted, albeit tentatively, to move beyond the purely SPP focus of the previous Cancún meeting and establish a broader North American agenda. Leaders shared perspectives on global, multilateral, and hemispheric issues (Canada, Prime Minister's Office 2007a). As well, leaders agreed to work on a series of other initiatives to do with addressing shared environmental challenges, consumer protection, and assuring both efficient and safe borders (Canada, Prime Minister's Office 2007b). Since the 2007 Montebello Summit, there has been less and less official focus on the SPP. It was last mentioned in the 2008 North American Leaders' Summit in New Orleans where the leaders directed their ministers charged with responsibility for the SPP to renew and focus its work in the areas of competitiveness, smarter and more secure borders, energy security and environmental protection, food and product safety, and emergency response (Lake and Villareal 2009: 2).

The SPP and Smart Border policies are based on the idea that countries must co-operate to reduce and even abolish duplication of efforts, thereby diminishing costs and improving efficiency. Work is also geared to finding regulatory compatibility – that is, establishing consistent practices so that all countries may benefit. The aim is thus to do away with cumbersome differences and, for instance, develop a common set of wash-care symbols for clothing, or implement commonly agreed-on technical requirements for companies (Canada, SPP 2006).

To a certain extent, Smart Border pacts, the SPP, and many initiatives that predate them, are in some ways examples of the functionalist model in action. In a narrower, bureaucratic and administrative sense, Smart Border policies simply extend and build on already pre-existing initiatives such as the 1995 Canada–US Shared Border Accord and the 1999 Canada-US Partnership (CUSP). The SPP also responds to this same logic by building on the Smart Border pacts, but extends it by introducing new measures that move beyond the security and trade facilitation focus of the Smart Border to focus on a variety of new policy areas such as energy, North American food safety, public health and pandemic co-operation, and trans-boundary environmental co-operation – reflecting how co-operation in one area leads to, or 'spills over' into co-operation in other areas. However, this does not necessarily amount to political integration. These initiatives, and a host of other initiatives like them, act as a framework for co-operation on issues of shared concern like security and trade.

I maintain that co-operation thus more accurately captures what is taking place between Canadian, Mexican, and US officials. The concept of co-operation emerges out of the neo-liberal institutionalist school of thought. Keohane defines co-operation as the 'process through which policies actually followed by governments come to be regarded by their partners as facilitating the realization of their own objectives' (1984: 51–52). He goes on to say that in the act of co-operation, the behaviours of separate states 'are brought into conformity with one another through a process of negotiation' (Keohane 1984: 51).

Clarifying the definitions of 'co-operation' and 'integration' is important because, in the North American context, what I argue to be co-operation has been confused with integration, a concept that is closely linked with developments in Europe but does not accurately describe what is taking place in North America. Co-operation can occur without the existence of formal institutional structures. Countries can engage in collaborative practices while at the same time pursuing sovereign agendas. The SPP and Smart Border plans are indeed characteristic of how Canada, the US, and Mexico do this – through a complex and pragmatic, bureaucratic-led policy-making process that is informed by some of the socio-political obstacles that characterize North America.

Complex, Bureaucratic-led Policymaking

The SPP is not a formal institution; neither is it an international treaty that legally binds the three governments to certain commitments. As such, instead of creating a new top-down institutional architecture, European style, the SPP works within the parameters of existing legislation and simply acts as a framework for co-operation between the three countries (Ackelson and Kastner 2005: 3). The SPP accomplishes its principal objectives through a complex process of interagency co-operation through both bilateral- and trilateral-level working groups which are tasked with developing work plans with set deliverables attached to them and reporting semi-annually to leaders on progress.

This complex style of policy-actor interaction across levels is expressed by the term 'multi-level governance', a concept that arose in the European context and describes a style of co-operation that, although endorsed at higher political levels, requires the work of elaborate networks horizontally across federal bureaucracies of the three countries, and vertically at lower levels of provincial and state government (Rosamond 2000: 89–92).

The bureaucratic style of integration that characterizes the SPP is in tune with the political realities of the NAFTA region. For one, there is little political appetite to create an EU-style North American community with common markets, social policy co-ordination, and common institutions. Domestic impediments and sovereignty concerns in all three countries would prevent such a political community from ever developing. Of all three countries, Mexico, for social and economic reasons, has been more outspoken about a stronger North America, albeit in a much more muted way since 9/11.

Thus, by operating within the boundaries of the federal governmental agencies of the three countries, the SPP avoids being bogged down by a formal institutional structure that may force them to cede power. Put differently, the SPP avoids institutions but institutionalizes co-operation and government interaction, which suggests that collaboration can take place without a formal organization structure attached to it. The SPP regularizes and routinizes co-operation and exchanges of information on a trilateral basis. In this way, messy and politicized discussions related to loss of sovereignty concerns are supposed to be bypassed and complicated debates that put the three governments in the public spotlight are circumvented.

Incrementalism

In a paper presented at the 2005 meeting of the Association for Canadian Studies, Ackelson and Kastner suggest that integration *à la Nord-américaine* can be described as incrementalist rather than 'big-bang' European-style integration (2005: 2). While I suggest that it is co-operation rather than integration that is really occurring, I agree with the authors that it is taking place gradually, through incremental steps.

As I have mentioned, the SPP builds on and advances already existing agreements and frameworks for co-operation. For instance, although presently little current information exists on the SPP, in its initial 2005 iteration the SPP contained specific initiatives on the prosperity and security agendas that appeared either to replicate what already existed under Smart Border plans or to extend work already taking place. For instance, to facilitate the speedy and secure movement of legitimate travellers and business, the SPP contained specific references to the development of more fast lanes (for example, the FAST and NEXUS expedited border-crossing programs) that were initially articulated in Smart Border Policies and even before them. Further in the area of traveller security, the SPP simply elaborated on Point 6 of the *Secure Flow of People* pillar of the Canada-US Smart Border Declaration. Point 6 made reference to VISA policy co-ordination and tasked the two countries to jointly review visa waiver lists and share look-out lists (Department of Foreign Affairs and International Trade Canada, Canada–US Smart Border Declaration 2001).

The Canada–US Smart Border Declaration in turn specifically builds on agreements like the Canada-US Partnership (CUSP). CUSP was initiated in 1999 to consider issues to do with shared border management. The goals of CUSP resonate in both the Canada–US Smart Border Declaration and the SPP Objectives:

- streamline and harmonize border policies and management;
- expand co-operation to increase efficiencies in customs, immigration, law enforcement, and environmental protection at and beyond the border;
- collaborate on common threats from outside Canada and the US (DFAIT, Canada-US Partnership 2000).

Initiatives like CUSP, Smart Borders and the SPP all build on each other and expand upon already existing collaboration in a pragmatic step-by-step fashion. They follow a model first established through NAFTA. Christopher Sands of the Washington-based Center for Strategic and International Studies recalls that

> [i]n NAFTA, the three governments established working groups on the operation of NAFTA rules of origin and custom classificatory procedures, on standards-related measures, on trade and competition policies, and on temporary entry for business persons. The SPP builds on this structure by creating new working groups and giving them renewed endorsement by the political leaders. (Sands 2006)

Incrementalism also functions in a second instance. By pragmatic incrementalism I am also referring to the way officials negotiate deliverables. After identifying a variety of specific practical areas on both the prosperity and security agenda, officials negotiate in an incremental fashion in order to make measurable progress that reconciles standards and ensures compatibility between procedures and rules. Through small agency-to-agency projects, officials create momentum toward future-oriented events and are able to meet deadlines and achieve concrete deliverables.

Two-speed Co-operation

Finally, the SPP and its Smart Border corollary institutionalize a two-speed model of co-operation. Both adopt a flexible framework that recognizes that two countries can co-operate on a specific issue and a third can join later. Indeed, especially in matters of security, the SPP advances a number of initiatives that are bilateral in focus. For instance, the most recent SPP update, released at the 2008 North American Leaders' Summit in New Orleans, only mentions separate work at Canada/US or US/Mexico border crossing points, as well as specific Canada–US work on finalizing a framework agreement to 'govern cross-border maritime enforcement operations in shared waterways' (Canada, Prime Minister's Office 2008).

Smart Border policies also entrench bilateralism. For one, Canada and the US, and the US and Mexico, developed similar, yet separate, bilateral border arrangements. The Canada–US version is also more advanced than its US–Mexico counterpart. For instance, the US–Mexico plan has only 22 points of agreement compared to the 32 points contained in the Canada–US plan. This incongruity can be explained by an extra section in the Canada–US plan that deals with the integration and co-ordination of functions between both countries. The US–Mexico agreement is missing a similar section because the US and Mexico have not yet reached a point in their relationship where they can begin to undertake these tasks (Gabriel, Jimenez and Macdonald 2003).

The explicitly bilateral nature of Smart Border policies and sections of the SPP reflects the complexities that characterize the North American relationship and the broader co-operation project, especially given the political and economic differences between Canada and the US on the one hand, and Mexico on the other. The dual bilateralism that defines these initiatives is also a reflection of the historical specificity of the US–Mexico and Canada–US relationships. Although highly institutionalized in a number of sectors, the US–Mexico relationship has been historically characterized by conflict and misunderstanding (Serrano 2003: 48). The tense nature of the relationship can be explained by factors such as the fact that each country has its own distinct culture, language, and heritage. Additionally, the US has a long history of intervention in Mexican affairs that has only served to deepen Mexico's mistrust of its northern neighbour. In contrast, Canada and the US, although certainly at times having experienced strong moments of disaccord, have shared a more peaceful and positive relationship. Both countries share similar norms and values, and this has allowed them to establish a consensual and institutionalized approach to the management of joint areas of concern (Thompson and Randall 1994: 72). These distinct historical backgrounds inform the Smart Border pacts and the SPP, and expose one of the defining features of co-operation in North America – its bilateral nature.

The SPP: Challenges and Implications for Governance in North America

When the editor of this volume wrote in his *Introduction* that 'this book is about North America' he was inviting us to imagine the region as a coherent entity, with convergent forces contributing to the making of this whole.

In large part, I agree with this statement. A more clearly defined North America emerges especially when the continent is viewed through a social lens. In fact, viewing from the bottom up, one could make the case that *de facto* integration is already taking place. Think of migration patterns, labour markets, family and social ties, cross-border networks, and the like: the people of the three countries have been integrating the continent for some time by making individual decisions to live, study, work, and visit each other's countries.

However, at the government level, the picture that emerges is fuzzy and less clear. Part of the challenge when contemplating what is taking place in official channels is that many of the parameters that frame the debate about processes underway in North America have been derived from the European experience evoking some kind of top-down supranational system of governance. It thus becomes difficult to imagine something different than the EU.

I argue that many of the socio-political variables that define the region make it unlikely that anything outside the realm of co-operation is taking place – at least at the level of government. The SPP, and other initiatives like it, are frameworks that facilitate co-operation, exchange of information, and discussion. I would even go as far as to argue that these initiatives don't go far enough: that they will never get beyond what can be called 'useful plumbing' exercises and that North America does need the occasional dose of grander visionary EU-style integration to address questions pertaining to the future of North America.

The fact is that governments must work together to deal with common transnational challenges to do with the environment, security, health, natural disasters, and so on. And what is wrong with jointly working to remove duplications, thereby reducing costs and finding consistencies with practices used in one country that might apply to the other? What is wrong with – as Prime Minister Harper famously stated at the press conference after the 2007 North American Leaders' Summit at Montebello – eliminating the differences in jelly bean content rules in the three countries? Wouldn't it be logical to have just one standard for jelly beans across North America? Is this not just common sense? Maybe so. But even if this is simply practical policy-making, the SPP and the particular brand of North American model of co-operation that it engenders still face a number of challenges that may hamper its effectiveness in the long run.

A number of criticisms can be levelled at the SPP, many of which arise precisely because of some of the features that define the region: asymmetries and the predominance of bilateral relations. The SPP debate is effectively about the nature of the changing governance landscape of North America. Critics in the three countries take issue with essentially how the SPP has been implemented by governments and the absence of any processes that would legitimize the SPP through broader consultations.

The first criticism – by some critics – is that the SPP is a prelude to some type of North American union, that it is a secret plan for continental integration threatening the sovereignty of each country. The SPP is not a secret scheme for continental integration. Far from it. It is simply a mix of bilateral and trilateral working groups, many of which existed before the SPP was launched in 2005. What's more, the SPP has been more or less publicized; each country has a Web site, albeit not a very visible one, dedicated to the initiative. Critics strike a much stronger chord and make a more powerful and reasoned contribution when they rightly question two aspects of the SPP: its closed-door nature, and the values, interests, and views it is seen as advancing or privileging over other views and interests.

In 2006, the then heads of state and government of Canada, the US, and Mexico invited a group of CEOs from North America's leading corporations to form the North American Competitiveness Council (NACC). The NACC is made up of business leaders from across the three countries and functions as an advisory group that offers recommendations to governments on issues to do with North America's changing competitiveness and a host of other issues that touch upon economic efficiency (US Chamber of Commerce 2007). The NACC last met with leaders to present its recommendations at the 2008 North American Leaders' Summit in New Orleans. It has since appeared to retreat from public view. Some speculate that the NACC has been institutionalized and that its work continues (Trew 2009).

Whatever the case may be, it still has been *the only non-governmental group* allowed full access to trilateral meetings. It should be noted that at the last leaders' summit in Guadalajara, in 2009, the leaders did state in their joint statement that they welcomed the feedback of 'business ... and those of civil society groups, non-governmental organizations, academics experts and others'. The joint statement also went on to say that ministers had been tasked to 'engage in such consultations as they work to realize the goals we have set for ourselves in Guadalajara' (United States. White House 2009). Nevertheless, it remains to be seen whether any mechanisms have or will be established to include stakeholder participation.

The second criticism is related to the first, in that if the private sector is the only non-governmental group granted access to the process, then it's the private sector's views and interests that will dominate and likely be advanced over other broader public interests. In her contribution to this volume, Brodie argues that post-9/11, 'deep integration by stealth' has been advanced by a powerful group of transnational business leaders, influential think tanks, and political actors.

McDougall explains the rationale behind recent business efforts to do away with the border. He states that 'the single most important qualitative change leading to deeper integration between the two countries has been the extensive rationalization of multinational firms over the past two or three decades. This has intensified the commercial and managerial interest in eliminating the effect of the border' (McDougall 2004: 13).

McDougall notes that in the late twentieth century, the main player lobbying for the liberalization of markets is the transnational corporation (TNC). The TNC is effectively what is operating in North America. It consists of a rationalized regional production system in which a parent company, situated in this case in the US, manages the various aspects of a firm's production process located throughout North America in order to derive benefits from comparative advantage (McDougall 2004: 14). This creates enormous pressures for the speedy and efficient movement of goods across national boundaries and makes the adoption of similar policy environments and the retrenchment of national differences attractive to the business community (McDougall 2004: 14–16).

It is beyond the scope of this chapter to evaluate whether or not co-operation between business and political elites is tantamount to some sort of political integration. However, what remains clear is that by privileging certain groups and excluding others, and failing to engage citizens of North America in a debate about the benefits of co-operation and decisions concerning that process, governments ensure future public backlash and legitimacy problems. But the SPP still exists. It is technical enough to function on its own. Presently, officials in the three countries responsible for the SPP have intentionally decided to relegate the initiative to the background to avoid further public discontent. A concerted effort has been made to decouple the SPP from the broader North American agenda. Recent trilateral leaders' statements look to be carefully crafted, with co-operation being framed and anchored within the wider agenda. The three governments' reluctance to address the fears and concerns of the public head on, and their mismanagement of the SPP in general, is symptomatic of what I believe to be a stalled and stagnant North American agenda, at least when viewed through a government lens. Canadian, US, and Mexican public officials seem unable or unwilling to move it forward. No vision of North America and its future exists.

I have maintained that many of the initiatives underway are more about co-operation than about integration. Having said that, one could argue that if many of the initiatives articulated in the SPP are actually instituted, it will result in some form of integration (Ackelson and Kastner 2005: 21). This argument is used especially in the security sphere by critics who maintain that even if there is no explicit mention in the agreement of a North American security perimeter or a common market, the myriad of incremental changes implemented through the SPP will result in the very same objective. In other words, small changes implemented over time will cumulatively lead to political integration. It is unclear as to what exactly this type of process would lead to. However, unlike Europe, it is unlikely to lead to the creation of supranational institutions. Presently, the North American governments are engaged in a process of exchanging information, but the execution of policy is not necessarily co-ordinated and remains in the hands of each government. Nevertheless, only in a wider public debate with the citizens of North America can governments make decisions about processes underway in the region.

The SPP and Smart Border policies are to a certain extent products of sociopolitical variables that define the region. For instance, the SPP entrenches a two-speed model of integration more advanced along the Canada–US track than along the US–Mexico track. Of course, as noted earlier, this just reflects the political reality of the North American relationship that in effect it is made up of two bilateral relationships. Is this necessarily a bad thing? Maybe not. However, without any explicit and conscious effort made to ensure that Mexico eventually reaches a point in its social and economic development where it can participate equally alongside its NAFTA partners, the danger is that the asymmetries that define North America are further reproduced and entrenched. Indeed, the Canadian government's gradual delinking of Mexico from its vision of North America (and its concentration on the Canada–US relationship) only further contributes to the asymmetries. Canada's focus on consular issues with Mexico, security concerns, and its recent imposition of a visa for all Mexican citizens wishing to travel to Canada, is an indication of how the Canadian government views Mexico.

Another telling side of the asymmetries in the SPP is its security orientation at the expense of other issues. The SPP's security focus leaves out important issues like migration, development, and social inequalities; and regarding prosperity and the quality of life, the focus is on disaster preparedness, pandemics, and ensuring a safe food supply free of threats – all initiatives that seem security centred. Similar, Smart Border policies also focus on security at the expense of key social and political factors important to Canada and Mexico. Indeed, US dominance in the process has meant that security has been defined along more narrow, traditional, and territorial interpretations. The Mexican case demonstrates that security defined along human terms is also important. Abraham Lowenthal, president of the Pacific Council on International Policy thus states: 'For example, being kidnapped for profit, drug abuse, death in the course of migration, suffering from the effects of trans-border environmental pollution ... There is much more to security than border controls, Smart customs proceedings and security checks' (Lowenthal 2003).

Conclusion

In conclusion, I have argued that at least with regard to government interaction, what is taking place is more accurately described as co-operation rather than integration. I suggest that features like bureaucracy-led policymaking, incrementalism, and dual bilateralism are particularities that define the North American complex and limit anything beyond co-operation from taking place, at least for the moment. And while the SPP is not synonymous with North America, it represents an important framework for co-operation between the three partners on matters that have significant implications for governance in the continent. Additionally, an examination of the SPP uncovers important concerns about the research agenda on North American integration: much of the main integration literature simply assumes that economic integration will result in political and social convergence. Specifically, some of the core integration literature deriving from the European case argues that political integration (defined as the existence of a centralized decision-making structure, shared institutions, common policies, and a shared identity) is the end point. However, as an analysis of the SPP reveals, economic integration does not have to result in political integration – at least not in the way it has resulted in Europe. The pressures for collaboration and co-ordination induced by economic integration and security events do not necessitate the substitution of supranational structures for national political systems. Policy actors can accomplish objectives 'through mutual but independently enacted adjustments to national policies that do not involve significant transfers of authority from national to international levels' (McDougall 2004). These types of actions require debating in a wider forum that includes the public, so that important decisions regarding the future of governance in the continent can be made. Perhaps the North American leaders will take the opportunity in the next summit to rethink the architecture of North America.

Chapter 5
The Security and Prosperity Partnership: The Short History of a Strategic Bargain

Janine Brodie[1]

Introduction

In late May 2010, Mexico's President Felipe Calderón paid an official visit to his northern neighbours, the US and Canada. Speaking to both houses of the US Congress and then to the Canadian Parliament the next day, Calderón asked the legislators of each country to join with Mexico in making North America the most competitive region in the world (Calderón 2010). Calderón's appeal echoed an earlier moment in the decade, in March 2005, when his predecessor, President Vicente Fox, US President George W. Bush, and Prime Minister Paul Martin unveiled the Security and Prosperity Partnership of North America (SPP) and applauded it as a bold and visionary plan for the continent. However, only four years later the SPP was quietly abandoned.

As this chapter explains, the SPP was the product of a relentless campaign directed largely by Canadian corporate leaders, business-funded think-tanks, and their political allies to achieve deeper continental integration in the aftermath of the 2001 terrorist attacks on New York and Washington. US borders were immediately closed, and then made progressively more cumbersome as layers of security measures were imposed on borders both to and within North America. This NAFTA successor agreement, as this chapter explains, was crafted as a strategic bargain, fusing together Mexican and Canadian anxieties about diminished access to the US market with US preoccupation with national security in the wake of 9/11. This chapter tracks how consensus was shaped around this strategic bargain in the months following 9/11 and how it ultimately failed to deliver on its twin agenda of security and prosperity for North America.

The chapter unfolds in three parts: first, it describes what is meant by deep integration (DI), and reviews various explanations for why DI strategies have intensified in the early years of the twenty-first century. Next the chapter explains the importance of spatial imaginaries, discourses, and performances in the process

---

[1] I wish to thank Isabel Altamirano, Jason Bisanz, and Malinda Smith for their helpful contributions to this chapter. This research has been supported by both the Canada Research Chair Program in which I hold a Tier 1 Chair in Political Economy and Social Governance and the Pierre Elliott Trudeau Foundation which awarded me a fellowship in 2010.

of contemporary transnational region-making. Finally, it recounts how the SPP project unfolded through three stages – agenda setting, consensus building, and consolidation – and outlines the contradictions that led to the official abandonment of the SPP.

The Road to Security and Prosperity

The determined promotion of deep continental integration in the post-9/11 era originated within the same networks, indeed, often among the same people that led the successful campaigns for both the Canada–US Free Trade Agreement (CUFTA 1989) and the North American Free Trade Agreement (NAFTA 1994). Both of these agreements were sold to the Canadian public, and could *only* be sold to the Canadian public, as trade deals that would not interfere with national culture, identity, and sovereignty. During the 1988 free-trade election, for example, a broad coalition of civil-society organizations and the weight of public opinion firmly opposed the idea of compromising the political and symbolic border between Canada and the US in the name of enhanced continental trade and competitiveness. Concerns about continental integration and eventual assimilation, however, were always countered with assurances from the proponents of free trade that the goals of CUFTA and NAFTA were limited to trade and to securing firmer access to the US market. As NAFTA's preamble underscored, the deal intended to 'create an expanded and secure market', 'reduce trade distortions', and 'enhance the competitiveness' of the North American region in a globalizing economy (quoted in Pastor 2001: 96).

CUFTA found its genesis in the recurring economic crises of the 1970s and 1980s. During these years, rising oil prices, competition from newly industrializing countries, the economic revival of Asia–Pacific and European regional economies, and stagflation (inflation + unemployment) combined to erode the logic of post-war economic strategies in both the US and Canada. Growth stalled and, facing a growing balance-of-payments deficit, the US increased tariffs and offered their multinational corporations tax concessions to bring investment and jobs back to US soil. In response to rising US protectionism, Canadian officials quickly began to search for new international trading partners, but proponents of the so-called 'Third Option' soon discovered that there was little room for Canadian goods in the increasingly powerful trading blocs of Europe and the Asia-Pacific (Sharp 1972). Seemingly without alternatives, in 1982, the Trudeau government appointed Donald Macdonald, a former Liberal finance minister, to head the Royal Commission on the Economic Union and Development Prospects for Canada (the Macdonald Commission) and charged the commission with recommending 'appropriate national goals and policies for economic development' (Canada 1985: Appendix A). The commission considered many options for national economic development, but in the end opted for freer trade with the US, reasoning that

'Canadians are wealthier because of the Americans, but we are also vulnerable to changes in their fortunes' (Canada 1985: 271–82).

A comprehensive free trade agreement, the Royal Commission assured Canadians, need not compromise national political and social norms. Rather, a trade deal promised to reduce the exposure of Canadian exporters to US trade barriers and countervailing duties, increase access to the US market, and enhance the productivity and competitiveness of Canadian firms in North America and globally (Canada 1985: 313, 323–24; see also Inwood 2005). The crafting of NAFTA was very much an encore performance of this trade-centred discourse. Canada, it was argued, needed to be at the negotiating table with Mexico and the US to ensure that the gains achieved in CUFTA were not compromised with the inclusion of an additional continental trading partner. It is important to underline here, however, that neither CUFTA nor NAFTA were celebrated as the foundations for extensive continental policy harmonization, the pooling of national sovereignty, or the eventual creation of a North American community. Opponents repeatedly warned that Canadian sovereignty would be compromised by these agreements, but the free-traders insisted that DI was not on the bargaining table. The trade deals were primarily about the exchange of raw materials and finished goods rather than the creation of a new transnational region resembling the European Union (Hale and Blank 2010: 23).

In many ways, both CUFTA and NAFTA were examples of shallow integration (McDougall 2004: 5) and what Ayres and Macdonald call shallow governance (2006). The framers of these documents explicitly rejected the model of DI that had been incrementally developed in Europe over the past half century. The European Union rests on pooled sovereignty, supranational democratic institutions, a burgeoning transnational bureaucracy, regulatory harmonization often by means of mutual recognition, common external borders, and a common currency. The North American model, in contrast, relied on constitution-like international agreements which limited the powers of signatory states to deploy tariff and non-tariff barriers on goods and investments from partner countries, to favour national companies in their economic development strategies, and to, directly or indirectly, appropriate foreign holdings.

In principle, then, shallow integration/governance only minimally reduces the capacity of national governments to develop and enforce national public policies, which are responsive to national electorates, with respect to (among other things) domestic social and cultural policies, protective regulation and product standards, immigration and asylum practices, foreign policy, and border management. In other words, shallow integration allows for a wide spectrum of border effects to continue (Helliwell 1998). The primary rationale for many of the instruments of DI, in contrast, is to erase as many border effects as possible, especially those posing some sort of friction on the free movement of goods, capital, and services across national boundaries. Although DI can take different forms, ranging from a customs union to full-blown political integration, its overarching goal is the creation of a 'seamless economic space' with a common interface with the global economy through the elimination of nationally-specific regulations, standards, and practices, and the harmonization of new public policies (McDougall 2004, Campbell 2005).

By the early 2000s, a select group of academics, business leaders, and neo-liberal think-tanks began to float the idea that some form of deeper integration for North America was a logical and inevitable consequence of NAFTA. Some pointed to growing social and economic interdependence, especially between Canada and the US. Citizens in these countries consumed the same products, watched the same TV shows and movies, and read the same books. Moreover, North American supply and value chains accounted for ever-larger proportions of GDP and employment (McDougall 2004: 5; Randall 2000: 33). These multiple and increasingly diverse cross-border linkages, DePalma confidently asserted in his book *Here: A Biography of the New American Continent*, 'are leading inevitably toward the integration of North America into a single, seamless entity' (2002: 14). Such predictions of the inevitability of deeper integration relied on the wisdom of a popular vein of international relations theory: neo-functionalism, which holds that transnational regionalism is a likely outcome of economic interdependence. Drawing on the European experience, this incremental model of transnational region-building contends that free-trade or limited sectoral integration 'spills-over' in an evolutionary sequence to a customs union, a common market, an economic union, and ultimately, political integration and transnational institutionalization (Haas 1961, Hettne 2005: 546). Others argued that North American integration was inevitable because it was a manifestation of globalization, which also was represented as an inescapable trend in the international political economy of the late twentieth century and beyond (Hoberg 2002: 4).

Emily Gilbert, however, argues that the growing chorus of predictions about the inevitability of deep North American integration was skilfully and strategically deployed by region-building elites in order to narrow the range of policy alternatives on the table and 'downplay concerns regarding the loss of political sovereignty and the transformations to state-society relationships that would result from the new North American economic space' that was being proposed (2005: 202). For example, Thomas d'Aquino, head of the Canadian Council of Chief Executives (CCCE), often repeated variations on the following theme: 'We feel that "Free Trade One" was sort of a transforming chapter in the relationship between Canada and the United States ... I would say that this [DI] is the second chapter of that transformative initiative' (quoted in Staples 2004). 'North American integration,' the CCCE's 2004 policy paper, *New Frontiers,* asserted, 'is now well advanced and is irreversible' (CCCE 2004: i).[2]

---

2   Previously called the Business Council on National Issues, and a flagship campaigner of both CUFTA and NAFTA, the CCCE identifies itself as Canada's premier business organization, and is composed of the chief executives officers of 150 leading corporations in Canada. See www.ceocoucil.ca.

After more than a decade of free trade, however, there was little evidence that the Canadian public was ready to open a new and more deeply textured chapter in continentalization. Indeed, if the initiators of CUFTA and NAFTA anticipated that popular resistance to deep integration might erode over time, and as ever-increasing economic interdependence became the 'new normal' in economic life, they surely were disappointed. By all indicators, the values structuring Canadian and US public opinion diverged rather than converged with free trade. In his popular book, *Fire and Ice* (2003), for example, Canadian pollster Michael Adams compared Canadian and US public opinion during the 1990s on a broad range of issues. He concluded that 'Canadian social values are not becoming indistinguishable from the United States. Rather ... we find a picture of startling dissimilitude, and – even more startling – ongoing divergence. The two countries are actually becoming more disparate' (2003: 72–3). The 2000 election and 2004 re-election of George W. Bush, widespread Canadian opposition to the Iraq War, and ongoing trade irritants also created friction among North America's neighbours. A December 2004 *Globe and Mail/CTC* poll, for example, reported that fully 80 per cent of Canadians agreed that they were fundamentally different in values and outlook from people in the US (while 50 per cent of Americans accepted this statement) (Galloway 2004: A10). Another *Globe and Mail* poll conducted in March 2006 reported that 48 per cent of Canadians had negative perceptions of the US compared to 36 per cent in 2002 (Laghi 2006: A1, A7). The sum of these findings amounted to what Alain Noël at the time termed the 'paradox of integration'. 'Canada has never been so economically integrated with the US,' he wrote, 'yet, at least on the cultural/value plain, it has never been so different' (quoted in Macdonald and Rounce 2003: 51).

From the perspective of public opinion, then, these were not especially promising foundations upon which to build a case for deeper integration with the US. It would be a mistake, however, to conclude that, after almost two decades of freer trade with the US, some form of value convergence and political support for deeper continental integration simply failed to materialize. It is more likely that the pollsters were looking in the wrong place and asking the wrong people. A different picture emerges when we shift our focus upward to elites and over to the corporate sector – in other words, to a different scale of integration and a different sector. Polling data as well as the official missives of business-funded think-tanks consistently revealed that corporate elites were far more likely than other Canadians to endorse closer ties with and becoming more like the US. This was not simply an expression of admiration for the US cult of free enterprise, which flourished under George W. Bush's presidency. For many business leaders, North America had become their place of business and their point of reference, which they viewed as being increasingly threatened by national regulatory regimes and competition from emerging markets.

According to John McDougall, the continentalization of the corporate sector was free trade's single most important political impact (2004: 13). Intra-firm transfers, comprising fully one-half of Canada–US trade, integrated board rooms, the expansion of networked production and distribution systems, the proliferation of cross-border supply and value chains, and myriad other firm- and industry-level integration had created a powerful coalition of continental capitalists who identified as North Americans and considered any national border frictions as detrimental to their security and prosperity. As important, over half of the members of nominally 'Canadian' business associations, often the most powerful ones, were US companies with headquarters in the US. It was through these processes that free trade brought structural economic integration to many sectors of the Canadian economy (Hale and Blank 2010: 22, McDougall 2004: 17). These transformations signalled that 'rather than selling things to one another', North American businesses were increasingly 'making things together' (Blank 2005: 2). This new reality prompted North American elites to begin to re-imagine North America on a new scale and as something more than a free trade zone.

Imagining North America: Discourses and Performances

All economic development strategies promote specific assumptions about how to achieve economic growth (through governing assumptions and regulatory practices), where in real geopolitical space and in what sectors that growth should occur, and at what scale rules will be made and enforced (for example, local, national, regional, and global) (Keil and Mahon 2009). Although, for most of the twentieth century, economic and political agendas were predominately set at the national scale, it is important to remember that the national scale was an invention of discourses and the outcome of prolonged political struggles. Consensus surrounding a particular scale of governance is 'the outcome of social struggle for power and control' and is always negotiated, contested, and regulated (Swyngedouw 1997: 140–141). In other words, scales of governance are the products of political imaginations, persuasive discourses, and political struggles among concrete material interests.

For many decades, struggles over space and scale have been neglected in thinking about economic development strategies. This is because, for much of the history of modern capitalism, both geographical space and governing scales were usually imagined and performed as national, that is, as coterminous with the territorial boundaries of the national state. When I say 'performed', I mean both acting out a script as well as bringing an entity into being through acts of imagination, naming, and regulation. The twentieth-century Keynesian state, for example, was performed on a national scale with discourses and policies that affirmed and reproduced a national economy, national state, national citizenship, and national society (Jessop 2002: 54, 74). Jessop calls this kind of congruence a 'spatio-temporal fix' and argues that all accumulation/development strategies, implicitly or explicitly, advance one, even if it is partial, provisional, and unstable (2002: 48–9). Over time, the shifting parameters of both the domestic and the international political economy combine in ways that destabilize conditions for economic growth, provoking a search for new growth strategies, new institutional compromises, and an alternative 'better' spatio-temporal fix. Moreover, as Jessop emphasizes, these alternatives are invariably cast in terms of an 'imagined general interest', which, by definition, privileges particular scales of governance and political interests (2002: 30).

Doreen Massey's work on globalization provides critical insights into how new STFs are discursively constructed and performed as imagined geographies in an imagined general interest. Globalization, as Massey contends, conjures up visions of inevitability, 'total unfettered mobility', 'free and unbounded space', 'instantaneousness', and the 'annihilation of space by time' (1999: 33). Although there has been widespread and uncritical acceptance of this account of globalization, it is not particularly accurate (Massey 1999: 36). Capital and information may indeed flow instantaneously through and above national boundaries, but borders remain formidable barriers for people, especially for those in the South seeking to escape abject poverty, insecurity, and exploitation (Gabriel and Macdonald 2003). Sassen similarly observes that two sets of rules govern globalization: one set facilitates the flow of capital while another set regulates the flow of people (1998: 60).

Massey argues that it is not simply sloppy social science that explains the many discrepancies between, on the one hand, accounts of globalization as the irreversible transcendence of national borders, and on the other, the reality of increasingly fortified borders, especially in the prosperous North. Instead, she explains that the vision of globalization as inevitable transnational flows is 'not so much a description of how the world is, as an image in which the world is being made', not the least through the neo-liberal discourses and enforcement of liberalized trade policies. Having been raised and installed, this powerful imaginative geography legitimizes 'in the name of (though of course without saying so) the powerful' and 'justifies the actions of those who promulgate it'. Moreover, Massey explains, this geographical imagination ignores 'the structured divides, the necessary ruptures and inequalities, on which the successful projection of the vision itself depends' (1999: 40, 36–7).

John Urry also emphasizes the importance of discourses, ideology, and performance in bringing globalization into being. Understanding globalization as an ideology, he argues, focuses on the role of economic interests, transnational corporations, and international financial institutions (such as the IMF and the WTO) in promoting the idea that globalization is both inevitable and irreversible. More important for our purposes, the concept of performance understands globalization *as an effect rather than as a condition*, that is, as a project to be achieved instead of an entity or process to be described. For Urry, the global is not so much a "cause" of other effects but an effect … It is continuously reconstituted through various material and semiotic processes … It is something that is made' (2003: 6).

These observations about the performance of globalization also apply to the envisioning and performance of a relatively new form of transnational governance termed as the 'new regionalism'. Students of the new regionalism argue that countries integrate into larger economic regions or blocs as a strategic response to the exogenous forces of globalization. It is a 'new' regionalism, not simply because this form of governance has proliferated only in recent decades, but also because it is fluid, variable, and not yet well understood (Brodie 2012a). There is agreement, however, on two fundamental points: first, transnational regionalization is a strategic response to the global economy which, as Larner and Walters importantly emphasize, is understood as a space of competition, investment, and trade flows that traverse national states (2002: 408). Second, the new regionalism is typically invented through the discourses of the exclusive clubs of region-building elites (Neumann 2003). In this global era, as Jessop further explains,

> new places are emerging, new spaces are being created, new scales of organization are being developed and new horizons of action are being imagined – all in the light of new forms of (understanding) competition and competitiveness ... The number of scales and temporalities of action that can be distinguished is immense but far fewer ever get explicitly institutionalized. (Jessop 2002: 179–80)

The new regionalism literature thus emphasizes that DI projects are not the inevitable outcome of either economic interdependencies or globalization, but instead, political artefacts, which are constructed through dominant imaginaries and strategic actions (and reactions) and which may or may not be successful. The next section of this chapter describes how this interplay of imaginaries, discourses, and strategic action unfolded in North America in the aftermath of 9/11. In particular, the chapter tracks how the eventual strategic deal that gave birth to the SPP moved from an agenda-setting period in which various representations of a new North America were tested, to a period of consensus building, and, finally, to the consolidation of partial and contradictory performances of North America as a security space. Tables 5.1, 5.2 and 5.3 below offer a panoramic view of how these three periods unfolded.

Security and Prosperity as Performance

Agenda Setting

The campaign for a new governing framework for North America did not begin with the events of 9/11. Instead, the aftermath of the terrorist attacks 'merely intensified the determination of most Canadian business leaders to reduce the practical significance of the border between the two countries to a minimum' (McDougall 2004: 5). By the late 1990s, there was a growing consensus among North American corporate leaders that NAFTA no longer adequately governed the continental economic spaces that it and CUFTA (1998) had helped create. From Canada's perspective, NAFTA had failed to discipline the US to abide by trade tribunal rulings. As Andrew Jackson, an opponent to continental integration,

Table 5.1   Setting the agenda

Time Period	Event
October 2001	Coalition for Secure and Trade-Efficient Borders
April 2002	C.D. Howe Institute commissions *Border Papers* series
December 2002	House of Commons Standing Committee on Foreign Affairs and International Trade releases report on public hearings, Partners in North America: Advancing Canada's Relations with the United States and Mexico
2002–03	Conference Board of Canada calls for debate on customs union with US
January 2003	CCCE launches North American Security and Prosperity Initiative
June 2003	Senate Standing Committee on Foreign Affairs releases report from hearings
October 2003	Institute for Research on Public Policy starts Thinking North America project

Table 5.2   Building consensus

Time Period	Event
April 2004	Canadian Council of Chief Executives (CCCE) goes to Washington with group of Canadian corporate leaders
April 2004	CCCE releases report, New Frontiers: Building a 21st Century Canada–US Partnership in North America
October 2004	Independent Task Force on the Future of North America is launched
November 2004	President Bush and Prime Minister Martin sign 'new partnership agreement'
March 2005	Thomas d'Aquino undertakes 10-city speaking tour in the US to highlight the benefits of 'deep integration'
March 2005	Prime Minister Martin and President Fox meet with President Bush in Texas and sign SPP
May 2005	Independent Task Force on the Future of North America releases its report, Building a North American Community

Table 5.3 Consolidating North America as a security community

Time Period	Event
2001 (December)	Smart Border Initiative
2002	US unilaterally creates Northern Command – establishing a security perimeter from the Arctic Ocean to Guatemala and Belize, and the Caribbean basin
2003	External Advisory Committee on Smart Regulation
2005 (January)	Implementation of Canada–US harmonization of visa, immigration, and refugee policies (3rd-party refugee agreement)
2005 (March)	Waco Summit stresses security interoperability with 'real time information sharing on high risk individuals', sharing data of terrorist watch-list and single mechanism for making decisions on who can enter or transit in North America
2005 (April)	Smart Regulation: Report on Actions and Plans
2005 (April)	International Policy Statement
2005 (June)	Progress Report to leaders – Deputy Prime Minister McLellan and US counterparts announce 300 initiatives designed to enhance trilateral security and trade, including unifying testing standards for all three markets
2005 (October)	PM Martin tells Wall Street that his government's priority is regulatory harmonization with US
2006 (March)	North America Competitiveness Council launched
2007	Ministerial working groups to present North American Regulatory Cooperation Framework Agreement

pointed out in 2003, 'from lumber to agriculture, the US still actively uses its countervailing and anti-dumping trade laws to selectively harass and penalize Canadian exporters' (2003: 23). NAFTA also was ineffective in reducing non-tariff barriers to continental trade such as differing rules of origin and national regulatory regimes. This 'tyranny of small differences', the corporate community complained in chorus, undercut the ability of North American entrepreneurs to effectively compete in continental and global markets (Doern and Johnson 2006). More broadly, NAFTA decreasingly provided a relative advantage in global markets because tariffs were progressively declining everywhere (Stewart-Patterson 2007) CUFTA and NAFTA had been configured as specific responses to an emerging global economy, but its contours were rapidly changing as developing economies such as China and India reconfigured patterns of economic growth, consumer demand, trade, and investment.

A variety of proposals for the reform of NAFTA were floated in both Canada and Mexico in the months preceding 9/11. The US, in contrast, was conjuring a different spatial imaginary – a Free Trade Agreement of the Americas (FTAA). Early in 2001, some prominent Canadian economists as well as the new governor of the Bank of Canada speculated about the potential advantages that might be gained through the dollarization of the Canadian economy. Similarly, in the spring of 2001, David Zussman, a one-time principal advisor to Prime Minister Jean Chrétien, called for a debate on such issues as common perimeters and regulatory harmonization, which, he argued, 'until a few years ago, were completely taboo in respectable Canadian society' (quoted in Gutstein 2009: 26). During these same months, Industry Canada published a research paper that called for an investigation of the implications of harmonization pressures in a wide range of policy areas (Clarkson 2008: 374). In Mexico, Vicente Fox put the idea of deepening North American integration at the centre of his successful 1999 electoral platform. His 'NAFTA-Plus' proposal called for greater trilateral institutional development, agreements to promote the continental flow of labour, the creation of a development fund to help Mexico catch-up to its more affluent northern partners, and eventually, a common market. Both President Bush and Prime Minister Chrétien gave nodding agreement to the proposal that continental strategies should be devised to deal with the obvious problems of continental labour mobility and uneven economic development. Moreover, the Guanajuato Agreement between Presidents Fox and Bush (February 2001) explicitly recognized the need to narrow the economic gaps between the NAFTA partners and to deal with ongoing migration issues (Clarkson 2008: 385). This nascent continental imagination, however, quickly ground to a halt when the World Trade Towers collapsed.

It was one thing to be dissatisfied with NAFTA for any number of reasons but quite another to watch the flow of exports from Canada shut down at the border and then slow to a trickle. On 9/11, US borders were immediately closed; travellers and transport trucks were trapped in long queues and manufacturers lost millions of dollars every hour that the border remained closed (Council of Foreign Relations 2005: 3). As memory of those tide-turning events fades, it is useful to recount the chaos and uncertainty that marked the Canada/US borders then, in particular, the busiest, the Detroit-Windsor crossing. As Edward Alden recounts:

> Within two days, the queue of trucks and cars at the Ambassador bridge had swelled, by different accounts, to anywhere between ten and twenty miles long. Trucks spilled onto the city streets of Windsor, and truckers abandoned their rigs and went to look for food and coffee … The Ontario Provincial Police brought in portable toilets, while the Red Cross and the Salvation Army provided food and water to stranded truckers and travellers. (2009: 43)

The private sector, at first dumbstruck, quickly formed the Coalition for Secure Trade and Efficient Borders, a coalition of Canadian business organizations, and in December 2001 released an action plan. It bore a distinct resemblance to the Smart Border Declaration, negotiated between the Canadian and US governments that appeared later in the same month. This 30-point plan, some of which had already been set in motion through the 1995 Canada–US Shared Border Accord, included co-ordinating strategies to better secure the flow of people and goods across the border, information-sharing, new surveillance technologies, and enhanced interoperability among border officials and agencies (Hale and Marcotte 2010: 103, Gabriel and Macdonald 2004: 88–9). But it soon became apparent that these measures were not going to quell US security concerns. US politicians continued to point an accusing finger at Canada, condemning it for having porous borders and slack asylum policies that opened a door to the continent for terrorists.

The subsequent intensification of border surveillance generated more uncertainty for manufacturers and policy makers who began to fear that the secure border initiatives would discourage new investment in Canada. Why would foreign investors invest in Canada if access to the US market was impeded by thicker and stickier borders? And how might another terrorist attack on the US further sever the supply and value chains that had been cultivated during two decades of free trade? Contemplating these questions, corporate elites and their political allies quickly became convinced that deep integration, specifically the erasure of border effects for the free movement of goods, capital, and services, was the only solution to the serious vulnerabilities of the continental economy exposed by the 9/11 attacks. But, if some new mechanism was needed to advance North American integration, a way to sell any new transformative initiative, either to the increasingly inward-looking US or to a suspicious Canadian public was not immediately obvious.

The following months saw a flurry of experimentation with ways to frame a new strategy to accelerate deep integration within North America. The House of Commons Standing Committee on Foreign Affairs and International Trade, for example, conducted a national consultation on North American relations, releasing its report in December 2002. While business groups were frequent contributors to these parliamentary hearings, they too commissioned a series of reports aimed at transforming the North American economy and politics. The C.D. Howe Institute, a business-funded neo-liberal think-tank, launched its *Border Papers* series to examine the broad spectrum of economic and security issues affecting the NAFTA partnership. In December 2002, the CCCE announced that 'redefining Canada's role and responsibility in North America [was] the country's most urgent priority', and, a month later, launched its North American Security and Prosperity Initiative. In October 2003, the Institute for Public Policy, headed by Hugh Segal, a former advisor to Brian Mulroney, launched a research and conference agenda entitled Thinking North America, with the resulting product published as a boxed set in 2005.

During this agenda-setting stage, there was little consensus about what a new governing framework might look like or how it might be quickly advanced. Indeed, after its extensive national consultation, the House of Commons Standing Committee concluded that 'the North American project, whatever it turns out to be, is still to be defined' (Canada 2002: 21). Moreover, it found 'no reason to assume that common or harmonized policies are inevitable, necessary, or even desirable' (Canada 2002: 31). In this early stage, however, Wendy Dobson's controversial April 2002 contribution to the C.D. Howe Institute's *Border Papers* series generated the most attention. Dobson, then director of the Institute for International Business at the University of Toronto, argued that, however much Canadian business might want to reduce border effects, 'Canada risks a dialogue of the deaf if it pursues an economic goal of deeper bilateral integration without taking account of US security preoccupations' (2002: 5). Dobson proposed that the terrorist attacks opened a 'door of opportunity' for Canada to correct for the limitations of NAFTA and the growing security barriers at the borders, if it were willing to seize the initiative and present the US with a strategic bargain that they could not refuse (2002: 18).

Dobson's 'Big Idea' was that the Canadian government acquiesce to US concerns about borders, terrorism, and energy security in exchange for some relaxation at the borders and harmonized policies that would ease the flow of Canadian goods and services into the US market (Dobson 2002: 24). In this vision, the Canadian objective was first and foremost to reduce obstacles to the freer flow of goods, services, capital, technology, and people in a North American economic space (Dobson 2002: 27). Dobson also proposed that the deeper North American integration should initially exclude Mexico, because it presented different kinds of security problems (2003: 25). She advised that Canada take the leadership in creating this truncated North American region, not the least because the spectre of US leadership 'would be too threatening as we have seen in the past with free trade ideas' (2003: 24).

Consensus-Building

Dobson's proposal was deceptively simple: to keep the US from buttressing its borders, there should be no border at least with respect to the movement of North American goods and the integrity of supply chains (Pickard 2005). The US preoccupation with national security following the 9/11 attacks simultaneously threatened Canadian economic security and thus provided a rationale for pursuing a deep integration agenda that otherwise seemed beyond the political reach of Canadian business interests. This marriage of convenience between security and harmonization was quickly embraced and embroidered by the CCCE when, at its January 2003 annual meeting, Thomas d'Aquino told the gladiators of the corporate sector that 'North American economic and physical security are indivisible.' 'Building the idea of a North American community', he announced, required Canada to take the lead in promoting a 'five-part strategy for a new Canada–US partnership within a common North American vision' (2003). 'The execution of the strategy' would involve the following measures:

- reinventing the border (e.g., a shared North American identity card, shared systems of commercial processing, shared policing);

- maximizing economic efficiencies (e.g., regulatory harmonization, tested-once standards, open-skies agreements);
- building resource security (e.g., further continental integration of oil, natural gas, electricity, coal, uranium, primary metals, forest products, agriculture);
- sharing continental and global security (e.g., co-operation with the US in defence and security of the continent, rebuilding the Canadian armed forces to enhance their capabilities in 'confronting the terrorist challenge and promoting world order');
- developing twenty-first century institutions (e.g., a rejection of European-style supranational institutions in favour of specialized joint commissions and bureaucratic regulatory process) (CCCE 2003);

After establishing the core elements of the new agenda for North American governance, the CCCE took the lead in building consensus around this five-point plan. Throughout 2003 and 2004, it consulted business and government officials in the three NAFTA countries and met privately with a number of key members of the Bush administration. Later in the summer of 2003, d'Aquino took George Bush Sr. on a fishing trip to Labrador. D'Aquino reportedly later recounted to a room of high level government officials how he pitched the CCCE's North American Security and Prosperity Plan to the former President. Bush Sr. was sceptical at first, d'Aquino recounted, until he suggested that the plan would make North America an island of prosperity and security. Bush Sr. reportedly replied, 'Now this is something that Americans would be interested in' (quoted in Staples 2004).

In April 2004, the CCCE released the results of its consultations on its North American Security and Prosperity Initiative (NAPSI) in the form of a discussion paper entitled New Frontiers (CCCE 2004). The working document proposed a 'comprehensive' new partnership with the US that would fuse Canada's aspirations for deeper continental integration with US security concerns and broaden the sphere of continental policy harmonization to include a continental energy strategy, a defence policy review, investment in a 'credible military capacity', and North American defence institutions (CCCE 2004: 26–8). Unveiling this blueprint for a new North America in Ottawa only a few weeks before Prime Minister Martin was to make his first official visit to Washington, d'Aquino announced that 'our goal in the months ahead is to help foster a powerful consensus that it is in the interests of both countries to move forward urgently in developing and implementing an ambitious practical agenda' (Goar 2004: A3).

This exercise in consensus building involved different actors but only one purpose (Brodie 2008). Shortly after releasing New Frontiers, d'Aquino took Canada's corporate elite to Washington to engage in private meetings with its US counterpart, the Business Roundtable, leading members of the U.S. Senate, and such key Bush administration insiders as Tom Ridge, first director of the Department of Homeland Security (DHS), and Richard Perle, one the architects of Bush's pre-emptive strike doctrine and the Iraq War. According to press accounts,

The Short History of a Strategic Bargain 99

the Bush team told the CCCE delegation that security was their non-negotiable priority and that any new trade initiatives would have to mesh with and advance this priority (Clarke 2004). The often out-spoken American Ambassador to Canada at the time, Paul Cellucci, put it more bluntly: 'security trumps trade' (Gutstein 2009: 27, Cellucci 2005). This pronouncement would later haunt the architects of the deep integration initiative of the early 2000s.

The CCCE's intense lobbying around its DI agenda was followed, in October 2004, with the launch of the Independent Task Force on the Future of North America (ITF) by the US Council of Foreign Relations (CFR). While the ITF was represented as an autonomous research and consultative effort, it comprised a small group of prominent political and business elites from all three NAFTA members, most of whom were already on the record as favouring deeper integration. Indeed, only one member (from Mexico) of the 31-member task force was widely recognized as an opponent of NAFTA (Pickard 2005: 8). The ITF was chaired by John Manley (former Canadian deputy prime minister charged with security after 9/11),[3] Pedro Aspe (a former Mexican finance minister), and William Weld (a former governor of Massachusetts with close ties to the Bush camp). Co-chairs included Thomas d'Aquino, Robert Pastor (an American academic and prolific promoter of North American integration), and Andrés Rozental (president of the Mexican Council of Foreign Relations). The task force also included Michael Wilson, a former Conservative finance minister who had negotiated NAFTA and was later appointed by the Harper government as Canadian Ambassador to the US.

The ITF held three meetings in preparation of its report: in Toronto (October 2004), New York (December 2004), and Monterrey (February 2005). Importantly for our purposes, an internal memo leaked from the Toronto meeting showed that the task force members were clearly cognizant of the importance of performing North America as a security community. This first meeting agreed that, unlike previous trade negotiations, they should consider nothing to be 'off the table' but also recognized that 'contentious or intractable issues will simply require more time to ripen politically' (Pickard 2005: 8). The leaked Toronto memo also indicated that 'members generally agreed that Task Force *recommendations will be taken most seriously to the extent that they are placed in the context of heightened concern about security*: for example, increasing regional cooperation on energy could be presented as addressing security-related concerns' (Pickard 2005, emphasis added). The confidential memo also underlined the importance of creating a 'shared North American identity' and the need to develop a 'North American brand name – a discourse and a set of symbols designed to distinguish the region from the rest of the world' (Pickard 2005: 10).

The release of the final report of the ITF, Building a North American Community, in May 2005 following a year of research and consultations, was somewhat of an anti-climax considering that the SPP had already been launched two months earlier. However, a draft of the ITF report had been given to the

---

3   In January 2010 John Manley replaced Thomas d'Aquino as head of the CCCE.

three North American leaders weeks before their historic meeting in Waco in March 2005 (Gutstein 2009). The ITF pushed the DI agenda even further than the SPP had dared, in many ways charting the path to be followed after the initial foundations for deeper integration had been set. The ITF report called for 'the establishment by 2010 of a North American economic and security community, the boundaries of which would be defined by a common external tariff and an outer security perimeter' (ITF 2005: vii). Not surprisingly, considering its neo-liberal bloodline, the ITF recommended that this new North American community should rely on market forces rather than on representative bodies, and that a tri-national competition committee be established also by 2010 to 'promote healthy competition' (ITF 2005: 22). Other ITF recommendations included the creation of a North American border pass with biometric identifiers, preferential migration, harmonization of visa and asylum regulations, sharing data on foreign nationals, and additional border measures. As the report emphasized, 'the three governments should strive toward a situation in which a terrorist trying to penetrate our borders will have an equally hard time doing so, no matter which country he elects to enter first' (ITF 2005: 8).

Consolidation and Performance

The official launch of the SPP in Waco in March 2005 marked the beginning of the consolidation and performance stage of the strategic bargain that North American corporate actors had crafted in the months following 9/11 and then refined during two years of consultation and collaboration with the executive branches of all three NAFTA governments (Brodie 2006) Echoing the script that had been performed across North America in the preceding two years by the CCCE and other business-funded think-tanks, the 2005 Inaugural Leaders' Communiqué explained that 'Our Partnership ... is a trilateral effort to increase the security, prosperity, and quality of life of our citizens' (SPP 2005b, Office of the Press Secretary 2005). Almost perfectly mirroring the recommendations of the CCCE's NASPI and New Frontiers discussion paper, and the recommendations of the ITF final report, *Building a North American Community*, the new partnership committed North American leaders to pursue a continental approach to regulatory harmonization, the integration of North American energy resources, and the formation of a North American security strategy. One of the few differences between the CCCE's 2003 and 2004 agenda-setting documents and the SPP was that the latter (as well as the ITF report) included Mexico as a key player in this performance of a new North America. This fact was not lost on President Vicente Fox who, on the flight home from the Waco summit, explained to the press: 'I would like you to understand the magnitude of what this [the SPP] means. It is transcendent, it's something that goes well beyond the relationship we have had up to now' (quoted in Pickard 2005: 1).

The SPP agreement enumerated a broad inventory of targeted initiatives under the broad thematic umbrellas of security and prosperity. The security agenda committed the three NAFTA partners to adopt new definitions of insecurity, new surveillance technologies, and new configurations of North American borders. In effect, the SPP sought to de-border and then re-border North America without changing the formal territorial boundaries of its partner countries. Specific security initiatives promised to accomplish the following:

- further streamline the secure and efficient movement of legitimate, low-risk traffic across our shared borders;
- implement common border security and bio-protection strategies;
- improve the legitimate flow of people and cargo at our shared borders;
- reduce the costs of trade through the efficient movement of goods and people;
- develop and implement a North American traveller strategy;
- develop and implement a North American cargo security strategy;
- develop and implement a strategy to enhance North American transportation and port security;
- identify, develop, and deploy new technologies to advance our shared security goals and promote the legitimate flow of people and goods across our borders (SPP 2005a).

The SPP's prosperity agenda promoted the mobility of goods within North America through regulatory harmonization, which typically strips products of their national markings, lubricates cross-national supply chains and selected sector integration, and reduces friction at border crossings. Targeted prosperity initiatives included measures designed to achieve the following:

- ensure compatibility of regulations and standards and eliminating redundant testing and certification requirements;
- strengthen regulatory cooperation ... to minimize barriers;
- lower the transaction costs of trade in goods;
- increase competitiveness by exploring additional supply chains options;
- identify measures to facilitate further the movement of business persons within North America (SPP 2005a).

At the same time, inter-ministerial working groups were charged with identifying areas for immediate action and to report back to North America's leaders within three months. A progress report, released in June 2005, identified approximately 300 actionable initiatives relating to smart borders and smart regulations, liberalized rules of origin, information-sharing, product safety, textile labelling, temporary work entry, and aviation safety (Canada FAC 2005).

It is beyond the scope of this chapter to provide a detailed account of the many different and often partial regulatory changes that were launched during the short life of the SPP. Suffice it to say that the prosperity agenda launched an ambitious strategy for regulatory harmonization. At the 2006 North American Leaders' Summit in Cancun, the SPP leaders established the North American Competitiveness Council (NACC), comprising ten corporate leaders from each partner country, to help identify regulatory obstacles for North American businesses. The creation of something like the NACC was one of the key recommendations of the ITF report as a mechanism that could monitor 'harmful subsidy practices' and promote 'healthy competition' within North America (CFR 2005: 22). The NACC was an executive-appointed trilateral private-sector advisory body, supported by secretariats and located in and funded by the private sector. According to one American CEO, this blue-ribbon panel was essentially given free rein to set the substance and timetable for the prosperity agenda. Lockheed Martin executive Ron Covais explained that the guidance that the business leaders received from the SPP political leaders was, 'Tell us what we need to do to make things happen' (quoted in Patterson, 2007: A7).

Mobilizing quickly in August 2006, the NACC established its three priorities: cross-border facilitation, standards and regulatory co-operation, and continental energy integration. Meeting in Ottawa six months later, in February 2007, the NACC presented 51 recommendations for 'enhancing North America's competitive position in the world economy', complete with an implementation timetable, to nine SPP ministers from Canada, the US, and Mexico (NACC 2007a). These recommendations, in turn, provided the core of the NACC's report to the SPP Leaders' Summit held in Montebello, Quebec in late August 2007 (NACC 2007b). The summit also unveiled a North American Regulatory Framework and a template of Common Regulatory Principles. Despite this initial flurry of activity on the prosperity agenda, by 2008 there was a growing consensus, especially among corporate leaders and think-tanks, that progress on the prosperity file was too slow. In fact, many of the early supporters of the SPP soon derided the agreement for its 'piddling efforts to move red tape' (Patterson 2007: B1) and its 'sluggish' progress in eliminating barriers to continental commerce (d'Aquino 2009). Others argued that tentative steps toward North American regulatory harmonization in Canada owed more to national initiatives, in particular, the 'Smart Regulation' policies launched by the Martin government in 2003, than to the tri-national partnership (Clarkson 2008: 445, Brodie 2009).

The consolidation and performance of the SPP's security agenda was an entirely different story. In the period coinciding with the official life of the SPP (2005–09), there was an unprecedented upsurge in the implementation of security initiatives designed to regulate the mobility of things and people to and within North America. Many of these initiatives were designed and implemented unilaterally, often by the US Department of Homeland Security (DHS), some in response to the recommendations of the 2004 US 9/11 Commission (Hale and Marcotte 2010: 105–06). Nevertheless, the broad commitments to enhanced continental security contained in the SPP, as well as the sheer dominance of the US in the North American partnership, effectively committed the governments of Canada and Mexico to acquiesce to a growing battery of US security initiatives. This growing list included the Secure Border Initiative, a no-fly list, the Western Hemisphere Travel Initiative, the Maritime Transportation Security Clearance Program, US Visitor and Immigration Status Indicator Technology, the Integrated Cross-Border Maritime Law Enforcement Operations 'ShipRider Program', and the Customs Trade Partnership Against Terrorism to name just a few important initiatives that were implemented in a relatively compressed time frame.

The most critical story to be told about the SPP during this consolidation and performance stage was that the security agenda quickly overpowered the prosperity agenda. By expediency as much as by planning, the SPP was configured as a strategic bargain, a trade-off, in which Canada and Mexico agreed to participate in the securitization of North America in order to free up the movement of goods and people across its internal borders. What was not acknowledged or perhaps even fully recognized at the time was that the US saw the SPP as on opportunity *to push its own national security perimeter* to the edges of the continent (Clarkson 2008, Brodie 2012b). The US had taken important steps in crafting North America as a security community in the years leading up to the launch of the SPP. Its unilateral implementation of a Northern Command (NORTHCOM) in 2002, for example, had been instrumental in drawing a de facto security perimeter around North America while the Smart Border agreements, signed by both Canada and Mexico in the immediate aftermath of 9/11 and enhanced under the SPP, further consolidated this transnational security regime. The combined effect of these security measures meant that, during the short life of the SPP, North American borders became thicker and stickier for goods, supply chains, and travellers. These were precisely the conditions that the designers of this deep integration process sought to correct with the SPP.

After only four years of implementation, it was increasingly apparent that the SPP's dual agenda of security and prosperity had contradictory, indeed antagonistic outcomes. This deep integration project had fused together two very different understandings of security and prioritized different kinds of expertise and governing technologies in post-9/11 North America (Brodie 2012b). One, deferring to corporate interests and the tenets of neo-liberalism, conflated the idea of security with the economic security that could be achieved through open borders and regulatory harmonization within North America. The other advanced a non-negotiable vision of security as an extension and securitization of borders to and within North America. Within only a few years of implementation, it was all too apparent that this spatial imagination of a new North America had backfired – and badly. Business leaders and their organizations soon demanded that their governments do something about the thickening of the borders, which was a by-product of the new security regime. In 2008–09, both the NACC and Canada's Competition Policy Review Panel impressed upon the federal government that the thickening of the borders was the most pressing issue on the North American agenda (Grady 2009: 48). Thomas d'Aquino lamented to the 2008 annual meeting of the North American Forum that 'the central issue of North American competitiveness boils down to how we manage our borders ... but these days, it seems every attempt to speed the secure flow of legitimate traffic runs into a brick wall' (2008). Stephen Clarkson similarly concluded that 'the new approach in which "security trumps trade" directly jeopardizes the previous decade's project of building an integrated North American market' (2008: 371). Thus weighed down by its internal contradictions and obvious failure to realize its vision of a seamless North American economic space, the SPP was quietly abandoned in late 2009.

Conclusion

The short life of the SPP tells a story about the failure of an idea to materialize as it was initially imagined. This attempt to embed a more expansive model of continental governance than that provided by NAFTA began as a strategy to secure cross-border mobility in a post-9/11 North America. This hastily contrived experiment in transnational governance, however, has helped underwrite precisely the opposite outcome. Rather than the seamless economic space that was envisioned by the framers of the SPP, borders to and within North America have been transformed into formidable obstacles to the movement of both goods and people. In fact, North American enterprises are arguably more vulnerable to border effects after the implementation of the SPP than they were before.

The demise of the SPP, however, does not signal the end of the North American DI project, although prospects for its revival in the immediate future appear remote. The underlying pressures that initially gave rise to the SPP, increasingly integrated continental production processes, and intensifying global economic competition, continue to challenge North American policy-makers. This said, new DI initiatives will have to take, as their point of departure, the transformed political and regulatory geography that the SPP helped set in place. Even nominal failures in governance irrevocably transform the spaces that they act on. As the first decade of the twenty-first century closes, Canadian region-building elites are already floating new ideas such as a common North American security perimeter and voluntary compliance with American regulatory practices as ways to circumvent the impasses that consolidated under the SPP.

The short life of the SPP also tells a broader story about the fluid, experimental, and contradictory nature of transnational regionalization in the contemporary international political economy. As discussed earlier in this chapter, many different kinds of transnational entities have been proposed in recent years, but few of these imaginaries have been institutionalized and, as the SPP example shows, even fewer realize their intended effects. The unfolding of the SPP raises important questions about the growing and contradictory frictions within globalization between national security, global mobility, and economic liberalization. It also begs the question of whether, over the span of a decade, the focus and character of the North American governance project has shifted from economic integration to continental securitization. If security has indeed trumped trade in North America as a result of the failed deep integration project tracked in this chapter, Canadian region-builders may find that they have few cards to play in new negotiations on the future of North America.

Part III
Migration

Chapter 6
A Dialectical Understanding of the Vulnerability of International Migrants

Jorge A. Bustamante

The US/Mexico Border

If there are geographical areas that have been particularly affected by the events of 9/11, they are the international borders of the US. It is understandable that a country that has come under attack would react by closing its international borders. Such immediate reaction has now been replaced by a more strict control over everything that crosses the border; in effect, everything has been drastically slowed. Eventually, normalcy will return, but for a long while, life at the border will not be the same.

The intense interaction of more than 12 million people from the two sides of the US/Mexico border have allowed us to live in many instances as if the border does not exist. This is the case among many of us in the way we practice family life. For the planning of weddings, birthdays, reunions, and other ceremonies, the border is more virtual than real. This is reversed as we approach the space where institutions – the laws and the governments – interact and remind us that there is a line that marks the beginning and the end of two different nations.

One of the effects of what happened on 9/11 is that we border people have been confronted with an increase in the number of instances when we are reminded that the border makes a difference. We might continue to have a lot of things in common with the people on the other side, but we are more frequently reminded that we are not the same. Indeed, the divisiveness of our borders may be now more keenly felt. Perhaps that is the nature of the concomitant relations between sovereignty and the nation's borders. It is understandable that a country whose sovereignty has been violated as viciously as was that of the US on 9/11 wants to make sure that its international borders are protected, regardless of how good the relations are with its neighbouring countries. Taking care of the integrity of national sovereignty is certainly not something that a country could delegate to a neighbouring country: there is nothing more internal or domestic than taking care of one's own borders. An international border cannot be the same during conditions of war than during conditions of peace; therefore, Mexico and Canada will have to wait until the conditions of war declared by the president of the United States are significantly modified, to see border life restored to what it was before 9/11. The 11 June 2002 issue of *Time* magazine (152 (23)) provided lengthy coverage about the border.

The main thesis of that unusually broad coverage was how promising the US/Mexico border region was as a place of convergence of the best opportunities for economic growth that the process of globalization and trilateralization had brought to the three NAFTA countries. *Time* magazine writers of that issue portrayed a very optimistic scenario based on the realities of a thriving process of integration of the three NAFTA economies: most particularly between that of Mexico and the US, and even more particularly between the border regions that we share. That optimistic scenario was one of the many casualties of the terrorist attack. Consequently, we border people will have to make adjustments as a different meaning of the border emerges from the actual war of the US against terrorism.

However, vital needs at the borderlands will not change. We still have to eat; we still have to provide for our families; we still have to seek the co-operation of our neighbours on the other side for the common tasks that geography imposes on us, such as a shared environment; we still have to seek on the other side what we are lacking on ours. We will continue to have things that the people on the other side need. We still have to barter and exchange and share markets across the border. We still have to produce together the rules of the game. We need to be understanding and patient with the measures of control that the US have taken and will be taking to protect itself against terrorism. The existence of the border makes us the closest foreigners to the US. There are times when this is an opportunity. There are also times when this is a problem. Always it is a challenge. The way in which we interact on the two sides of the border will be an example for the whole of our two countries. We have to make an effort to improve our mutual understanding of the way we are, because no matter how smart we get, we are not going to be able to change geography.

The Historical Context of Labour Migration from Mexico to the United States

Let me now change gears to a more specific aspect of the US/Mexico border relations that will have an impact over all aspects of border life and of bilateral relations in general. That is the question of the immigration of Mexicans to the US.

I would like to start my reflections on the phenomenon of Mexican migration to the US with a historical perspective on how it is that we are where we are in this regard and where it's likely that we will go from here.

Before 9/11 it appeared that the governments of Mexico and the US were closer than ever before to an agreement on the question of migration. This raises a common sense question: Why has it taken so long? It is only rational that a bilateral agreement is the path to follow for a bilateral problem that is caused by factors located on the two sides of the border. On the US side, there has been a persistent demand for Mexican labour – a demand that has been totally endogenous. It has always been in a process of interaction with a labour supply coming from Mexico. History shows however, that the US government has consistently tried to solve this bilaterally shaped problem unilaterally.

There has not been enough debate about this question in Mexico. Neither is there enough historical awareness about those elements that have made the rational option of a bilateral agreement so difficult to reach. It is certainly not because such an option has escaped the minds of the leaders of the two nations (Olloqui 2001: 7–19). I have suggested elsewhere that the answer to such an absence of a meeting of their minds is in the asymmetry of power between the two countries. Indeed there is not enough awareness in Mexico of the extent to which such an asymmetry of power has to do with the US history of labour relations: particularly with the way in which agricultural workers were excluded from the benefits of the first US labour laws in favour of US industrial workers. I am referring, for instance, to the famous Wagner Labour Act of 1935. This law established the legal framework within which labour relations were to be conducted in the US. It was good news for the industrial workers but bad news for the farm workers. They were not included in the new legal framework under which labour rights were granted to industrial workers. The important point here is that such labour legislation excluded farm workers from the legal definition of 'employee' to whom the rights of this law were granted (see, 29 USC Section 151 sec 152(3). The law was amended by the Taft-Hartley Labor Act passed by the US Congress in 1947 and then amended by the Landrum-Griffing Act which was passed by Congress in 1959. However, the original exclusion of agricultural workers from the right to organize and bargain collectively through representatives of their own choice remained unchanged. This in fact signified a discrimination against farm workers through the legal basis upon which industrial workers were to be treated by US employers. The development of such a structural context of asymmetry of power between farm workers and their employers in the US lies behind the inability of the US and Mexico to reach an agreement on the migration question.

As demonstrated in Dr Ernesto Galarza's classic study of the *bracero* program, in his book *Merchants of Labor; A History of the Bracero Program* (1964), the political leaders of the two countries thought the *bracero* agreements were a rational solution to the migrant workers question. However, as Dr. Galarza so eloquently explained, far from being a rational solution for the migrant workers, the *bracero* agreements became an instrument in the service of the US growers. US agribusiness used the *bracero* agreements to legitimize and perpetuate the exploitation of the Mexican migrant workers in the US (Galarza 1996: 47–49).[1] This is not to suggest the same peasants were treated any better in Mexico. The post-war years were a time when peasants as a social class were increasingly abandoned by the Mexican government and by Mexico's emergent middle and upper classes, in the context of a dramatic change in the nation (Torres 1979). At the middle of the twentieth century, Mexico changed from an agrarian society to a new urban society with an economy based on industry and services.

---

1   As reported in Galarza's compilation of migrant workers' complaints, included in a memorandum prepared for the president of Mexico, cited in Mraz and Vélez-Storey 1996: 47–49).

In Mexican government circles there was for many years the notion that the *bracero* agreements constituted a model to be followed to regulate the migration situation. This notion derived from the reading of the written terms of the first *bracero* agreement signed by the two governments in 1942. Indeed, the written texts of that first agreement spoke of vary favourable conditions for Mexican migrant workers (Olloqui 2001: 12). There was, however, an enormous distance between the written text and the reality. Ernesto Galarza tried very hard to persuade the Mexican government of this fact at the end of the Second World War, as one can read in his memoranda to the President of Mexico, found in the Mexico's National Archives by Jaime Vélez Storey and partially published with John Mraz (Mraz and Vélez-Storey 1996: 49). Through a series of articles published by the prestigious journal *El Trimestre Económico* in the 1950s, Galarza again tried to persuade the Mexican government that the words of the first *bracero* agreement were something substantially different from the reality lived in the US by the Mexican migrant workers.[2] The imbalance of power between them and their US employers determined the abysmal difference between the words and the reality of the *bracero* agreement.[3] The history of such an imbalance derived from a historical context in which the US government persuaded an initially reluctant Mexican government under the presidency of Manuel Ávila Camacho (1942–46) to sign the first *bracero* agreement negotiated and approved by Mexico under the geopolitical conditions in which the US entered the Second World War (Ojeda-Gomez 1971). The Mexican government was not in a position to challenge the rising power of the US, and I have argued for a long time that the asymmetry of power between the migrant workers and their US employers was rooted in the asymmetry of power between the governments of the US and Mexico (Bustamante 1992: 28).

The realities of that asymmetry were reflected in the racism about the Mexican immigrants expressed at the highest circles of the US government ever since the beginning of the twentieth century. John Nance Garner, who was US vice president years later, once said: 'The Mexican race as inferior and undesirable as US citizens as they are, should not worry any one because they are *genetically determined* with a *homing pigeon* instinct of always return to where they came from.'[4] The Mexican government did not have the power or the will to protect its people against such anti-Mexican ideological statements, nor to set the record straight that what the US was referring to as an immigration policy was in reality a US labour policy.

It was early in the twentieth century when the US developed ambivalence about the presence of immigrants from Mexico: that is, ambivalence between wanting the immigrants as cheap labour and not wanting them as members of American society. This is seldom discussed in the US, no matter how politically important

---

2 Galarza Ernesto, *El trimestre Económico*.
3 Galarza, *Merchants of Labor*.
4 This, and other equally racist arguments can be found in, US Congress. House Committee on Immigration and Naturalization, *Seasonal Agricultural Laborers from Mexico*, 69th Congress, 1st Session, 1929, pp. 6–62.

the issue of immigration (let alone undocumented immigration) has become in the decision-making process determining the laws of the land in the US Congress. That ambivalence has blinded Americans from seeing the objective realities of a US labour demand which shapes the undocumented Mexican immigration phenomenon as the result of the US labour demands.

It is not a lack of information that explains American blindness to the fact that Mexican immigrants are wanted so badly in the US. In 1994, Proposition 187 – the most anti-Mexican anti-immigrant law in the history of US–Mexico relations (this is elaborated below) showing how deeply rooted was the hate against Mexicans in California – was passed by two-thirds of that state's electorate. That same year, the findings of a scientific study published by the US Department of Labor was not only recognizing the undocumented immigrants' labour demands but empirically defining their function in US agriculture as 'a subsidy' to the US economy. The conclusive remarks of that study are included the following paragraph:

> In effect, migrant workers so necessary for the success of the labor-I U.S. agricultural system, subsidize that very system with their own and their family's indigence. The system functions to transfer costs to workers who are left with income so marginal that, for the most part, only newcomers and those with no other options are willing to work on our nations' farms. (US Department of Labour 1994: 40)

The findings of this scientific report (released in the midst of a widely publicized propaganda campaign to garner votes for 'Prop. 187' as a part of the re-election campaign of then Governor Pete Wilson) were virtually invisible both to its proponents and to the two thirds of the electorate of California who voted in favour of the proposition.

The story of how Pete Wilson supported Proposition 187, resorting to Californians' anti-Mexican prejudices to bolster his political ambition, is reminiscent of the words of George Wallace's inaugural speech as governor of Alabama in 1963: 'Segregation now! Segregation tomorrow! Segregation forever!' Pete Wilson was less dramatic in his use of racist ideologies for political purposes, but no less inclined to appeal to anti-Mexican prejudices in his time than Wallace was in his appeal to anti-Black sentiments. Pete Wilson endorsed Proposition 187 which, as it was written for the ballots, stated:

> Section 1 "Findings and Declarations":
> The people of California find and declare as follows: That they have suffered and are suffering economic hardships caused by the presence of illegal aliens in this State. That they have suffered and are suffering personal injury and damage caused by the criminal conduct of illegal aliens in this State.[5]

---

5   See http://ca94.election.digital.com/e/prop/187txt.html.

Further on in Section 5, entitled 'Exclusion of Illegal Aliens from Public Services', a Section 10001.5 (c) was added to the State's Welfare and Institutions Code, citing the obligation of state officials to denounce to the immigration authorities any person on the basis of 'his or her *apparent* illegal immigration status' (emphasis added).

The contradiction between the paragraphs quoted above includes empirical evidence of the extent immigrant undocumented labour is not only wanted, but needed, in California. It also demonstrates the existence of an anti-Mexican ideology that substitutes a definition of the Mexican immigration's reality, based on scientific research about the nature and impact of Mexican immigration to California, with myths based on prejudices and racial hatred. Such myths were enough basis to criminalize a whole ethnic group (the Latino) ideologically identifiable in California by the colour of their skin. In a state where INS statistics show that, for decades, more than 90 per cent of apprehensions have consisted of Mexican nationals, the term 'illegal alien' is socially synonymous with Mexican. Under the social conditions where this is possible, the most visible a priori indicator of an 'apparent' illegal immigration status is the colour of the skin. This explains why there is such an enormous inconsistency between the US Immigration and Naturalization Service's (INS) estimate of the proportion of Mexican nationals in the total of INS's statistics of apprehensions and the estimates of the US Bureau of the Census regarding the proportion of Mexican nationals in the US in the total number of undocumented immigrants from all countries. The latter is less than 60 per cent, whereas the former has been more than 90 per cent. Such a difference suggests some sort of a 'police profiling' behind the apprehensions of Mexican nationals by the INS.

The criminalization of those who appear to be illegal aliens by ethnic profile, as implied in Proposition 187, did not cease after it was declared unconstitutional by a federal court decision in California. Some of the same proponents of Proposition 187 in California ten years ago were behind Proposition 200 in Arizona in 2005 and behind James Sensenbrenner's Bill 4437 in December of 2005.[6] The way undocumented immigrants are criminalized in the latter essentially replicates the approaches of the two propositions, thus showing the persistence of both anti-Mexican ideologies and the way in which an asymmetry of power between the two nations is transferred to an asymmetry of power between US employers and Mexican migrant workers.

The Myth of an 'Escape Valve'

The question of Mexican emigration to the US is not free of ideologies in Mexico. This is the case of what I have called the ideology of the 'escape valve'. In Mexico the majority of the population at the beginning of the Second World War consisted

---

6   Border Protection, Antiterrorism and Illegal Immigration Control Act of 2005, H.R. 4437. Passed by House of Representatives. Co-sponsored by Republican Representatives James Sensenbrenner and Peter King.

of very poor farm workers who were viewed as less than equal citizens by the upper income social classes. So, by the time the US government put pressure on the Mexican government to sign the first of the *bracero* agreements (1942–64) as a way to supply the labour force needed by the US at the time of the labour shortages produced by the war effort, the recruitment of the temporary workers made under the terms of the bilateral agreement consisted basically of peasants from that underclass of Mexican society. By the end of the war, there was an increasing gap between the interests of the Mexican peasants and the interests of the Mexican government. This was particularly the case under the administration of President Miguel Alemán (1946–52) (García-Cantú 1978).[7] Such a gap explained the beginning of the notion that the emigration of Mexican peasants to the US was an escape valve. Under this notion, the emigration of Mexican migrant workers to the US was seen in Mexico as a sort of solution to the pressures, both real and potential, derived from the increasing abandonment of increasingly impoverished peasants by the Mexican government. There was an inverse relationship between the support the government gave to a new social class of industrial entrepreneurs who led the beginning of the industrial economic growth, and the abandonment of the countryside, both by the government and by Mexican civil society. Behind the 'push factors' of the emigration from Mexico to the US were Mexico's lack of capabilities to achieve modernization through industrial development without abandoning its agricultural sector and its farm workers. Mexico as a nation became enchanted with the illusion of modernization by turning its back on its past as an agriculture-based society.

In effect then, the emigration to the US of Mexican peasants was viewed by Mexican elites as necessary to alleviate the pressures and the costs of the abandonment of the peasants' social class. The notion of emigration to the US as an escape valve became a predominant ideology of the Mexican government. Such an ideology obscured the realities of the exploitation and rampant violations of human and labour rights of Mexican immigrants in that country throughout the *bracero* period (1942–64).

The decade of the 50s was the period in which the Mexican government found that there was no political cost to doing nothing for the Mexican migrant workers in the US. This marked the context in which the Mexican government tried very hard to cover up the conditions under which Mexican migrant workers were treated in the US. I had an argument with a Mexican consul in a US border state right after I posed as an undocumented immigrant in 1971, as part of the research for my doctoral dissertation. He had flatly denied there were Mexican undocumented immigrants in the US. I had to refer him to my recent experience as a participant observer. When I asked him why he had to deny the existence of what I just had witnessed, he reluctantly proposed that if I were to give him my word that I would never reveal his name, he would let me read a *circular* (internal memo), from the Secretariat of Foreign Affairs of Mexico. The memo's instruction

---

7   See also, Bortz 1992: 228.

to all Mexican consuls in the US was very clear: not to expressly recognize, or to make any statement alluding to, the illegal presence of Mexican immigrants in the US. Before 1964 and years after, a top priority of the Mexican government was to persuade the US government to renew the *bracero* agreements; a fact that explained why the government was so complacent about the impunity with which frequent incidents of violations of the human and labour rights of Mexican immigrants were taking place, mostly in Texas and California. Indeed, there was an increasing indifference on the part of the government about the distance between the written terms of these agreements and the realities lived by the Mexican migrant workers. This mindset was supported by increasing corruption as a norm at all levels of the Mexican government and by the political control of the Mexican peasantry through the Confederación Nacional Campesina (CNC). The CNC proved over the years to be a very efficient mechanism of manipulation of the Partido Revolucionario Institucional's (PRI) 'peasants' sector' through a mixture of populism and corruption which gave rise to *caciques* (regional bosses) who ruled the countryside of Mexico with a combination of patriarchal protection to supporters and an iron hand, full of impunity, to manage opponents. This way the PRI ruled most of Mexico from 1929 until 2000.

The works of Ernesto Galarza explained the conditions under which Mexican emigration to the US became functional for the two sides. They maintained an escape valve for the Mexican government through the emigration of an increasingly impoverished, unemployed, uneducated, unorganized underclass of Mexicans, and they maintained, in the interests of US agribusiness, a source of cheap labor (Galarza 1970). This explains why, at the end of the last *bracero* agreement in 1964, the Texas and California growers' associations and the Mexican government became the most persistent proponents of the renewal of the *bracero* programs (Craig 1971).

The ideology of an "escape valve" inhibited the Mexican government from defending or actually protecting the Mexican migrants in the US, other than through rhetorical references. Far from being a solution to the problems associated with migration between the two countries, the *bracero* agreements became concomitant with the rise of officially undocumented migration. As it was documented in Julian Samora's book *Los Mojados, The Wetback Story* (1972), by the end of the last of the *bracero* agreements in 1964 there were more Mexicans crossing as undocumented immigrants than the number of *braceros* contracted through the bilateral agreements.

The absence of a political cost for the Mexican government in doing nothing for the Mexican migrants in the US was not independent of Mexican civil society's general indifference about their plight. I have studied that indifference and I have come up with this hypothesis: that such indifference was not unrelated to a generally unacknowledged Mexican racism. It was not until the 'Chiapas rebellion' of 1994 that the question of Mexican racism virtually came out of the closet as a deeply entrenched part of Mexican culture. Mexican migrants have been viewed by the Mexican middle and upper social classes as distant and distinct from themselves: it is as if the plight of the Mexican migrants – the constant violations of their human and labour rights in the US and in Mexico – was something happening on a different planet, or something that was happening to people with whom the middle and upper classes of Mexico had no connection. It was certainly not racism in any pure form: the disdain of the Mexican middle and upper social classes for the problems of Mexican migrants in the US contained elements of classism. This explains why the plight of the Mexican migrant workers was never taken to the streets by any Mexican organization, particularly by any one of those who claim to protect or defend the interest of the Mexican poor. It has not been until very recently that public institutions such as the Mexican Catholic Church have expressed concern and have begun to support a few programs in defence of the Mexican migrants. Such concern however, follows behind the actions and public statements of several US archbishops. For many decades the principal institutions representing Mexican civil society (the Churches, the unions, the political parties, and the students' organizations) reacted with no more than rhetoric when an incident of abuse of the human rights of the migrants reached the mass media, and usually this tended more to reflect anti-American sentiment than sincere concern for the migrants.

This long-standing indifference of Mexican civil society to the plight of the Mexican migrants has not been adequately studied; it remains as a gross incongruence. The dependence that the national economy of Mexico has had on the remittances of US dollars made by the migrant workers in the US had no congruence with the rampant indifference of the Mexican middle and upper classes to the problems of the migrant workers. Only exports of Mexican oil have produced an income of US dollars per year for the Mexican economy higher than the close to US$20 billion that the Central Bank of Mexico has estimated as the total of remittances generated by migrant workers from the US in 2005–06 (Olloqui 2001: 17). There is not enough consciousness in Mexico of what the social consequence of the exhaustion or even diminishing of migrant workers' remittances from the US would be on their economy.

Returning to the years of the *bracero* program, a paradox should be noted. The end of the *bracero* programs was basically due to the pressures exerted by the American Federation of Labor (AFL-CIO) (Mexico, STPS 1964). Through several decades the AFL-CIO was one of the most important anti-immigrant forces in the US (Garcia 1980). Not only were they successful in ending the *bracero* programs, but also for decades they were the principal proponents of anti-immigrant legislation.[8] That situation ended on 17 February 1999 when the executive committee of the AFL-CIO, in a meeting in New Orleans, made a 180-degree change of course. From then on, the AFL-CIO has become the most

---

8 US Congress, Hearings before the Committee on Immigration and Naturalization, 1926. Washington, DC: US Government Printing Office. 1926; US Senate, Subcommittee of the Senate Committee on the Judiciary, S1917. Appropriations Hearings 1953; Taylor 1981.

vocal proponent of a 'blanket amnesty' for undocumented immigrants. To be sure, this change was not incidental; behind it was the surging of a newly arrived Latino leadership in the upper echelons of the AFL-CIO.[9] These new leaders conveyed the message to the top that an inclusion of undocumented immigrants in the rank and file of the AFL-CIO would bring not only a new source of union fees but also a new dimension of international involvement and political clout to the otherwise weakening political strength of the AFL-CIO. This change came about as a result of the observation of the demographic trends of the Latino population in various circles of American society.

An important factor in the absence of a bilateral agreement on the migratory phenomenon between Mexico and the US has been the distance between the predominant definitions of this phenomenon in the governmental circles of the two countries, as well as within the political elites and the predominant views of public opinion about the presence of undocumented immigrants from Mexico within the US. From the first economic recession of the twentieth century in the US, in 1907, to all the subsequent recessions, a pattern has always appeared consisting of the following sequence:

- The rise of unemployment rates and other signs of a recession catch the public attention.
- Politicians make an association between the rise of unemployment and the presence of the immigrant workers.
- There is a social construction of immigrant workers as scapegoats' of the recession.
- Politicians then propose anti-immigrant measures as a solution to the economic crisis.
- The vulnerability of immigrants as subjects of human rights increases together with the impunity of the abusers.
- The economic recession subsides.
- The anti-immigrant furor ends.

The 'Silent Invasion' Issue

The recession that came about as the result of the oil cartel action taken by OPEC countries in 1974 was not an exception to such a pattern. Those were the years when General Leonard Chapman was appointed as commissioner of the US Immigration and Naturalization Service (INS). He coined the phrase 'silent invasion' in reference to the presence of undocumented immigrants from Mexico.[10] He also testified before various US congressional committees about estimates of 20 million undocumented immigrants from Mexico. It was only after the end of his tenure as commissioner of the INS that his successor, Leonel

---

9   This was confirmed in a letter from the AFL-CIO representative in Mexico City.
10 US House of Representatives, Report No. 94-506, 1975, p. 5.

Castillo, lowered previous estimates to 3 million. The enormous difference in the estimates that two successive commissioners of the INS presented to US congressional committees made evident the extent to which previous estimates had been a fabrication made to substantiate the notion of a silent invasion. It was under General Chapman that the rise of anti-immigrant sentiments in the US crystallized in a definition of the phenomenon of Mexican immigration to the US as a crime-related phenomenon. This became a predominant definition in US government circles where there was a consensus to reject any recognition of the existence of a demand in the US for the labour force of the undocumented immigrant, particularly in the agricultural production of California and Texas.[11] This social construction of Mexican undocumented immigrants as criminals led to the notion in the US that the only solution to a 'problem' defined as having a criminal nature was either a police or a military one (Bustamante 1983). This notion was concomitant to another: that the only solution to the 'Mexican illegal question' should be unilateral.[12] Such a position prompted a delayed reaction of the Mexican government during the presidency of Carlos Salinas (1988–94) expressing opposition to what was termed an unfair and unjustified 'criminalization' of the undocumented immigrant from Mexico. Through the Secretary of Foreign Affairs, Fernando Solana, the Mexican government produced a contrasting definition of the undocumented immigration from Mexico to the US as derived from a *de facto* international labour market. The Mexican reaction defining the phenomenon of undocumented immigration of Mexicans in the US as basically a labour issue contradicted the predominant definition of the same phenomenon in US governmental circles. The net result of this contradiction between the predominant definitions in the two governments about the same migratory phenomenon was a maintaining of the status quo, since the position of the Mexican government during the 1990s never got beyond the confinements of the rhetorical.

President Ernesto Zedillo (1994–2000) saw that whatever degrees of freedom he had in negotiating with the US were crippled very early in his administration by the Mexican economic crisis of 1994. This not only provoked a drastic devaluation of the peso but a close call for the forfeiture of the Mexican foreign debt. A collapse was avoided by President Bill Clinton's decision to bail out the Mexican government with a loan of US$20 billion. Indeed, President Zedillo owed so much politically to President Clinton that he couldn't find room for any criticism in spite of the deaths of Mexican migrants due to the introduction of 'Operation Gatekeeper' in 1994. This was designed not to stop the entry of undocumented immigrants from Mexico into the US, as one would expect from an immigration law enforcement agency, but to deviate the routes of their entries toward areas away from the visibility of urban eyes like those of San Diegans. As the chief of the border patrols recognized in a written testimony

---

11 Meissner, Doris (Hearings).
12 Senator Simpson (quotation).

to a US congressional committee, Operation Gatekeeper was designed under the assumption that undocumented immigrants would be discouraged by the risk of death at the crossing points to which their routes were deviated.[13] These were in mountainous terrain east of San Diego; in the deep irrigation channels, such as the All American Canal; or in the inhospitable desert areas between California and Arizona, where soon enough the number of migrant deaths began to climb. Risks of dehydration in the desert lands, hypothermia during the winter months, or drowning in the irrigation channels did not discourage the inflow of undocumented immigrants.

Very soon after the implementation of Operation Gatekeeper in 1994, the number of migrants dying in the area where the operation was put into effect showed clearly that the assumption based on which the operation was designed, was wrong. This was a conclusion reached by a report of the US Government Accountability Office after conducting an investigation into the extent to which Operation Gatekeeper had reached its stated objectives.[14] What really happened to the immigration flows of undocumented immigrants from Mexico was not a diminishing of the volumes of their flow to the US but a change of places of entry toward the west from the traditional areas through San Diego. In that process, the number of deaths of migrants in the area covered by operation gate keeper climbed at an average rate of more than one migrant killed per day, to a total of 3,800 deaths of migrants from 1994 to 2006. Some non-governmental organizations such as the Rural Legal Foundation of California and the American Civil Liberties Union of San Diego & Imperial Counties criticized their own government for the violation of human rights that Operation Gatekeeper implied, alleging that its implementation was in violation of the charter of human rights, originally drafted by the Pan American Union (now OAS). No Mexican institution, including the Mexican government, reacted in solidarity to such a criticism made by US NGOs and by US citizens. In fact, when president Zedillo was invited by Governor Gray Davis to visit California in May of 1998, he declared to the Spanish daily *La Opinion,* on the verge of his visit, that the deaths of the migrants were a responsibility neither of the US nor of Mexico.

Vicente Fox Defeats the Partido Revolucionario Institucional in 2000

These and many other things changed with the emergence of the political leadership of Vicente Fox. He was able to correctly judge that Mexicans were fed up with the ruling of the Partido Revolucionario Institucional (PRI), which had been in power for the last 71 years. Vicente Fox ran a political campaign for president based

---

13 US Border Patrol, "Border Patrol Strategic Plan 1994 and Beyond". Prepared testimony for a Congressional Hearings, see, www.stopgatekeeper.com.

14 US General Accounting Office, Report to Congressional Committees, "INS' Southwest Border Strategy; Resource and Impact Issues Remain after Seven Years," August, 2001, Washington, DC, US Government Printing Office, 2001, 24.

on a promise of change, particularly a change from corruption in the practice of government. As a governor of the State of Guanajuato and as a prosperous rancher in that state, he was familiar with the phenomenon of emigration of Mexicans to the US Guanajuato is one of the Mexican states where this is something of a tradition.

Early in the twentieth century, Guanajuato had a comparatively high concentration of population. At that time the US Congress decided to appropriate some monies to fund the recruitment of Mexican workers. The First World War had stopped the influx of immigrants from Europe. Blacks had gone north from the deep South to substitute for European immigrants in the lowest paid occupations. US anti-immigrant laws had succeeded in expelling first the Chinese, then the Japanese, and then the Filipinos in the wake of the 'Asiatic barred zone'. The conditions of the First World War had produced a massive need for agricultural production for exports. It also had produced some labour shortages, particularly in Texas and California. This created a sort of a vacuum of cheap labour in the West, the sensitivity of which was taken to Washington by some congressman from California who, after the first economic recession of the twentieth century in 1907, argued in the US Congress that the Mexicans should be sought after as immigrant workers for which purpose public monies should be appropriated. The US congressional records tell the story. The idea was approved and recruiters were sent south to Mexico. Congressmen from California argued that the 'Mexican race' was shorter and closer to the ground, and thus physically suited for stooped labour, as opposed to members of the taller white race who were born for stand-up work, and thus more suited for the industrial production (Feagin 1999: 301). Racist ideologies of White supremacy had penetrated the ivory towers of US academia at the turn of the century, and ideas of White supremacy were incorporated into the mainstream of US social science (Feagin 1999: 385).

The goal of the US recruiters was to attract Mexican workers to fill the cheap labour vacuum caused by the restrictions against immigrants from Asia. However, the recruiters could not find concentrations of people in Mexico right across the border, because some of the most populated communities near the Mexican northern border, like Tijuana, didn't exist as urban settlements at the beginning of the twentieth century. As a result, the US labour recruiters had to go farther south until they found higher concentrations of population. That is why they reached Guanajuato, thus initiating what soon became a tradition in that state: emigrating to the US in search of higher wages.

As governor of Guanajuato, Vicente Fox knew the importance of remittances of dollars from the US by the Mexican migrant workers. Therefore, in his political campaign for the presidency, he called migrant workers 'heroes', recognizing for the first time the importance of migrant workers remittances in the Mexican balance of payments. According to Banco de México's estimates in the year 2004 these represented more than US$13 billion per year, placing them among the top sources of dollars for the Mexican economy. Calling migrants heroes was quite a change from the ideology that saw migrants as an escape valve.

Vicente Fox visited the US and Canada in August of 2000 after his electoral victory that made him president. During the visit, he surprised many Mexicans when he said that the deaths of migrants at the border would be 'intolerable' to his administration. He also surprised the US with his audacious proposals of an open border for Mexican migrants following sufficient closing of the wage gaps between the US and Mexico. The idea was not accepted in the highest circles of the US government, but it certainly made Americans think. Fox's proposals on migrant labour had the legitimacy of a 'democracy bonus' that had come from an electoral victory under the freest elections in the history of Mexico. The image of Vicente Fox as a champion of liberal democracy, after having been in his past a regional director of Coca-Cola for Mexico and Central America, was not a difficult concept to swallow for the American media. Fox came to the US as president-elect, free of the strings attached to previous negotiations led by President Zedillo. Soon enough it became clear that Fox had a powerful ally in the US president, also a former rancher, who became a president almost at the same time as Vicente Fox.

None of the US presidents before George W. Bush, including his father, had deviated from the notion that the 'illegal aliens' were criminals. This is why the different position taken by President Bush during his visit with Vicente Fox at his ranch in Guanajuato represented such a significant change in US immigration policies. Bush's speech on that occasion included a recognition, for the first time, of US labour demand as a factor that shaped the phenomenon of the immigration of Mexicans to the US. His speech also included references to the human and labour rights of the Mexican immigrants in the US, and perhaps most importantly, to the need to negotiate a bilateral solution to the immigration question. The most serious obstacle to a bilateral agreement on the migrant question had been removed. Some very efficient diplomacy under Fox's Secretary of Foreign Affairs, Jorge G. Castañeda, in preparation for this presidential meeting in Guanajuato, was probably an important contribution to what was accomplished. Before this change happened, there was an irreconcilable contrast between the predominant perception in the US of the presence of undocumented immigrants from Mexico as a crime-related phenomenon – one that could only be contained unilaterally by the police or military – and the predominant perception in Mexico of the same phenomenon as the interaction between the factors that create a US labour demand and the factors that create a Mexican labour supply. A power asymmetry between the governments of the two countries had maintained the status quo of that contradiction for more than 30 years, since the years when General Leonard Chapman, as high commissioner of the INS, coined the term 'silent invasion' that, judging from references in the US mass media, permeated the US political culture. Under this ideological environment, the abuses of human and labour rights against the Mexican immigrants came to the surface through the mass media showing the impunity with which US law enforcers from the local to the federal level were involved in incidents of violence against Mexican immigrants.[15] These were years when extreme cases of exploitation were reported by the US media, such as that which provoked legal action with charges of slavery against one US employer.

During the decades of the 70s, 80s, and 90s when the Mexican government was incapable of doing anything concrete against the increasing vulnerability of Mexicans in the US, the most important source of legal protection of Mexican immigrants came from Mexican American organizations in the US. These organizations included the Mexican American Legal Defense and Educational Fund (MALDEF), National Council of La Raza, League of United Latin American Citizens, and GI Forum, in addition to numerous community organizations in California, Texas, Colorado, Illinois, and New Mexico. The litigation of *Brown v. Texas Board of Education* involved lawyers hired and paid by Mexican American organizations who were concerned for the vulnerability of Mexican migrants as subjects of human and labour rights. Such was the case in which a federal court in Houston declared it unconstitutional to exclude from public schools the children of undocumented immigrants from Mexico. The author was an expert witness in that trial, which represented an important victory for the immigrants after a fair recognition that the majority of them pay taxes and social security while they work in the US.

The role of Mexican Americans in the protection of the human and labour rights of Mexican immigrants has not been sufficiently recognized in Mexico except for the award *Águila Azteca*, which is the highest decoration granted by the Mexican government to non-nationals for services to Mexicans: to Antonia Hernandez, president of MALDEF (Aexican American Legal Defense Fund); Julián Samora, professor at the University of Notre Dame; and Blandina Cárdenas, civil rights activist and scholar from Texas.

There was however, a gradual change from rhetoric alone to positive action during the administration of Carlos Salinas de Gortari, when the Mexican government reinforced consular protection. Political appointees whose performance demonstrated this change from rhetoric to action occupied some of the most important Mexican consul general offices in the US. They established more conspicuous and closer contacts between the new Mexican consuls and the

---

15 *Los Angeles Times* published a series of reports from April 22 to April 24, 1993, including the following text: "Some agents complain that commanders place so much emphasis on amassing drug seizures—thus impresing top brass and law makers in Washington—that supervisors turn a blind eye to evidence of wrongdoing by agents ... Managment will let you do whatever you need to do to get the job done to stop drug smuggling, said Thomas A. Watson a five-year Nogales veteran who was fired this month for complicity in the cover-up of a fellow agent's fatal shooting of a suspected trafficker. Drugs are what the chief wanted. Drugs made the headlines ... Many agents admit that they prefer drug duty – waiting in remote canyons with automatic weapons to waylay traffickers along backcountry trails—to the more prosaic task of apprehending illegal immigrants" April 23, 1993, p. A26.

local communities of Mexican origin in the cities of Los Angeles, San Diego, Chicago, Houston, and San Antonio as the predominance of self-denominations was shifting from Mexican Americans to Chicanos, to Hispanics, to Latinos.

By the time Vicente Fox was elected as president of Mexico the 'Latino vote' had surfaced in the political scene of the US as a political force to be reckoned with. The close victory of Ms Loretta Sanchez over her Republican opponent in 1996 in the district that includes Orange County in California was a clear indication of the difference that the vote of formerly undocumented Mexican immigrants could make after they had become US citizens. That election, in what used to be a stronghold of the Republican Party, showed a pattern. Undocumented Mexican immigrants became legal residents of the US and then US citizens, and the overwhelming majority of them joined the Democratic Party.

President Fox had shown a particular sensitivity to the US population of Mexican origin referred to by themselves and others in the US as 'Latinos'. The fact that more than two thirds of them are descendants of Mexican nationals led President Fox to explicitly include them as a part of the Mexican people whom he said he would serve as president of Mexico. It could be argued that this was not a very orthodox view if one takes into account that the majority of Latinos are US citizens. A Mexican citizen who acquires another country's citizenship can no longer invoke Mexican citizen's rights, particularly the right to vote in Mexican elections, unless he or she expressly resigns the other country's citizenship. Fox however, has contributed to the blurring of national identities which began in the preceding *sexenio* (six-year term) with the constitutional reform in Mexico that instituted a virtual 'double nationality'. In fact, this was a constitutional reform which established that Mexican nationality would be considered in Mexico as permanent, regardless of the acquisition of other nationalities by Mexicans. This reform of Mexican nationality left untouched the constitutional rules for Mexican citizenship. Thus, there can be a dual nationality but not a dual citizenship for Mexicans. This distinction is confusing in the US where it is common to equate nationality with citizenship. This is not the case in Mexico, where nationality implies certain patrimonial rights given in exclusivity to Mexican nationals by the Mexican Constitution, such as the right to own land within the zone 50 km parallel to Mexican borders and 100 km parallel to Mexican coastal lines (Article 27 of the Mexican Constitution). President Fox's insistence, in fact an express promise, of granting voting rights to Mexican citizens who reside outside of Mexico in presidential elections only, contributes to the confusion, particularly in the US. This remains a very controversial issue in Mexico, given the fact that there are more Mexican citizens in the US (probably 19 million) than in any single Mexican province except the Federal District (the metropolitan area of Mexico City). Part of the controversy in Mexico derives from the technical possibility that an electoral victory that decides who will be the president of Mexico might come from the way Mexicans citizens residing outside of Mexico would vote.

It has been my opinion that Mexican citizens residing abroad, on a permanent or temporary basis, should have the right to vote in Mexican presidential elections.

It is the implementation of such a right to vote, particularly in the US, that I think President Fox and other proponents of this idea have not thought out carefully. To my knowledge, none of the proponents of the right to vote for Mexicans abroad have addressed, for instance, the fact that there are laws in the US which require a license issued by the US federal government to conduct political activities for other countries within the US territory, with penalties of fines or prison for violators. Nor has it been resolved how the Mexican electoral campaigns in the US could escape from being subjected to US electoral laws, particularly for the electoral propaganda, financing, and conducting of an electoral campaign. Even worse, which country's judicial system will decide in the final instance the eventual electoral controversies? Could it be that the US Supreme Court could decide who will be the president of Mexico? These and many other questions should be answered in Mexico and in the US before the rules for the implementation of such a right to vote for Mexicans abroad allows for its actual exercise unless communication technologies allow for an electronic vote that would overcome the international principle against the extraterritorial implementation of a national law. Again, the events of 9/11 only exacerbated the difficulties of these and other matters pertaining to the realm of the sovereignty of the US and that of its neighbouring countries.

The general indifference in Mexico to the migrant workers' plight has prevented a more significant participation of the political parties in a public discussion about the mentioned options for a US–Mexico agreement on migrant workers. In fact, there has not been a comparable debate in Mexico about the options debated in the US Congress on the subject, in spite of president's Fox unprecedented attention to their plight. There are however, important implications for the Mexican migrants. The option that would be more convenient for the average Mexican migrant worker is whatever comes closest in meaning to the term 'amnesty', a term not accepted by either of the two governments. There has been some confusion in the US over the terms 'legalization', 'regularization', and 'amnesty'. In reality, since they seek the same consequences, the three terms essentially have the same meaning: namely, making the 'undocumented' the 'documented'. This means that the undocumented person becomes empowered when he or she becomes documented; that is, the individual gains a non-restrictive access to the protection of the law, such as the police or the court system in the US, without taking the risk of being deported.

This empowerment has not taken place under previous temporary-migrant US visa programs, particularly under the old *bracero* programs, as it was argued above. The main reason has been that none of the temporary visa programs (H1, H2, H2A, etc.) have significantly modified the asymmetry of power between the migrant worker and his or her US employer. To the extent that amnesty-related options could lead to US citizenship and full voting rights, such options could indeed signify empowerment, which would present a way out of the conditions of vulnerability attached to being an undocumented immigrant. This is not the kind of migrants' empowerment the US growers would be interested in pursuing. Notwithstanding the greater benefit for migrants that could be derived from a 'legalization' or an amnesty-related option, the reality is that this is the option least likely to be palatable to the US negotiators. In fact, President Bush stated that he would not sign any amnesty law.

Geopolitics between Mexico and the US have never been so overlapping as they are today and as they will continue to be in the near and not-so-near future. If there is one factor even more important than a renewal of NAFTA for such a future, this would be the Latino vote. With the exception of California's gubernatorial election of 2004, when Arnold Schwarzenegger was elected, previous elections in California have shown the political cost that Republican candidates could suffer by supporting anti-immigrant measures. Both the elections of 1996 and more clearly the election of 1998 showed how the Latino vote of California punished the candidates of the Republican Party by giving the victory to Democrats such as Governor Gray Davis and Lieutenant Governor Cruz Bustamante.

The emergence of the Latino vote in California was the result of a paradox derived from the re-election campaign of Pete Wilson in 1994, which was based on the support of Proposition 187. The preference of its proponents for extending the limitations established for the undocumented immigrants to all 'aliens', that is to say, to all Mexicans in California including those with a US visa of legal residence, instilled a serious fear in all of the population of Mexican origin in the state, including US citizens. This reminded many Latinos of the anti-Mexican campaign in the 1930s when US citizens of Mexican origin were deported from California back to Mexico, as documented by Abraham Hoffman in the US and Carreras de Velazco in México.[16] The paradox was that a law (Proposition 187) that was intended against the undocumented Mexican immigrants produced fear among all Californians of Mexican origin. Those among them who were US citizens went to the following elections (1996, 1998, 2000) in California, ready to vote against all candidates of the Republican Party whose political platform had included strong anti-immigrant proposals ever since the Party's convention at which George Bush Sr. was elected candidate to the present, as illustrated by the Sensenbrenner Bill.

Public debate on Proposition 187 was marked by the court's main argument in its first and final decisions about its unconstitutionality, namely, its violation of the 'supremacy clause' (immigration matters are the exclusive jurisdiction of the federal government). This was perhaps the main reason why there was not an in-depth discussion of Proposition 187's basic premises. It is argued here that Proposition 187 was based on biased perceptions tainted by racist and xenophobic ideologies, and that its basic provisions represent instances of institutionalised racism against people of Mexican origin, identified as such by the colour of their skin. It is further argued that Proposition 187 was made possible by the

---

16   The two best studies on the massive expulsion of Mexicans during the years of the Great Depression are Mercedes Carreras de Velazco 1974 and Hoffman 1974.

conditions of vulnerability in which an ethnic minority of Mexican origin in general, and Mexican immigrants in particular, have lived in the US. This argument has acquired renewed relevance with the protest marches of March, April, and May 2006, which occurred for the first time in the history of the US, in more than a hundred cities in the US and involving more than a million and a half migrants and their supporters, including other US citizens and many from other countries. Many of the banners in these protest marches targeted the Sensenbrenner Bill HR 3447, which is very similar to Proposition 187 of California and the so-called Law 200 of Arizona. The three legislative pieces proposed by Republican politicians implied various ways of criminalizing US immigrants, including the empowerment of any police officer in the US to arrest and expel any person who, at first sight, may look suspicious of being an 'illegal alien'. By the beginning of May 2006, approval of the Sensenbrenner Bill was still pending in the US Senate.

The most relevant point of the concluding statement in the 1994 US Department of Labor's report quoted above (1994) is the positive impact of migrant workers on the US economy, to the point of referring to the presence of Mexican immigrants as a 'subsidy' to the US economy. This research finding was, and is, completely contradictory to Proposition 187, and equally contradictory to the main propositions of the Sensenbrenner Bill, approved by the US House of Representatives in December 2005. This explains why there is a reference to 'findings' in Proposition 187, with no reference to their source. It is important to point out that the same US Department of Labor study reports that 94 per cent of the migrant farm workers included in its research were Mexican nationals. Mexican immigrant labour is not only necessary for a return to business as usual in the US, it is necessary for the recovery of the US economy. It is known that by the year 2020, more than 70 million Americans (the baby boomers of the late 1940s and 1950s will leave the US labour force. Republicans will hear voices from their own party and certainly from the competition, speaking about the need to rationalize what so far has been a *de facto* labour market between Mexico and the US: one in which the US demand for immigrant labour is as real as the supply of it.

I mentioned two factors in the return of the bilateral relations to where they were before 9/11. I referred to the sharing of a bilateral *de facto* labour market as one factor. The other is of a different nature; it is the Latino vote. As this is growing as a consequence of demography, it was expected to be of crucial importance for the intermediate elections of November 2006 where a change of a political control of the majorities in the US Congress was likely to occur. The November 2005 elections in California, in which all of Governor Schwarzenegger's proposed amendments failed, taught an important lesson: The Latino vote is not impartial to immigration policies. Latinos vote in favour of proponents of pro-immigrant measures and they vote against the proponents of anti-immigrant measures. It is true that Latinos have had a history of low voting records, but it is also true that those ethnic differences tend to disappear when educational levels have been raised. As Latinos' education levels continue to improve, they will be voting in greater numbers. Thus, presidential candidates of the two parties are going to try hard to obtain the Latino vote in the whole US. This will work in favour of an end to unilateral approaches to solving the migration issue, which is in fact shaped by the two countries.

A Theoretical Framework

Figure 6.1 depicts a social process from which two implications may be drawn:

- A socio-legal inclusiveness that arises out of a dialectical process between two legal notions of sovereignty;
- The social construction of conditions of vulnerability for international migrants who are mobilized across international borders by the dynamics of the international relations arising from the globalization[17] of international markets.

This diagram conveys a theoretical framework of a socio-legal inclusiveness. It addresses an apparent contradiction between a notion of international migration and a notion of human rights. The first is generally understood as partially corresponding to the sovereign right of a country of destination, as far as it implies the right of a country to determine who can enter its borders and who cannot. On the other hand, there exists a notion of human rights derived from the UN Universal Declaration of Human Rights which implies rights for all human beings, regardless of national origin. To the extent that countries of destination of international migrations decide to accept the need to protect the human rights of all people regardless of their migratory status, the sovereign decision to do just that implies a self-imposed limitation, if not an apparent contradiction, between the exercise of a sovereign right in two opposite directions.

---

17 Malcolm Waters' comments on Giddens' definition, quoted below, help to clarify the meaning of globalization implied in the diagram: "This definition usefully introduces explicit notions of time and space into the argument. It emphasizes locality and thus territoriality and by this means stresses that the process of globalization is not merely or even mainly about such grand, center-stage activities as corporate mega-mergers and world political forums but about the autonomizations of local life worlds. Globalization, then, implies localization, a concept that is connected with Giddens' other notions of relativization and reflexivity. The latter imply that the residents of a local area will increasingly come to want to make conscious decisions about which values and amenities they want to stress in their communities and that these decisions will increasingly be referenced against global scapes. Localization implies a reflexive reconstruction of community in the face of the dehumanizing implications of rationalizing and commodifying" (Waters 1995: 4–5).

A Dialectical Understanding of the Vulnerability of International Migrants   129

The diagram suggests the use of 'dialectics', as proposed by G.W.F. Hegel, as an analytical tool with which to analyze this apparent contradiction. Understanding the diagram requires making the following three assumptions: First, the dialectical relations between the two acts of sovereignty correspond to a social process. Second, this social process takes place over a long time span in which a set of contradictions originates from two opposite acts of sovereignty. Third, the evolutions implied on each side of the diagram are relatively independent of each other, except that both evolutions are moved by the international relations that are implied in the concept of globalization. The notion of a clash between the evolutions on the two sides of the diagram implies a growing process of maturity and a dynamism that reaches its maximum force as it is confronted by another force from an opposite side. That is, a clash between the vulnerability of the migrants, depicted on one side of the diagram, and the empowerment of the migrants coming from the opposite side. Behind the notion of a dialectical clash is the assumption that there is a point of maximum vulnerability of the migrants that is characterized by the impunity of those who violate their human rights. There is a point where that impunity is stopped by its encounter with an opposite force. That force comes from the empowerment of the migrants. This empowerment has been evolving as a result of pressures coming from the international community, or what is known as globalization. An illustration of this process and this outcome is the granting of voting rights to legal immigrants in local elections that has occurred in several nation states of the European Union.

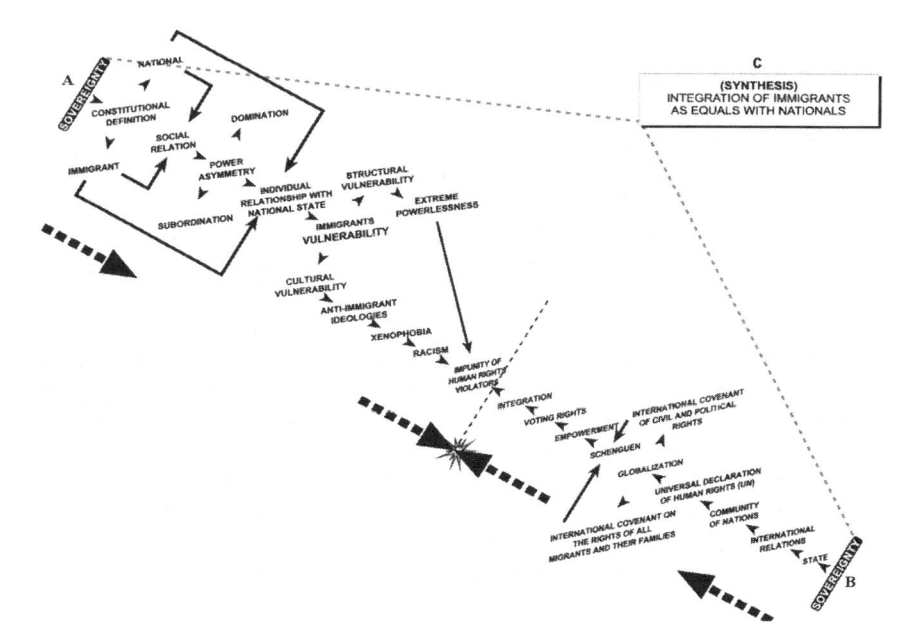

Figure 6.1   Dialectic of migrants' vulnerability

Following the model proposed by Hegel's dialectics, the clash between a thesis and its antithesis gives way to a synthesis, which to Hegel consists of elements from the two colliding forces. This is the way integration (as explained below) is understood in the diagram as (C) or, as the dialectical synthesis of (A) and (B). The following parties are the main actors of the social process implied in the diagram:

- immigrants (understood as foreigners);
- nationals of a country of origin;
- nationals of a country of destination;
- the State, respectively of both the country of destination and the country of origin of international migrations.

This social process begins when a country of destination, exercising its sovereignty, decides to include in its constitution a distinction between nationals and foreigners by establishing a definition of who is one and who is the other. This act of sovereignty, identified in the diagram as (A), enters into a long-term process that ends up in an apparent contradiction, defined in the diagram as dialectically opposed, to another act of sovereignty. This is when a sovereign decision is made by a country of destination to commit itself to respect and protect an international standard of human rights, regardless of the national origin and migratory status of individuals, and then constitutionally remake that international standard into a law of the land. This is when it becomes (B) in the diagram. As such, it is in contradiction to (A), which preceded it. The decision to make a constitutional distinction between nationals and immigrants (as foreigners) implies the emergence of a basis for a social relation between those enacting the constitutionally defined role as nationals and those enacting the constitutionally defined (by default) role as foreigners. These two exercises of sovereignty depicted in the extremes of the diagram as dialectically opposed become interrelated in the practice of international relations arising from the phenomenon of globalization.[18] Thus, the thesis in this Hegelian dialectical process is (A), and the antithesis is (B). More will be said below about the synthesis (C), namely, integration.[19]

---

18   For the purposes of this chapter, Anthony Giddens definition is the most fitting. "Globalization can ... be defined as the intensification of worldwide social relations, which link distant localities in such a way that local happenings are shaped by events occurring many miles away and vice versa. This is a dialectical process because such local happenings may move in an obverse direction from the very distant relations that shape them. Local transformation is as much part of globalization as the lateral extension of social connections of time and space" (Giddens 1990: 64).

19   There are two contrasting notions of *integration*. One, predominant in the United States, derives from the studies of Robert Ezra Park, whose followers, according to Michael Haas, have argued "that differences between ethnic groups are a function of attitudes of prejudice" (Haas 1992: 61). This thesis assumes that such differences can be removed through intense interethnic interactions, which could lead to a colour-

As I have said, the diagram starts from the Hegelian notion of dialectics, but this is not to be confused with 'dialectical materialism', a term coined by Hegel's rebellious student Karl Marx after he had criticized Hegel's dialectic as one that was 'standing on its head', which necessitated 'turning it right-side-up' again. He claimed to have done just that by creating what he termed 'historical materialism'. The diagram of Hegel's dialectic at work has nothing to do with Marx's 'correction' of his mentor's philosophy of history. Here, Hegel's dialectic is viewed as a social process that is taking place between two exercises of sovereignty, each with different objectives and opposed to the other as a *thesis* opposes an *antithesis*, out of which a *synthesis* emerges. Implicit in this use of dialectics as a tool of analysis is the inclusiveness of two cognitive domains, namely, law and sociology. One is of a legal or normative nature and the other of a social nature. The bridge between the two dimensions is implied in the passage from a norm – an 'ideal construct' – into actual human behaviour in the empirical context of social relations.

The diagram assumes such inclusiveness in alluding to a social process in which the main actors are those defined constitutionally as nationals, and those defined legally and socially as foreigners or immigrants. The main feature of this inclusiveness is the dialectical dynamic, energized by the international relations of globalization. In that relational context emerge the conditions under which the vulnerability of international migrants comes into being. This vulnerability, then, is understood here as a condition of powerlessness to which an international migrant is socially consigned in the society, the economy, and the culture of a country of destination. A condition of vulnerability of a migrant in his or her country of origin is of a different nature, as is discussed later. The shaping of an international migrant's vulnerability as it is understood here begins with an ultimate act of sovereignty, namely the Constitution, when it includes a definition of who is a national and who is not. By establishing this dichotomized definition, the Constitution of a country of destination is establishing a criterion for a social asymmetry between nationals and foreigners. Regardless of how consciously this is done, the fact of the matter is that when such a Constitutional distinction is transferred to the context of a social relation between actors who assume their roles claiming the authority of the Constitution, the asymmetry of power implied in the Constitutional distinction becomes enacted in the empirical reality of the social relation between a national and an immigrant/foreigner. To the extent that an unequal power is implied in the constitutional distinction for the two of them

---

blind society. About this assumption, Haas comments: "There are at least four flaws in integrationism. First, it is a theory of assimilation. The closer an ethnic group resembled the dominant culture, the more it would be 'tolerated' and ultimately 'accepted' and 'admitted' to equal status ..." The other notion of integration, predominant in Western Europe, is more recent. This is epitomized by the Schengen Agreement, binding for member states of the European Union, where integration means equal rights for nationals and foreigners. The latter notion is the one adopted in this chapter.

(nationals and foreigners) respectively, a distinctive access to the social forces of society allows for the rise and development of anti-immigrant ideologies or social constructions whose function is to justify, reinforce and promote the power differentials originally assigned to the constitutional distinction. The rise of anti-immigrant ideologies is a direct result of the power differentials derived from the asymmetry of power established by the constitutional distinction between national and foreigner. A social outcome of such a power differential is a pattern of discrimination against immigrants.

This is particularly evident in the labour relations of Mexican immigrants in the US where employers tend to be US nationals and workers are Mexican immigrants. Perhaps the best example of the labour relations between them is the California economy, in which Mexican immigrants make up more than 90 per cent of the total of the labour force employed in that state's agricultural production. (California's agricultural production is equal to one third of the total of agricultural production in the US, according to the US Department of Labor NAWS survey, published in 1994.) In the study of this labour market, one finds empirical evidence to substantiate the existence and operation of a power structure in which the basic social relations of nationals (US employers) and immigrants, as depicted in the diagram, have entered into the fabric of a national system of agricultural production in the US. The following paragraph, from the aforementioned 1994 US Secretary of Labor research report, supports this:

> In effect, migrant workers so necessary for the success of the labor intensive U.S. agricultural system, subsidize that very system with their own and their family's indigence. The system functions to transfer costs to workers who are left with income so marginal that, for the most part, only newcomers and those with no other options are willing to work on our nation's farms. (US Department of Labor 1994)

These remarks, based on scientific research, not only empirically support the notion of a power asymmetry between migrant workers and their employers in California; they also illustrate the strength of US demand for immigrant labour and the degree of vulnerability that is imposed on migrant workers to whom the costs of agricultural production are transferred in order for the US agricultural system to function.

The fact that the publication of the research findings from which the above quotation is taken took place before the appearance of Proposition 187 illustrates the dynamics of a social process on its way to a growing impunity for the violators of immigrant human rights, which is supposed by the diagram at some point will be stopped by the empowerment of the immigrants. Before that is understood, the apparent contradiction between international migrations and human rights requires analysis of its historical context.

It is assumed here that there is an evolution of the asymmetry of power derived from the constitutional distinction between nationals and foreigners.

That evolution follows paths similar to those which have followed other socially constructed 'distinctions' out of which discriminatory behaviour against a social group has been subjectively justified. That has been the case in racism, sexism, homophobia, and xenophobia.

Integration, as it has developed in the European Union, becomes a true Hegelian synthesis of the dialectical opposition between (A) and (B), to the extent that it eliminates the inequalities implied in (A) between nationals and foreigners. By the time an exercise of a sovereign right turns (A) into its opposite (B), the new notion of human rights has erased the previous inequalities between nationals and foreigners. The emergent product of the dialectical relations between (A) and (B), namely integration, implies that human rights apply equally to both nationals and foreigners. Such is the meaning of the Schengen agreements.

There seems to be a distance of light years between the empowerment of migrants through legislation enfranchising immigrants in local elections, such as the Schengen Agreement enacted by countries such as Spain, the Netherlands, and Denmark, and the vulnerability of migrants such as those exposed by 'Operation Gatekeeper' at the US/Mexico border. However, when one takes into account the time it took for European countries to evolve from the Treaty of Rome in 1957, to the Schengen Agreement, to speaking about 'voting rights' to immigrants, one could hypothesize that immigrants' rights will follow in the US the evolutionary line marked by their history in Europe. That is the hypothesis behind the dialectics of vulnerability implicit in the diagram.

The dialectical contradiction between (A) and (B) suggests that all nation states have the sovereign right to define who is a national and who is a foreigner, as well as the sovereign right to control their borders. In both cases, the implication is to define the frontier between the essential inner and outer components of a nation. Most democratic nations have these rights written in their constitutions. Although such legitimate distinctions, in most of the cases, do not explicitly place the foreigner[20] in a subordinate position *vis-à-vis* the national when they interact socially within the receiving country, the duality (national–foreigner) is nevertheless very often transformed or socially constructed into an object of *de facto* discrimination against foreigners by nationals. As Robert Miles[21] discusses extensively, this distinction is implicit in the origin of all kinds of discriminatory practices against foreigners as such, at the personal, group, and institutional levels. This implies a power structure wherein nationals are more likely to occupy dominant positions *vis-à-vis* foreigners, and the latter are more likely to occupy subordinate positions.

---

20 The terms "foreigner" and "immigrant" are used interchangeably in this chapter.

21 For a discussion of the dominant/subordinate relation of nationals/immigrants assumed in most recipient countries, see Robert Miles, *op. cit.* (particularly in reference to what he calls the problem of "Euro-racism"), pp. 207–15.

In this metamorphosis from the normative to the social lies the virtual contradiction between immigration and human rights. But in reality, there is no contradiction. The sovereign right that is implicit in the definition of each concept respectively is of the same legal nature: two different instances of an exercise of sovereignty, in two different times, in the history of a country of destination. The opposition between these two exercises of sovereignty is dialectical. Such a dialectical opposition was generated from the dynamics of international relations implied in the process of globalization. To the extent that international migrations are a consequence of globalization, the international community acquires an acting role in the evolution implied in each side of the diagram. However, this acting role is manifest on a level of abstraction that requires the analyst who would understand it to look at the history of the specific international relations between countries of origin and destination, and to focus on the microcosm of the social relations between the international migrant and a national of the country of his or her destination.

In the past, as human societies have confronted problems of power and authority, the source or locus of authority has moved from God, to the State, to the people. The definition of sovereignty[22] has been based chronologically on these three sources. At their origin in medieval times under the doctrine of Christian unity, the concepts of 'sovereignty' and 'sovereign' were one and the same, except for the semantic distinction between an attribute and the subject of its enactment.

The diagram above starts from the Hegelian notion of a dialectic process. Here, this process consists of two opposite exercises of sovereignty, each with different objectives and opposed to each other as a thesis opposes an antithesis, and out of which a synthesis emerges. Implicit in this dialectic is the inclusiveness of two cognitive domains: law and sociology. One is of a legal or normative nature and the other of a social nature. The bridge between the two dimensions is the passage from a norm to actual human behaviour in the empirical context of social relations. The diagram assumes such inclusiveness in alluding to a social process in which the main actors are those defined constitutionally as nationals, and legally and socially as foreigners or immigrants. The main feature of this inclusiveness is the dialectical dynamic, energized by the international relations of globalization. In that context, the vulnerability of international migrants becomes the focus of a contradiction between (A) a 'classical' notion of the sovereign right of nations to define who is a national and who is not, as well as to control immigration by controlling their borders; and (B), a 'modern' notion of sovereignty susceptible to self-controls through a state's sovereign decision to adhere to international standards of human rights.

---

22 For an in-depth analysis of the historical context in which the notion of *sovereignty* has evolved, see Bartelson 1995.

This is a similar paradox to what is implicit in all international agreements that become of a higher legal order than norms of internal legislation by virtue of the exercise of sovereignty, namely the Constitution.

Part IV
The Democratic Deficit

Chapter 7
Canada and North American Integration – Bringing in Civil Society?

Laura Macdonald[1]

> Encouraging public interest and understanding of international trade is critical to establishing policies that reflect Canada's priorities and interests, and our commitment to fairness, stability and good governance as citizens of the global community.
>
> Canada's experience has shown that consultations, whether at the domestic or the multilateral level, greatly reinforce public awareness and understanding of the importance of trade, and ensure that citizens' priorities and interests are reflected in the development of trade policy objectives, policies and positions. By mobilizing popular opinion and keeping people fully informed of the issues and the direction of trade negotiations, transparency and engagement combine to establish the legitimacy, consistency and the durability of policy decisions and outcomes.
>
> 'Why We Consult', Foreign Affairs and International Trade Canada[2]

In recent years, the role of civil society has become an increasingly prominent part of the discussion of international trade agreements. Citizens have become increasingly concerned about the implications of arcane trade discussions for sustainable development, equity, labour standards, and democracy. Civil society organizations argue that it is important for actors outside of business and government to be able to play a role in discussing the important issues that will affect many aspects of the lives of North Americans. As the introduction to this volume suggests, a common political space has emerged at the transnational level in North America, despite the remaining obstacles to co-operation among governments. On one hand, big business actors from the three countries have coalesced in a common project of promoting deeper economic integration. On the other hand, non-business civil society actors representing a wide range of concerns

---

[1] I thank the Social Sciences and Humanities Research Council of Canada for their financial support, as well as Julián Castro-Rea and an anonymous reviewer for their helpful suggestions.

[2] Department of Foreign Affairs and International Trade Canada, "Why We Consult," accessed at http://www.international.gc.ca/trade-agreements-accords-commerciaux/goods-produits/why-consult.aspx?lang=en on 2010-03-30.

and interests have come together in opposition to this project. Whatever their differences, these civil society groups are united in opposition to what they see as the exclusionary and secretive manner in which decision making has occurred to date in the North American region.

In the next chapter, John Foster reviews the turbulent politics of civil society protest against North American trade policies. This chapter examines the arguments that have been made for the inclusion of civil society in discussions of international trade agreements, and will provide an overview and critique of the structures (or lack thereof) for consultation with civil society regarding the evolving North American relationship. As the quotation that begins this chapter indicates, the Canadian government rhetorically champions the advantages of widespread consultation. I argue, however, that despite the Canadian government's relatively good record in attempting to create a more inclusive model of consultation for a wide range of trade agreements, the participation of civil society has been quite limited in decision making about North American integration, probably because the stakes in this domain are highest for Canada. As demonstrated in Canada's recent involvement of (the now concluded) Security and Prosperity Partnership of North America (SPP), mechanisms for the participation of civil society in decision making seem to be becoming increasingly rare, while the involvement of big business has become more institutionalised. While big business is an important actor with legitimate concerns that should be addressed, the exclusion of other perspectives means that governments risk ignoring broader public concerns about a 'democratic deficit' in North America.

Civil Society, Consultation, and Trade Policy

Many factors have combined to push governments to take into account the interests of actors outside of the State when making decisions around trade policy. Keohane and Nye argue that international governance was in the past characterized as a 'club model' of decision making, where high-ranking officials would make the rules of the global economy behind closed doors.[3] This old club model is breaking down in the context of increased public concern about the scope of the decisions being made in trade talks. While earlier trade negotiations in GATT primarily focused on cutting tariffs, more recent trade discussions have broadened to include such complex and wide-ranging issues as quotas, countervailing duties, intellectual property rights, trade in services, and investment (Weston 2005). As a result, new models of consultation have been developed to take into account the views of both business and non-business civil society actors, as well as other departments of

---

3   Robert Keohane and Joseph Nye Jr, "The Club Model of Multilateral Co-operation and Problems of Democratic Legitimacy," in Porter, Sauvé and Subramanian and Zampetti 2001. See also discussion in Ayres and Macdonald 2006.

both the federal and provincial governments that would not normally be involved in trade discussions.

Brian Hocking argues that most countries have moved away from the old club model toward new positions located along a spectrum of increased transparency and inclusiveness. As Hocking puts it, 'No longer can trade issues be dealt with as a brand of technocratic politics, insulated from the mainstream of political dialogue, a game for an elite operating behind closed doors, removed from prying eyes and the glare of publicity'(Hocking 2004: 3). The next stage away from the club model is what Hocking calls the 'adaptive club model', in which business interests are directly represented in the policy process. As we will see below, this is the model which has come to dominate North American relations. However, civil society representatives have expressed profound concern about policy processes in which only business actors gain privileged access to decision makers. In response to such criticism, some countries have moved to a 'multi-stakeholder model', which includes representatives of civil society as part of the policy process, even though their impact on policy may be limited.[4]

Canada is often seen as a global leader in the move away from the old closed model of trade policy decision making toward a newer, more inclusive model (Wolfe, R. 2006). Dan Ciuriak, former deputy chief economist, Department of Foreign Affairs and International Trade, claims that after an initial us-versus-them response to the mobilization of civil society around trade issues, during the debate on the Canada–United States Free Trade Agreement (CUFTA), government policy embraced 'transparency', one of civil society's major demands.

In fact, Canada has been at the leading edge internationally in responding to this demand. For example, even prior to the WTO Ministerial meeting at Seattle in November/December 1999, Canada submitted a proposal to the WTO on transparency. At Seattle, Canada instituted regular briefings for Canadian civil society representatives. Canada also brokered agreement to make public the draft text of the Free Trade Area of the Americas (FTAA) process, and recently published its negotiating position in the GATS (Ciuriak 2004: 215).

According to Ciuriak, the club model of decision making on trade policy in Canada was relatively short-lived; by as early as the Kennedy Round of the GATT negotiations (1963–67), successive Canadian governments had to try to 'sell' trade by expanding the model of consultation (Ciuriak 2004: 216n). As a result, what Ann Weston calls the Canadian model for public participation in trade policy formulation was launched. As trade agreements moved away from discussions on tariffs toward measures that affect areas that previously were viewed as within domestic jurisdiction, trade officials were forced to adopt a series of measures to consult with affected areas of government within Canada. Consultative measures inside of government include consultations by officials from the Department of Foreign Affairs and International Trade with other government departments

---

4 Cited in Weston 2005: 9–10; Hocking 2004: 3–26. See also the concept of "input-oriented legitimacy" in Montpetit 2003.

and agencies whose interests might be affected by ongoing negotiations and the 'C-Trade' process that brings together representatives from the provinces and territories four times a year to discuss trade issues that might impinge on provincial jurisdiction (Ciuriak 2004: 221–222; Weston 2005: 16–17).

More significantly for this discussion, Canada made the shift away from the club model toward Hocking's adaptive club model of decision making during the negotiation of CUFTA in the mid-1980s. This shift occurred in part because of Canadian business's dissatisfaction with their relationship with the State in the Trudeau years, which led them to seek a more unified voice on macroeconomic policy and greater access to the decision-making process. An International Trade Advisory Committee (ITAC) and fifteen Sectoral Advisory Groups on International Trade (SAGITs) were created to structure consultation with the business community on international trade. The ITAC was designed to provide general advice on macroeconomic policy; SAGITs were designed to provide expert advice on the impact of trade negotiations on specific economic sectors (Ciuriak 2004: 222; Macdonald 2002: 202–3). Business groups thus gained privileged and institutionalized access to the decision-making process. As well, an Academic Advisory Council was created in 1998 to provide input from leading academic experts on trade issues.[5] As Hocking notes, shifting away from the club model to the adaptive club model was not terribly difficult because of the high degree of consensus between business and government trade officials. However, bringing in other actors has proved much more difficult.

As indicated above, the Canadian government has in recent years moved toward Hocking's multi-stakeholder model in some aspects of trade policy. Multi-stakeholder consultative meetings are held several times a year to discuss trade issues with participants from a wide range of organizations. Parliamentarians also play an important role in consulting with the public on trade issues, through the House of Commons Standing Committee on Foreign Affairs and International Trade and the Standing Senate Committee on Foreign Affairs. The government also uses the internet to communicate with the public about its positions in trade talks, and also calls for comments on a wide range of ongoing trade issues. Canada has also pushed for greater transparency and public consultation in several trade negotiations, like the WTO and the FTAA. By and large, however, these consultations with civil society actors outside of business appear to be aimed more at legitimizing and gaining public support for Canada's trade policies than at incorporating advice from non-business civil society actors.

Robert Wolfe argues that interest in consultation on trade policy in recent years has waned. There are a number of reasons for this: the routinization of consultation which means civil society no longer needs to fight for this principle; the possibility that civil society groups are exhausted by the number of ongoing consultations;

---

5   Ann Weston reports that it was decided in 2005 to reduce the number of SAGITs and to create a process in which expert groups are created on a temporary as-needed basis. According to the government website, there are currently 12 SAGITS (Weston 2005: 5).

the change in the substantive trade negotiation away from the WTO and FTAA toward concern with access to the US market after 9/11; the cost of participation in consultation processes; and, possibly, a lack of public support for the anti-globalization agenda. Wolfe discusses another interesting factor that may have led to a reduction in the Canadian government's interest in consultation:

> By inviting more players to the table, the government has, to some extent, changed the game. Business leaders, who were quite interested in trade policy in the late 1980s and 1990s, may retreat from formal consultation because of the influx of third sector or civil society organizations, some of whom disagree with the fundamental principles of trade liberalization. (Wolfe, R. 2006: 10)

Trade policy expert Sylvia Ostry similarly claims that the value of consultation is diminished as the trade ministry

> tries to be seen to be including the desires of every diverse interest group ... My sense is that the business community is finding less and less value in participation as they are asked to input at the same time as any NGO and seemingly have no more weight in their advice. (Ostry 1999)

Ironically, then, civil society's limited success in gaining access to the processes of decision making on trade may have led big businesses to search for other ways of influencing the policy process.

Civil Society and North American Integration

For Canada, agreements on free trade with first the US and later Mexico would serve as a trial by fire for long-standing models of trade policy decision making. Unlike other areas of trade policy where the stakes are much lower for Canada, the Canadian state has jealously guarded entry into the decision-making process on as important and controversial an issue as the trade relationship with its major trading partner.

As suggested above, Canadian trade relations with the US were traditionally governed by the club model of decision making, in behind-closed-doors meetings between Canadian and US officials. The Canadian state adopted an adaptive club model of decision making by creating the SAGITs shortly after the announcement of the bilateral trade negotiations. This outcome was partly the result of a shift in the nature of Canada's business community: as a result of the economic crisis of the 1980s and years of tariff cuts under GATT, Canadian business moved away from its earlier protectionist policies toward a neo-liberal position that embraced free trade with the US, despite the risks involved for less competitive Canadian businesses. Indeed, Canadian business's embrace of the free-trade option under the leadership of the Business Council on National Issues and the

Canadian Manufacturer's Association was a major factor in the Brian Mulroney Conservative government's decision to opt for free trade (Macdonald 2002: 202–4). This ideological convergence between business and the State facilitated the shift toward a new model of trade-policy decision-making.

While the Conservative government was eager to include business in the decision-making process, its attitudes toward civil society participation were much less accommodating. As John Foster discusses in his chapter, the announcement of the decision to pursue a trade agreement with the US resulted in the unprecedented coalescence of new ties among a wide range of civil society actors, including trade unions, nationalists, women's groups, social agencies, development groups, Indigenous peoples, farmers, environmentalists, and social justice groups like the mainstream churches. Shut out of government consultation processes, these very diverse actors came together for the first time in a coalition called the Pro-Canada Network (later renamed the Action Canada Network) around a wide spectrum of concerns ignited by CUFTA. CUFTA was also opposed by both the Liberal Party of Canada and the New Democratic Party in the so-called free trade election of 1988, and a majority of Canadians voted against the government, but the split in the opposition vote resulted in the re-election of Prime Minister Mulroney (Ayres 1998; Foster, J. 2005: 209–29). CUFTA therefore came into effect in 1998.

The civil society movement opposed to CUFTA re-emerged during the negotiation of NAFTA, and also developed ties with its counterparts in the US and Mexico, as well as the Quebec coalition, the Réseau québécois sur l'integration continentale (RQIC). These alliances remained shut out of the official mechanisms of consultation with business on the trade discussions. Again, the coalitions were unsuccessful in blocking the signing of NAFTA. The so-called 'Red Book', which outlined Liberal Party policies prior to the 1993 election campaign, said that a Liberal government would call for a review of the side agreements and a renegotiation of both CUFTA and NAFTA to obtain a subsidies code, an anti-dumping code, a more effective dispute resolution mechanism, and the same energy protection as Mexico had acquired in the NAFTA agreement (Gabriel and Macdonald 2004b: 71–91). These demands reflected public concerns about NAFTA as well as the demands of civil society organizations. However, once elected and after talks between his government and US officials, Prime Minister Chrétien neglected this earlier promise. Civil society actors did have some impact on the eventual shape of the NAFTA agreement, not because of consultation processes in Canada, but rather because of the politicization of trade issues in the US. While the bilateral agreement with Canada excited little interest in the US, the inclusion of Mexico awoke widespread concern among civil society and political actors in the US. As had happened earlier in Canada, a diverse coalition of civil society actors opposed to NAFTA emerged during the debate. Because of the more porous nature of the political system in the US, these actors were able to exercise considerable pressure on the political system, particularly within the Democratic Party. Bill Clinton supported the NAFTA agreement negotiated by President Bush Sr. However, to retain support from labour unions, environmentalists, and fellow

Democrats, in his campaign for the presidency he called for the negotiation with Canada and Mexico of side agreements on environmental and labour conditions. Once he was elected president in the 1992 election, these agreements – the North American Agreement on Environmental Cooperation (NAAEC) and the North American Agreement on Labour Cooperation (NAALC) – were negotiated despite a lack of enthusiasm from the Canadian and Mexican governments.

The side agreements were opposed by many civil society actors because they lacked strong enforcement standards, and because the standards established for labour and environmental conditions were those already existing in the national legislation of each member state; they did not impose new, higher standards on any of the members. However, it could be argued that the two NAFTA side accords did create some new supranational architecture with the potential to promote new spaces for citizen engagement. The labour side accord received little support from North American trade unions, apart from the official Mexican unions, which were closely tied to the Mexican state. As a result, there was little input from labour into the design of the institution established under the NAALC, and relatively little provision for citizen participation in the review of labour standards on the continent. Partly as a result, it is widely agreed that the agreement on labour has had minimal impact on the promotion of labour rights and improved labour standards in the region. The NAALC has permitted civil society organizations to publicly challenge governments over their lack of enforcement of their labour laws, and has created some public pressure on corporations to abide by existing legislation, for example in the case of pregnancy screening of female *maquiladora* workers (Dombois, Hornberger and Winter 2003: 421–40). However, there is widespread disappointment with the responses given by the National Administrative Offices in each country to the submissions filed (Dombois, Hornberger and Winter 2003) and the number of submissions, never high, has dropped. The overall impact of the NAALC has been underwhelming, according to Dombois and Winter:

> While it is true that the NAALC has, for the first time, made social policy issues the subject of international and transnational communication and cooperation in North America, the activities have had little visible or more general regulatory effects, even though they might have been influential in individual disputes. And even the expected 'sunshine effect' and impact on public discourse have been very modest. Altogether, the NAALC seems to have run out of steam and certain strategically important actors of civil society have turned aside in disappointment. (Dombois and Winter 2003)

The ineffectiveness of the NAALC in promoting labour rights is attributable not just to its weak capacity for enforcement, but also to the lack of common understandings and strategies among governmental and non-governmental actors in the three countries of the region. The three governments of the region designed the agreement to maintain their sovereign control over labour issues, and non-state actors like unions and NGOs have been highly sceptical about the labour side agreement, and reluctant to appear to seemingly contribute to its legitimacy by working through the NAALC institutions to promote labour rights in the region.

Although environmental groups were split in their views on NAFTA and the NAAEC, considerable numbers of environmental NGOs did support the side agreement, and it has prompted some lively debates and research concerning the connections between trade and environment in the North American region. The NAAEC also differs from the NAALC in the establishment of a Joint Public Advisory Committee (JPAC) which forms part of the North American Commission for Environmental Cooperation (CEC). The NAAEC thus broke new ground by 'including a public, nongovernmental advisory group as one of its components';[6] it is designed to carry out public consultations to advise the commission, and also to 'ensure active public participation and transparency in the actions of the Commission'. This type of language is virtually unique in the institutions of governance of the North American region, and it comes close to Hocking's 'multistakeholder model' (Ayres and Macdonald 2006). In particular, the side accord on the environment and the existence of transnational activism by North American environmental NGOs (ENGOs) has contributed to a significant opening of new political spaces in Mexico for Mexican ENGOs' participation in domestic decision making processes (Torres 2009: 195–210).

Overall, while the NAFTA side accords do provide some limited room for civil society participation in governance, the bulk of the NAFTA regime retains its exclusionary character in which processes of decision making are elite-based and non-transparent.

Deepening NAFTA? The Security and Prosperity Partnership

Prior to September 11th, some actors, most notably the government of Mexico, but also some business actors, were feeling that the existing model of integration under NAFTA had largely achieved its objectives, and that deeper forms of integration were required in order to achieve greater benefits. President Vicente Fox, elected in Mexico's first truly democratic elections in 2000, was pushing for a 'NAFTA-plus' model that would create a North American community similar to the European community, including labour mobility and structural funds. Fox's proposals met with little support in Washington or Ottawa. However, the 9/11 terrorist attacks launched a new stage in the process of North American integration, although not in a manner consistent with Fox's proposals.

The virtual closure of the Canadian and Mexican borders by the US government after the attacks dramatically demonstrated the high level of dependence of both countries on secure and easy access to the US market. Canadian business organizations and authors associated with conservative think tanks launched a

---

6 See: http://www.cec.org/who_we_are/jpac/pub_consult/index.cfm?varlan=english, accessed August 16, 2005.

series of proposals to 'deepen' North American integration. Thomas d'Aquino, former president of the Canadian Council of Chief Executives, and Wendy Dobson of the C.D. Howe Institute proposed different types of strategic bargains, in which Canada would accept many elements of US policy around continental and global security, and access to Canadian resources, in return for secure access to the US market. Advocates of deep integration supported the construction of a continental energy pact, a common market, common regulatory standards, and the virtual elimination of border controls (Jackson 2005; Gabriel and Macdonald 2004: 79–100).

Some aspects of the proposals floated by business civil-society actors – a common market and the elimination of border controls, for example – were extremely ambitious but politically untenable. However, other aspects, especially regulatory harmonization, were picked up in the announcement of the Security and Prosperity Partnership of North America (SPP) at the summit of the three leaders in Waco Texas in March 2005. The leaders' statement announcing the SPP stated that the partnership represented a 'trilateral effort to increase the security, prosperity, and quality of life our citizens'. It set out objectives such as common border security and bio-protection strategies, enhancing critical infrastructure protection, and announced the creation of a North American steel strategy and the Canadian Automotive Partnership Council (2002).[7]

Commentators on the SPP differed on the extent to which the SPP truly represented the consolidation of a 'deep integration' agenda, since many of its elements were quite modest, and the policy style was incrementalist, in contrast with the dramatic steps advocated by writers like Dobson and d'Aquino. Nonetheless, even if the SPP did not represent a step forward to deep integration, the policy style adopted clearly did not represent progress in achieving a multi-stakeholder model and greater non-business civil society consultation. The SPP was adopted without public consultation, or even parliamentary debate. Critics of the process charge that the manner in which the SPP was promoted represented an attempt to bypass citizen involvement. Mexican activist Miguel Pickard notes:

> When NAFTA was negotiated in the early 90s, civil society had little chance to provide input. In Mexico there was no public consultation. The Mexican congress at the time, still controlled by the Revolutionary Institutional Party (PRI), held perfunctory debates. Today civil society in the three countries is better informed and mobilized. In Mexico the congress no longer rubber stamps bills sent by the president. This explains in part why deeper integration is taking place through a series of regulations and executive decrees that avoid citizen watchdogs and legislative oversight. Activist civil society organizations have to work overtime to keep up. (Pickard 2005)

---

7 "Security and Prosperity Partnership of North America Established, March 23, 2005, Waco Texas," accessed at www.pm.gc.ca.

In addition to the lack of consultation with civil society actors leading up to the creation of the SPP, the North American leaders created a new form of privileged access by business actors to decision-making. The leaders of the three countries invited 15 CEOs from large corporations to the summit in Cancún in March 2006. After the summit, the leaders created the North American Competitiveness Council (NACC), initially made up of 30 senior private sector representatives, 10 from each country. According to Prime Minister Harper's office, the Council

> has a mandate to provide governments with recommendations on broad issues such as border facilitation and regulation, as well as the competitiveness of key sectors including automotive, transportation, manufacturing and services. The Council will meet annually with security and prosperity ministers and will engage with senior government officials on an ongoing basis.[8]

The SPP was implemented through the establishment of a series of working groups in the areas of both security and prosperity. The working groups, made up of representatives of government departments from the three countries, were mandated to consult with 'stakeholders' in each of their areas of interest. It remained unclear, however, whether the term 'stakeholders' included groups other than businesses and municipalities.[9]

The tri-national coalitions that opposed NAFTA also organized in opposition to the SPP. After the creation of the NACC, the national chairperson of the Council of Canadians, Maude Barlow had this to say:

> This latest development clearly puts business leaders in the driver's seat and gives them the green light to press forward for a North American model for business security and prosperity ... How truly accountable is the Harper government to the Canadian people when it gives preferential treatment to the big-business community in the design of its policies?[10]

On 6 June 6 2006, representatives of civil society networks from Canada, the US, and Mexico, as well as sympathetic legislators from the three countries announced a collective plan to 'bring an end to deep integration and replace NAFTA with a people-centred trade model'. This was the second North American

---

8 "Prime Minister announces Canadian membership of North American Competitiveness Council," June 13, 2006, accessed at http://pm.gc.ca/eng/media.asp?id=1200 on March 29, 2010.

9 In 2007 the U.S. SPP website was adapted to allow comments by visitors to the site on a comment form, perhaps reflecting public criticism of the lack of substantive consultation mechanisms. Accessed at www.spp.gov on October 29, 2007.

10 Council of Canadians, "Competitiveness Council formalizes power of big business leaders, says Council of Canadians," accessed at www.KnowledgeDrivenRevolution.com, June 19, 2006.

Forum; the first was held in Washington in May 2005. The group announced plans to create a North American secretariat, introduce simultaneous legislation in the three countries to replace NAFTA, and build opportunities for public engagement regarding the issue of continental integration.[11] Protesters also gathered during the third annual meeting of the SPP leaders in Montebello Quebec in August 2007. A large public event initially scheduled to take place near the summit site was moved to Ottawa when the Quebec provincial police instructed the manager of the local municipality to cancel access to its community centre. The New Democratic Party's trade critic, Peter Julian, criticized the lack of public outreach around the SPP:

> There has never been any real public consultations and we're talking about an agenda that touches about 300 different areas…What we are saying is this needs to come out in the public domain, we need to have full and meaningful consultations, we need a parliamentary vote before anything else is negotiated away.[12]

Perhaps in response to public opposition, the SPP was quietly concluded in 2009. Civil society groups hailed the SPP's disappearance as a victory. Stuart Trew, the trade campaigner for the Council of Canadians, declared that 'the NAFTA-plus agenda died at the latest North American Leader's summit … we killed it and we should be singing that from the rooftops' (Trew 2009). It is likely that it was the Obama administration that pulled the plug on the SPP initiative, but civil society opposition likely played a role in discrediting the SPP, particularly among strong Democratic constituents like labour unions.

Conclusion

The latest phase of the process of integration in North America brings out many of the tensions and problems of earlier phases. In contrast with its rhetoric and, to some extent, its practices in other international trade agreements, when it comes to relations with its most important trading partner, the Canadian government has consistently followed an exclusionary model of decision-making. This model, which Brian Hocking calls the adaptive club model of trade policy decision making, incorporates business participation in decision making, but systematically excludes participation by civil society actors that fail to share the fundamental assumptions and beliefs of government and business. As discussed above, in recent years many forces have combined to push governments to incorporate

---

11 "Legislators and civil society groups of the North American region call for halt to Security and Prosperity Partnership and replacement of NAFTA," press release, June 6, 2006.
12 "Protests begin before SPP summit," CTV.ca, August 19, 2007.

some degree of participation by civil society actors in decision making in order to legitimize and gain public support for controversial trade measures. In fact, the Canadian government has been recognized as a leader in this shift toward a multi-stakeholder model of decision making. Nevertheless, the governments of the region did not engage in consultation with civil society actors on the creation of the SPP, and instead institutionalized a new mechanism for consultation with big business, following Hocking's adaptive club model. The style of decision making adopted in the SPP clearly showed the limitations of this model, since the clear inclusion of big business and exclusion of other civil society actors acted to discredit the whole SPP initiative. It is unclear, however, whether governments will move toward more inclusive mechanisms of decision making in the wake of the SPP. Indeed, a return to the elitist 'club model' of backroom consultation seems quite likely in future discussions of North American co-operation.

Chapter 8
Making Room for Democracy: Three Moments in the Struggle Against Trade and Investment Regimes in the Americas

John W. Foster

Introduction

This chapter is based on the experiences of a researcher and writer with a long history of engagement and activism in the movements and processes described. These include being a participant in the movement against the original Canada–United States Free Trade Agreement (CUFTA), in Common Frontiers, and in a tri-national coalition against NAFTA, as well as an observer in the growth and development of the Hemispheric Social Alliance.

While having the vantage point of early 2006, the chapter depends, in part, on earlier work.[1] References to a few relevant more recent events and commentaries are found in the footnotes. The author has recently published a subsequent treatment: 'NAFTA and After: The Triumph of Bilateralism,' in *The USA and Canada 2012*, edited by Neil Higgins (Abingdon: Routledge, 2011).

* * * * *

The issues we are dealing with are in no way restricted to the study of civil society, but involve the social, economic, and governmental future of the Americas and the future of Canada itself.

The Americas remain a highly polarized and unequal domain. Despite 25 years of following the Washington Consensus, Latin America has experienced a spectacular failure of economic growth from the perspective of the average person – less than 0.5 per cent per capita average income growth since 1980. Even the *Wall Street Journal* admits that 'the rise of Mr Chávez and other more moderate leftist leaders in Latin America, reflects the disappointing results of the so-called

---

1 My chapter John W. Foster, "The Trinational Alliance against NAFTA: Sinews of Solidarity", in Bandy and Smith (2004), as well as two speeches "Imaginary Citizens" prepared for KAIROS, in 2005 and "When Big Ideas go Bad", presented to the Labour College of Canada (2005) (manuscripts in the possession of the author). See also Foster, with Krudniewicz (2005).

Washington Consensus, a set of market-oriented policies like trade liberalization and privatization that the region ... embraced'.[2]

Canada, although you would never know it from the 2005–06 and 2008 election debates, is on a course of 'deep' integration with the US, a version of what the Mexicans call 'NAFTA Plus', in good part a product of a successful if quiet effort on the part of the Canadian Council of Chief Executives to pre-empt debate over our future.[3]

* * * * *

Three Windows

This review highlights three fairly distinct periods in approximately 15 years of civil society engagement in issues of continental and hemispheric integration.

- The first is the initial engagement with the NAFTA negotiations, from roughly 1990 to mid-decade, in which the primary actors are nationally-based social coalitions allied in an informal tri-national alliance of civil society organizations and networks.
- The second extends generally from the Miami Summit of the Americas (1994), through the Santiago (1998) and Quebec (1991) summits to Mar del Plata in November, 2005, in which a hemisphere-wide association of coalitions developed, the Hemispheric Social Alliance, or *Alianza Social Continental*.
- The third is quite contemporary, and I would date it in some ways from 2001 through to the election of President Obama late in 2008. It is highlighted by the birth of the SPP in Waco (March, 2005) and in which organizational responses involved, in part, a renovated tri-national civil society alliance.

---

2 As quoted by James 2005.

3 For the difference between Canadian 'deep integration' projects and Mexico's 'NAFTA Plus' proposal, see Janine Brodie's chapter in this book. Some journalists and academic observers downplay the process, pointing out that it is largely 'bureaucratic' and 'technical'. A further argument is that the SPP was an unfortunate tactical approach to what should be 'inevitable' institutional changes (see for example, Ibbitson 2007). Those who discount the process are offset by the testimony of figures like the head of the US section of the North American Competitiveness Council, Lockheed-Martin's Ron Covais, who stated to *MacLean's* Magazine 'The guidance from the ministers was, "tell us what we need to do and we'll make it happen,"' and that rather than going through the legislative process in any country, the Security and Prosperity Partnership must be implemented in incremental changes by executive agencies, bureaucrats and regulators. 'We've decided not to recommend any things that would require legislative changes, because we won't get anywhere.' (Council of Canadians, *Backgrounder: the North American Competitiveness Council.* Ottawa, February, 2007). See also Foster 2011.

The Obama administration and its trade, investment, and military policies in the hemisphere usher in a new period, with the emphasis on bilateral relationships with Canada and Mexico and the civil society response still incipient.

This examination focuses on one locus within civil society: social organizations, movements, and coalitions actively engaged and in tension with the dominant government–corporate-sponsored generation of trade, investment, and intellectual property agreements. Even more specifically, I am speaking of those bodies that were primarily oppositional in position, while recognizing that there were other strata of organizations, some of them government-supported, that were engaged in ways more sympathetic to official approaches. Some scholars simply characterize the first as 'outsiders' and the second as 'insiders', although there are contradictions as well. For example, the Canadian government in both the Toronto Trade Ministers meeting of 1999 and the Quebec Summit of the Americas provided funding for some outsider activities.

The NAFTA Engagement

The highly articulated battle over the Mulroney–Reagan CUFTA brought together marvellous coalitions of social actors in Canada, part of a majority of Canadians who voted against Prime Minister Mulroney and his 'deal'. Yet they were out-financed and out-gunned in the campaign and battered after the 1988 election. The prospect of a further negotiation, involving Mexico, seemed more potential than real, but began to be operational sooner than many expected.

The occasion of a public debate over free-trade prospects in Mexico City in 1990, organized by the right-wing PAN party with the passive support of the governing Salinas PRI administration, brought together about a dozen opponents of the bilateral agreement from Canada with an equal number of advocates, including Quebec's Bernard Landry and one or two from Alberta. The opponents from a variety of Canadian labour, environment, women's, Indigenous, Church, and farm organizations took the opportunity to meet with Mexican counterparts, organized by the independent union *Frente Auténtico de Trabajo*. Not long afterward, several of the same groups met with US counterparts in Washington.

Within months, an informal tri-national alliance of coalitions opposing the proposed NAFTA had developed.

- In Mexico, the *Red Mexicana de Acción frente al Libre Comercio* included a variety of independent labour, social, environmental, agricultural, and academic bodies, some with close links with Cuauhtémoc Cárdenas and the *Partido de la Revolución Democrática*.
- In the US, what was later named the Alliance for Responsible Trade (ART) grew out of years of work on labour and human rights and included a

portion of the environmental movements, the major labour federation AFL-CIO, and development-oriented organizations like the Development Group for Alternative Policies among others.
- In Canada, the key group was a coalition of labour, Church, human rights, and environmental groups called Common Frontiers, working with the predecessors of the Council of Canadians and others.
- In Quebec, a *Réseau québécois sur l'intégration continentale* (RQIC) emerged, with trade union, women's, nursing, development, and other organizations.

These four groupings as well as an additional electorally-focused coalition in the US composed an informal tri-national alliance working against NAFTA (see Foster 2004).

The alliance took opportunities to engage with politicians, particularly in the US Congress and in the context of Mexican electoral politics: it sought to make the negotiations transparent and to publicize and educate, and it assisted Mexican organizations in opening up space for dialogue with officials and advocacy which had not previously existed. In the US, it was part of a public movement and electoral challenge which was sufficiently pungent that the Clinton administration moved effectively to buy off organizations, in particular splitting the environmental movement. The promise of side agreements on labour and the environment and of specific attention to border concerns in southern California were all used in the effort.

The alliance followed the NAFTA negotiators at each stage of their process, organizing protests, seeking dialogue, engaging the media, and exposing what could be learned about the texts and sensitive issues under discussion. It worked at developing common tri-national positions and critiques, often through joint declarations, involving detailed and sometime fractious negotiation. Each alliance partner used spokespersons from its partners in advocacy and media work, and sponsored exchanges, in particular visits of trade union and other representatives to Mexico, and, for example, a US program where those threatened by runaway shops were taken to Mexico to 'visit their jobs'.

The alliance, particularly in moments of joint lobbying and large conferences, provided a space for intense debate. Not all issues and emphases were by any means subject to consensus. Areas like auto part production and migration sparked tense debates between Mexican and US participants. The Mexicans, and to some extent the Canadians and Québécois, were interested not only in the details of the trade and investment clauses, but in what they termed the 'social agenda': agreements that would fight poverty and encourage social development, among other themes. US participants tended to be influenced by the more iterative and incidental processes of the US Congress, finding broader visions less attractive, if engaged at all.

The alliance did, however, establish durable, flexible, and productive cross-border working relationships, despite significant linguistic barriers and the inexperience and ignorance of many actors about the history, politics, and social reality in partner countries. Further, it provided a context in which the sophistication and capacity of many organizations to monitor, analyse, and advocate around the complexities of the new generation of trade, investment, and intellectual property agreements developed considerably, contributing as well to the development of positive alternative propositional thinking and action. It assisted in opening up trade negotiations to public scrutiny and to understanding their far-reaching implications.

Finally, for some of the groups involved, particularly the unions and Churches, the process of working together against NAFTA led to ongoing exchanges, agreements, and solidarity which continued for at least a decade after the US Congress had approved the deal. The analytic talents developed around NAFTA were applied to the raft of bilateral and regional agreements which followed, in particular to the successful battle against the proposed Multilateral Agreement on Investment in the late 1990s, and the wide-ranging continental effort against the proposed Free Trade Area of the Americas (FTAA).

Nevertheless, NAFTA was passed and signed in all three countries. On the drizzly night of the Congressional vote, on 20 November 1993, representatives of the opposition coalitions gathered at the Capitol. As corporate lobbyists celebrated NAFTA's passage under chandeliers inside, members of the tri-national alliance coalitions, including figures like Jesse Jackson, huddled outside on the steps, in damp defeat.

The Free Trade Area of the Americas and the Hemispheric Social Alliance

The second phase under review began essentially in May 1997 in Belo Horizonte, Brazil. The occasion was a hemispheric trade ministers' meeting, implementing the decision of the 1994 first Summit of the Americas in Miami, with the FTAA project at the centre of the agenda. A parallel Third Trade Union Summit was held at the same time. These events, as counters to the trade ministers, were, in retrospect, the moment of conception of the Hemispheric Social Alliance (HSA), from a diverse gathering of trade-union, anti-poverty, environment, and other NGOs in Belo Horizonte, Brazil.

The various groups drafted and signed the Declaration of Belo Horizonte, which challenged the FTAA agenda in the following ways:

- There should be no agreement along the lines of the NAFTA; there should be instead a development agreement based on strengthening national economies and national development models.
- Any trade agreement should not be an end in itself but a means to combating poverty and social exclusion.
- There should be no FTAA unless it includes a social agenda, including broad-based citizen participation in the negotiation and ratification by

democratic means, unless there is respect for and improvement of the social and economic rights of workers, women, *campesinos*, Indigenous peoples, and migrant workers.
- Competitiveness must not be based on workers' exploitation, social dumping, and downward harmonization. ILO conventions on freedom of association and collective bargaining should be the foundation, and there should be a Charter of Social and Economic Rights for the Citizens of the Americas.
- There must be protection for the environment and food security, including support for small-scale farmers and small and micro-enterprise.
- There must be protections against instability caused by speculative capital, controls on capital flows, and performance requirements on foreign investors as well as relief of foreign debt.

Those associated with the original declaration included the members of the original tri-national alliance, the Chilean Network for a People's Initiative, the Brazilian Association of NGOs, the National Union El Barzón (Mexico), the Coalition for Justice in the Maquiladoras (US), the National Indigenous Council of Mexico, and the Inter-American Regional Organization of Workers.

The HSA that developed out of this meeting, and the declaration, were the springboard to convene summits of the peoples of the Americas to coincide with the summits of the Americas, held in Santiago in 1998, Québec in 2001, Mar del Plata in 2005, and Port of Spain in 2009, as well as a meeting with FTAA trade ministers in Toronto in 1999. The HSA developed a detailed alternative proposal for regional integration, the product of collaborative research entitled Alternatives for the Americas.[4]

Alliance member organizations set out to mobilize national efforts against the FTAA agenda. The US campaign to defeat fast-track legislation, and the Brazilian civil society plebiscite on the FTAA, which involved millions of participants, along with the people's activities at the Quebec Summit of the Americas were among the most notable elements. There were also seminars and demonstrations at the suddenly truncated 2003 eighth meeting of trade ministers in Miami.

Initially, there was considerable continuity of actors between the NAFTA and the early FTAA battles on the civil society side. The diversity of actors increased with the entry of the regional trade union federation, the *Organización Regional Interamericana de Trabajadores*, into the formation of the HSA, and with the engagement of peasant, human rights, women's and Indigenous networks, among others. However, it can be argued that continuity was a central feature of the formative four or five years.

Until early in 2002, the strategic leadership of the HSA lay with a triumvirate of organizations and personalities, based in Mexico City, Washington, Ottawa, and

---

4 Hemispheric Social Alliance, *Alternatives for the Americas.* At www.web.net/comfront/alts4americas/eng/eng.html.

Toronto,[5] who remained in frequent and regular contact, planned agendas for larger HSA formations, monitored events, suggested initiatives, and kept the mechanism in shape, albeit with extremely limited resources. However, other centres of activity in the Americas, notably Brazil (the *Central Única de Trabalhadores* trade union federation and the *Rede Brasileira para a Integração dos Povos* and Quebec's *Réseau québécois sur l'intégration continentale* were coming to play greater roles.

The veterans of the struggle over NAFTA at the core of the HSA represented a considerable body of experience in dealing with the negotiation processes and the negotiators, in using relevant and timely analytic resources, in dealing with their own organizations, and in working with the press. They also used strategy effectively, particularly in recognizing the essential political importance of transparency of negotiations, and in refusing to take pro-forma consultations with officials as being anything more than that.

Nevertheless, it can be argued that the effects of these stratagems, initially at least, were marginal. A civil society 'committee' was added to the negotiating structure, although movement observers recognized that it was little more than a 'mailbox', in that no reply could be expected. The trade ministers met, formally, with a sizeable representation of HSA participants in Toronto in 1999, where they heard alternative proposals, and engaged in a brief debate. And some governments developed consultative practices and staff liaisons to deal with HSA members and other civil society advocates. Some governments, including Canada and the US, funded what might be called 'insider' civil society processes, favouring groups that accepted the basic FTAA agenda.

After a relatively limited prelude at the Windsor Assembly of the OAS in 1998, the high point of mobilization and confrontation occurred in Quebec City, around the heavily-guarded Summit of the Americas in April, 2001. The arrival of more than 60,000 citizens in a massive march, together with the much more graphic confrontations between youth and security forces with tear gas and truncheons, exceeded any popular manifestation that had occurred during the NAFTA negotiations. Despite the strength of this mobilization and the increased media attention to the arguments made by the HSA members, analysts could specify little shift in the framework or detail of key issues in negotiation. The HSA could, however, claim the victory of forcing government officials to make public the draft negotiating text and to respond to an increasingly probing press.

In Canada, there had been a growing hope that given its almost indefensible character, the investor–state mechanism in Chapter 11 of NAFTA might be revised and the possibility of its inclusion in an FTAA forgone. Executive statements at Quebec City soundly dashed those hopes. The HSA devoted a good deal of the

---

5 The primary actors in the alliance were Common Frontiers (Canada with members in Toronto, Ottawa and some other centres), RQIC (Quebec), ART (Washington) and RMALC (Mexico). There were other groups pre-occupied with the same problematic, most notably Washington-based Public Citizen, who acted independent of the common understandings of this alliance.

post-Quebec period to debating and developing a strategy for mobilizing public opposition. This has taken form in a series of parallel but not identical initiatives, including demonstrations and dramatizations, public consultations, and unofficial plebiscite soundings. By the end of 2005, participants could claim they had 'stopped the FTAA'.

The transfer, early in 2002, of the secretariat of the HSA from Mexico to Brazil, the continued contribution to the HSA of the Brazilian *Central Única de Trabalhadores*, and the symbolic and motivational power of the Brazilian-based World Social Forum expressed a similar shift in movement emphasis.[6]

From a Canadian civil society perspective, the locus of initiative, political priority, and nuance shifted from the early days of formation of the HSA to the climactic moment of Mar del Plata. Symbolic and real, the move of the secretariat of the HSA from Mexico City to São Paulo pre-dated but suggested the gravitational shift. Originally a reflection of the relative power and resource of the Brazilian trade unions and social organizations and the rise of Luiz Inácio da Silva ('Lula') to power, it served the increasing shift toward the social movements of South America, whether in Brazil, Argentina, Bolivia, or Ecuador.

As mentioned, this shift was facilitated and fed by the Brazilian-led World Social Forum at Porto Alegre. This forum brought tens of thousands of primarily young and motivated activists together. It was an occasion for education by the HSA and its components and allies, for a myriad of intense analysis, strategy, and planning sessions, and for large multi-sectorial public demonstrations against the FTAA and neo-liberalism. At its most visionary, the forum injected into political language the phrase 'Another world is possible', and at its most practical it multiplied the constituencies motivated by the experience of popular or participatory budgeting as pioneered in Porto Alegre's municipal government itself.

But perhaps more important was the shift of the agenda from reaction and opposition to the US, Canada, and the FTAA integration model, to another focus. That focus was not merely couched in opposition to the US and Canadian approach, but was increasingly rooted in South American or pan-Latin American orientations. Initially the Cubans played a key role in facilitating these discussions, but the torch was taken up with enthusiasm and greater resource capacity by Venezuela.

Mid-way in this shift came the 2003 Cancun WTO Ministerial Conference failure which is important in this discussion as symbolizing the crisis of the Mexican approach, caught between its enthusiastic adoption of the US–Canada trade and investment agreement model and the new geopolitics of trade. The political weight of other 'southern' initiatives coming from Brazil, India, and the southern G-20 formation of countries, reinforced by avid pressure from international NGOs

---

6 In mid-2007 the Secretariat of the HSA transferred to Bogotá, Colombia. In part this symbolizes the change in "front" from fighting a comprehensive FTAA to dealing with specific bilateral US-led trade and investment agreements (Colombia, Peru, Central America, etc.). See www.asc-has.org/.

present, created resistance to previous assumptions of 'northern' leadership and the operation of select invitational groups in manipulating the agenda.

Mar del Plata, in 2005, like Quebec City, was a festival of civil society workshops and events, with an estimated 12,000 participants and a closing assembly of over 5,000 people. Like Quebec City, it concluded with a demonstration of tens of thousands, with participants like Silvio Rodríguez, Diego Maradona, Adolfo Pérez Esquivel, the Mothers of the Plaza de Mayo, Evo Morales, and Hugo Chávez, in a massive 'funeral' for the FTAA.

Hugo Chávez, in his weekly television talk show, said in November 2005: 'In the future, we will speak of US–Latin American relations in terms of the era before Mar del Plata, and the era after it.' In a four-hour show, he provided clips of the speeches of government representatives from Mexico, Argentina, Canada, and the US among others. Observers have commented that the Canadian performance was embarrassing in its failure to reckon with the new moment in Latin America.

What Chávez was signalling was not only the victory of more or less progressive governments in Brazil, Uruguay, Argentina, Bolivia, Venezuela, and Chile, and the possibility of a left victory in Mexico, but a focus on Latin American or Latin American–Caribbean approaches, rather than those led from Washington or Ottawa. The Bolivarian Alternative for the Americas (ALBA), a Venezuelan initiative grounded in a framework of commitment to complementarity, solidarity, co-operation, and respect for sovereignty, is one of his challenges to the FTAA agenda, along with other steps such as Petrosur (an initiative of Venezuela, Brazil, and Argentina to undertake co-operative petroleum projects in the region) and Telesur (a pan-Latin American television and satellite network). Venezuelan domestic social initiatives in improving the lives of the poor, social services, and education have engendered a great deal of popular interest outside the country, as well as condemnation from governments, pundits, and media sympathetic to neo-liberalism.

The shift in locus was not limited to Venezuela, but even with the charges and challenges that the Lula administration faced, the role of Brazilian diplomacy in trade, development, and such specific theatres as the combat of HIV/AIDS was significant. Brazil's role as co-chair of the FTAA negotiations high-lighted the ambiguity of its position, not necessarily as an ideological opponent of the project but as a government with a significant interest in a better deal. The inter-play between the prospects of the moribund FTAA and the ongoing WTO negotiations, particularly in the area of agriculture, continues. Given the Mar del Plata failure, OAS head José Miguel Insulza has said that without a breakthrough in the WTO, the hemisphere can either scrap the FTAA or negotiate a regional deal on subsidies. Mexico's Fox suggested an FTAA without Mercosur and Venezuela. Washington is still probably asking too much in return for its producers and service providers to gain support for a regional deal.

This period ended with another declaration, at the III Peoples' Summit of the Americas in November 2005, involving social movements from Canada to Patagonia, 'to deepen our resistance to the neoliberal calamities orchestrated by the imperial power from the north and to continue the construction of alternatives.'[7] The opposition noted that although the Quebec City Summit had promised an FTAA by January of 2005, it was then late in the year with no agreement, with negotiations 'irreversibly stalled ... We are here today to celebrate this!' The declaration noted that the agenda of the hegemonic power had not ceased, that it not only worked through bilateral FTAs and the WTO negotiations but through the extension of military bases, the continued use of external debt as blackmail, and ongoing polarization. In addition to calling for immediate suspension of FTAA negotiations and those of bilateral FTAs and investment agreements, the declaration included the following, among other things:

- All agreements should be based on principles of respect for human rights, the social dimensions, respect for sovereignty, complementarity, co-operation, solidarity, and the consideration of economic asymmetries so that the least-developed peoples are favoured.
- Support is pledged to the alternative projects such as the Bolivarian Alternative for the Americas.
- Illegitimate, un-payable, and unjust debt should be cancelled.
- A commitment to the equitable distribution of wealth and social justice.
- Protection of food sovereignty, native seeds, agrarian reform, and sustainable agriculture.
- Rejection of militarization of the continent and the doctrine of co-operation for hemispheric security, as well as of the state terrorism of the Bush administration.

More recently, many of the approaches raised in Alternatives for the Americas and at Mar del Plata have been taken on in the Ten Principles of the People's Trade Agreement put forward by Bolivian President Evo Morales in 2006.[8]

NAFTA 'Plus' or 'Minus' and the SPP

On 27 June 2005, nine cabinet ministers – three each from each from Mexico, the US, and Canada – presented a report of progress to their chief executives on the SPP. The partnership had been celebrated March 23 at a meeting of the 'three amigos' – Bush, Fox, and Martin – in Waco, Texas and at the presidential ranch in Crawford.

The SPP, in brief, was an agreement to enhance sectorial co-operation both on security concerns and on economic issues through ministerially empowered

---

7 "Final Declaration of the III People of the Americas Summit in Mar del Plata". Common Frontiers.

8 "A People's Trade Agreement" pamphlet, Common Frontiers, June, 2006 www.commonfrontiers.ca.

harmonization discussion in such areas as energy, transportation, financial services and technology, the costs of trade, and issues of environmental standard. There was agreement to continue the North American Steel Trade Committee and to construct the Automotive Partnership Council. It established more than a dozen tri-national working groups and a 90-day target for initial reports, which the nine ministers conveyed in June 2005.

The ministers stated that there had been meetings with business, roundtables with stakeholders, and briefings for legislators. Note the three words – meetings, roundtables, and briefings. When asked for a list of participants, none has been forthcoming and conversations with staff convey that it was all quite 'informal'. Two challenges to this approach should be noted:

- One was expressed in the Statement by North American Social Networks on the Future of NAFTA, issued on the eve of the Waco summit – what might be regarded as a restatement of the 'social agenda'. It posited that the summit was organized in NAFTA's image, and that there was little or no evidence in NAFTA that merited deepening it. It argued that the presidents and the prime minister should be discussing human security in such areas as ending poverty in all three countries; protecting and improving the environment; guaranteeing universal access to health services; committing to food sovereignty, food safety, and decentralized farmer-peasant production; and the ratification and implementation of international human rights as the foundation for democratic governance.[9]
- The other challenge is the governance model expressed in the agreements celebrated in Waco and in the June progress report: essentially a model of integration by executive fiat, advised by corporate leadership.

The model continued through the following years with summits in Cancún (2006), Montebello, Quebec (2007), and New Orleans (2008). The tri-national emphasis has atrophied since the election of Barack Obama late in 2008, the SPP website has announced that there will be no new postings, and the US has shifted emphasis to *bilateral* relations with Mexico and Canada.[10]

---

9 "The damage done to human security by NAFTA should be at the top of their agenda: Any discussion on deeper integration or 'NAFTA-plus' is premature" from *Statement by the North American Social Networks on the Future of NAFTA. The Martin-Bush-Fox Summit in Texas*. March 22, 2005. www.commonfrontiers.ca.

10 See, for example: Stuart Trew "SPP to be dismantled say friends in the U.S., Guadalajara leaders forum to be coordinated by the National Security Council." July 27, 2009. www.canadians.org See also the section on North American Security and Prosperity in the website of the Canadian Council of Chief Executives. www.ceocouncil.ca. See also Foster 2011.

A Reflection: Taking the Torch to Democracy, and Other Means

In Montreal, on the night of 25 April 1849, a mob broke into the new Parliament buildings of what was then the province of Canada, ripping down hangings, breaking furniture and smashing gas lights.

The speaker of the Parliament ensured that a proper motion of adjournment was passed, and the members filed out of the burning building as the historian puts it 'in ordered dignity' (Careless 1967: 125). The mob which attacked the Parliament, as described by the British colonial governor of the time, Lord Elgin, was not spontaneous. 'The whole row is the work of the Orange Societies, backed by the commercial men who desire annexation and the political leaders who want places.'[11] In October of 1849 these 'commercial men' published the Annexation Manifesto. The classic Canadian historian A.R.M. Lower terms this part of his story 'Tory Treason'; those who had been most loyal to the British crown, as he says, gave living proof to the saying that 'where the treasure is there is the heart also'.

The incident is a reminder that business-led annexationism in Canada has deep if oft-forgotten roots, and sometimes ends up with unexpected allies. But this anecdote also introduces the new annexationism, which Canadians confront in this land today, masked in bland rhetoric about 'deep integration'.

It is no longer necessary to burn legislatures to attempt to win your case; much better to quietly evacuate them of meaningful jurisdiction and power. Lest you consider this an idle jest, consider a speech made by the head of the Canadian Council of Chief Executives a couple of years ago in a session on integration at Carleton University, where he stated proudly, 'Canadian sovereignty should be exercised, it should be exercised in the act of giving it away.'[12] A companion element in the argument is the recurrent use of threat, essentially the spectre of a US-initiated closing or harmful 'slow-down' of the 'undefended' border. A largely unpublicized core element is the issue of US entitlement to priority access to Canadian petroleum resources.[13]

CUFTA (1988) was a major step in this regard, particularly in areas like energy resources. NAFTA went much further, particularly in enhancing corporate and

---

11   Lord Elgin to Earl Grey, 30 April 1849 as found in Lower 1964: 277.
12   The author was present and witnessed the address.
13   With regard to the threat see Roger Gibbins, "Adding barriers borders on folly," *The Calgary Herald*, October 20, 2007. On the core importance of the energy sector of the SPP see the statement of a lead US negotiator: "To many, the SPP agenda for energy integration is now sacrosanct and incontestable". In 2005, Joseph Dukert, an independent US energy analyst and adjunct fellow at the Centre for Strategic and International Studies, explained that continentalization of energy "makes all three countries ever more sensitive to each other's energy problems." At that time trilateral co-operation in energy was so well entrenched that he suggested "it would be a counterproductive international provocation if a future government in any of the three countries tried to back out of the SPP" (Dukert 2005).

investor power and legal recourse, setting an international precedent in Chapter 11. The attempt to fast-track those corporate privileges into universal application helped stimulate the successful people's movement against the Multilateral Agreement on Investment in the late 1990s. However, pressure to include and extend the same privileges in bilateral and regional investment agreements continues apace. These agreements, like the 1995 WTO, have come upon citizens so quickly that only years later were key studies of their implications on our constitutions and our democracy made available, documenting and elaborating what some of us charged during the negotiations themselves.

A key Canadian reference in this regard is Stephen Clarkson's *Uncle Sam and Us: Globalization, Neoconservatism, and the Canadian State*, which examines the far-reaching constitutional implications of the trade and investment agreements at national, state/provincial, and local levels (Clarkson 2002). Clarkson deals with long-term and deep impacts, but there are immediate effects of which we should be aware. During the Chrétien and Martin governments, the Canadian Environmental Law Association drew our attention to an internal federal government directive regarding regulation across departments. This directive instructed civil servants, when drafting regulations for the daily operation of the government of Canada, to keep in mind our obligations under trade treaties – NAFTA, CUFTA, the WTO, and certain maritime agreements. Other treaties and covenants we have signed and ratified, and their relevant obligations on Canadian behaviour, whether in human rights, environment, gender, or the conventions of the International Labour Organization, are not even mentioned.[14] The task forces set up by the recent trinational accord in Waco follow very much in this line.

The central concern of civil society critics is not so much to review the wording of NAFTA or details of what might become NAFTA-plus, but to concentrate instead on how these things come about and on the fundamental issues of democracy – on how we will govern ourselves.

'Imaginary Citizens'

Responding to the attempt by the political establishment and the two right-wing parties in Mexico to prevent him running for president in 2006, then-Mexico City Mayor Andrés Manuel López Obrador reflected on the motivations of those who joined him in rejecting and resisting the manipulation. The mentality of the people has changed, he said. 'Once we were imaginary citizens. Now we are real. And we are not going to go back.' To demonstrate their concern and in support of the mayor, more than a million real citizens marched through Mexico City in the largest public demonstration in Mexican history.

---

14   Privy Council Office, *Government of Canada Regulatory Policy, Appendix A: International and Intergovernmental Agreements: Obligations for Regulators*. As accessed May 15, 2005.

In the Canadian context, one recalls the popular response to the Asia–Pacific Economic Cooperation meeting in Vancouver a few years ago. Our government, the host, described the official gathering not as a meeting of countries or nations, and certainly not one of peoples, but as a meeting of 'economies'.

Nothing could better describe the way in which the advocates of deep integration in North America approach their agenda. It is put forward as essentially a problem of economic management, the sort of thing that top managers and CEOs can handle, with a little help from their political allies. As for anyone else – citizens … peoples – they are imaginary: just not there!

There is a great deal of rhetoric at the intergovernmental level about 'partnership'. The bilateral Canada-Mexico partnership agreement, for example, celebrates the many things the two countries have in common, and charts the way forward with this strategic relationship. It states that 'The Partnership will be a high-level public–private forum which will strengthen bilateral economic and policy cooperation and promote private and public sector dialogue at senior levels.'[15]

So we have a general idea of the public side of this, but what about the private? Reading further, the participants are outlined: 'Bringing together business leaders, key economic actors and senior policy makers in this way will foster strategic networks and partnerships.' This is to sustain prosperity and improve our competitiveness 'while enhancing our security and improving the quality of life of our citizens.'[16]

The 23 March 23 2005 meeting that inaugurated the SPP gave the proponents of deep integration, like Tom D'Aquino, head of the Canadian Council of Chief Executives (CCCE), a great deal to celebrate. The Waco agreement and the SPP embodied a recovery of elite commercial and governmental momentum for deep integration.

The CCCE and a number of business-supported think tanks had been arguing since 9/11 that Canada should seek a strategic bargain with the US, offering whatever guarantees the Bush administration and Congress desired in areas of security concern, from defence to borders and immigration, in return for the long-desired guarantees in areas of market access, freedom from trade retaliation, and further integration of energy and other key sectors. In April 2004, the CCCE published a comprehensive strategy paper on this proposal,[17] took executives to lobby Washington, and co-sponsored a trilateral Independent Task Force on North America with the Council on Foreign Relations and the *Consejo Mexicano de Asuntos Internacionales*. The latter recommended annual summit meetings of

---

15   Canada–Mexico Partnership, October 25, 2004. Online Canada-Mexico Partnership (CMP), http//:www.canadainternational.gc.ca/mexico-mexique/assets/pdfs/CMP-PCM2004-en.pdf, 1 (accessed 1 June 2011).

16   *Ibid.*

17   CCCE, New Frontiers: Building a 21st Century Canada-US partnership in North America. April, 2004. www.ceocouncil.ca/en/view/?document_id=365.

political chief executives, ministerial working groups and the establishment of a North American advisory council to explore new ideas and be a public voice for North America. A great deal of this approach was taken on in the Waco partnership agreement.

As west-coast journalist Murray Dobbin points out, the advocates of deep integration have succeeded in moving their agenda from the CCCE through a tri-national elite panel sponsored by the US Council on Foreign Relations and right into the declaration of the two presidents and the prime minister, without pausing to consult the citizens of any one of the three nations. And Mr D'Aquino, many of whose chief executives are heads of American-owned and -controlled corporations, calls anyone who disagrees with the agenda 'nationalist extremists.' In 2003, the CCCE launched what they called the North American Security and Prosperity Initiative. At the March 2005 Waco meeting, the three heads of government issued a statement entitled the Security and Prosperity Partnership of North America, a considerable achievement for a sectoral lobby.[18]

The March 2006 meeting of the three heads of government in Cancún, Mexico gave birth to an extension of the SPP: the North American Competitiveness Council, a tri-national grouping of 30 business executives with an agenda of 'broad issues', which met annually with security and prosperity ministers and engaged with senior government officials on an ongoing basis. The council continued making agenda proposals to the leaders' summits through the Guadalajara leaders forum in 2009, but whether it would survive the transition to greater concentration on bilateral rather than trilateral approaches was an open question.[19] There may be laudable objectives here, but it is a relationship which is being constructed and appears as distorted as a marriage of convenience. Consider whose interests will prevail.

In terms of governance: the forces that triumphed in Waco do not want North American democratic structures (the European model); they want something that is institutionally 'light'. With regular consultation between top corporate managers and their political counterparts, and with the executive branches implementing agendas agreed with business at the top, not a great deal more is required. When he was foreign minister, Lloyd Axworthy momentarily raised the issues of how we should govern the 'North American "community"'. Of the various proponents of the 'big idea', or strategic bargain', only former Quebec politician Pierre-Marc Johnson, and now Senator Hugh Segal, have raised ideas of institutional development beyond areas of policy and regulatory harmonization and technical economic management. It can be argued that it is far past the time for the debate

---

18   Murray Dobbin, "CEOs Sell Out the Nation," *Georgia Straight*. April 7, 2005. www.straight.com/content.cfm?id=9320.

19   The Canadian Council of Chief Executives continues to refer to itself as the Canadian secretariat for the NACC. www.ceocouncil.ca. The US-based Council of the Americas indicates that it and the U.S. Chamber of Commerce are jointly the secretariat for the US, however no recent documents are posted.

to be engaged about the appropriate democratic and participatory means of further shaping the relations among all the peoples of North America. So far, statements about social involvement have not gone very far into the realms of governance, sovereignty, and democracy.

A direct application of the European model is unlikely, given the sensitivities of the US Congress among others, and the simple lack of public knowledge and enthusiasm. However some people have considered what might be useful.

David Bonior, former Democratic whip in the US Congress, and Carlos Heredia, former opposition foreign affairs critic in the Mexican Congress, have suggested a couple of items which are worth considering:

- A common human rights declaration or convention. This is more challenging than one might think, as neither Canada nor the US have ratified the relevant hemispheric convention, and the US has not ratified the International Covenant on Economic, Social and Cultural Rights. My view would be that a joint citizen's effort to achieve common ratification and build a common tri-national instrument on that foundation could have the effect of renewing attention and focusing the priority on human rights.
- A tri-national parliamentary assembly to deal with issues such as migration, environment, drug trafficking, etc., which particularly transcend borders.[20]

Jeff Faux, founder of the Washington, DC-based Economic Policy Institute has taken up these ideas and others in a consideration of a new 'cross-border politics to support the democratic redesign of globalization beginning with the new integrated economies of Canada, Mexico, and the United States.' His approach is integrationist with a social democratic flavour (Faux 2006).

Proposals for new institutions on a pan-North American basis may be technicolour dreams, but why should the conversations about the future of North America be restricted to how we can ensure that more trucks move faster?[21] There is no particular reason why discussions about social development, human rights, and environmental enhancement should not transcend the decline of the NAFTA/SPP focus. Debate on, and development of, democratic responses for the future of the continent are overdue and urgent.

---

20 NDP MP Peter Julian has taken the leadership, along with allies in the US and Mexican Congresses, in forming a network of legislators opposed to NAFTA and favouring a "people's" trade and investment agenda.

21 In fact, in a post-Kyoto world, we need to think about how we have fewer trucks, consuming less carbon-based fuel moving in our environment, and find ways of sustaining our economy with lower energy consumption.

Conclusions

This rapid voyage through recent history and personal experience leads to at least a few concluding destinations:

- The claim that the HSA stopped the FTAA in its tracks is probably a considerable over-statement, but the alliance partners certainly contributed significantly to national resistance to the FTAA agenda, in such countries as Brazil and Argentina, and to political coalitions exercising greater influence in several other nations.
- The US components in the alliance have been instrumental in ending 'fast-track' authorization for a period, and in the near-defeat of DR–CAFTA.
- The HSA was an early pre-cursor and signal of the political change which has swept a number of Latin American republics, and which continues today.
- The HSA, like the tri-national alliance, took major steps from opposition to proposition with the international collaborative work on Alternatives for the Americas and various interim declarations and public letters.
- The tri-national alliance contributed directly to more public access and transparency regarding trade negotiations in Mexico, and the securing of the FTAA negotiating text at the time of the Quebec City Summit.
- The tri-national coalition which fought NAFTA made use of some pre-existing liaison links between Canadian and Mexican social actors, but created and reinforced new ones, particularly in the trade-union and religious sectors.
- The leadership of partner organizations in coalition, particularly in Canada, has tended to be sustained and long-lived, which has encouraged durable trust relationships. However it faces, since the mid-2000s, significant generational challenges.
- The centre of gravity for Canadian organizations shifted after 2005 to a focus on NAFTA, NAFTA–plus, SPP issues, and the tri-national alliance, with less emphasis on the hemispheric HSA.
- The end of the SPP as a formal/public format for tri-national relations is in good part due to the activities of the tri-national NGO/labour alliance and its allies, as well as to clear failure in design of the initiative which left it open to charges of exclusivity and elitism, making it unpalatable for the Obama administration.[22]
- Despite repeated calls for Canadian (and US) ratification of the American Convention on Human Rights and the complementary Protocol of San

---

22 This conclusion is based on interviews with staff of the US Congress, Wilson Center, Canadian American Business Council and others. John W. Foster, "Two Days in DC", 26-04-09 Rev.1 Notes of a two day visit and interviews in Washington DC, manuscript in the possession of the author.

Salvador on Economic, Social and Cultural Rights, neither government has moved.
- Some actors used the HSA linkages and occasions like the World Social Forum to involve their members more deeply in hemispheric affairs and to build personal and experiential links, including such groupings as ecumenical Church participants, youth, and several trade unions.

In overall terms, as is clear from the third section of this examination, while civil society social organizations have made considerable advances, their resources are limited and their political access is often limited, conditional, or non-existent. At the same time, the CCCE and the NACC have enjoyed much greater shares of both, and the further joy of seeing a good deal of their approach embodied in executive agreements at an international level.

For civil society organizations, and social, labour, and environmental movements, it can be argued that the essential issues are either not found or are found only in the details of trade, investment, and intellectual property agreements. Although those are far reaching-domains, the essential issues are found in the terrain of governance and the democratic challenge.

The fundamental question civil society organizations face is whether they are content to be treated as simply invisible – as effectively not being there – or whether they are ready and willing to turn imaginary citizens into actors with imagination, actors who must be reckoned with, who will construct and fight to reclaim democratic sovereignty and for an agenda of human rights, environmental protection and sustainability, health, and equality on this continent.

PART V
Identities in Flux

Chapter 9
Slippery Borders: Negotiating North American Hybrid Identities

Victoria Ruétalo

Addressing the audience in multiple tongues, the *brujo* or wizard appears, wearing a multitude of symbols taken from Mexican, Latin American, and US popular culture such as the Posada-inspired dangling skeleton earrings, a banana necklace *à-la*-Carmen Miranda, a *pachuco* hat, and a popular culture-influenced jacket adorned by a Batman symbol alongside a button of a painting by Mexican artist Frida Kahlo. He sits before an altar surrounded by votive candles and other paraphernalia while he calmly describes his dream: '[A] map without borders where the Latin American archipelago reached all the way to the *Nuyorrican* barrios of Boston and Manhattan, all the way to the pockets of Central American refugees in Alberta and British Columbia' (Gómez-Peña 1993: 77). His epiphany, performed in a meditative state, reminds us, the spectators, of the dream of unity, what will contrast with his abrupt recognition of its impossibility. The *brujo* opens his eyes to describe the harsh realization that beyond economic ties, there is resistance to any unity. He concludes: 'And when I dream like this you suffer, my dream becomes your nightmare and pot your only consolation' (Ibid.). National borders are physical indicators of psychological fears, ones only pacified with comforting drugs.

The above description details a section titled 'Language is a Border' from border artist Guillermo Gómez-Peña's video version of *Border Brujo*. The performance, produced in 1988, and enacted in such diverse spaces as art galleries, museums, theatre festivals, youth centres, migrant worker centres, community events, and political rallies, began as a live performance that was later archived into video. Gómez-Peña is a writer and experimental artist born in Mexico who immigrated to the US in 1978. Since then he has been exploring border issues, cross-cultural identity, and US–Latino relations through multimedia in his performances, radio art, video, bilingual poetry, and installation art. He has been cited as an example of border culture and hybridity by scholars across the world, from Homi Bhabha in the United Kingdom to Roger Bartra in Mexico. For Bhabha, Gómez-Peña is an example of a resistance strategy that 'deploys the cultural hybridity of [his] borderline conditions to "translate" and therefore reinscribe the social imaginary of both metropolis and modernity' (Bhabha 1994: 6). Meanwhile, Bartra sees in Gómez-Peña a place of confrontation that challenges the nation, particularly the Mexican nation (Bartra 1993: 11–12).

The *Border Brujo* performance features '15 different personae, each speaking a different border language. The relationships among these personae are symbolic of those between North and South, Anglo and Latin America, myth and social reality, legality and illegality, performance art and life' (Gómez-Peña 1993: 75). For this performance, Gómez-Peña adopts an epiphanic voice full of insight and revelation to contrast his utopian vision with the reality of this dream. Gómez-Peña's inclusion of Canada in this dream compels us to go beyond the usual focus of the US/Mexico border to think about the concept of hybrid identities in the context of North America and within globalization. By drawing on examples from Canadian, US, and Mexican culture, I will try to think through the term 'hybrid identities' within this context. The main goal of this discussion is to historicize the notion of hybrid identities and bring it back to the particular location on which this book focuses: the North American context. I will argue that the term 'hybridity' has been stripped of its political value, and will attempt to reformulate its use since NAFTA and 9/11 with the help of performance artist Guillermo Gómez-Peña's theorization of borders, a notion that can still prove useful for the ever changing reality of North America with its constant flows of new immigrant groups.

Defining the Slippery Term 'Hybridity'

Before tackling the issues outlined above, it is necessary to define and contextualize the term 'hybridity'. These reflections by no means will be exhaustive, first because I do not wish this article to solely be a theoretical exercise. Second, to properly theorize hybridity, it is imperative to refer to terms that express very similar ideas (e.g., creolization, trans-culturation), all of which have their own genealogy and specific contexts. For a more exhaustive discussion of these and other similar terms see Lull's article in this anthology. However, lack of space restricts me from dabbling into these terms and to focusing only on hybridity.

The word 'hybrid' has biological and botanical origins referring to the offspring of two animals or plants of two races, varieties, or species. In the nineteenth century, hybrid was imbued with racist scientific thought. What was once an offensive insult acquired an emancipated function as post-colonial theorists re-appropriated the word to refer to racial, ethnic, and cultural mixing. Hybridity explains the access an individual has to two or more cultures through the negotiation of difference, describing the cultural crossings, interactions, and mixtures existent in today's 'multi-temporal and multi-cultural societies', to borrow a phrase from anthropologist Néstor García Canclini (1995). It is the space between zones, and an ongoing condition of all cultures that contain no zones of purity because they undergo a continuous process of mixing and influence – in a sense an antidote to the belief in the purity of race, ethnicity, or national culture. There is a danger of de-contextualizing hybrid identities in referring to anything that may blend two or more distinct elements. For this reason, post-colonial theorists place it specifically within the context of colonialism and post-colonialism: societies that continue to maintain colonial structures despite their apparent break with the colony. For our purpose here, North America and its three sovereign nations while historically post-colonial societies in the strict sense also re-enact a post-colonial relationship between them. It is worth keeping in mind, as Castro-Rea argues in the introduction to this book, that the stark socio-economic disparities between the three nations have created equally disparate power relations.

One of the problems with the term 'hybridity' is that it automatically assumes that the new hybrid product evolves from two distinct categories. Paradoxically, as the term tries to resist the essentialism of the origin through its significance, it nonetheless must accept the idea of origin in order to make its point. Be this as it may, I will demonstrate how the term, despite its limitations, still proves useful. Furthermore, critics have argued that in some uses this theory ignores the historical and material conditions of colonial discourse. For the sake of our argument here I am going to avoid this concern by placing my discussion within particular social and material contexts (the confrontation between first and third worlds) as I speak about hybrid identities while bearing in mind this recent history. Precisely for this reason, and furthermore because it is a useful context for the sake of thinking about our location (North America), I will examine hybridity as it relates to borders in North America and focus on southern migrants, particularly from Mexico as they begin to encroach on the north, as but one example of other encroachments from other parts of the world.

To begin somewhere within our context, we can trace the idea or concept of the hybrid all the way back to the colonial period (without seeing this as an absolute origin, what can prove a counterproductive exercise): the first and violent confrontation between the European 'adventurer', the Indigenous communities of the Americas, and later the uprooting of African slaves. This interaction and mutual discovery produced a new world culture, a direct product of the new realities created by what Mary Louise Pratt calls 'the contact zone' (Pratt 1992). This contact zone yielded the first generation of American hybrids in racial terms. 'Colonial desire', as Robert J.C. Young argues, led to a more disjointed concept of identity, one that becomes clearer as we think about the two different readings of the word hybridity: hybridity as creolization or mestizaje, a productive space that tends toward fusion, but contrarily, hybridity as raceless chaos which produces no stable new form but a restless uneasy in-betweeness (Young 1995: 18). In the first example, a whole is produced from the parts; in the second, what is considered an entity is divided into two or more parts, turning sameness into difference. In this second case hybridity evokes contrafusion and disjunction. This hybrid difference is transformed by critic Homi Bhabha into an active moment to challenge and resist dominant cultural power and authority (Bhabha 2004), thereby denying the imperial power its authority and its claims to authenticity by rejecting the notion of what is pure (purity of blood, purity of race), authentic, and original in the mother culture and race. This model of hybridity is most useful in our current analysis because it constantly makes us aware of borders between peoples and borders within peoples. This understanding of precisely these borders, I suggest, is a key to thinking about what we can call North American hybrid identities, while it offers a more complex rather than celebratory model that helps to question the very border it maintains.

Border Lessons or Lessons from the Border

> The US-Mexican border *es una herida abierta* where the Third World grates against the first and bleeds ... Borders are set up to define the places that are safe and unsafe, and to distinguish us from them. A border is a dividing line, a narrow strip along a steep edge. (Anzaldúa 1991: 3)[1]

For anthropologist Néstor García Canclini, the US/Mexico border provides the best field of study for the concept of hybridity because of the constant deterritorialization and reterritorialization[2] of culture that occurs there on an ongoing basis.[3] This wall, fence, and natural border is due to the terrain of the region, which physically separates two distinct and different nations. Ironically, it also opens up a space for the symbiotic, or hybrid identities which no nationalist or chauvinist critique can contain despite attempts to do so. The physicality of the border translates into a head-to-head confrontation between first and third worlds, what by some standards can constitute a threat to each others' distinctive identity. On the other hand, the border itself is a material reality that keeps people in or out, depending on one's point of view. Crossing to the other side is feasible as long as one possesses the necessary documents to do so. Close to one million undocumented crossers from Mexico to the US are caught each year by the Border Patrol, but how many do manage to cross on a yearly basis is still unknown: estimates range between 10,000 and 3 million people.[4] This 3,140-km boundary is the most frequently crossed international border in the world. For this reason there exists a border patrol dedicated to 'work tirelessly as vigilant protectors of our Nation's borders,' as the web page informs.[5] After the implementation of NAFTA, the vigilant presence of the border patrol increased in many of the twin city areas. Operation Hold the Line (in El Paso 1993) and Operation Gatekeeper (in San

---

1 Anzaldúa always uses language as a barrier. She purposefully includes Spanish in her work to ensure that the unilingual reader only understands some of the text, which is wholly readable to the bilingual reader.
2 See definition of these concepts in Lull's chapter in this volume.
3 See García Canclini (1995).
4 In 2004 an article in *Time* magazine stated that 3 million people had entered the United States illegally that year. The figure was echoed all over the press. However, this is an exaggerated number that has no basis in fact. Experts believe that this figure falls between 350,000 and 500,000. See Winograd 2004, 114–15.
5 See *US Customs and Border Protection*, 13 January 2006. <http://www.cbp.gov/xp/cgov/border_security/border_patrol>.The Border Patrol has been functioning since 1924 but the border with Mexico has been patrolled as early as 1904.

Diego 1994) were successful in decreasing the number of persons who were able to penetrate; however, this suppression at these target areas has forced many determined crossers to more dangerous terrain. This increased security clearly produces a parallel increase in the number of deaths occurring in more dangerous alternative border routes.

The US government enactment of the Secure Fence Act on 26 October 2006 mandated the construction of 1,100 km of double-reinforced fence along the border with Mexico, across cities and deserts alike, in the states of California, Arizona, New Mexico, and Texas in areas that have experienced drug trafficking and undocumented migration. It further authorizes the installation of more lighting, vehicle barriers, and border checkpoints, while putting in place more advanced equipment like sensors, cameras, satellites, and unmanned aerial vehicles. Even before this project is completed, it has dramatically increased the risks to migrants, pushing them further to more dangerous border crossings.

In the year 2000 alone, 356 people died crossing the border, a figure higher than the 1993 number of 115 crossers that died that year. Despite recent efforts to tighten borders, the US economy thrives on the work provided by so-called illegal aliens. Alan Greenspan, Chairman of the US Federal Reserve Bank from 1987 to 2006, acknowledged that migrant labour in the 1990s allowed the US economy to grow faster and with less inflation (Cunningham 2004: 337).

> Although unauthorized migrants represented just 4.9 percent of the total labour force in 2005, they represent large proportions of the workforce in several specific occupations: 24 percent in farming occupations, 17 percent in cleaning occupations, 14 percent in construction, and 12 percent in food preparation.[6]

Despite globalizing agreements such as NAFTA, meant to open boundaries between distinct nations, the social reality proves that people and immigration are not deemed important enough to be included in these treaties.

Gómez-Peña's art makes us aware of the border as a marker of difference and the spatial contiguity between bi-national cities and fluid populations. He calls into question the notion that there exists a discrete national identity to be protected on either side of the line. To return to his performance in *Border Brujo*, it is the figure of the *brujo*'s 'dis-narrative' that replicates the border experience by inviting comparisons between his personal crossing of different borders and that of millions of undocumented migrants on the basis of a shared traumatic ritual. Hybridity in this sense must be interrogated, particularly its redeeming potential. The most important lesson that we will learn from his performance is the ability to destabilize the very specific idea of creating a new identity. Gómez-Peña turns sameness into difference, Bhabha's active moment to challenge and resist dominant culture. His brand of hybridity never accepts this mixing as completely

---

6 See *Economic Report of the President* (February 2007), 28 October 2007. <http://www.whitehouse.gov/cea/2007_erp.pdf>, 194–195.

redemptive; it is a constant struggle within the individual and one the individual frequently faces in society. Therefore, he calls for a complex and situational hybrid subject conscientious of the dangers involved in crossing and transgressing to the other side. Crossing implies more than the physical act: it entails a psychological trauma, a national displacement, and a questioning of the very sense of a fixed identity, albeit national or otherwise.

What happens when we look at North America's other border? Can Gómez-Peña's ideas about hybridity and identity help us understand the other important border in the continent? The political divide between Canada and the US stretches 8,891 km. This longest undefended border in the world is known as the International Boundary. The events of 9/11 may have changed the inherent openness of the border, as more law enforcement officers are placed on patrol. While Canada has had a long-standing border patrol, only in 2003 did Canada establish a more obtrusive entity, the Canada Border Services Agency, to better guard the increasingly vulnerable Canada/US border. Thus far, no wall or barrier has been erected to demarcate the 49th parallel; however, in its outset Canada's agency upholds its core values (Integrity, Respect, and Professionalism), which are quite different from the US Border Patrol's motto ('Honour first').[7] Nonetheless, the border differentiates the asymmetrical relationship between Canada and the US: for Canada the border is the space where the nation ends – and the doorway to the bigger US market. With the increasing threat of drugs and terrorism entering the nation from the north, the US has only since 2001 shown any interest in the border's existence.

The Nation Reconsidered

To better illustrate Canadian secret desires to erase the hegemonizing threat from the south I will refer to Greg Curnoe's painting titled *America* (1989). Greg Curnoe (1935–92) was a Canadian artist and an ardent nationalist who believed in the importance of working from a particular locale; in his case London, Ontario. His body of work reflects his attachment to place, a celebration of London which defies the culture of the metropolis, and is known for its effervescent pop art, saturated with colour. In his map, *America* (1989, see Figure 9.1), he eliminates the threat to national sovereignty by eradicating the world power, while furthermore making considerable geographic changes to the rest of Canada (Toronto disappears as more marginal places, such as Manitoulin Island, take a more pronounced role on the map). Most notable in his version of America is the unification of two more marginal nations: Mexico and Canada. Although it is by no means typical of the contemporary Canadian world-view, his exaggerated

---

7 Both websites reiterate the mottos and values of each organization. For the Canadian version see *Canada Border Services Agency*, 13 January 2006. <http://www.cbsa-asfc.gc.ca/agency/menu2-e.html>.

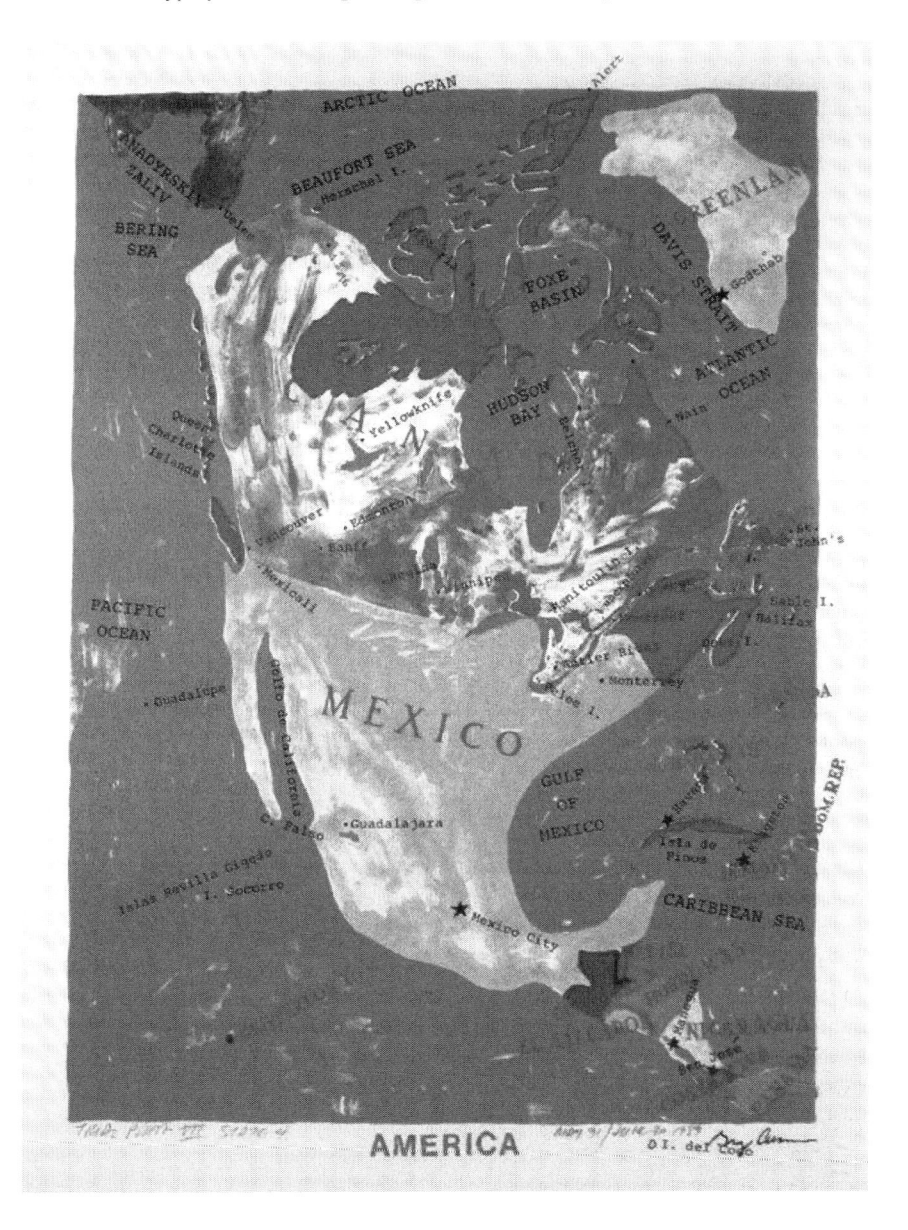

Slippery Borders: Negotiating North American Hybrid Identities 177

Figure 9.1 *America* (1989), by Greg Curnoe. Printed with permission from Ms Sheila Curnoe and the Thielsen Gallery, London, Ontario Canada.
Source: thielsengallery.com, available at http://viewoncanadianart.com/2008/06/20/underrated-canadian-artist-greg-curnoe.

and idealized reconceptualization of space raises crucial questions that did reflect anxieties in 1989 when the CUFTA debates were taking place.

Furthermore, within the context of NAFTA Curnoe raises further problems as he reorders the border: would power relations between Canada and Mexico remain somewhat symmetrical? How is this plausible when despite the towering presence of the US no parity exists between Canada and Mexico? It is rather difficult to imagine that this new visualization of the border would not recreate similar patterns found in the present border between Mexico and the US, even after its move northward towards the forty-ninth parallel. Would not Canada take the place of the US despite its arguably less imperial history with Latin America, or would the border itself drive more imperial actions on the part of Canada? The answers to these questions are of course unknown because spatially speaking this border has never materialized. While Curnoe's vision thinks from a particular place, the nation, it thereby ignores the possible implications of a Canada/Mexico border. The Canadian reaction to CUFTA, which was implemented on 1 January 1989 (the same year as the painting was finished), did not foresee the future ratification of yet another agreement. NAFTA took effect on 1 January 1994 and did indeed unite Canada with Mexico, without obliterating the US from the equation. NAFTA perpetuated old problems for Canada (trade areas of dispute such as softwood lumber) and Mexico alike, causing the uprising of the Zapatista movement precisely on the day of NAFTA's implementation.

Latin America has produced similar visceral reactions to US hegemony that date back to the nineteenth century when the US would justify its manipulation of hemispheric politics with 'manifest destiny', the belief that the country had a divinely inspired mission to expand. Latin American nations would alternatively strengthen national cultures by thinking of themselves as mestizo, trans-cultured, or hybrid (although the latter two are more recent terms) – in other words a fusion of two or more elements. In this embracing model of hybridity, which I discussed earlier, hybridity is posited as a productive space that tends towards fusion. By the 1930s, the growth of the culture industries (popular radio and film) would heighten that national consciousness thereby resisting the imperial policies of the north. In today's globalized world is it feasible to think of a hybrid strategy evolving from a post-national space? Cultural studies practitioners continue to find in the nation the place of resistance to imperial power relations, and thus prefer to link or unite culture to a national consciousness and identity. However, this rhetoric persists and filters through the issue of the border: to Mexican advocates, the border represents vulnerability of the Mexican nation before US imperialism. Canadians, like Curnoe, whose idealized border outright eliminated such a threat, show similar fears and paranoia. In Curnoe's vision, Mexico replaces the US, and cultural and ethnic diversity help to strengthen Canadian identity. While within the US perspective the border means a loss of US jobs to Mexican workers – a blow to the already moribund American dream and the threat of complete penetration, which literally leads to racial and ethnic mixing. Is there a way of thinking of the border and its hybrid identities beyond these national conceptions of space?

In his analysis of Emily Hicks's *Border Writing*, Marxist critic Neil Larsen sees the importance of the spatial marker both literally and figuratively for the conceptualization of a post-nationalist cultural space. Hicks is continually redrawing 'the border within and across both the local and global text/culture' (Larsen 1995). She is constantly crossing borders herself, exceeding the colonial/post-colonial and centre/periphery binaries. Much like Guillermo Gómez-Peña, Hicks thinks, speaks, and writes from the border despite her physical location. There is very little coincidence that these two have so much in common. In fact, they were once married. At this time, their theories came together in a performance titled *Tijuana-Niagara* (1988), which as its title suggests made explicit the Mexico–Canada connection through a return to each border (Gómez-Peña 1994a: 91). This performance-pilgrimage produced a juxtaposition between two 'marginal' nations while travelling in a mobile temple made up of religious kitsch and pseudo-Indigenous souvenirs purchased in these border towns. While both physical borders are referred to in this performance, the main object of attack is the commodification of ethnicity in the tourist industries found in border towns in general. Canada and Mexico, both sharing a border with the US, also share in the values of a capitalist-driven tourist industry and their need to sell their distinctive national identities to US and foreign consumers/tourists. This performance was carried out in border towns on both shores of the Niagara River. By setting their performance on the Canada/US border, Gómez-Peña and Hicks bring together Mexico and Canada, much as did Curnoe. However, unlike Curnoe's map, this juxtaposition is mobile, which leaves many unanswered and apprehensive questions. The mobility and the performative actions (auctions for border art, spiritual consultations for tourists, photo sessions with authentic border shamans and witches, begging for money in costume, broadcasting bilingual poetry with huge megaphones) contrasts as well as unites both borders while they redraw their delineation beyond the nation. These performances in fact have at their forefront the historical, political, and material contexts of borders, what Curnoe ignores from the place of the nation, and what others who embrace hybridity as merely a fusion quite easily forget.

Gómez-Peña's early work with the group Border Art Workshop/*Taller de Arte Fronterizo* was at first located on the border though an art focused on the idea of place. However, at this time he was also beginning to express ideas about liminal subjectivities. As a founding member of the San Diego/Tijuana-based group (1984) made up of Mexican, Anglo and Chicano artists who engaged in collaborative, multimedia, and interactive arts projects about the US/Mexico border, the group addressed border issues such as immigration, human rights violations, and racism (Fox, C.F. 1999: 122). His move from the local art of place to a more global vision of the border took place during the filming of *Border Brujo* and would influence the work following this performance. For critics such as Claire Fox, Gómez-Peña's globalized border "[o]verlooks the specificity of regions such as the US-Mexico border, where nation-states continue to enforce differences within urban space. Making the border the global metaphor of an oppositional politics also falls prey to facile appropriation by an equally globalizing US nationalist expansionism" (*Ibid.*: 136). While the second part of her statement has some validity, the first part is precisely what is needed to bring the specific US/Mexico border into the NAFTA context. Fox, like other US-based critics, ignores that these global issues are not limited to the physical space delineating the US from Mexico, but can be useful to think about our context in North America, and beyond. This view limits the focus over the greater problem. The performances taking place between 1992 and 1994, published into a collection under the title *The New World Border: Prophecies, Poems and Loqueras for the End of the Century*, echo this vision of a 'multi-centric, hybrid American culture' (Gómez-Peña 1994a: 1). When referring to America, Gómez-Peña is not limiting himself to any one nation or its limits. He states:

> Let's get it straight: America is a continent, not a country. Latin America encompasses more than half of America. Quechuas, Mixtecas and Iroquois are American (not US citizens). Chicano, Nuyorrican, Cajun, Afro-Caribbean and Québécois cultures are American as well. Mexicans and Canadians are also North Americans. Newly arrived Vietnamese and Laotians will soon become Americans. US Anglo-European culture is but a mere component of a much larger cultural complex in constant metamorphosis. (Gómez-Peña 1994b: 18)

Identity and culture for Gómez-Peña, then, are open systems not limited through their authenticity but in a constant process of transformation, redefinition, and recontextualization. Theoretically, in this sense the border subject defines itself as an American carrying an ambiguous hybrid identity while unable to continue existing on either side, but still unwilling to give up the border for fear of placing it back in the domain of Eurocentrism's false universe. In fact, Claire Fox questions Gómez-Peña's general motives: 'The idea of alternation among personae, spaces, and languages is so integral to the performance that it raises the issue whether Gómez-Peña would really like to see borders eliminated, or whether his work is indeed dependent upon borders to uphold the oppositions he critiques' (Fox 1999: 124–50). For Gómez-Peña this is not a problem because the border (or borders in general) will never cease to exist; even if the physical frontier between Mexico and the US were some day to become more permeable, allowing freer movement of not only goods but people, other borders will surface to become more visible and equally problematic. Gómez-Peña's border is more global, more flexible, and geographically dislocated; it belongs to a continental map of communities in motion and cultures in context but it will never cease to exist. While beginning within the context of the US/Mexico border, Gómez-Peña's border is much broader and deals with identity from a global perspective, while not excluding the specifically local problems. In Curnoe's map, the politicized space of the US/Mexico border, a historically constituted location, disappears to be replaced by a northern utopian border. The border, as conceptualized by Gómez-Peña, on the other hand, produces a different map, one that maintains historically located places while literally inverting the conception of the world to question the stagnant position of these locations. This inversion places hybridity as a restless uneasy middle ground that is constantly in flux.

Hybridity as Fusion?

For some critics, hybridity is simply everywhere, in the hybrid symbolic products that are 'created through the reflexive mixing of various "realities" by "blending in the same discourse ... messages entitled from [various] levels of existence"' (Lull 2001: 134). By generalizing the term and applying it to any type of mixing, what is left is a 'hybridity' as a productive space that tends toward fusion, not much different from the creolization and *mestizaje* paradigms I mention above and that Lull explains in more detail in his contribution to this book. Hybridity has certainly been used by international multimedia and other conglomerates to sell their products, stripping it away from its socio-historical context and thereby denying its ability to provoke. This goes hand in hand with the belief that globalization is opening up markets and producing more connections that lead to more hybrid possibilities. Yet, as anthropologist Hilary Cunningham argues, 'Borders, in fact, might rapidly be emerging as the next floating signifiers of globalization' (Cunningham 2004: 333). The quick and facile embracing of hybridity on the part of global corporations and critics alike does not deny that political borders remain a physical reality. These borders are being protected more and more as we get caught up in globalization's concentric force.

We need only look at some examples in Canada and the US. For instance on 1 May 2006, International Workers Day, millions of illegal immigrants and their supporters took to the streets for what they called 'A Day without an Immigrant' to protest bill HR4437, which classified illegal workers and those who aid them as criminals. The protesters were claiming amnesty and attempting to show US society the importance of immigrants' work. On 15 May 2006 President George W. Bush addressed the nation on this very issue. He presented his reform of the immigration issue by denying amnesty to those in the country, adding 6,000 National Guard troops to patrol the border (this was a temporary measure until 6,000 more Border Patrol agents were hired in 2008), increasing funding for technological methods to secure the border (this includes building a high-tech fence, roads, and cameras, as stipulated in the Secure Fence Act), increasing funding for state and local authorities, and creating a temporary worker program – a project that remains very vague. In Canada with the election of a Conservative government in 2005, immigration has resurfaced as a key issue in politics. During the elections the party had campaigned on increasing deportation and decreasing the amount of illegal workers. Since then more resources have been spent on immigration enforcement. In a span of a few weeks in 2006, hundreds of Portuguese, Latin American, and other undocumented workers were caught and deported to their country of origin. Their respective communities rallied and protested throughout the city of Toronto.

The government of Portugal even got involved questioning Canada's actions. In the summer of 2009, visa requirements to visit Canada were imposed on Mexican citizens. In both cases, making the borders within North America more permeable seem distant dreams, as the '*brujo*' above has already suggested.

In a more recent Gómez-Peña video, *The Great Mojado Invasion, Part 2 (The Second US–Mexico War)* images juxtapose to narrate the future history of the Great Mojado (Wetback) Invasion of the US from the south. This vision actualizes the real US fear of the border: the re-conquest of a once-lost territory and the conquest of US women by macho Mexicans, which in both scenarios produces or makes way for racial and cultural hybrid identities. Gómez-Peña's spectacle of difference reminds its viewer that he and Latinos in general are here to stay and it is better to begin developing a pact of mutual cultural understanding. He explains: "'[W]e want understanding not publicity." We want to be considered intellectuals, not entertainers; partners not clients; collaborators not competitors; holders of a strong spiritual vision, not emerging voices; and above all, full citizens, not exotic minorities' (Gómez-Peña 1994b). This implies a dialogue without sacrificing identity to hegemony. As an alternative to NAFTA he suggests a free-idea zone between Mexico, the US, and Canada, a zone of multi-lateral co-operation, cross-cultural dialogue, and interdisciplinary artistic antithesis. This third way avoids the traps of nationalist chauvinism and homogenizing global consumerism. This alternative cultural model opposes NAFTA's jurisdiction only over mass media industries and trade in fine art and antiquities, and thereby includes all other cultural outputs in the exchange, not forgetting people in the process. This new zone calls for a three-way communication between equal powers, a micro-universal expression of international communication which has never existed between first and third worlds. With the ever-growing populations of immigrants, particularly from Latin America, Asia, and Africa in both Canada and the US, Guillermo Gómez-Peña's version of hybridity reminds us that despite the borders that will always exist, North American hybrid identities have been forming both inside and out for a very long time and they will continue to do so.

Hybridity is a political question, which is not about mixing or embracing the 'fusions', but rather about exposing those borders that exist between nations, across peoples, and within individuals. Hybridity is a problem that can help us think through our identity in North America: a constant confrontation between first and third worlds.

Chapter 10
Our North America: A Continent of Cultural Change[1]

James Lull

The contemporary pop music form *reggaetón* can serve as a conversation starter for a broad discussion about the cultural complexities of 'Our North America'. As a musical form, *reggaetón* derives mainly from Puerto Rican and Cuban salsa, *merengue* of the Dominican Republic, reggae and dance hall from Jamaica, *soca* from Trinidad and Panama, and rap from the US. The ability of *reggaetón* to animate dance floors around the world results from its distinctive, catchy beat to be sure, but also from the power and audio clarity of sound systems made in Europe and Japan through which the music passes, and from brilliant recording techniques used by producers in San Juan, New York, Los Angeles, and London. In every sense, reggaetón is a remarkable contemporary cultural hybrid, not unlike Guillermo Gómez-Peña's performances, explained in Victoria Ruétalo's chapter in this volume.

Reggaetón's classic anthem is *Gasolina* from the album *Barrio Fino* by the Puerto Rican artist Daddy Yankee (Figure 10.1). The album reveals how cultural hybridity infuses much more than various musical influences into the particular mixture of *reggaetón*. The very name, Daddy Yankee, symbolically reverses power relations between the US and its colonized island territory, Puerto Rico. The singer appropriates the insignia of the New York Yankees baseball team on his cap to promote his own image. Spanish and English alternate throughout the lyrics. The globally-recognized aesthetic of the US dollar, Puerto Rico's imposed currency, adorns the edges of the CD cover.

The album title, *Barrio Fino*, plays on the realities of social class difference in Puerto Rico; the 'refined neighbourhood' where Daddy Yankee grew up is extremely poor. Daddy Yankee's rise as the most successful *reggaetón* artist is driven by an in-your-face countercultural ideology, multiple appropriations of dominant symbolic forms, and dramatic reversals of cultural territory and social categories that are articulated through the seductive power of an especially infectious form of body-oriented human expression.

Like so many architects of popular culture, *reggaetón* artists exercise symbolic creativity by cutting, mixing, sampling, and mashing up a selection of the cultural resources available to them – the world of constantly-expanding mobile symbolic

---

1   Parts of this chapter were first published in Lull 2000.

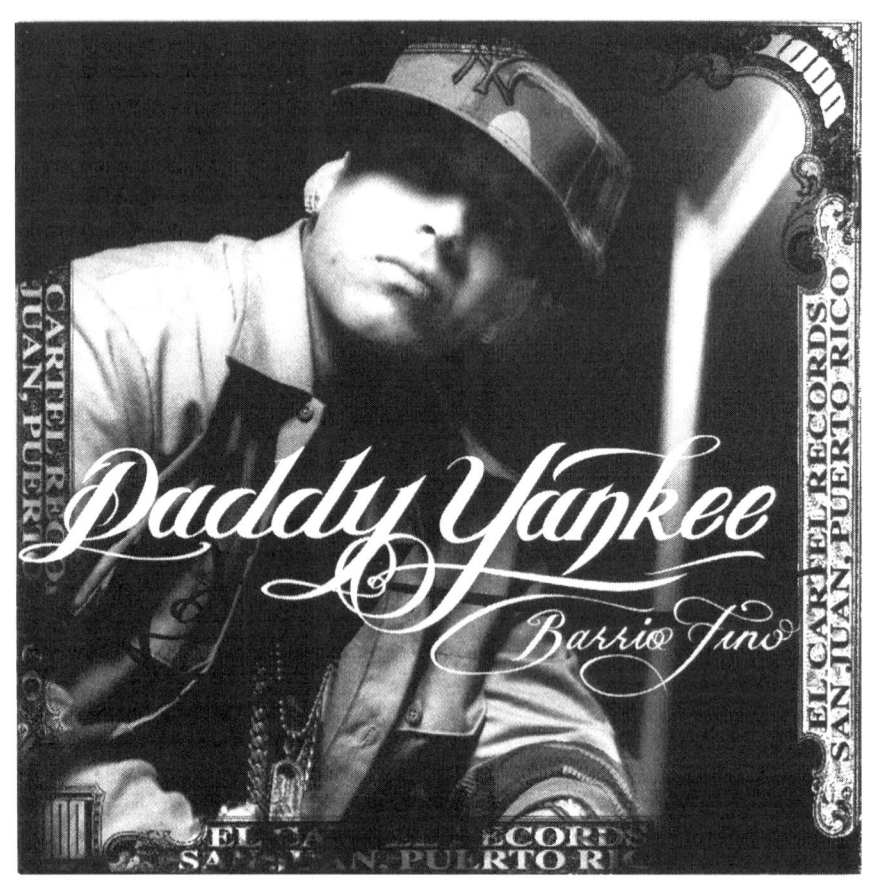

Figure 10.1 *Barrio Fino* **album cover, Daddy Yankee (2004). Produced by the artist's own record label: EL CARTEL RECORDS. This album was a significant contribution in music industry**

forms. Cultural hybridization lies at the heart of such transformative experiences and shifting identities in North America and everywhere else. Music's flexibility, availability, and corporeal intimacy make it a potent ideological and cultural force.

Music fans play their part in cultural hybridization too. Distinctions traditionally made between producers and consumers of cultural products have broken down because of advances in technology that democratize cultural production, authority, and power, and the accessibility of popular music forms, including *reggaetón*. The proliferating culture industries today make the spread of such forms possible. As *Newsweek* magazine explained *reggaetón*'s sudden popularity, '[T]he real force behind the invasion of *reggaetón* is a rapidly evolving, globalized music industry driven by two catalysts: satellite radio and the internet' (Beith 2005).

I spent a week in residence at the Guadalajara campus of Mexico's huge private university, the *Tecnológico de Monterrey*. Lecturing to undergraduate students, I played the famous *Gasolina* to jump start the discussion. I asked the students a simple question to initiate the session: 'Is *reggaetón* Latin music?'

I asked that question because just a few months earlier at the annual Latin Grammy Awards held in Los Angeles, quite a fuss had been made about whether or not *reggaetón* qualifies as a true Latin American musical genre. Should *reggaetón* have its own musical category? Is *reggaetón* too Caribbean to be Latino? Too black? Too hip hop? Finding categories for constantly emerging music styles has always been a challenge for awards committees, retailers, and programmers of radio and television outlets. Even within the circumscribed terrain of 'Latin Music', Grammies are given for *Tejano*, *Norteño*, *Banda*, Regional Mexican, Christian, Alternative, Contemporary Tropical, *Merengue*, Folk, Pop, Salsa, and Rock. Spanish-speaking Latinos have always struggled to place Brazil in the cultural mix, finally settling on MPB, *música popular Brasileira* – a category that crunches two vastly different traditional genres, samba and *pagode*, together into a single category. If that degree of cultural confusion is not enough, consider this: the winner of the 2005 Latin Grammy for best Female Pop Album was Laura Pausini, an Italian, who defeated Bebe, a Spaniard!

What was the fate of Daddy Yankee and *Barrio Fino* at the Latin Grammies that year? It was named Album of the Year, besting fellow *reggaetón* artist Don Omar's *The Last Don*, but not for a *reggaetón* category; there is no such thing, yet. The album won the award as Best Latin Urban Album of the Year. That was an honour the students in Mexico did not believe was warranted. The vast majority of them say they don't consider *reggaetón* to be Latin music.

The Global Cultural Mix

The confusions and contradictions of hybridization, the emergence of new cultural forms such as *reggaetón*, and the role of mass media and the cultural industries in the creation and spread of these forms brings about a vibrant cultural mix at the global level, often with a Latin inflection:

- A Peruvian band playing traditional Andes folk music at a tourist restaurant in Playa del Carmen, Mexico, suddenly breaks into the English band Queen's *We Will Rock You* to the delight of Canadian girls in the audience.
- Many New Yorkers born in the Dominican Republic regularly return to that Caribbean island nation to vote in national elections, and say they consider themselves as much Dominican as American.
- More than 400 million people worldwide, in countries including Russia, Tunisia, Zimbabwe, and Switzerland, regularly watch TV soap operas that originate in Spanish-language nations.

- The two top-rated radio stations in Los Angeles broadcast only in Spanish. One of them features *banda* music – regional Mexican folk music blended with traditional Bavarian rhythms and instruments including the tuba.
- The police department in Santa Barbara, California patrols the Latino section of town in a police car customized with air-brushed door panel murals, metallic sparkle, and magnesium wheels to resemble the 'lowrider' vehicles young Latino men drive.
- The Argentine veejay on MTV Latin America explains to Mexicans, Colombians, Venezuelans, and other Latinos why Black Sabbath was such an important influence on Korn.

Globalization does not mean that some universal, technology-based super society covers the globe and destroys local social systems and cultures. Despite technology's awesome reach, we have not, and will not, become one people. It is true that potent homogenizing forces such as English, Chinese, Spanish, Arabic, and other dominant languages; military weaponry; advertising techniques; internet protocol; media formats; international airports; and fashion trends undeniably affect consciousness and culture in every corner of the world. Such spheres of influence unquestionably introduce and reinforce certain standardizing values and practices. But these political-economic-cultural influences do not enter cultural contexts uniformly. They always interact with local conditions to produce diverse and dynamic consequences. Languages are great examples of linguistic hybridity and cultural borrowing. And just as TV programs, films, and popular music don't turn individual consumers into passive dupes in any single society, the power to transmit information worldwide likewise does not stimulate automatic imitation or conformity. To the contrary. By delivering culturally-rich symbolic resources, television, the internet, and all other mass and micro media open up and extend the possibilities of cultural work in every direction – invention, creolization, and retrenchment.

Forces of modernity and globalization no doubt have changed the face of world cultures and influenced political-economic relationships. But the overall effect is 'more an organization of diversity than a replication of uniformity' (Hannerz 1990). Local and regional ways of thinking and living do not disappear in the face of imported cultural influences. While globalization is irreversible, the global has not destroyed or replaced the local. The very concept of culture presumes difference. British sociologist Anthony D. Smith points out:

> If by 'culture' is meant a collective mode of life, or a repertoire of beliefs, styles, values, and symbols, then we can only speak of cultures, never just culture; for a collective mode of life, or a repertoire of beliefs, etc., presupposes different modes and repertoires in a universe of modes and repertoires. Hence, the idea of a 'global culture' is a practical impossibility. (1990: 171)

The nation state often serves as a way to demarcate important ideological, social, and cultural differences. Presumably, the nation state protects cultural interests. Arjun Appadurai, for example, wonders 'if the nation state disappears, what mechanism will assure protection of minorities, the minimal distribution of democratic rights, and the reasonable possibility of the growth of civil society?' (Appadurai 1996: 19). But the very idea of the nation state represents a historical construction that often covers up important cultural and political differences that exist within geographical territories. The nation state refers to a population that enjoys recognized political autonomy, effective legal codes and systems, geographical boundaries, a means of defence, and symbolic features like flags and anthems. Nation, on the other hand, has more to do with cultural identity and identity politics. People who make up a nation frequently believe they also have a right to freedom and autonomy too, and often struggle mightily for their cultural and political independence (Edgar and Sedgwick 1999). Mass media and the circulation of symbolic forms play key roles in such nationalist campaigns.

The Quebec separatist movement in Canada is a good example of how physical geography, political legitimacy, and communications media can resonate with and reinforce each other in nationalist struggles. The imagination of separatists from Quebec galvanized and accelerated when the first French language television channel appeared on the federal, state-supported Canadian television system, CBC), in 1952. The French-speaking channel with its culturally attractive media content over the years has arguably reinforced and further inspired separatist leanings by many French-speaking Canadians. Today, the explosion of more and more culturally specialized media channels on cable and satellite TV, French-speaking radio and print media, video, and popular music together with the internet and other information technologies make it even easier for French-speaking Canadians who are so disposed to imagine themselves as members of an alternative interpretative community – a symbolic nation that some hope will eventually become politically viable too. Modern nations depend on mass communication for just such symbolic presence and continuity (Anderson 1983, Chaney 1994).

Cultural globalization is best considered a complex set of interacting and often countervailing human, material, and symbolic flows that lead to diverse, heterogeneous cultural positionings and practices which persistently and variously modify established vectors of social, political, and cultural power, or, as Jesús Martin-Barbero puts it, 'the steady, predictable tempo of homogenizing development is upset by the countertempo of profound differences and cultural discontinuities' (1993: 149). Culture oscillates dialectically between permanence and change, between tradition and innovation. How people organize these cultural stresses is key to understanding modern personal and social stability.

Néstor García Canclini joined the chorus of contemporary thinkers who no longer accept the argument that political-economic-cultural realities are dominated and manipulated by large metropolitan consortia. He points out that theories of cultural imperialism do not account for the ways ideological and cultural images are created and distributed by the centres of production. The subjectivity and creative unruliness of the arts, mass media, and cultural production generally prevent cultural homogenization and manipulation: 'The aspirations of artists, journalists, and all types of cultural workers to function as a mediator between symbolic camps and in relations between and among diverse groups contradicts the motion of the market toward concentration and monopolization' (1989: 344).

Deterritorialization and Migration

The first step in the formation of new cultural territories is "deterritorialization". This refers to 'the loss of the "natural" relation between culture with geographic and social territory' (García Canclini 1989: 288), or 'the release of cultural signs from fixed locations in space and time' (Rowe and Schelling 1991: 231). In Anthony Giddens' (1990) terms, deterritorialization means the 'disembedding' (lifting out) of people and symbolic forms from the places we expect them to be. Deterritorialization is the partial tearing apart of cultural structures, relationships, settings, and representations.[2]

The migration of Third World peoples into more developed countries – a social uprooting that provokes major cultural disruptions and adaptations – is one primary and often troubling form of deterritorialization. Economic incentives usually are at the heart of such human movements, as Jorge Bustamante explains in his chapter in this volume. The African and Asian slave trade in colonial North America, Brazil, and the Caribbean region centuries ago, for example, was inspired by a search for cheap labour. Today the market for menial labour attracts poor immigrants to wealthy societies. For instance, California money routinely tempts Mexican farm workers and domestic help to leave home despite the dangers of doing so.

Conflicting immigrant groups often maintain and even increase their hostilities in their new lands. Chinese students from China, Taiwan, and Hong Kong, for example, form their own student organizations on California college campuses, and Chinatown neighbourhoods and social groups often divide up by origin. Young Mexican immigrants to the US form gangs according to their geographical origins in Mexico ('northerners' v. 'southerners') and export these contrived hostilities back to Mexico, a development that is reinforced by media images, especially movies, that depict and glorify the gang wars.

Not all human migrations are unwanted or forced by political or economic necessity. Professor and student temporary exchanges and relocations are common. International tourism, among the most profitable of all global industries, and employment reassignments for multinational corporations and federal governments also account for a tremendous number of people living outside their native lands. Modern forms of transportation and communication have made all types of human migration faster and easier.

---

2 See Tomlinson (1999) for a comprehensive discussion of the complexities of deterritorialization.

Cultural Melding and Mediation

> Immigrants cross the city in many directions and install, precisely in the crossings, their baroque places of regional sweets and contraband radios, their curative herbs and videocassettes (García Canclini 1989: 16).

When Angolans relocate in Brazil, Indians in Zimbabwe, Koreans in Japan, Mexicans in Canada and the US, and Jamaicans in England, for example, they certainly don't keep strictly to themselves, especially not the young adults and children. In one way or another deterritorialized peoples mix in with their new surroundings. What results is a kind of cultural give-and-take. These cultural interactions are variously termed transculturation, hybridization, and indigenization. Each concept emphasizes a different aspect of cultural melding and mediation.

Transculturation and Hybridization

Transculturation refers to a process wherein cultural forms literally move through time and space where they interact with other cultural forms and settings, influence each other, produce new forms, and change the cultural settings. Such syntheses often result from the physical movement of peoples from one geographic location to another. But we must not think of transculturation simply as the consequence of shifting populations. Many cultural crossings are also made possible by the mass media and culture industries. Some of the most significant and vast cultural territories and movements are mediated, symbolic lands and migrations.

Modern technology reconstructs the essential axes of cultural distance – space and time. This is most obviously the case in terms of physical space. Transmission and reception of information and entertainment from one part of the world to another inspire new cultural syntheses. But communications technology also permits new perceptions and uses of cultural time. Film, still photography, kinescope, audio tape, video tape, and today's sophisticated digital audio and video information storage and retrieval systems provide access to the symbols that make up cultural histories. Electronic and digital media preserve culture in ways print media can never do, and make it available for creative reinterpretation. People today can experience, edit, and use cultural symbolism in new temporal and spatial contiguities, greatly expanding the range of personal meanings and social uses. Mixing the traditional with the modern is fully reasonable and practical. Cultural archives of symbolic forms can be creatively accessed and reconstructed using consumer communication technology. Transculturation processes synthesize new cultural genres while they break down traditional cultural categories. Modern communications technology and the culture industries facilitate the creative process.

The information superhighway travels through contexts of both cultural production and reception as it simultaneously moves many directions in space and time. Certain genres, images, and stories appeal quite universally and move rapidly from one cultural space to another. Not all categories of information or entertainment travel at the same fast speed, however. For example, most national and local news, even juicy scandals, are far more provincial, and therefore more likely to occupy an information dusty county road than a superhighway (Tomlinson 1997). Transculturation produces cultural hybrids – the fusing of cultural forms and genres that are popular almost by definition.

Indigenization

The concept 'indigenization' helps explain how transculturation and hybridization occur. Indigenization means that imported cultural elements take on local features as the cultural hybrids develop. The exotic, unfamiliar, and foreign is domesticated. For example, consider what happens when rap music is exported to a place like Indonesia, Hong Kong, or Spain. The unfamiliar, imported cadence and attitude of rap is appropriated by local musicians. The sounds become indigenized at the same time. Indonesian, Hong Kong, and Spanish rap is sung in local languages, with lyrics that refer to local personalities, conditions, and situations. The resulting musical hybrid is an amalgam of American Black culture and Indonesian, Hong Kong, or Spanish culture. This popular creativity serves the cultural and political interests of local artists and activists while also furthering the economic interests of the culture industries that produce the hybrids.

Hybrids such as these never develop from 'pure' cultural forms in the first place. American Black culture has already been strongly influenced by African cultures and by European-American cultures, while Indonesia, Hong Kong, and Spain reflect long and complex histories of cultural influence too. They were hybrids themselves long before they met each other.

Although transculturation, hybridization, and indigenization may indeed bring about 'the mutual transformation of cultures' (Rowe and Schelling 1991: 18) as well as considerable input into cultural creativity from both sides, the transformations often entail unequal economic power relations between the interacting cultures. Multinational corporations often drive the process to their advantage, incorporating local cultural features into their products in processes of exploitative appropriation. One extremely visible and often criticized symbol of global popular culture for this and other reasons is the McDonald's restaurant chain. McDonald's picks up local culinary themes and blends them into their lines of products for those markets. So we get the mutton-based Maharaja Mac and vegetable nuggets in India, the Teriyaki Mac in Japan, McSpaghetti in the Philippines, and so on. McDonald's has become the paradigmatic instance of how a Western concept, fast food, and an ensemble of specific food products can combine to damage local cultures. But there is another less obvious side to this story as well. McDonald's provides liberating input to local cultures by offering alternatives to familiar food which can also break down the repressive insistence on blind allegiance to local foodstuffs and the managed, undemocratic rituals of eating (Watson 1997).

Cultural indigenization also takes place within national boundaries. The spectacular Brazilian cultural tradition, *Carnaval*, is telecast throughout the country on the national TV system, Globo. But rather than imitate the famous Rio version of *Carnaval*, people throughout Brazil modify the 'TV stimulus' (not only of *Carnaval*, but of national TV fare generally) by diffusing it in ways that integrate local preferences and traditions (Kottak 1990: 174). Furthermore, the Brazilian audience, especially lower middle class, working class, and lower class viewers, definitely prefer Brazilian programs over imported television shows. Imported television programs that succeed anywhere in the world usually resonate harmoniously with local cultural orientations or represent universal genres such as melodrama and action. Doing so, of course, they make money for their distant sponsors.

Reterritorialization and Diasporas

Deterritorialized by modernity and globalization, people attempt to re-establish a new cultural 'home' wherever they go (Tomlinson 1999: 148). These cultural ambitions and activities compose the processes of 'reterritorialization'.

Fusing imported traditions with resources in the new territory, immigrant groups all over the world create local versions of distant cultures: diasporas. Diasporic cultures can be formed and maintained much more easily today than ever before. Cultural goods such as food, clothing, and domestic items of all kinds flow much more rapidly around the world now, thanks mainly to transportation advances and market incentives for global import/export businesses.

Communications media, information technology, and culturally-relevant symbolic forms such as popular music, videos, newspapers, magazines, books, and computer software are extremely important in reterritorialization processes generally, and in the establishment of diasporas in particular. Culture, communication, and connectivity are essential ingredients in the formation of 'diasporic public spheres' (Appadurai 1996: 21). The 'ethnic media' are especially useful to diasporas in the US for sharing information about immigrants' legal rights and opportunities, for example. Meeting the informational, entertainment, and cultural needs of diasporic communities has become a modern growth industry. Deterritorialization and reterritorialization create new markets for entrepreneurs of all types, but especially for those in the media and culture industries who 'thrive on the need of the deterritorialized population for contact with its homeland' (Appadurai 1990: 302). In the slow and painful process of cultural assimilation to a new geographic space, particularly in the alienating, huge metropolises where immigrants and exiles tend to congregate, popular culture products from 'back home', as well as local materials produced in the native language and reflecting core cultural values from the homeland, are crucial for creating peace of mind and ethnic solidarity for reterritorialized peoples. These cultural materials are not rented or sold in department store or video outlet chains, but in 'ethnic' grocery stores and video rental shops. There is also a growing market for videos, pop music, and software produced in exile and sent to the home countries.

Connecting to traditional values, religion, popular arts, and language, communications media help to maintain, enliven, and transform cultural life for cultural diasporas. Older members of deterritorialized peoples often use traditional cultural materials to reinforce their cultural identities, preferred modes of living, and social statuses within their new communities. Many senior Chilean immigrants in Canada, for example, organize festivals that feature the Andean folkloric music that was fashionable at the time of their arrival in the 1970s, celebrate the Chilean popular culture stars of that bygone era, and even repeat slogans such as 'socialism or death' that characterized the politics of the past. Younger members of the various diasporas may find comfort in traditions like these too, though they are just as likely to form their reterritorialized cultural identities at least partly in opposition to imported values, ways of life, and cultural products, which they often find outdated, uncool, or otherwise uninteresting.

Widespread, affordable point-to-point consumer communication technologies facilitate mediated interpersonal communication that is used to construct hybrid satellite cultures in new locations and maintain ties to cultural homelands. Immigrants who live thousands of miles away from their places of geographic origin regularly use e-mail and telephones to nurture relationships with family and friends back home, and to expand their cultural territory in new geographical locations. Communications technology sustains and enlarges the very nature of a given cultural field by facilitating social interaction that is not bound by physical space. Put another way, culture can be actively reterritorialized by the ability of communications technology to facilitate social interaction that transcends physical distance.

A tremendous advantage of reterritorialized immigrant culture is that the perceived good things about the 'old country' can be preserved in the new locations without having to directly confront the typical repressive political and economic realities back home. Heavy nostalgia – a highly selective, fond remembering of the distant culture – is common for reterritorialized peoples as they seek emotional comfort in their new lands. Dominant cultural values and familiar behaviours back home are reduced to memory traces and figments of the imagination. Immigrants usually face co-cultural or sub-cultural status in their new territories, a reduced role that is frequently difficult to accept.

Ethnic shopping malls have become the new meeting grounds for California's immigrants, providing culturally-familiar merchandise and food, negotiations in their own languages, and most important, a place to meet friends. The ethnic mall has become a social support system and centre for self-sufficiency – much like the original urban enclaves – that helps immigrants make the transition to life in the US. But of course this changes with time too. One immigrant to the Silicon Valley, for instance, told a *San Jose Mercury News* reporter that first generation immigrants spend 85 per cent of their leisure time at the ethnic malls, the second generation 50 per cent, and the third generation 25 per cent with the remaining time spent at McDonald's and Pizza Hut!

Circular Migration

Immigration need not be a one-way, permanent state of affairs where mediated cultural forms become the only contacts with the original culture. Some people move back and forth frequently between national cultures, functioning well, often in quite different ways, in both. This is 'circular migration', a phenomenon that is very common in all of North America.

Learning how to live in multiple places and spaces is a kind of cultural competency in globalization. Some Puerto Ricans, Jamaicans, Dominicans, and Mexicans travel from South to North and return South, or vice versa, several times every year. Even specific Indigenous peoples, such as Zapotecs and Mixtecs from Oaxaca, Mexico, move back and forth, and have created specific cultural and social links between California and their homeland; as documented in Isabel Altamirano-Jiménez's chapter in this volume.

The Latinos often share common neighbourhoods in New York, Miami, Toronto, Vancouver, and Los Angeles, where they interact and influence each other. Spanish language television, radio, cinema, and dancehalls in the US bring Latinos together physically and symbolically. Mexican kids whose parents work in the US legally can attend school half the year in Mexico, the other half in the US, and receive a legitimate joint diploma. The positive syntheses forged among the reterritorialized cultures, as well as the conflicts that emerge in contested social and cultural space in America, are then exported back to the Caribbean, Mexico, and Central and South America as cultural products (popular music especially) and as perceptions of the Latino 'other'.

Case Study: Singing to the Heart of Mexico

> Our bilingual, bicultural, binational experience is a form of schizophrenia, rich and poor, sun and shadow, between realism and surrealism. To live on the border is to live in the center, to be at the entrance and the exit; to inhabit two worlds, two cultures, and to accept both. (Burciaga 1993: 66)

> If you want us to come back, hire a Mexican player (Banner held by Mexican immigrants to northern California at a San Jose, California professional soccer match)

Divorced in time and space from the familiar terrain of everyday life back home, Mexican immigrants to the US depend greatly on symbolic links to their imagined native ways of life. Mexico is by no means just a geographical place. More than anything it is a cultural space, and nostalgic journeys to that space are taken by people as they establish their new cultural territories.

Those types of symbolic connections to romanticized Mexico are very strongly felt when Juan Gabriel Mexico's greatest composer and singer of popular music performs concerts in California. The state's huge Latino community, composed mainly of Mexican immigrants, connects intimately to the cultural feelings that he inspires. Gabriel performs songs such as *The Mexico That has Left Us* (*El México que se nos fue*), a particularly emotional portrait of political and cultural tensions between Mexico and the US. The song laments the transformation of Mexican towns and villages in the wake of immigration, the devastation of the Mexican economy since the recent peso devaluation and recession, industrialization and contamination of the countryside that has been accelerated by hemispheric trade agreements, and the modernization and commercialization of life in general. Gabriel sadly describes the replacement of adobe homes with cement structures in Mexico, the breaking up of nuclear families, even the preference of television over local music groups for entertainment in Mexican villages.

Juan Gabriel presents a poignant Mexican interpretation of the downside of modernization and globalization. He creates a vivid, nostalgic view of old Mexico which may not promote Mexican economic development, but touches the hearts and souls of Mexican immigrants those with and without legal papers who reside and toil in California. His concerts are attended almost exclusively by Mexican Americans and Mexicans in the US. He draws huge crowds without advertising in the English-language media. Like the Vietnamese and other cultural groups in California, Mexican Americans learn about their cultural events mainly through alternative media and informal social networks. They really don't expect much more.

What Juan Gabriel offers his compatriots in the US is access to their own sense of cultural well-being, hopes for the future, and potential to enjoy popular pleasures. Performers like him are unifying resources of enormous importance. For thousands of immigrants to countries all over the world, symbolic representations of culture such as music are much more accessible and democratic than traditional political, economic, or coercive power because they help individuals from all walks of life exercise real influence over their experiences and feelings.

Because culture is constructed and mobile, it is also synthetic and multiple. The abundance, power, and convenience of modern communications technology give reterritorialized peoples opportunities to keep their ethnic identities alive. This is true for Mexican immigrants in northern California who watch three Spanish-language cable TV stations in the Bay Area, listen to many Spanish-language radio stations, rent the same video classics their friends and families view in Mexico, and buy the latest Juan Gabriel, Molotov, Julieta Venegas, Café Tacuba, or Alejandro Fernández LP. Because of the robust and efficient US market, many Mexican cultural materials are actually easier to find and less expensive in California than they are in Mexico.

Mexican towns and neighbourhoods have grown up all over California. These settlements often have profound attachments to particular parts of Mexico. Their inhabitants make frequent journeys back and forth between their homes in the US and their homes in Mexico. Aguililla, Michoacan (Mexico) and Redwood City, California is one such pair of communities. Aguililla is known as 'Little Redwood City' in Mexico, and Redwood City is 'Little Aguililla' in California. The Mexican national economy depends on dollars coming in from labourers working in the US. Because Mexicans living abroad have the right to vote in Mexican elections, Mexican politicians come to California and Texas to campaign for votes.

The transnational flow of communications technology and cultural materials helps make Mexicans feel more Mexican in Mexico too. For instance, when famous popular music groups like *Los Tigres del Norte, Bronco,* or *Los Tucanes de Tijuana* play their hits in outdoor stadiums in Mexico, they depend on Japanese, German, and US audio technology to amplify the music with minimal distortion. The effect is loud, pure, sound that drives Mexican emotions, feelings, language Mexican culture deep into the bones of concert goers. Far from destroying Mexican culture, the imported equipment enhances the *puro mexicano* cultural experience.

The sites and styles of cultural territories have changed in the late modern and post-modern world, but people still organize themselves culturally in order to carve out their personal identities and feel secure. No doubt, the 'disembedding [lifting out] ... of social relations from local contexts of interaction and their restructuring across indefinite spans of time and space' can be very disorienting and intimidating (Giddens 1990: 21). But by developing new cultural territories and 're-embedding' (inserting) social relations in new contexts, people can overcome the depersonalizing tendencies of fractured postmodern life to find emotional relief and security (*Ibid.* 141–2). New ways of conceptualizing time, space, and culture thus provide one basis for refashioning stable social relations (Giddens 1991: 17). Cultural reterritorialization is not something done to people over which they have no control.

Surfing the Cultural Shores of Our North America

Cultural environments today are made up of material and symbolic elements, of the highbrow and the popular, of the personal and the mass, the public and the private, the here and there, the familiar and the strange, of yesterday, today, and tomorrow. People draw ambitiously from all available cultural domains to construct the worlds they inhabit.

Culture has never been motionless; it is invariably modified by subsequent generations. From a cultural perspective, then, we might ask, is 'Our North America' best described as a continent or as a continent of cultural change? The latter description comes closer to the truth. Charles Darwin noted more than 150 years ago that change is biologically indispensable to the evolution of all species (Darwin 1859/1979). Some of the best fossil evidence supporting Darwin's claim, the Tiktaalik roseae – a 375-million-year-old-species of fish that was transitioning from water to land – was discovered in 2006 in North America's own northernmost terrain, the Nunavut territory in the Canadian Arctic. Indeed, our North America has been undergoing a multidimensional cultural transformation of endless making long before human beings traversed its soil. It couldn't have happened any other way.

Part VI
Intergovernmental Relations

Chapter 11
Canada–US Relations: The Contemporary Imbalance

Tom Keating

Introduction

Canada's bilateral relationship with the US has been a perennial issue of discussion in Canada. Historically, Conservatives and Liberals in Ottawa fought over this important bilateral relationship with the former defending Canadian sovereignty in the face of American imperial ambitions and the Liberals arguing for ever-closer economic relations. Canada's two major parties have altered their positions somewhat since the mid-1980s, when Brian Mulroney's Conservative government led Canada into a free trade agreement with the US. During the 2006 federal election campaign, the Liberals tagged Conservative leader Stephen Harper as a Canadian version of George Bush and presented themselves as the party that would defend Canada's distinctiveness and sovereignty in the face of the neighbouring behemoth. The New Democratic Party, for its part, has based much of its foreign policy platform on resisting close relations and acting independently from their southern neighbour. The election of Barack Obama as the forty-fourth president of the US has altered this picture, as Canadian party leaders saw his popularity on both sides of the border and were glad to align themselves with the new American administration. The winds of change may not be as great as first believed, so the question of how to manage this most complex of bilateral relations remains at the forefront.

Playing the US card in an election campaign is a bit of a gamble, even in 2006 when many Canadians were clearly troubled by the foreign policy excesses of the Bush administration and upset over the American government's persistent refusal to respond constructively to repeated NAFTA decisions on softwood lumber. As much as Canadians were concerned about such practices, they were equally troubled by the apparent deterioration in amicable relations between Canadian and American leaders and concerned about a whole series of potentially negative spin-offs from American policies on bilateral economic and border issues. Indeed, a public opinion poll taken shortly after that election revealed that the foreign policy issue of most concern to Canadians was the poor state of bilateral relations. Interestingly, in the same poll, the second most frequently cited foreign policy concern was protecting Canada's sovereignty. This suggests the somewhat schizophrenic approach that Canadians have exhibited on relations with the US.

The attention given to these relations in the 2006 campaign was indicative of a widely held view that there was a problem in the relationship, and given its importance to Canada, a pressing need to find some way to fix it.[1] This concern has dissipated somewhat as the Harper government worked to improve the relationship and as Barack Obama's arrival in the White House made Canadians a little more comfortable being close to the US. Yet given the importance of the US for Canada, many Canadians continue to worry that too little attention has been given to the management of Canada's most important bilateral relationship.

Canada's relations with the US are among the most intensive and extensive in the world. It is the largest bilateral trade relationship in the world. The flow of commercial and human traffic across the border persists around the clock every day of the year with commercial exchanges of more than US$1.5 billion a day alongside an estimated 300,000 people crossing the border daily. The importance of the relationship is most pronounced on the Canadian side of the border. Not only is the US the dominant power in the global political economy, it is also the most critically significant market for Canada's trade-dependent economy. While Canada's trade dependence has declined and its total merchandise trade with the US has fallen significantly over the past five years (from 71 per cent in 2005 to 63 per cent in 2009), the US remains Canada's most important market and Canada's economic prosperity continues to depend on reliable access to American markets. The sheer size of these exchanges and their significance for Canadian prosperity have led to repeated arguments for the establishment of a more permanent institutionalized relationship with the US.[2]

Others have called attention to the importance of the US in supporting Canadian security. It is commonly argued that Canada is incapable of defending itself against military threats, let alone of reassuring the US that we are capable of doing so. Indeed as Frank Harvey notes, in the security-conscious America of the post-9/11 environment, 'Ottawa will be incapable of spending enough to convince Americans that our commitment to their security is reliable' (Harvey 2006). This has led to proposals for defence spending increases and for closer integration between the American and Canadian militaries in such areas as continental defence, ballistic missile defence systems, and interoperability.[3] Many of those concerned about the state of the bilateral relationship also argued that members of the Canadian government should be less critical of the American government and its policies, more attentive to American concerns, more supportive of their initiatives including their interventions abroad and the war on terror, and alternatively less

---

1   There are no shortages of suggestions for improving the bilateral relationship. For a sample see the selection of source documents at the CBC's 'Canada and the New American Empire, Economic Integration and Security' at http://www.cbc.ca/empire/integration.html and http://www.cbc.ca/empire/security.html. Also see Goldfarb 2003b, Granatstein 2003, Cox 2005; and the more sceptical view of Barry 2003.
2   For a review of the various proposals see Goldfarb 2003b.
3   See for example, Jockel and Sokolsky 2006.

persistent in the face of US opposition to Canada's own initiatives such as the landmines treaty and the International Criminal Court.[4] The argument runs that, in approaching foreign policy choices, Canadians should first and foremost consider the ramifications of those choices on the bilateral relationship with the US, and that the government should avoid pursuing policy choices that will create problems in the bilateral relationship, either because they challenge American foreign policy objectives, or because they offend important political interests in the US. All of these, of course, fall within the responsibility of the Canadian government as the University of Calgary's David Bercuson explained:

> Americans don't expect Canada to be a military superpower, but they do expect Canada to do as much as a wealthy and advanced democracy can do to help the United States defend itself and the democratic world. This is no more than Americans expect of their European allies. President Obama will want the same from Canada; if his administration is disappointed, it will not go out of its way to accommodate Canadian needs in other areas. (cit. in Burney 2009: 23)

The assumption is that Canada must continuously do something to demonstrate its support for the US expecting that, in return, the US government will be more responsive to Canadian interests and objectives. The most commonly referred-to 'something' since 2001 has been border security and Afghanistan. In the past NATO and Cold War security concerns played a similar role. The arguments have not changed significantly since the election of Barack Obama despite the emergence of somewhat different policy priorities in the US. There is a prevalent view that the bilateral relationship with the US has been problematic and needs to be fixed. It is also commonly accepted that the problem, such as there was one, was in Canada, and that changes needed to be made in Canadian foreign policy. Both assumptions can be questioned.

The election of Stephen Harper's minority government in 2006 brought about a change in tone and style that has persisted following its re-election in 2010. The change in the US administration following the election of Barack Obama in 2008 has also alleviated the concern among some Canadians about the costs of good relations with the US. Yet despite these developments, many remain worried about managing Canada–US relations and continue to argue the need for a significant realignment of Canada's approach to its most important bilateral relationship.[5] In considering whether it is necessary to reorient Canadian foreign policy as a way of maintaining good relations with the US, it makes sense to take another look at the 'problem' in order to consider what Canada could or should do to manage bilateral relations with the US.

---

4   See for example, Granatstein 2003.
5   See for example the essay by Burney 2009 and the report from Carleton University 2009.

In much of the discussion on managing Canada–US relations, there has been less concern with the extent to which the emergence of problems in the bilateral relationship might be the result of changes that have occurred in the US; changes that have served to make the relationship more difficult to manage and create more opportunities for conflict between the two countries; and most importantly, changes that are beyond the control of the Canadian government and will likely make the relationship increasingly problematic regardless of the position that any Canadian government of the day might adopt on specific policies.

This chapter argues that changes in the US, evident in both its domestic and foreign policy, have resulted in an altered domestic policy-making environment that is less conducive to the sort of senior-level management that has been used in the past. The net result is that bilateral issues are less amenable to executive-level management and that the foreign policy activities of the two countries are more likely to come into conflict in the global arena. For these reasons, in examining Canada's relations with the US, it is first worth considering that one of the significant reasons for the deterioration in bilateral relations has been the significant changes that have occurred in the US. These changes have substantially altered the domestic context in the US in which Canadian–American relations are conducted. Equally important have been policy shifts in the way in which the US and Canada engage with the rest of the world. These policy shifts have put Canadian and American foreign policy more significantly out of synch than has traditionally been the case. To suggest that Canada should adapt in order to respond to these changes because of the overwhelming importance of the US to Canada, and especially the Canadian economy, is to overlook the fact that such changes would force an alignment on Canada's part to merge its foreign policy with that of the US. The Obama election also raises the question of which policies to adjust as American policies undergo their own transition. Moreover, if domestic conditions in the US are most important in shaping those aspects of bilateral relations of most concern, trying to devise a convergence of policies or appeal to the US by supporting its most urgent security or foreign policy concerns may do little to alter the less hospitable domestic environment which confronts Canadian interests in the US, and to generate little of real value in resolving bilateral differences. Before considering the implications of these developments for Canadian foreign policy and Canadian–American relations, the chapter will briefly examine the evolving policy-making environment in which these relations are conducted.

A Changed Partner: The Domestic Setting

In considering the changes that have occurred in the US, it is important to bear in mind that these changes are not solely the result of the administration of a single president, though some were brought into sharp relief under the Bush administration. Nor are these changes entirely new, as some have been developing for a number of years.

[The turning point] wasn't the free-trade agreement, the end of the Cold War or 9/11. These events shook up the bilateral relationship, but the pivotal moment was really the early 1970s, when the Vietnam War and Watergate smashed the 'imperial presidency' and fragmented control over U.S. foreign policy. America's ability to recognize and adhere to postwar diplomatic culture was irretrievably lost, and the relationship became more confrontational, complicated and unpredictable. (Bow 2010)

These domestic developments, however, took on greater significance as Canada's commercial relations with the US expanded under the free trade agreements and as a result of the significant global shifts underway since the end of the Cold War and the terrorist attacks of 9/11.

Christopher Sands identifies three sources of change in the domestic policy-making environment of the bilateral relationship (Sands 2005: 483–96). The first is the passing of a generation of Americans that had worked with Canadians through the 1940s and 1950s and shared 'a common outlook as parochial North Americans shedding their isolationist past and building institutions to stabilize a new world order' (*Ibid.*: 487). These American multilateralists have given way to a new generation less committed to the network of institutions established after the Second World War and less conscious of the significant participation and commitment of Canadians during this period.[6] Sands also notes that there has been a significant shift in power that has resulted in Canadian issues being decentralized from the president to the various agencies of the federal government, to lower levels within these agencies, to the US Congress, and to state and local authorities. This has left the American executive with considerably less influence over the substantive policy decisions that affect the bilateral relationship. It also means that personal interventions at the executive level are less common and often less effective. As Derek Burney has written, 'the personal qualities and the interpersonal chemistry between leaders can ... affect the tone and can help set the basic direction for bilateral relations but they cannot override the system of governance on issues' (Burney 2005). The combined effect of these various changes has been to diminish the degree and effect of influential interventions by the executive and other senior officials in many aspects of Canadian–American relations. Sands argues that less executive control over the outcome of specific issues in the Canadian–American relationship has also reinforced the elite competition between different governmental and non-governmental actors within the US, as a variety of local and private interests compete for control over policy outcomes. This is enhanced even more when there are differences at the political level. 'As the official Canada–US relationship has become strained, the private relations between our citizens have become more important (Sands 2003). This third source of change has been reflected on the Canadian side as

---

6 Philippe Sands (2005) has also noted the changed attitude towards international law and institutions that has crept into American policy making circles.

Canadian provinces and business elites compete for a greater voice in the bilateral relationship, in part in response to a perception that the federal government in Ottawa loses its ability to manage the relationship effectively in the face of the shifting policy-making environment in the US.[7] Proposals from the CCCE for reforming the bilateral relationship, greater private sector input into the SPP, and the addition of provincial government representatives from Quebec, Alberta, and Manitoba in the Washington embassy are indications of this trend.

These changes have had a direct influence on the bilateral relationship. They have been complemented by other developments in American politics that have repercussions for the US government's approach to Canada. These include a shift in the geographic and demographic location of political influence in the US political process to the South and West and to the growing presence of Hispanic and Asian groups within American society. This shift has created a geographic and demographic gap between Canada and the US that compounds the Canadian government's ability to gain a hearing in Washington. American policy makers who need to draw their political support from the South and the West are going to look to these regions to set the policy priorities. US political elites are also increasingly populated by individuals from these regions who are less familiar with the forty-ninth parallel and the country and politics that lie to the North. The growing influence of Hispanics and especially Mexican–Americans also has made Mexican–American relations *the* bilateral relationship that receives most attention from government officials.

Brian Bow has identified three different models for managing bilateral relations (Bow 2006–2007). The intergovernmental model involves executive–executive diplomacy and is the one most affected by interpersonal relations. The transgovernmental model involving cross-national bureaucratic interaction had for a number of years been the means for conducting much of the 'business' between the two countries. Increasingly, a third model has become more influential, wherein transnational relations involving extensive cross-national societal actors affect the policy process and ultimately the policy itself. The general pattern of relations over time suggests a movement away from intergovernmental towards the transnational, but at different times in different policy sectors each retains some relevance. While one can identify proponents and detractors for these different approaches, Bow argues that there has been no well-researched assessment of their relative effectiveness. What Bow does note is that, as one moves from the intergovernmental through the other options, the relationship becomes increasingly more complex and complicated. The record would also suggest that the Canadian government has not been more or less successful under any particular approach. Obviously good relations at the executive level are important, but the camaraderie among leaders often does not resonate with members of Congress, let alone with state and local officials. Moreover, even the most popular president has only so

---

7 A good discussion of this changing provincial role can be found in Kukucha 2008.

much credit to use on recalcitrant members of Congress, and Canadian interests are seldom a high priority.

The changed policy-making environment has, if nothing else, complicated the Canadian government's efforts to influence US policy decisions affecting Canada. It is not only more difficult to be heard, it is also more difficult for Canadians to find a receptive ear. This is not to suggest that US policy officials are antagonistic toward Canada, but that their attention is focused elsewhere and that the sort of privileged access and sympathetic hearings of the past have given way to a more competitive and business-like environment. This is not completely new, as Sands suggests, or necessarily a negative development. However, it has become more pronounced. It also seems improbable that Canada can do anything to change this situation. Thus, while we need to adapt to how and with whom we interact, it does not necessarily mean that we need to modify our interests or policies to coincide with those favoured in some quarters in the US, for there is no longer a guarantee that anyone will notice or care. The new environment will mean that the relationship will be more difficult to manage, but the difficulty is as much a result of these structural changes in the US policy environment as they are of the policies being pursued by Canada. Under the circumstances, it seems questionable to suggest that one way of addressing this new reality is to bring selected Canadian policies such as border security and immigration, among others, more into line with those of the US.

A Changed Partner: Dancing to a Different Tune on the World Stage

In addition to the changed domestic environment, there have also been changes in US foreign policy that have placed Canada and the US on different paths and have, at times, exacerbated the bilateral relationship. There have been some noteworthy developments that owe their appearance to the 9/11 attacks, mainly on the side of border security, but even more noteworthy has been the persistence of patterns and practices that were in motion before that day. Regardless of their source, US foreign policy initiatives increasingly diverged from those favoured by Canadians, increasing the potential for conflict between the two countries.

One important development has been the unprecedented accumulation of power by the US, especially military power, since the end of the Cold War. As Canada and some European states cashed in on the post-Cold War 'peace dividend', US military power has expanded across a number of different dimensions, by many indicators unprecedented in relation to other states in the world. The US spends almost as much as all of the other major countries combined on defence (about 48 per cent of the world's total military expenditures), but this represents only 4 per cent of its gross national product.[8] The US economy is larger than the next three national economies combined. The US has only 5 per cent of the world's

---

8 Data are drawn from Shah 2007.

population, but generates 25 per cent of the world's production and 35 per cent of the world's research and development.[9] In addition to what Paul Kennedy referred to as an unprecedented concentration of power, the US government has also embarked on what appears to be a plan to use this power to shape the globe in its interests. For example in a speech at West Point in 2001, President Bush said that the US strategy should be to 'keep military strengths beyond challenge, thereby making the destabilizing arms races of other eras pointless.'[10] In emphasizing 'beyond challenge' the US has displayed the pursuit of dominance as a foreign policy objective. This implies that the idea of a balance of power or even an element of superiority is no longer enough. There is little indication that such a mission has been abandoned by the Obama administration, given its announced defence budgets and the 2010 National Security Strategy.

There are some who have suggested that US power is not on very secure foundations, given its dependence on foreign oil, foreign funds to finance its debt, and especially after the financial collapse of 2008. Yet, this has not halted the attempt to assert this power, nor has it shaken the desire to accumulate it. The drive to dominance suggests a different approach from the hegemonic aspirations of the US after World War II. At that time, there seemed to be more attention given to bringing others along in support of US policy and a greater consideration of securing US power within an institutional framework. Since the end of the Cold War, and particularly in the aftermath of events in Somalia, Bosnia, and Kosovo, the US has been more inclined to resist formal institutional connections and alter its approach to multilateralism, partly on the assumption that given its preponderant power it can. The accumulation of this preponderance of power has been part of a shift to a contingent multilateralism that depends on its ability to support US interests.[11] The willingness to proceed with military action against Afghanistan and then Iraq in the absence of institutional support suggests a preference for unilateral action, even at the expense of additional resources and political support. This has, at times, been combined with a hostile critique of the multilateral processes and institutions that governed much of the post-1945 period and that have been such an important forum for the pursuit of Canadian foreign policy objectives. The rhetoric of the Obama administration indicates a return to a more collective enterprise, but there are at least three grounds for questioning its staying power: one is the past practice in which such intentions have proven difficult to sustain. A second is the persistence of isolationist sentiments that are a constant feature of American foreign policy culture. A third will be the US

---

9 See http://fcw.com/articles/2010/01/19/national-science-board-research-and-development.aspx.

10 George W. Bush, Address to Graduation Exercise of the United States Military Academy, West Point, New York, June 1, 2002, reprinted in Scott, Jones Jr., and Furmanski 2004, p. 53.

11 The author would like to thank an anonymous reviewer for suggesting the term contingent multilateralism.

government's willingness to share policy making along with its implementation and the willingness of others in Europe and Canada to come out in support. Early indications in Afghanistan in 2009–10 suggest that it may prove difficult to elicit both of these, which would leave the US government once again to take its own course. On balance, 'Washington values multilateral institutions for their burden sharing and legitimating functions, but only if these allow it to exercise significant control over the agenda, preserve its margin of manoeuvre, safeguard U.S. sovereignty, and increase the likelihood of success' (Stewart 2002:12).

In the immediate aftermath of the Cold War, then US President George Bush Sr. displayed an interest in developing multilateral coalitions to support US foreign policy objectives. This was reflected in the pulling together of a coalition of states at the time of the Gulf War, and with the UN Security Council's sanctioning of the use of military force by this coalition. This support for multilateral consultations and institutions has been superseded by a more ambivalent approach. In the early months of the Clinton administration, there was talk among his national security advisors of American support for assertive multilateralism, but this soon gave way – in the aftermath of events in Somalia – to Presidential Decision Directive (PDD) 25 which confirmed that the US government would support only multilateral initiatives that were clearly in their interest and under their control. The emphasis given to unilateralism in the administration of George W. Bush was even more pronounced. In the summer of 2001, Charles Krauthammer described the spirit of the new administration: 'The new unilateralism seeks to strengthen American power and unashamedly deploy it on behalf of self-defined global ends' (Krauthammer 2001). In the immediate aftermath of 9/11, there were indications that this tragic event might serve as an opportunity to restore US commitment to multilateralism, much in the way that Roosevelt tied US power to multilateral institutions after the Second World War. When terrorist attacks jolted the post-Cold War complacency of the US and their closest allies, including Canada, the member governments of NATO for the first time in the history of the Alliance invoked Article 5, and the editor of *Le Monde* declared 'we are all Americans now.' The US received an outpouring of support from around the globe, as governments from all corners of the globe committed themselves to the fight against terrorism. In this atmosphere, it would seem unnecessary for the US president to lay down the threat 'You are either with us or against us', when much of the world had already signed the pledge. But the threat was issued and the flirtation with multilateralism vanished more quickly than it had appeared.

The preference for unilateral action was evident in the US military response in Afghanistan and in its approach to the war against Iraq in 2003. Calls for patience, caution, and more evidence were rejected and the US government intensified pressure on members of the Security Council to support military action. The pressure combined with the 'you are either with or against us' approach generated considerable criticism. 'We find it extremely irritating to be treated with utter contempt' was Mexico's foreign minister's Jorge Castañeda's response to such tactics. And in the words of Vladimir P. Lukin, former Russian ambassador to

Washington, '[W]hat kind of compromise can you have if the US doesn't want to hear anybody?' (Cited in Tyler 2003). Tony Judt concluded that '[w]hen a great power has to buy its allies, bribe its friends, and blackmail its critics, something is amiss' (Judt 2003). A British and very belated Canadian effort to postpone the inevitable in the hope of gaining Security Council approved were tossed aside. The net result of the ultimately futile debate at the UN was to reinforce American suspicions of or animosity toward the institution.

In addition to this contingent multilateralist approach for addressing international issues, which is the second trend in recent US foreign policy, Washington also more directly challenged international institutions and international agreements. For example, it rejected various international agreements on biological weapons investigations, climate change, and the International Criminal Court, among others. The administration not only renounced the Rome Statute of the International Criminal Court, a rather unusual move, but 'Arms Control Undersecretary John Bolton's statement that signing the letter renouncing the Rome Statute was "the happiest moment of my government service" told more about the administration's ideologically driven campaign against multilateral constraints on US power.'[12]

A third trend in American foreign policy was to increase the use of military force as an instrument of foreign policy.[13] It is perhaps not too surprising to see this development, as the temptation to turn to military power has been strong, given the technological and material advances that the US has made in this area relative to other states. The international political environment has also been more conducive to the use of military intervention since the end of the Cold War. Throughout the 1990s, the US continued to develop the capacity to project its military force throughout the globe. During the NATO-sanctioned campaign against Serbia in defence of Kosovar Albanians in 1999, the US military recognized its clear superiority over its own allies. With the arrival of the Bush administration, the US government not only continued to develop their overwhelming military capacity; they also embarked on a policy to deliberately seek an unmatched preponderance of military power and to retain this for the foreseeable future. The terrorist attacks of 9/11 consolidated political support behind a major expansion in US military spending and helped to secure support for a further development of such things as ballistic missile defences and new nuclear weapons. Military spending continues to grow under the Obama administration, fuelled in part by the ongoing conflicts in Iraq and Afghanistan. Nevertheless, it is indicative of the persistent commitment to the central role of military force in US foreign policy.

A fourth and final trend in US foreign policy, one that was reasserted after the Cold War and especially pronounced under the George W. Bush administration, is a strong sense of moral conviction in the pursuit of foreign policy objectives. Once again this is neither unique to recent administrations in the history of US foreign

---

12 Tom Barry, "The US Power Complex: What's New" at http://www.fpif.org/fpiftxt/913.
13 See Bacevich 2005.

policy, nor limited to the US. It does, however, raise another point of difference between the US and its allies and complicates the resolution of international conflicts. Former US Senator William Fulbright understood this pathology:

> Power tends to confuse itself with virtue and a great nation is particularly susceptible to the idea that its power is a sign of God's favor, conferring upon it a special responsibility for other nations – to make them richer and happier and wiser, to remake them, that is, in its own shining image. Power confuses itself with virtue and tends also to take itself for omnipotence. Once imbued with the idea of a mission, a great nation easily assumes that it has the means as well as the duty to do God's work.[14]

Cox has argued that this has shaped recent policies in many areas:

> This conviction of being bearers of an exceptional historic mission is expressed in the paradox that combines an atavistic cultural isolationism with a messianic expansion-defending the purity of one's own culture while aiming to convert those of other cultures. It has led American leadership with public acquiescence, to refuse to ratify the Kyoto accord on environmental protection, the treaty to abolish the use of landmines, and the International Criminal Court. American exceptionalism affirms in practice that the US is not a state like all the others and that American officials, the agents of this special responsibility, cannot be subject to other than US law. (Cox 2005)

While Canadian policy officials have generally steered clear of such moral imperatives, they are not completely immune to the temptation.

These trends in both the domestic political environment in the US and in its foreign policy activities have very much changed the context for conducting Canadian–US relations and Canadian foreign policy. While Canada and the US continue at present to share many common values and objectives, these developments have placed the US on a different path, one that is generally less familiar and less comfortable to Canadians, and in Cox's view, in opposition to Canadian preferences.

> The United States, meanwhile, has been moving in the opposite direction, towards a unipolar concept of world power in which the United States has emerged from the global conflicts of World War II and the Cold War as a the paragon of economic, social, and political order with a mission to transmit its values and its order to the rest of the world, both for the benefit of other peoples and to ensure the security of its own way of life. In part, this evolution of American values has been encouraged by the collapse of the Soviet power

---

14 Senator William Fulbright cited in Jim Lobe, "The Arrogance of Power," at http://www.fpif.org/commentary/2002/0209arrogance_body.html.

and the vision that this has left the American way as the 'end of history' beyond which no fundamental change is conceivable. In part, it arises from the domestic power shift within the United States from the northeast, with its historic links to Europe ad European thought, to a southwest more susceptible to the idea of American 'exceptionalism' and more impregnated by the certainties of Christian fundamentalism as to the absolute and evident nature of good and evil. (Ibid.)

It is too early to tell whether the economic collapse of October 2008 or the coming to power of the Obama administration is a significant change or merely a moderation in this longer-term trend. Obama and others in his administration have given more rhetorical attention to the importance of multilateral co-operation, and have made some initiatives to alter US policy and reach out to other states on climate change and on economic reforms. Yet as indicated here, other aspects of US domestic politics and foreign policy seem untouched by the change in government. The uncertainty itself as to future direction reflects the underlying difficulty for Canadian policy makers in deciding which US foreign policy to support.

Canada under Harper: Playing in a Bush League

Responding to these changes has clearly been a matter of concern for Canadian officials and has motivated much of the commentary on how best to manage the bilateral relationship. It is evident, however, that Canadians have little ability to alter these broad forces at play within the US and in the US's orientation to the global community. The question is then one of how to balance the need to maintain good relations so as to secure important bilateral relations while maintaining a Canadian foreign policy for the global community. In examining the historical record, one finds that Canada has chosen a variety of responses when confronted with these competing interests in the past. These responses range from co-operation to resistance. They also include efforts to engage US foreign policy within multilateral frameworks that serve both to contain US power and legitimize it within the broader international community.

Policies of co-operation between Canada and the US are common. In large measure, this is because the two countries share numerous values and interests, and for much of the twentieth century these were in close alignment. There is still much on which citizens of the two countries agree. More significantly, there have been repeated efforts to find policies of convergence since the end of the Cold War, even when public support has been lacking. As the US has turned toward a greater use of military initiatives outside of the UN, Canada has often moved alongside the Americans, as for example, Chrétien's willingness to support the bombing of Iraq in 1998, to join NATO's campaign against Kosovo in 1999, and to send Canadian forces to Afghanistan to fight with the Americans in 2002 and again in 2006. John McDougall has written:

Canada was, next to the US, one of the most active bombers of Serbia and contributed ground and naval forces to the American effort against hostile forces in the Afghan campaign. These interventions have to be regarded as departures from the classic peacekeeping model ... and service in them is better regarded as an extension of membership in NATO and Canada's allegiance to the US than as an expression of Canada's traditional UN peacekeeping commitment. (McDougall 2006)

and further that these 'commitments seem to be more about shoring up its partnership with the US than keeping faith with its longstanding tradition of international peacekeeping' (McDougall 2006: 306). The US government's support for such NATO initiatives brings Canada's overseas contributions more in line with the priorities in US foreign policy.[15] While these shifts in security policy were in progress prior to the election of Harper's minority Conservative government in January 2006, this 'me too' approach has been extended into other areas.

Closer to home, the incidents of co-operation have also been common in such areas as border security in December 2001, the trilateral Security and Prosperity Partnership (SPP) of 2005, and the renewal and expansion of NORAD to include a maritime component in 2006. The Harper government has also been inclined to pursue opportunities for bringing Canadian policy into line with that of the US by, for example, abandoning commitments under the Kyoto protocol and pursuing free trade arrangements with Colombia and others. The government's willingness to challenge US unilateralism faded as it has moved closer to American security policy. A perception that Canadian foreign policy was distinctive from that of the US through such practices as UN peacekeeping operations, foreign aid, or human rights, is no longer tenable as policies in these areas are increasingly indistinguishable from those of the US.

These decisions, while generally supportive of US foreign policy objectives, have been defended in part as being consistent with Canada's own interests. For example, in a statement in the House of Commons in 1998, Chrétien defended his government's willingness to join US and British air attacks against Iraq by stating: '[W]e believe that a military strike against Iraq would be justified to secure compliance with Security Council Resolution 687 – and all other Security Council resolutions concerning Iraq.'[16] This has been echoed most recently by Stephen Harper when at the time of Obama's visit to Ottawa in February 2009, he said: 'There is no such thing as a threat to the national security of the US which does not represent a direct threat to this country.' This desire to align Canadian policy with that of the US is based on the assumption that such an alignment will yield benefits in the bilateral relationship, a quick resolution for outstanding trade disputes, and

---

15 See for example, Harvey 2005.
16 Prime Minster Jean Chrétien in the Canadian House of Commons, February 9, 1998.

concessions on border access. A strategy of co-operation not firmly rooted in a strong domestic consensus can only be justified on its effectiveness in securing the desired objectives. As suggested earlier, it is not evident that such objectives have been achieved.

In contrast to these co-operative efforts, and despite occasional objections from Washington, the Canadian government has also sought to pursue its own foreign policy priorities in such areas as UN reform, the establishment of the International Criminal Court, the Ottawa Treaty in support of banning anti-personnel landmines, and promoting such principles as human security and the responsibility to protect (the 'R2P' international security and human rights norm). Such initiatives have at times brought Canadians into conflict with US officials. One of the most sustained challenges occurred over US concerns about insulating American leaders and soldiers on UN peace-keeping operations from the International Criminal Court (ICC). The US even sought to restrict UN peacekeeping operations until US soldiers who might be involved could gain an exemption from the jurisdiction of the ICC. Eventually a compromise was reached in the form of Resolution 1422 which 'provides for a one-year deferral of potential war crimes prosecutions before the ICC against personnel from states which have not ratified the court treaty. As such it is a substantial retreat from the initial US demand for permanent blanket immunity for any US personnel' (Borden 2002). The compromise did not remove Canada's objections or its extreme frustration with US policy. 'Canada's U.N. Ambassador Paul Heinbecker started the session with a warning that the credibility of the council, the legality of international treaties, and the principle that all people are equal and accountable before the law were at stake' (*Associated Press* 2002). One spokesperson for DFAIT was quoted as saying: 'This is a frontal attack on international law and rule of law. The US proposals are unnecessary and Canada urges the Security Council to reject them.'[17] Such cases reflect the divergence between Canadian and US approaches to international law and indicate the increased potential for conflict between them on the global stage. The continued rejection of the ICC by the Obama administration suggests little real change in this area, despite a less harsh rejection of international law by officials in his government. At the same time, the Canadian government's withdrawal from its role as an active promoter of the Court and principles such as R2P suggest a concern for avoiding policies that might further antagonize bilateral relations.

Rare have been the cases where the Canadian government has directly challenged US foreign policy initiatives. That is one reason why the government's decision not to support the US-led invasion of Iraq in the Spring of 2003 came as a surprise to some, like the editors of *The Economist*: 'How could the superpower's neighbour and biggest trading partner be against?' they asked (*The Economist* September 28, 2002). The decision to refuse to support the invasion of Iraq and the subsequent decision to reject participation in the US national missile defence program both demonstrated an ability on the part

---

17 Nancy Bergeron, cited in Edwards 2002.

of the Canadian government to resist US pressures for co-operation in areas that were clearly priorities for the government in Washington. It is clear that both decisions carried some political costs for the Canadian government, as witnessed by the cancellation of high level meetings involving US President Bush and Secretary of State Condoleezza Rice, but there is little evidence that there were substantial long-term effects on the bilateral relationship. Once again, it is as difficult to translate such actions into policies that punished Canadian interests as it is to demonstrate any rewards for supporting US policy initiatives. This would suggest that more involved bilateral issues are governed by a different set of concerns and that there exists a considerable amount of room for independent action on the part of the Canadian government.

What remains less clear is whether close alignment brings any potential to influence the direction of US foreign policy. Burney, for one, has suggested that: '[o]ur commitment and sacrifice in Afghanistan give us unique credibility and relevance in Washington and should be a catalyst for new strategic approaches to North American defence and to global conflict issues where we have common concerns' (Burney 2009: 23–4). It is less than clear that the government has taken advantage of such an opportunity, if in fact it exists. There is little in the US government's actions that suggest any interest in what the Canadian government might contribute to developing policy toward Afghanistan, let alone North American defence or other global conflicts.

At the present juncture, given the tendencies in US foreign policy which, in many respects, challenge and undermine certain core elements of Canada's traditional liberal internationalist foreign policy orientation, and that have not been substantially reversed by the Obama administration despite some rhetorical shifts, Canadian policy officials are confronted with a more difficult environment. Foreign policy options such as supporting international law and working through the UN, that have traditionally been a procedural interest for Canadian policy makers, are not as easily pursued when the US is openly hostile to the institution. The sort of defence of the UN mounted by the Mulroney government in the 1980s is also less likely given the UN's own problems. In response, Drache has argued: 'Disengagement, skepticism, prudential self-interest, building new strategic alliances, and support for international law and the UN offer a constructive alternative in uncertain times' (Drache 2005). The possibility of new strategic alliances raises an interesting option, but it is not clear whether the investment in such an initiative will produce a constructive response or yield any significant benefits. Repeated suggestions on the desirability of enhancing Canada's relations with Mexico have, as suggested in subsequent chapters, yielded little by way of tangible government or private-sector action. The Harper government's bid to launch a new Americas initiative to develop broader ties within the hemisphere may be more successful than earlier efforts, but seems too limited in scope to generate much interest, especially given shifting trends on that continent. In addition to marginal economic benefits from existing and proposed free trade agreements with Chile and Colombia, there is potentially room to pursue broader political interests in areas such as human rights, security, and peace-building if the government wants to give them attention. It could be an opportunity for a distinct Canadian contribution from that of the US, but, and perhaps more likely, it will tend to reinforce an alignment with US interests and policies.

Conclusion

The current state of the bilateral relationship presents a difficult set of challenges for Canadians and their government. Though it remains very significant, Canada's economic dependence on the US has begun to decline. Canadians are still closely tied to the American economy, but they are also increasingly active on a broader global stage. For many it is essential to maintain a close, stable, and friendly relationship with their economic support system, and to reinforce the north–south linkages between the two countries, their economies, and their governments. At the same time, the US has been realigning its foreign policy in ways that increasingly diverge from that of other governments and from the multilateral processes, institutions, and values that Canadians have long supported. Yet given shifts in US policy, the environment is less hospitable to the sort of liberal internationalism that Canada has practiced in the past. We may, as Cox suggests, be at a critical juncture.

> Canadians should reflect now upon the historical options in their national life; the east-west and the north-south orientations towards the world. The north-south perspective pushing towards the so-called big idea in which Canada would be enclosed within a North American strategic and economic bloc, would limit Canada's horizons to one of the three main centres of world power at a time when that centre, the United States, is distancing itself in action and values from much of the rest of the world. Clinging to it would be an act of isolationism inconsistent with the outlook of most Canadians and inconsistent with Canada's potential role in the world. (Cox op.cit.)

In response, many Canadians have voiced concerns about a continued close alignment with US foreign policy. Supporting such values as the development of international law or a more activist UN may bring Canada into conflict with the foreign policy priorities of its southern neighbour. Canadian governments have adopted alternative options in response to US policies in the past and have been able to pursue their own distinct interests without too much damage to the bilateral relationship. The foreign policy options for Canada are not as narrow as sometimes presented and need not create a bilateral conflict.

The question for Canada has to be whether such moves as border security, NORAD renewal, and joint operations in Afghanistan will preclude the motivation for more independent initiatives in multilateral arenas and whether they will enable the government to resist pressure for co-operation in areas such as Iraq, about which Canadian interests and/or values diverge. Alternatively, those advocating for improved relations have been less likely to argue that Canada should change its policies on the oil sands, climate change, or the Arctic Council to appease US policy officials. This would seem to suggest that there is more at play here than simply a matter of appeasing US interests for the sake of good bilateral relations. The shift in aspects of American foreign policy since the 2008 election of the Obama administration and the concomitant response by selected Canadians suggests that one of the primary motivating factors behind much of the concern over the state of bilateral relations was as much about the direction of Canadian national and foreign policy as it was about bilateral relations. Conjuring fears of US retaliation or a deteriorating bilateral relationship are one means for securing policy changes in Canada.

John McDougall has argued that the issue confronting the Canadian government is a divergence between the views on Canadian–US relations held by the public and those held by Canadian economic interests who place a priority on a smoothly functioning bilateral relationship for commercial reasons:

> In sum, there may be more convergence of values taking place across the Canada–US border than most Canadians realize, especially among the business communities of the two countries, and the 'distribution of influence among domestic actors' may be detracting from the capacity of the rest of Canadians to promote politically the kind of future the majority of them wish they could choose. (McDougall op.cit.: 298)

McDougall goes on to suggest that 'Canadians may or may not be pleased to support military action that essentially consolidates existing economic and political power structures, especially if they perceive that such actions promote the interests of the US and its partners in the global economy rather than protect human rights' (Ibid.: 307). Drache shares these concerns when he argues that '[i]f Ottawa is to be a more effective actor globally, it needs to connect with the Canadian public in ways that it has not chosen to do. Increasingly foreign policy will have to reflect the social values of Canadian society, rather than, as in the past, the special interests of business elites'(Drache op.cit.: 130).

The decisions to refuse to participate in the invasion of Iraq and reject support for ballistic missile defences were taken amidst considerable amount of domestic opposition to the American initiatives and at a time when the government was highly vulnerable to such pressures. The persistent concern among Canadians with matters such as sovereignty claims in the Arctic, cultural policy, and, for a time, the Kyoto protocol also suggest support for a more independent approach to foreign policy. Such attitudes suggest that large segments of the Canadian public are concerned about converging with American policies with which they disagree and have some concern for an independent foreign policy for Canada (Bow and Lennox 2008). In the long term it may very well be these Canadians who will need to bring some balance to this special relationship.

Chapter 12

Saying 'NO' to North America: Canadian and Mexican Perspectives

Athanasios Hristoulas[1]

Immediately following the 9/11 attacks, leaders from Canada, Mexico, and the US began talking about security perimeters, NAFTA+, and the European Union of North America. In early October of 2001, Adolfo Aguilar Zínser, the then Mexican National Security Advisor, said that Mexico was working toward 'interdependent security with its NAFTA partners, including more co-ordinated customs procedures and increased intelligence gathering and sharing'. And in early November of 2001, US Ambassador to Mexico Jeffery Davidow told the Mexican press that high-level bi-national meetings scheduled for mid-November between Mexican National Security Adviser Aguilar and US homeland security czar Tom Ridge would focus on ways to create a regional 'security bubble' and the possible 'harmonization' of customs procedures.

Canada, for its part, issued International Policy Statement 2005 (the IPS) which dedicated an entire section to the future role of Canada within the context of North America. The section 'Revitalizing our North American Partnership' signals a shift in emphasis away from a global approach to foreign policy, to a more regionally based one. To be sure, the section privileged the role of the relationship between Canada and the US:

> [T]he bedrock of that partnership is the Canada–U.S. relationship, built upon more than two centuries of close economic, security and personal ties. Over several generations, Canadians and Americans have intermingled through migration, cross-border work and travel, and the exchange of ideas. Our joint achievements – the world's largest bilateral trading relationship and the world's longest demilitarized border – are the envy of the world.[2]

What was interesting about the document, however, was that Mexico was mentioned no less than 12 times. Canadian foreign policy seemed to shift toward closer co-operation not only with the US, but with Mexico as well. 'To ensure continued prosperity and security,' it read, 'Canada needs a more expansive

---

[1] The author would like to thank Julián Castro-Rea and the anonymous reviewer for their helpful comments. All omissions and errors are the responsibility of the author.
[2] See, http://www.dfait-maeci.gc.ca/cip-pic/ips/ips-overview4-en.asp, 10 June, 2006.

partnership with both the United States and Mexico that continues to reflect the unique circumstances of our continent.'³ More notably, the IPS stated that 'Canada will engage more actively with Mexico, bilaterally and trilaterally, to ensure that the North American Partnership is truly continental in character.'⁴ The document also emphasized that there must be increased collaboration with both the US *and* Mexico to protect North American territory and citizens from twenty-first century threats.

Finally, US policy makers spoke of the need to improve co-operation with both Canada and Mexico. George Bush argued that prosperity and security go hand-in-hand:

> [W]e've got a lot of trade with each other and we intend to keep it that way. We've got a lot of crossings of the borders and intend to make our borders more secure and facilitate legal traffic. We've got a lot to do, so we charged our ministers with the task of figuring out how best to keep these relationships vibrant and strong. (Bush, Fox, and Martin 2005)

Condoleezza Rice, speaking as National Security advisor, stated that

> thanks to increasing and increased cooperation after September 11th our efforts to have smart borders, to engage technology and better cooperation, I think we're making progress. But the terrorists are going to keep trying. They're going to keep trying in our southern border. They're going to keep trying in our northern border. And it's just the acknowledgement that we need to make certain that we keep working on this issue.

The apex of this trilateralization frenzy was the signing of the Security and Prosperity Partnership (SPP) in 2005. The leaders declared their desire to 'develop new avenues of cooperation that will make our open societies safer and more secure, our businesses more competitive, and our economies more resilient.'⁵ The calls for enhanced co-operation came not only from government circles, but from the private sector as well. For example, the US Council on Foreign Relations, the Mexican Council on Foreign Relations, and the Canadian Council of Chief Executives released a joint report at the time of the signing of the SPP arguing that 'The governments of Canada, Mexico, and the United States should articulate as their long-range goal a common security perimeter for North America' (Council on Foreign Relations 2005: 8). The report added: "The three governments should strive toward a situation in which a terrorist trying to

---

3   *Ibid.*
4   *Ibid.*
5   SPP. Security and Prosperity Partnership. 2005a. <www.spp.gov/2005_launch.asp.

penetrate our borders will have an equally hard time doing so no matter which country he elects to enter first'[6]

The terrorist attacks would serve as the event that triggered this move toward a more unified North America, but the end result would be three countries bound together not only by economic necessity, but also by a desire to co-ordinate security and political – maybe even social – policy.

Yet now, the North American agenda has changed. The SPP has failed and nobody talks about deep integration any more. Mention of the security perimeter has become taboo. What happened? This chapter seeks to answer that question by looking at Canada–Mexico relations after 9/11 and within the context of North America. First, the chapter will examine the regional security situation. This will help provide context for what follows, which is a discussion on why Canada and Mexico resoundingly said "NO" to North American integration. Finally, the chapter provides a discussion of what the future might bring in Mexico–Canada relations. The central conclusion of the chapter is that very little has changed in the nature of bilateral Mexico–Canada relations since 9/11. This is partly due to the fact that Canada does not see Mexico as a partner in North America and partly the result of the fact that Mexico's attention is almost wholly absorbed by internal problems, namely the war against drug cartels.

The Post-9/11 North American Security Context

The post-9/11 continental security discussions are designed to achieve two interrelated goals. The first, of course, is to free the North American continent of terrorists and terrorist organization and to make sure that terrorists hiding in Canada and Mexico, if any, are captured and/or not allowed to enter the US. Although unrealistic, because terrorist groups are very well embedded within diaspora groups in Canada and the US, to achieve this first anti-terrorist objective a number of proposals have been suggested, which include but are not limited to co-operation in information and intelligence gathering; the transfer of technology; the harmonization of immigration policy; jointly manned US-Mexican and US-Canadian border points; as well as the (possible) interoperability of military and public security forces.

The second objective of continental and border security – one that is much more important to Canada and Mexico – is the free flow of legitimate goods and legitimate business and leisure travel. Here policy makers and analysts alike are examining how mechanisms such as pre-clearance, fast border lanes, and North American travel identity cards can make travel more efficient in a world of 'just-in-time' commercial and industrial delivery.

From a US perspective, continental and border security will deal with perceived security threats emanating from the US's principal trading partners, Canada and

---

6   *Ibid.*

Mexico. Taking Canada first, US public opinion and policy makers alike see the country as a hotbed for terrorist activity. Although exaggerated because none of the 9/11 terrorists entered from Canada, this perception may not be all that far from the truth. Canada is primarily a 'venue of opportunity' to support plan or mount attacks elsewhere. It is estimated by Canadian sources (The Canadian Security and Intelligence Service) that there are at least 50 terrorist groups operating in the country, primarily in the areas of fundraising, planning and execution of terrorist activities elsewhere.

Alternatively, the US concern with respect to Mexico is that the country *might* represent a terrorist threat in the near future. Mexico does not have a large Muslim community where Islamic terrorists can easily 'blend in' as is in the case of multicultural Canada. Yet the fear is that Al Qaeda and other terrorist organizations might somehow reap the benefits of corruption, inefficiency, and archaic investigation techniques present in Mexican immigration, customs and public security forces. A second concern is that terrorist organizations will create strategic alliances with other criminal organizations such as drug dealers and '*polleros*'[7] in order to gain easy access into the US. Finally, a third concern is the porous nature of Mexico's southern border with Guatemala.

In response to these fears, both Canada and Mexico signed border agreements with the US (Canada in late 2001 and Mexico in early 2002). Both agreements outline bilateral mechanisms with regards to border infrastructure in order to secure the flow of goods and people. The agreements also placed special emphasis on the twin principles of co-ordination and information sharing as critical components of a secure common border.[8] Equally important was the meeting between George Bush, Paul Martin and Vicente Fox in 2005 which resulted in the signing of the SPP. According to the SPP web page, currently used merely as a document repository, the 'partnership is a trilateral effort to increase security and enhance prosperity among the three countries through greater co-operation and information-sharing.'[9] Through the formation trilateral cabinet level working groups, the agreement tasked the three countries to

> develop concrete work plans and specific timetables for securing North America and ensuring legitimate travellers and cargo efficiently cross our shared borders; enhancing the competitive position of North American industries in the global

---

7 Literally speaking a *pollero* is someone who transports and sells chickens. *Polleros* is a term referred to those paid individuals who assist Mexican migrants to cross the border. They employ trucks similar to those used for chickens. Further, people are packed in the trucks like cattle.

8 "Security and Opportunity at the U.S.-Canada Border", White House website, June 28, 2002.http://www.whitehouse.gov/news/releases/2002/06/20020628.html.

9 See US government official website Spp.gov.

marketplace; and, providing greater economic opportunities for all of our societies while maintaining high standards of health and safety.[10]

On a more general level, the Conference Board of Canada (2001) has argued that North American security can imply some or all of the following three elements. The first is the enhancement of border efficiency by exploiting more intelligent methods of processing border examinations for both people and cargo. This most basic form of *continental* security would turn the frontiers between Canada and the US and Mexico and the US into 'smart' borders (CBC 2001: 3). The second element involves rethinking the way borders are conceived to begin with. Here, Canada, Mexico and the US law enforcement agencies would work more closely together away from the physical frontiers in order to reduce the need for inspection at the borders themselves. The Conference Board refers to this strategy as moving away from the *Maginot line* of defence mentality to a *defence in depth* philosophy (CBC 2001: 4). A third potential scenario involves the harmonization of immigration and refugee policy, customs clearance, and even national and public security policy in order to remove border inspections altogether. This latter 'Fortress North America' scenario would also include common visa requirements (CBC 2001: 5).

Saying 'NO' to North American Integration

When it comes to global issues, Canada and Mexico can be considered strategic allies. At least with respect to rhetoric, both countries place heavy emphasis on multilateral relations and the peaceful resolution of conflict. Both countries also consider human rights to be pillars of their foreign policies. Further, within the context of the United Nations, both countries have worked closely together to push forward the Human Security agenda as well Security Council reform. Indeed, according to the Canadian Foreign Affairs web site, 'Canada and Mexico share the objectives of peace, order, good government, social and sustainable development, trade and investment liberalization, economic growth, and common prosperity.'[11] Along similar lines, former Mexican President Vicente Fox assured that 'Mexico ... like Canada, makes its voice heard in the most important issues on the international agenda such as the defence of multilateralism and human rights, the respect for international law, the promotion of co-operation to ensure development and peace, together with international security.'[12]

Hal Klepak once suggested that Canada and Mexico were natural 'allies' within the context of North America because of the similarity of their conditions: both were relatively small powers who neighboured a superpower. Given this similarity, Klepak argued that Mexico and Canada were in some sense 'strategic

---

10   *Ibid.*
11   http://www.dfait-maeci.gc.ca/mexico-city/extra/60/partenariat-en.asp.
12   http://envivo.presidencia.gob.mx/?Orden=Leer&Tipo=Pe&Art=9080.

allies' within North American and should therefore work much more closely together (Klepak 1996). There is a good case to be made in favour of Klepak's argument, especially in recent years where the two countries foreign policies have coincided in many areas. However, on a regional (North American) basis, a different reality presents itself. Here, Canada–Mexico bilateral relations have been hurt by a persistent fear on the part of Canadian decision makers that the inclusion of Mexico in the 'North American' agenda is not in the country's best interests. This is not a new phenomenon in Canadian foreign policy: during the negotiations leading up to the signing of NAFTA in 1993 Canadian officials repeatedly tried to torpedo Mexican inclusion fearing that their county could not compete against cheaper products produced in Mexico. More recently, bilateral relations have been hurt by Mexico's war against the drug cartels which entails an almost exclusive focus on the US with respect to foreign relations.

After 9/11, Canadian policy makers tried to differentiate their country from Mexico, arguing that the kinds of security threats present at the Canada/US border were different from those at the Mexico/US border and should therefore be treated separately. While Canada placed emphasis on bilateral US-Canada responses to the 9/11 terrorist attacks, Mexico pursued a trilateral approach, ironically trying to convince US policy makers to treat the country more like Canada. A further area of contention between Canadian and Mexican decision makers was the pace of change in response to 9/11. While Canada preferred an incrementalist piecemeal approach to dealing with the terrorist threat, Mexico wanted what the Mexican Foreign Minister of the time, Jorge Castañeda, called the 'whole enchilada', or a comprehensive renegotiation of the NAFTA agreement to include other areas such as security and migration. And while Canada rejected the idea of a North American Security Perimeter fearing, among other reasons, that it would send a signal to the international community that Canada was 'inside something' and that the rest of world was 'outside', Mexico embraced the perimeter terminology as an ideal starting point. It is the reasons for this divergence in foreign policy between Canada and Mexico that the chapter will now turn to.

A Canadian Perspective

With respect to Canada, early on in the debate over perimeter security (immediately following the 9/11) then Canadian Foreign Minister John Manley highlighted that Canada must be inside any such security perimeter because 87 per cent of the country's exports go to the US. It was, in his words, a 'no-brainer'. Yet in a policy shift, within weeks Canadian officials were arguing against a common continental defence. John Manley later expressed reservations telling a parliamentary committee that the notion that somehow or other Canada can solve a perceived problem by something called a perimeter is 'simplistic'.

One official explanation for this change had to do with Canadian sovereignty. The Chrétien administration began to argue that a common continental defence would adversely affect the right of self-determination of Canadians and their elected officials. Yet sovereignty did not appear to be an issue with respect to Canadian voters at the time. In a poll conducted on 15 October 2001 by Ipsos-Reid, a Canadian polling firm, 70 per cent of Canadians supported jointly manned border posts, 85 per cent believed that Canada should make the changes that are necessary to create a joint North America security perimeter, and 81 per cent said that the two countries should adopt common entry controls in treating refugees and immigrants. The same poll found that 53 per cent of Canadians supported the creation of a Canadian-US security perimeter even if it meant accepting US-made security and immigration policies. Admittedly, this poll was conducted almost immediately after the 9/11 attacks, when Canadians were extremely sensitized (and sympathetic) to the US anti-terrorist plight. Indeed more recent polls have found Canadian public opinion to express strong anti-George Bush feelings. For example, a poll conducted by EKOS in 2003 found that 62 per cent of Canadians believed Bush has made the world less safe since he became president in 2001. Interestingly enough, Canadians found the American president the world's third most dangerous leader, behind North Korea's Kim Jong Il and Osama bin Laden. The first poll does however, highlight the fact that Canadian public opinion was much less sensitive to the issue of sovereignty. Recent polls indicate that Canadians overwhelmingly approve of Barack Obama with an 81 per cent rating for the first African American president.[13] Interestingly, the same poll found that Canadians were worried that Obama might want to renegotiate NAFTA in order to protect American jobs. Although not directly related to the issue of sovereignty, the poll does suggest that Canadians are much more concerned about maintaining friendly economic and political relations with the US rather than defending Canadian sovereign rights.

Irrespective of the aforementioned poll, former Canadian Prime Minister Jean Chrétien remained opposed to doing anything in a dramatic way. In declaratory fashion, Chrétien was reluctant to acknowledge that anything about the relationship was in the process of changing arguing 'we have an excellent relationship with [the US] at this time. There are very few problems' (quoted in Wallace 1999). In operational terms, any notion of a grand vision in terms of re-thinking the relationship was played down. The focus was on ways the two countries could work more closely together to loosen cross-border controls, such as by streamlining and modernizing Canadian and US customs procedures, and routine forms of trade facilitation. In institutional terms, the management of the Canada–US relationship was left to an ad hoc and open-ended process.

Further, any notion of a North American security perimeter was rejected in favour of a series of incremental and piecemeal measures with the focus on the more efficient management of the Canada/US border. Indeed, any explicit endorsement of the phrase security perimeter was explicitly rejected by key

---

13   Canadians feel the love for Obama, but are lukewarm to his plans: poll, http://www.cbc.ca/canada/story/2009/01/18/obama-poll.html#ixzz0uuZcIGRY.

elements of the Liberal government. One problem is that by its tone the concept of a perimeter in the North American context explicitly privileges security over economic/commercial matters. As such it conditions (and legitimizes) a shift in perception – in conceptual terms – that sees the Canada–US relationship deepening through a realist selfhelp model rather than through the vantage point of complex interdependence.

A second problem concerned the image of Canadian foreign policy emanating from this change in focus. Any privileging of the perimeter concept necessitated a clear (and decisive) choice for Canada as to whether the country is either in or out – not only in terms of some forms of domestic harmonization but also in terms of Canada's role/status in the world. To concentrate on a perimeter would send a signal depicting an 'us and them' view of the world.

Another, more important reason for Canada's shift in policy – at least for the purposes of this chapter – had to do with the prospects of Mexico participating in the Perimeter. Bloc Québécois Member of parliament Stéphane Bergeron recognized this when he argued that what seems to bother the Canadian Minister of Foreign Affairs about the idea of continental security is that it would involve Mexico. He then went on to highlight that Canada has everything to gain in seeing the discussions go from bilateral to multilateral because Mexico is a partner of Canada within the context of NAFTA. In a quick and somewhat abrupt response, the then Foreign Minister stated that Canada and Mexico do not share any borders. What Manley was trying to convey at the time was that the issues facing Canada and the US were (and still are) the efficient flow of legitimate goods and travellers within the context of heightened US security concerns. On the other hand, the US/Mexican border was depicted as far more complex, characterized not only by a high level of trade, but also by the existence of illegal migration, drug trafficking and corruption. The negotiation of a trilateral security mechanism would require much more time and the introduction of a third actor – from a Canadian perspective – would unnecessarily delay the entire process or possibly stall it completely. Moreover, 'smart border' technology at the Canada/US border has been in place for a while, predating the terrorist attacks by a number of years. The same was not the case along the Mexican–US border.

Thus, Canada attempted to stick to the status quo. Unenthusiastic about explicit or implicit modes of trilateralism, Canada preferred to deal with the US strictly on a one-to-one basis. By design, therefore, it chose to differentiate itself (both in terms of issues and solutions) from Mexico. While this stance could be justified on technical grounds, it also underscored important symbolic/political factors, which depicted Mexico not so much as partner but as a complicating ingredient in the neighbourhood.

The Stephen Harper government has taken a different approach but with similar results with respect to the construction of a North American community. Harper has increased co-operation with the US at the expense of the relationship with Mexico. The Harper administration extended Canada's main military presence in Afghanistan until 2011, overturning the previous Liberal government's promise to bring the troops back home by the beginning of 2007. At times, Canada had up to 3,000 troops in Afghanistan engaged primarily in combat missions alongside US and other NATO troops.

With specific reference to North America (read 'bilateral relationship'), and in light of the North Korean nuclear tests, Harper's government has reopened the national debate on whether Canada will participate in the US ballistic missile defence program, once again something that the previous Liberal governments had rejected as not being in the country's national interest. If the Harper government decides that Canada will participate in missile defence – and it looks increasingly as though it will – this will require a renegotiation of the bilateral Canada–US NORAD treaty established in 1958.

NORAD monitors and tracks human-made objects in both countries' airspace. It is also tasked with preventing attacks on North American targets by airplanes, missiles, or space vehicles. The NORAD commander is chosen by and is responsible to both the Canadian prime minister and the US president. NORAD is headquartered at the Peterson Air Base in Colorado Springs, Colorado.

The 9/11 attacks produced a structural change in NORAD's organization. The terrorist attacks resulted in NORAD being incorporated in the US Northern Command (NORTHCOM). NORTHCOM's mission is to dissuade, prevent, and confront threats directed against the US, its territories and interests within its area of responsibility. This includes airspace, and land and maritime assets, in the continental US, Alaska, Canada, Mexico, and waters extending out to 500 nautical miles such as the Gulf of Mexico. Canada's role within NORTHCOM is to assist in the defence of airspace as stipulated in NORAD. It is important to note that NORTHCOM is not considered a threat to Canadian sovereignty. Indeed, because NORAD is now part of NORTHCOM, most observers agree that any renegotiation of the treaty will eventually result in closer military co-operation between the two countries not only with respect to air, but also to coastal and territorial defence. According to the Canadian Department of Foreign Affairs web site, 'the (Canadian) government will further develop Canada–US cooperation in other areas, involving other departments, including cooperation on maritime security ... and with regard to border issues.'

Canada and the US had also implemented the Integrated Border Enforcement Team Program (IBETS) at 23 points along the US/Canada border. This binational program permits five security agencies to exchange information and to work together on a daily basis with local, state, and provincial authorities. These agencies co-operate on matters such as national security, organized crime, and other crime committed along the Canada/US border. The agencies involved in IBETS include the Royal Canadian Mounted Police (RCMP), the Canadian Border Service Agency (CBSA), US Customs and Border Protection, the US Bureau of Immigration and Customs Enforcement, and the US Coast Guard.

Canada has also located four Integrated National Security Enforcement Teams (INSETS) in the urban centres of Toronto, Montreal, Vancouver, and Ottawa. The INSETS increase Canada's ability to collect, share, and analyse intelligence gathered by different Canadian security agencies. The INSETS include the RCMP, the CBSA, Citizenship and Immigration Canada (CIC), the Canadian Security Intelligence Service (CSIS), and other local and provincial authorities.

In sum, since Harper, Canada has done quite a bit in terms of constructing a North American community, but at the exclusion of Mexico. Indeed, it would not be inaccurate to say that the Harper government has no real strategy for the Americas outside of the relationship with the US. As a sign of this, Canada's assistance package for Mexico in the area of security adds up to a mere Can$16 million for fiscal year 2010.

A Mexican Perspective

In contrast to Canada's approach, Mexico took steps to politically demonstrate its solidarity with the US following the terrorist attacks. For example, in October of 2001, President Fox stated that Mexico 'considers the struggle against terrorism to be part of the commitment of Mexico with Canada and the US to build within the framework of the North American free trade agreement a shared space of development, well being and integral security' (Wallace 1999). Later that year, Jorge Castañeda, the then foreign minister, said 'Mexico would favour a continental approach to border security issues, extending a North American partnership that already operates at a trade level' (Canadian Press 2002). In the same speech, Castañeda signalled that the Mexican government would prefer to take perimeter security 'as far as possible, but that depends on the Canadians and the Americans.'

The Mexican government saw continental and border security as offering multiple opportunities in the areas of trade, security, migration, and even social development. Similar to Canadian concerns, Mexico worried that enhanced security at the border would hurt trade between the US and Mexico. But Mexico's interests went beyond simply trade. Mexico's strategy had been one of issue 'linkage' or the attempt to trade security for other types of benefits. A first issue of linkage directly related to the expansion of NAFTA to include other non-trade related issues. When Carlos Salinas signed NAFTA in the early 1990s, his administration argued that the trilateral trade agreement would result in the improvement in the standard of living of all Mexicans. Two administrations later, Vicente Fox was under tremendous domestic pressure to deliver on those promises. In the months following the terrorist attacks he repeatedly argued that as long as Mexico is a place where 40 per cent of the population makes less than two dollars a day, US borders will never be secure. The solution was either a migration agreement where the US legally absorbs a substantial number of Mexican migrant workers, or a North American social cohesion program similar to that in existence in the European Union, or preferably both. Taking the idea of linkage even further, Mexican officials even went as far as to argue that it was in the national security interests of the US to legalize the 10–12 million undocumented Mexican workers because it is better to know who they actually are, given the context of homeland defence.

Thus, migration is the key to understanding Mexico's strong support for continental security and the perimeter agenda. The hope on the part of Mexican decision makers was that by giving the US what they want in security positive effects would spill over into other areas of greater concern to Mexico. Yet in practical terms, Mexico only required the support of the US. 'Canada needs to be part of integration process', argued Gerónimo Gutierrez, the under-secretary of state for North American affairs in an informal discussion with the author of this chapter. '[F]or purely political reasons: it will be easier to sell it to Mexican public opinion.' For Mexican decision makers, border security is North America's equivalent to the European Coal and Steel Community. Canada's attitude was, understandingly, 'fair enough, but what's in it for us?' In that respect, Mexican decision makers saw Canada's continental security posture as disappointing, exclusionary, and even contrary to the long-term interests of Mexico. However, even though Mexico pursued its grand North American strategy politically, internal political issues prevented the country from implementing its policy. Mexico cannot keep up, either politically or operationally, with the changes in North America. Taking as examples the twin border agreements signed in late 2001 between Canada and the US and in early 2002 between Mexico and the US, it goes without saying that the Canada–US version is much more comprehensive in nature. Those areas of the Canada–US border agreement that focus on harmonization and co-operation – such as pre-clearance, joint training and exercises, integrated intelligence, and The Integrated Border Enforcement Teams (IBETS)[14] – simply do not appear in the Mexican–US version of the agreement.

A further three interrelated factors combined to limit the ability of Mexico to fulfil the promises made by President Fox immediately after 9/11:

The first obstacle is the capacity of the Mexican government to respond to the perceived threat. Beyond the fact that Mexico is a developing nation and by definition has less capacity than its other two North American partners, the US-driven criminalization of certain transactions (narcotics and labour markets) has radically altered the nature of corruption in Mexico and has also magnified the size of this problem, weakening in turn the institutional capacity of the State. The criminalization of these transactions rests at the heart of the problem of corruption and ultimately explains the difficulties recurrently faced in US–Mexico efforts at law enforcement co-operation.

---

14 According to Royal Canadian Mounted Police web page, http://www.rcmp.ca/security/ibets_e.htm, the IBETS program "is a multi-faceted law enforcement initiative comprised of both Canadian and American partners. This bi-national partnership enables the five core law enforcement partners involved in IBETS to share information and work together daily with other local, state and provincial enforcement agencies on issues relating to national security, organized crime and other criminality transiting the Canada/US border between the Ports of Entry (POE)."

Corruption in Mexico is now fundamentally driven by the drug trade, and the drug trade is in turn propelled by a widely promoted and enforced US policy of conceptualizing the drug trade as a threat to US national security. This has essentially externalized and placed the burden of the drug trade on other states such as Mexico and Colombia, when in fact it should also be viewed as an internal public health problem. Moreover, the price of drugs has increased dramatically because of this externalization policy, and this has made it a highly profitable endeavour for those willing to participate in the illicit market, further contributing to the corruption problem. Indeed, it is estimated that at least 250,000 Mexicans are involved in the drug trade with profits approaching US$5 billion annually (Aguayo 2008).

Second, the six years of President Fox's administration were characterized by intense political infighting between different ministries. In other words, intense interagency competition existed at the crucial moment when Mexico was deciding how it would pursue North American security co-operation. Combined with the fact that the Mexican Congress was (and still is) deeply divided, this led to a situation in which the country's leaders simply could not make any decisions of a substantial nature. The implications of this problem were fairly obvious: much of the decision-making structure of the State was heavily permeated by this personal and institutional competition. For all intents and purposes, it would not be inaccurate to state that the effect of this fragmentation was that President Fox essentially muddled through his presidency.

A classic example of this muddling through is the case of Mexico's national security strategy after the 2000 general election. When President Fox came into office, he tried to formalize the national security agenda of the country by creating the nation's first national security presidential advisor. The move signalled an attempt to develop a coherent national security doctrine that would rationalize the different agencies that were in charge of intelligence, which at last count included the Center for Intelligence and National Security (CISEN), Naval Intelligence, Army Intelligence, the Attorney's General's office (PGR), the Federal Preventative Police (PFP) and finally, the Federal Investigative Agency (AFI).

The president's policy failed because the national security advisor chosen, Adolfo Aguilar Zínser, was extremely unpopular with the agencies involved (he had previously been a senator from a left-leaning party). Indeed, Zínser's access to the intelligence community was purposely limited not only by CISEN (who didn't want him there because they saw him as a direct threat) but also by other intelligence agencies. Ultimately, the national security adviser left for a diplomatic post in New York, and more significantly, the President decided that no replacement was needed. In an ironic decision, Fox decided to formally name himself his own national security advisor. This decision was telling because Fox did not wish to appoint another individual who might create further problems. Thus, political infighting between the above-noted agencies as well as Fox's disinterest in the subject essentially doomed real restructuring of national security doctrine and intelligence services. The net effect of the national security advisor fiasco was that no clear mandate for Mexico's intelligence agencies was created.

If Mexican officials have a hard time dealing with one another, the situation along the northern border is even worse. Few, if any mechanisms for co-operation and communication exist between the authorities of both countries: both Mexican and US officials have deeply entrenched trust issues. Little communication and information sharing exists between the two sides. 'U.S. law enforcement officials often find themselves in frustrating situations, unable to deal with the inefficiency that often characterizes Mexican officials, while Mexican authorities are overly sensitive to U.S. unilateralism, and lack the technical expertise to foment the kinds of cooperative mechanisms that exist along the Canada–U.S. border' (Shirk 2002). The end effect is that 'no security confidence' exists along the US/Mexican border, and as argued by David Shirk, 'bi-national cooperation is typically focused on reducing cross border interagency irritants and misunderstandings rather than on coordinated operations, and while occasionally stronger at the local level of inter-agency cooperation, it tends to vary from place to place and time to time' (Shirk 2002).

The final obstacle is the use of nationalism and sovereignty by Mexican political actors to pursue their personal agendas. The recently signed bilateral Mérida Initiative (MI) serves as an example: The plan provides for US assistance to Mexico to fight drug cartels. 'While President Felipe Calderon's government has pursued US assistance, opposition politicians have argued the aid package would violate Mexico's sovereignty and polls show most Mexicans oppose the help. Calderon's political opponents have railed against the aid package, many to make political hay' (Schwartz 2007).

With the signing of the MI between Mexico and the US in 2007, Mexico has wholeheartedly placed its security emphasis on the US, at the exclusion of Canada. The MI is considered a turning point in bilateral US–Mexico relations. It is the first time the US has provided such a substantial sum of military and police assistance to Mexico. (Prior to the MI, Mexico would receive an average of US$30 million in assistance from the US through the International Narcotics Control and Law Enforcement agency.) Moreover, the level of co-operation between Mexican and US authorities, specifically in the area of training, is unprecedented. Indeed, more than an assistance package, 'the Mérida Initiative should be seen as a central element in a broader strategy of growing co-operation between the US and Mexico to address a shared threat presented by organized crime' (Selee 2008). Along similar lines, others have argued that the MI 'can serve as an important element in building confidence and cooperation between the two countries' (Olson 2008).

The agreement is designed to provide Mexico the sum of US$1.4 billion over a three-year period beginning in 2008. The initiative provides assistance in equipment, technology, and training for Mexico without a significant US military footprint in the country. Forty per cent of the money will be used to purchase fixed- and rotary-wing aircraft designed to facilitate interdiction and rapid response. The rest is for inspection equipment.

The final nail in the coffin of Mexico's plan for a trilateral North American security arrangement was the failure to obtain a migration deal from the US. This long-sought objective probably died as early as 2001, even before the 9/11 attacks. Mexico's president at the time proposed the so-called "whole enchilada", or a comprehensive expansion of NAFTA to include a social and political agenda that went far beyond the economics of North American co-operation. The plan was viewed as overly ambitious by Washington at the time, and probably politically impossible given the mood in congress. By 2007, the ambitious plan officially failed when the US Senate decided that there would no longer be any further debate on a comprehensive migration agreement.

Final Thoughts

The smart border agreements signed in 2001 and 2002 are indicative of the nature of North American security co-operation. Security relations in North America are likely to continue being disjointed and bilateral in nature. The North American security perimeter seemed to be an option when there was at least a minimal perception of a common security interest, namely, immediately following 9/11. The ten years since the attacks have shown that common perception has dissipated. Indeed, the findings presented in this chapter suggest that there is no inherent reason for the three North American partners to co-operate in a more enhanced manner, particularly in the area of security. As argued, Canada and Mexico have very different security concerns.

Canada's North American security focus does not go south of the Rio Grande, and to a great extent the country's decision makers are preoccupied with the war in Afghanistan. For its part, Mexico believed that the trilateralization of the war against terror would lead to other benefits, such as North American deep integration, but given the failure of that project for reasons discussed above, Mexico has reenergized its bilateral security relationship with the US within the context of the Mérida Initiative process.

The US, a country not discussed in this chapter, probably has the least 'North American' focus today. To the north, it worries about the potential terrorist threat coming from Canada's generous refugee and immigration laws. To the south, it worries about drugs and illegal immigrants in that order. When combining the interests of the three NAFTA partners together, we therefore see a multitude of security interests in the region with little potential for overlap. The business of North American security co-operation is, therefore, unlikely to evolve beyond the present status quo.

Chapter 13
A Critique of Mexico–US Relations: Beyond the Contemporary Impasse

Raymond A. Morrow

Introduction

The North–South Frontier: Beyond Official Discourses

Though the preceding two articles on intergovernmental relations provide instructive insights, they share a crucial limitation that reflects a widespread tendency: the assumption that Mexico can be treated comparatively – without strong qualifications – as a 'consolidated' liberal democratic state in the sense that is valid for the US and Canada. Tom Keating does not need to deal with this question because of his focus on a comparison of Canada and the US. The discussion of Mexican–Canadian relations, on the other hand, for rather different reasons does not adequately address the profound significance of the fact that as a form of society or social formation Mexico is qualitatively different, with profound implications for the nature of its politics. Nevertheless, in focusing on security issues, Athanasios Hristoulas can justifiably focus on intergovernmental relations relatively independently of the question of deeper differences. The precariousness of the assumption that Mexico is just another 'formal democracy' was implied by Obama's appointment of Carlos Pascual – an expert on 'failed states' – as the new ambassador to Mexico. As all concerned hastened to clarify, this appointment did not mean that Mexico was actually considered to be a failed state, a term more applicable to some post-Communist regimes.

To be sure, defenders of the current regime in Mexico have been particularly disturbed by questioning Mexico's status as an 'equal' partner in NAFTA and a legitimate modern democratic state. For example, writing in a *New York Times* article, the noted historian and commentator Enrique Krauze made the case against the increasing perception in the US that Mexico might 'fall apart':

> But since 2000, when the opposition National Action Party won the presidency, power has been decentralized. There is much greater independence in the executive, legislative and judicial branches of government. An autonomous Federal Electoral Institute oversees elections and a transparency law has been passed to combat corruption. We have freedom of expression, and electoral struggles between parties of the right, center and left. Our national institutions

function. The army is (and long has been) subject to the civilian control of the president; the church continues to be a cohesive force; a powerful business class shows no desire to move to Miami. We have strong labor unions, good universities, important public enterprises and social programs that provide reasonable results. Thanks to all this, Mexico has demonstrated an impressive capacity to overcome crises, of which we've had our fair share.[1]

The superficiality of each of Krauze's assertions as half-truths would be readily apparent to less ideologically apologetic experts who might make counter points such as the following: A small degree of political decentralization has been followed by re-centralization in the name of a war against organized crime and other crises. The Federal Electoral Institute has been increasingly called into question because of blatantly partisan and inconsistent decisions. Formal increases in electoral and press freedom have been accompanied by waves of political assassinations, including the murder of 57 journalists from 2000 through to 2009 (DPA 2009). To the extent that major institutions function, they do so in a crippled and often problematic form. The president's control of the military saw federal power used to undermine human rights in zones marked by drug conflicts, and criminalize social protest in the name of anti-terrorism. The Church has played an increasingly reactionary role, suppressing its critical wing (for example, the former Bishop Ruiz in Chiapas). The business classes are surrounded by private security forces and significant numbers have fled the country for fear of kidnapping. Labour unions have become progressively weakened and remain extensively corrupt and subjected to increasing abuses by business, as a number of recent court cases have shown. Aside from a few 'good universities' with research capabilities (most notably UNAM, rated in the top 100 in the world, and the rather small Colegio de México) and several others with respectable programs, the overall system of higher education has abysmally low standards and rates of participation, starvation wages for the vast majority of professors, and virtually no research. Moreover, all of the indices for inequality, health and education compete with Turkey for the bottom rankings of the OECD. None of Mexico's economic, social, or political 'crises' has been 'overcome' – aside from a formal 'democratic transition' with the election of non-PRI presidents – beyond the fact of the sheer survival of the Mexican nation-state. Many of these assertions will be documented in the pages that follow.

This chapter will not argue that Mexico is a failed state in the technical sense, but that it is a chronically failing, unconsolidated democratic state that has not managed to create a substantively adequate rule of law – or level of public standards in areas such as health and education – that satisfies even the minimal requirements

---

1 Krauze 2009. All citations from *La Jornada* can be obtained by date under the heading of "Servicios" under "Ediciones anteriores" at http://www.jornada.unam.mx/.

A Critique of Mexico–US Relations: Beyond the Contemporary Impasse   233

for a modern democratic society.[2] Though the State retains overall control, it does so from a position of increasing weakness and declining legitimacy. Nor does the Mexican state have any reasonable prospect of fundamentally overcoming these problems in the near future, given the bottleneck of contradictions that plague it from effectively linking a process of democratic consolidation with economic and social transformation. It will be argued that a candid recognition of this situation is the necessary foundation for understanding the larger context of Mexico–US relations, a theme that will be later used to identify some possible strategies to break the current impasse.

For those who may not be fully aware of the current situation, it is instructive to begin with several recent examples to illustrate the current tense relations between Mexico and the US that date from the Bush administration but will not disappear magically with Obama. The following kinds of tensions should not be surprising, given that the 3,000-km frontier between these two countries not only represents the greatest income differences across borders in the world (a ratio of around 8:1, enhanced by the extremity of the inequality), but also provides a dramatic example of the North–South divide in an increasingly gated world (Cunningham 2004):

- Approximately 2 million Mexicans illegally migrated to the US during the Fox administration from 2000 to 2006, bringing the total of undocumented Mexicans to more than 10 million with many estimates running much higher – nearly 60 per cent of illegal 'aliens' (Brooks 2005). Of the Mexicans, 38 per cent are now estimated to be from marginal indigenous areas (La Jornada de Oriente 2003). In the process, more than 2,000 Mexicans have died (more than 437 in 2007), and the cumulative total is now more than 10 times the tally of the infamous Berlin Wall (Brooks 2007, Román 2007). Though economic crisis in the US and stricter border vigilance has reduced the rate of flow, the basic situation remains the same in the Calderón administration.
- In February 2004, 1,500 soccer fans in Zapopan, Jalisco booed the *Star-Spangled Banner* and US players in a soccer match and repeatedly chanted, 'Osama! Osama! Osama!' The surprising part was that the game was against Canada. A later Mexico–US Olympic trial game in Guadalajara produced (less surprisingly) similar results. The tone of the resulting blogging frenzy on the US side is expressed by one single comment: 'Seal the borders with shoot to kill orders' (Little Green Footballs 2006).
- Beginning in July 2005, a small but vocal network of groups calling themselves the Minutemen began unofficial, vigilante border patrols in Arizona and California in search of undocumented migrants. Even though largely outnumbered by the anti-Minutemen groups who have confronted

---

2   With respect to law, see Rios and Shirk 2007. The weaknesses of other public institutions are discussed and often documented throughout this chapter.

them, the Minutemen have gained wide publicity and stirred up potentially violent and racist anti-Mexican sentiments.
- In early February of 2006, a business delegation of 16 Cubans was expelled from the Sheraton María Isabel hotel as part of an extra-territorial demand by the US to conform to the Helms-Burton sanctions against Cuba – without any official Mexican government protest.
- Finally, in the fall of 2007 the US passed legislation calling for the criminalization and expelling of illegal immigrants and the construction of an 1,100-km-long wall to keep out Mexican immigrants.

Though having a much longer history (Meyer 2001), such recent incidents point to the deeper conflicts between Mexico and the US that are obscured in official reports and mainstream journalism. Though political polarization makes such issues more visible in the US (even if the protagonists talk past one another), in Canada there is limited awareness of the realities of Mexico. To be sure, such issues have drawn some attention since several recent high-profile cases of Canadians confronted with the inadequacies of the Mexican justice system and the failure of the federal government to intervene effectively.

The first visit to the US of the new Mexican president Felipe Calderón, in early 2007, illustrates the fragile underpinnings of his claim that, following in the footsteps of his PAN predecessor Vicente Fox, he is making Mexico 'the best place in the world' to invest. His upbeat talk at Harvard University provides a standard list of ostensible accomplishments and goals that wither under closer examination (Walker 2008).

For example, he takes personal pride in having initiated the planting of 250 million trees – one quarter of the UN world goal for the year. However, closer examination reveals that though official estimates assumed a 50 per cent survival rate, even the environment minister has belatedly admitted that the survival rate would be closer to 10 per cent (Greenpeace México 2008). Not surprisingly, the program has been rejected on scientific and sociological grounds by both Greenpeace and forestry experts who argue that the money is misallocated because it does not provide support to communities for sustainable forestry, primarily serves local partisan interests, and distracts attention from failures across the environmental spectrum, such as making significant headway against deforestation that is fifth highest in the world, and given the fact that half of lumber production is illegal (Enciso 2008).

Calderón also claimed (at least before the economic crisis in the fall of 2008) there had been a significant reduction of extreme poverty, a suggestion based in part on dubious government statistical procedures that have been highly criticized.[3]

---

3 Criticism of official poverty statistics has been extensively developed in the writings of Julio Boltvinik at the Colegio de México; for a good summary, see Julio Boltvinik and Araceli Damián, "Derechos humanos y medición oficial de la pobreza en México," *Papeles de Población* enero-marzo, número 35 (2003).

Furthermore, such assertions gloss over the fact that more than half the population lives in 'ultra' poverty and that Mexican gains have been among the lowest in Latin America (Amador and Brooks 2007). Indeed, as one government-sponsored study has suggested, only 18 per cent of Mexicans have the means for fully adequate living standards, relegating the other 82 per cent to various categories of poverty (Enciso 2009).

Listeners were also presented with the absurd future projection of achieving universal health care within the five years left in his regime. What Calderón failed to point out was that the public system is in chronic economic crisis and disorganization linked with spending the lowest per cent of GNP in Latin America, and that more than half the employed are in the informal economy (58.7 per cent) and only about a third of workers are enrolled in the national system of social security (Cardoso 2010). Calderón's dubious claim about universal medical coverage is based on the expansion of a relatively new program, *Seguro Popular*, aimed at the very poor. Yet the untrustworthy official statistics suggest that even including the expansion of *Seguro Popular*, 18 per cent of the population remains completely outside the public health system.[4] But this figure is not only contested; it also ignores that this plan does not cover many major and chronic illnesses and is crippled by a lack of staff and resources. Since only 3 per cent have private insurance and the public system is avoided by those who can, at all levels of society people borrow large sums of money to pay for private care in emergencies, with the result that 55 per cent of health costs are covered out of the pockets of private individuals (Gómez Mena 2004). Symptomatically, the numerous perks for highest-level government officials include comprehensive private health insurance, thus bypassing the government health plan for public employees.

Mexico falls at the bottom of Organisation for Economic Co-operation and Development reports in virtually all areas, including education. While Calderón admits (by omission) that the quality of education remains a major problem, he fails to note that the middle classes who can afford it have abandoned the public system, thereby reinforcing the process of deterioration, and that his election was due in part to the support of the corrupt, autocratic leader of the national teacher's union.

Though viewed as a 'right-wing' president with conservative Catholic affiliations in the Latin American context, Calderón explicitly denies being a 'neoliberal'. Perhaps he has a semantic point, in part because in Mexico the exercise of ritualistic, cosmetic state-symbolic action is necessary for legitimation, a manipulative process that works in a nation of non-readers and a media system where newspaper and TV news production is dominated by the traditional elites. As part of a statistical pseudo-consensus based on an informal PAN and PRI alliance, Calderón perhaps stands in 'the middle of the road', *but one leading nowhere*, given the context of the constraints of NAFTA, his weakness in a disputed election

4   Such government claims have been seriously challenged by critics, e.g., Laurell 2010, Velasco 2009.

marred by corruption, the deterioration of domestic middle- and small-scale production, declining manufacturing employment, flat and more recent declining, per-capita growth, and the very limited degree to which tax and pension reforms will confront the looming intensification of the fiscal crisis of the Mexican state.[5] The war against organized crime has served as a classic diversion tactic.

Interpretive Perspectives: The Agenda

The present analysis stands outside the stand-off between the US and Mexico, taking a neutral position on a complex set of disputes that, it will argued, cannot be dealt with or resolved within the presuppositions and policies of the existing political elites. The Obama administration implicitly acknowledges the depth of the problem (now exacerbated by high unemployment) by not yet taking action on migration reform – to the dismay of Latino groups. The rest of this chapter will be developed around a longer-term diagnosis of the current standoff. Theoretically, a reflexive conception of critical social theory will inform the empirical analysis of social and political contradictions (Morrow 1994). Descriptively, the central theme of the resulting discussion can be conveyed in the melodramatic language of a Western B-movie. US–Mexican relations could be described in terms of the evocative metaphors of the 'spaghetti Westerns' portraying a southwest frontier where the stark distinction between good and evil, the good guys and the bad guys, dissolves into the murky distinction between 'the good, the bad, and the ugly'. On both sides of the border, defensive nationalisms, political contradictions, and self-serving platitudes have fuelled hatred and anxieties that only reinforce the difficulties of the current situation.

The first section will argue that classical 'realist' theories of international relations and neoliberal theories of globalization have helped create the current situation and provide little prospect for meaningful alternatives, especially from the perspective of those who bear the burden of its tragic consequences. In the process, the discussion will introduce a critical social theory of international relations and globalization as an alternative framework for analyzing these border disputes and the underlying social and cultural transformations they involve.

The second section, in applying this framework, will argue that the origins and persistence of the bad and the ugly can be identified with two intersecting systems of hegemony: US dominance at the inter-nation level, and within Mexico an internal system of hegemonic classes that largely complements this relation of dependency, even as the State publicly claims autonomy in the name of national interests. Further, it will be concluded that these relations will tend to reproduce their inhumane and unjust consequences over time without fundamental changes, even with the change of governing parties in the US. The resulting 'impasse

---

5   For extensive documentation of the failure of economic and social policy, see Cordera and Cabrera Adame 2008.

thesis' will argue that the existing crisis will persist indefinitely despite efforts at resolution within the logic of the present structural situation.

The final section will turn to potential alternatives to the bad and the ugly: to *the potential good* – to the longer-term emergent possibilities and transformative outcomes. Beyond its analysis of the structural contradictions of the current impasse, a critical social theory perspective attempts to shed new light on ways of thinking beyond the current deadlock of Mexico–US relations and its consequences for the millions who suffer from its effects on both sides of the border. Such considerations will require a shift of focus from the effects of the current structure of relations to the possibilities of agency, both actual and potential, especially on the part of non-state actors, as well as of normative considerations relating to justifications of the values of what 'ought' to be in 'the good (global) society'.

International Relations Theory and Globalization: Foundations for Rethinking Mexico–US Relations

Introduction: Debates in International Relations Theory

The preceding descriptive analysis has already begun to introduce some theoretical arguments that now need to be made more explicit. How can we reflect in more theoretical terms on making sense of the origins and future transformations of the border and immigration question and the on-going failure of the neoliberal Mexican model of development? The topic of Mexico–US relations can be analyzed at the intersection of two diffuse theoretical traditions that dominate current discussions. The oldest is that of international relations, a field dominated by political scientists and historians. The other, which emerged during the last three decades, is associated with the problematic of globalization and has been defined by several disciplines. A position on these issues will be briefly developed in this section to justify the perspective that will be used in the more analytical and constructive part of this chapter.

The classic polarization in international relations theory has been between so-called realism and its opposites, which have taken diverse forms characterized as idealistic and humanitarian. The point of departure of realism is that unlike the hierarchical, organized relations within societies, the relations among societies take the form of anarchic international relations with a focus on the capacities of states. Accordingly, states must exercise their sovereignty to make their basic interests and security the most fundamental goal of foreign policy, even if this runs against high-minded but unrealistic goals of international community and universal rights. Similarly, related neoliberal forms of globalization theory (or the ideology of 'globalism') offer another form of determinism based on the status quo that defines itself as the 'objective reality' to which we simply have to passively adapt. In the case of Mexico, this supposed imperative takes the form of accepting the necessity of accommodating to the official US vision of hemispheric 'solidarity' based on free trade, truncated forms of democracy, and the US hegemonic economic model. Such theoretical perspectives underpin the official policy discourse that defines relations between the US and Mexico.

In contrast, anti-realists – in the classical form of an idealistic liberalism – have contended that through education and the establishment of global institutions based on universal principles of solidarity, the anarchy of international relations can be overcome. The chronic failure of classical humanitarian internationalism and related forms of liberalism is that they do not adequately take into account the socioeconomic and structural conditions that make possible the extension of international co-operation and integration. In this respect, the realists have an important point in labelling such policies as idealistic and unworkable. At the same time, however, realists can also be criticized for simply taking the existing relations of power and interest as 'given' without any concern for longer-term fundamental re-structuring of relations within and between states.

As has often been pointed out, the future of the integration of the Americas of the north is confined to three options: First, a move toward closer relations going beyond free trade, of the type suggested by the European Union, championed by the early Fox administration, and cautiously explored by a wide variety of academics (Earle and Wirth 1995, Vargas Suárez, Gómez Arnau and Castro Rea 2001). The events of 9/11, the escalation of reaction against Mexican migrants, and now the domestic economic crisis make the US increasingly resistant to this option. Furthermore, there is little support or motivation for Canada to seek closer US ties. The second option is a retreat of the US to a 'fortress America' that includes a wall on the Mexico/US border and the further escalation of cross-border controls and economic protectionism. The most likely future option, even with the election of Obama, is an unstable status quo driven by the cycles of US domestic politics, and calls for reform that will remain cosmetic. At best, something resembling the earlier McCain–Kennedy bi-partisan migration proposal may eventually help relieve the hardship of many of the current undocumented immigrants, without really touching on larger issues. The biggest danger is the US tendency to identify Mexican reform with a simplistic process of 'Americanization', thus reinforcing a limited (polyarchal) elitist process of democratization that has little prospect of confronting the contradictions of Mexican development (Robinson 1996).[6] Instead, it will be argued that the contradictions within Mexico can only be confronted with a deeper process of democratization that in the longer run would create a new, more stable, and mutually rewarding foundation for Mexico–US relations.

Implications of Critical Social Theory

At the beginning of the 1980s, various alternatives to the opposition between realism (along with its neoliberal siblings) and classical humanitarian liberalism

---

6 In neo-Gramscian terms these adjustments reflect a "passive revolution" that restructures the mode of accumulation and its relation to the state; see Morton 2003.

began to emerge in international relations theory, a tendency reinforced by discussions of globalization in terms of theories of 'cosmopolitan democracy'. More recently, these more sociological alternatives to traditional liberalism have been grouped together under the heading of 'constructivist' theories of international relations. Though this term has been used rather inconsistently, it refers broadly to social theories of international relations that attempt to view the social construction of the international system much as one would analyze the construction of societies. In rejecting the classic realist assumption of international anarchy, it is argued that depending on the context, many forms of international society and community are already in existence. Such social forms have been widely discussed in relation to globalization research under the heading of such terms as global community, regional blocs, and transnational civil society. The confusing aspect of constructivism in international relations theory is that social theory itself has become defined by inter-paradigmatic differences, so there are bewildering variations among constructivist perspectives with respect to the dimensions of social inquiry.

The focus here will be on forms of constructivism associated with the often confusing label of 'critical theory'. Though largely marginalized in the elite international relations programs in the US, such discussions have been extensively developed elsewhere. Critical theory in this international relations literature has had three main associations: (1) the 'neo-Gramscian theory' of hegemony initiated in the work of Robert W. Cox; (2) the 'critical theory' initially associated with the Frankfurt School tradition but later transformed by the German theorist Jürgen Habermas and many others; and (3) the diverse 'critical' perspectives of various strands of feminist, poststructuralist, and postmodernist thinking. For the purpose at hand, the term 'critical social theory' will be used to designate an implicit alliance of approaches that is broader than the Frankfurt tradition, but not so inclusive as to directly incorporate poststructuralist and postmodern tendencies with often rather different deconstructive concerns. As social theory, such critical social theory has an empirical and explanatory dimension concerned with the historical origins of contemporary realities in the contradictions of contemporary capitalism and its relation to democracy. And it is 'critical' in the double sense of methodological (post-positivist) reflexivity in social science and addressing normative questions about values and social justice.

From the perspective of such a critical social theory, the neo-Gramscian approach to international relations and globalization can be viewed as generally complementary to the more normative and metatheoretical approaches associated with Habermas and others.[7] The discussion will follow in the path of those who have argued that the form of critical social theory proposed by Habermas provides the most helpful general framework for incorporating the issues of agency and ethics with empirical themes of political economy and cultural hegemony introduced by the neo-Gramscians such as Robert W. Cox, as well as potentially

---

7   For an example this form of hybrid critical social theory, see Neufeld (2001).

responding to issues relating to gender, difference and Eurocentrism raised by the third position.[8] The task of the rest of this essay will be to suggest how a critical theory of international relations and globalization might be used to inform thinking about the longer-term transformation of Mexico–US relations.

The US-Mexican Case: Two Theses on Structure and Agency

To simplify discussion, the analysis will be conceived in terms of two interrelated arguments about structure and agency. The structural argument will draw indirectly on neo-Gramscian theory and take the form of what will he called the 'impasse thesis based on the reproduction of US/Mexican border relations': given the current constellations of economic interests, dominant political discourses, and political regimes, there is an ongoing social reproduction of the status quo. This process will not only reinforce the internal hegemony of the dominant political classes in Mexico, it will also continue to sustain American hegemony and the suffering of those impacted by globalization from below represented by undocumented migration.

The agency argument will draw primarily upon the forms of critical social theory associated with Habermas, David Held, and others, and give particular attention to the construction of normative dialogues and forms of transnational civil-society networking that are distinct from state-centred forms of analysis. This agency argument will be referred to as 'the transformative thesis based on envisioning some of the conditions of possibility of longer-term possibilities' that might push the current border impasse based on American hegemony in new directions. A key aspect of this argument is that while it is grounded in awareness of the structural realities that characterize the current situation, it also attempts to take into account the possibilities that are already implicit or latent – immanent – within the existing paradigm as part of facilitating and nurturing them through social research and communicative practices.

Intersecting Hegemonies and the Impasse Thesis

Historical Introduction

The rhetoric of the NAFTA agreement has created the widespread illusion of the collaboration of three equal partners who, as modern democratic nation-states, have embarked on an immensely successful project of economic co-operation based on free trade. In this context, the Fox and Calderón administrations have embraced a policy of proactive, bi-lateral negotiation with the US that has been viewed as

---

8 For a defense of Habermasian critical social theory against Marxist critics, see Linklater (1990). Critical theory can also be adapted to include questions relating to poststructuralism, postmodernism and gender as suggested by Fuat Keyman (1997).

part of a new era of co-operation oriented toward mutual benefits (Bondi 2004). In contrast to such up-beat views, the evidence after more than a decade (to be discussed later) reveals that Mexico has in fact lost ground, especially relative to other Latin American countries. The initial argument here will be that one simply cannot understand the nature of current Mexico–US relations without taking into account the following two complicating factors beyond the divisive effects of competing nationalisms, despite a significant erosion of Mexican nationalism in its traditional forms: (1) the overwhelming bi-lateral dominance of the US within a hegemonic relation, hence the difficult negotiating position of Mexico confronted with the post-9/11 'homeland' crisis of the US; and (2) how Mexican hegemonic elites have maintained political power through two sustaining myths: an ideological interpretation of the theory of 'democratic transition' that concludes that the regime change defined by the end of PRI domination marks the beginning authentic democracy (as embodied in the Fox and Calderón regimes), and that NAFTA has catapulted Mexico into a new era of modernization, sustained growth, and poverty reduction, even though certain limited taxation and legal reforms are necessary (and sufficient) for consolidating this process.

US Hegemony: Irresponsible versus Visionary Power

In the case of Latin America, the historical record casts some doubt on the capacity of the US to engage in the responsible use of power, given its hegemonic aspirations (Slater 2004). Many social scientists avoid the term hegemony because of its provocative connotations and its association with the Marxist tradition, even though it is now employed by a variety of social theories. In political science, the cosmetic term 'asymmetric interdependence' is now often used, often evasively, instead of hegemony to describe such relations. Nevertheless, some authors may be more candid – to cite one example:

> [T]his structural asymmetry has given Washington significant policy leverage over its immediate neighbours, leaving them with limited space to manoeuvre. Here the United States largely sets the policy agenda and narrows the room for autonomous policy choices. In this precarious context, Canada and Mexico are like two scared mice next to a neurotic elephant. (Andreas 2003)

From the point of view of the mice, of course, this indeed sounds a lot like an abusive hegemonic relation.

In the present context, one could point to a number of issues that are ongoing topics of official debate in Mexico–US relations in the agenda set primarily on the US side: border water rights disputes; the Plan Puebla-Panamá that would open the door to transnational capital in southern Mexico and Central America through infrastructure construction; policies toward the supposed security threats represented by Castro in Cuba and Chávez in Venezuela; and issues relating to NAFTA, border security, drug trafficking, and undocumented migration to the US.

But it is these last three – security, drugs, and migration – that are actually widely recognized as dominating the current agenda. In the post-9/11 era there has been an increasing tendency to conflate all three of these under the heading of security, raising questions about the coherence of US policy. A symptomatic result in the fall of 2007 was a Bush proposal for a US$1.4 billion 'Mexican Plan' directed against drug trafficking along lines pioneered in Columbia, but delayed until the Obama administration.

South of the Border: Myths of Modernization and the Persistence of Internal Hegemony

The dilemma is that the more recent Mexican policy of co-operation and economic integration has not borne the expected results, and thus Mexico's capacity to respond to the US agenda has been drastically reduced. Though generally denied in official circles, it is clear from its negative effects that the neoliberal model for the economic development of Mexico based on NAFTA is largely bankrupt in its current form, as has been documented by recent research. This economic failure is part of a broader vulnerability that afflicts the capacity of Mexico to deal with its dependency or – to put it more politely – 'asymmetrical interdependence'. Three key "myths" underlie official policy and are repeated in much international journalism: (1) the myth of NAFTA as the foundation of a new economic miracle; (2) the myth of being a fully "modern" state in the sense implied by its participation in NAFTA and membership in the OECD; and (3) the myth that the election of Fox, reinforced by the subsequent election of Calderón, essentially completes or consolidates the process of democratic transition.

First, the current 'myth of NAFTA' obscures how the expansion of exports has been accompanied by the failure of the sustained expansion of domestic production and investment as reflected in slow expansion of employment (and actual declines in manufacturing), low and declining real wages, low R & D expenditures, extremely low technical innovation, and relatively unchanged per capita income (Nadal, Aguayo and Chávez 2003).[9] Increases in productivity have been concentrated in the export sector and have not been associated with any general wage gains. In short, a variety of economic and social indicators give little substance to the assumption that NAFTA has contributed to sustaining high levels of growth, let alone reduced poverty and increased economic equality. Whereas the Mexican economic 'miracle' based on an import-substitution model generated rates of growth averaging 6.2 per cent from 1933 to 1982, during the last five years of the Fox administration growth declined to an average of around 2 per cent. In 2005 even a 3 per cent growth rate placed Mexico 14th out of 19 in Latin America (Fernández-Vega 2005). Moreover, over the past 20 years real income has declined sharply, per capita income has not increased significantly (despite a demographic revolution and the flight of millions), and income inequality has

---

9   For a less polemical but largely convergent assessment, see Polaski 2004.

increased with the top 10 per cent of the population receiving nearly 40 per cent of all income. Consequently, more than 61–82 per cent of the population has been declared poor by a wide variety of researchers, with 15–39 per cent widely held to be in 'extreme poverty' (Boltvinik 2001). Or, to put it in more concrete terms, only 11.7 per cent of wage earners earn more than 5,600 pesos per month (or about US$430 – five times the minimum salary) (Zúñiga 2000).[10] In short, the 'middle class' is for all practical economic purposes confined to the top 18 per cent who can usually, with combined family incomes, satisfy their basic needs as defined in terms of international standards.

Further, even more ominously, these relatively poor results are linked with an unsustainable government reliance, both directly and indirectly, on artificial and vulnerable sources of income and foreign exchange. Using figures from 2005, the economy is sustained by an unstable combination of the following:

- oil revenue (US$32 billion, around 37 per cent of the federal budget that moved higher with the peaking of oil prices) based on reserves that are now declining rapidly;
- remittances from those working in the USA (more than 20 billion);
- tourism (11.795 billion);
- profits from drug trafficking (estimated at 13.8 billion); and
- direct foreign investment (17.8 billion) (Castellanos 2006, Castillo García 2006, González Amador, Rodríguez and González 2005).

Moreover, much of that foreign direct investment has little to do with actual expansion of production since it has been linked with the entry of American franchises in goods distribution (Walmart now controls 50 per cent of self-service business), fast food, and services (including the sale of the banking system to foreign investors at fire-sale prices and the public funding of previous massive bank debts). Similarly, the more than 20 billion in remittances (at its peak) was used primarily for direct consumption rather than investment.

In short, not only does the Mexican state already lack the capacity to tax at levels necessary for a modern state, it is confronted with a failed economic strategy and an emerging, explosive fiscal crisis that was fully revealed by the after-effect of the US economic crisis of late 2008, as well as a depreciation of the peso around 30 per cent and a recent lowering of international credit ratings. The decline of production in 2009 was 6.9 per cent – the worst in Latin America three times the average – which erased the meagre gains of the past four years (González Amador 2010). Foreign investment fell by 41 per cent and tourism by a projected 15 per cent (AFP and Reuters 2010, González 2009). Due to the decline of oil reserves and the drop in prices, there was a 40.7 per cent decline in petroleum exports,

---

10 This calculation was based on the assumption of a minimum wage of 56 pesos (regions vary from 54.47 to 57.46) per day in 2010, a 13 to 1 US exchange rate, and no significant change since 2000.

whereas remittances fell 16 per cent because of migrant unemployment in the US (Cardoso 2010a, Rodríguez 2010). To the extent that the war against organized crime is successful, that will also reduce foreign exchange and the stimulus of laundered money. The recent passage of the most important tax reform in 20 years – whose passage despite past divisions and business opposition reflects the urgency of the crisis – will postpone but not resolve the double crisis: falling oil reserves and revenues and the lack of a tax base necessary for a modern state. The introduction of a minimal flat tax will reduce loopholes, but not the exemptions granted to many large corporations, and it is estimated that the final version will increase government taxes by 2.3 per cent of GNP by 2012. But Mexico begins with one of the lowest rates of overall taxation (less than 11 per cent, compared to the South American average of 16 per cent and 25 per cent in advanced societies) (Malkin 2007, Méndez and Garduño 2007, OECD 2007). A tragic response to this most recent crisis, and the neoliberal orientation of the Calderón administration, has been the raising of taxes and reducing budgets in 2010, hence enhancing the cyclic downturn.

Second, despite the forms of a modern social democratic state and economy and considerable progress in institutional reform over the past two decades, Mexico is at or near the bottom of the OECD in terms of virtually every major indicator of modernization: educational achievement and participation rates; research and development; quality and distribution of medical and social services; income inequality and rates of poverty; environmental protection; corruption; freedom of the press; and crime rates and the effectiveness of the rule of law. And despite per capital production that is immensely greater than Cuba, the outcome is a 'human development' level that is roughly the same.

Third, the fragility of democratic consolidation is strongly reinforced by both the relative economic stagnation and the incomplete modernization just described. A series of factors reinforces the spectre of ungovernability, even if not a failed state in the strong sense: chronic rural and regional violence, including political assassinations; the infiltration of police forces by drug mafias; less powerful presidents without a legislative majority; inexperienced legislators who can only be elected for a single term; and a grossly overpaid supreme court with a dubious track record. Perhaps the most notable illustration of this fragility was the effort to use legalistic tricks in an a failed attempt to eliminate the mayor of Mexico City, López Obrador, as a PRD presidential candidate by a form of impeachment (a *desafuero*) by putting him in jail. Only international pressures and one of the largest demonstrations in the history of Mexico City forced the suspension of the trumped-up charges relating to the courts having overturned a city land expropriation measure for a hospital. Journalists are targets of rates of violence (57 murdered from 2000 through 2009) that are among the highest in the world. The state of affairs in Chiapas remains unchanged and the state of Oaxaca was brought to a standstill in the fall of 2007 by teacher strikes and occupation of the capital for months as part of demands for the resignation of the state governor. Police violence contributed to a number of deaths, culminating in federal military intervention to quell the violence. Confrontations among drug traffickers – closely related to military intervention – have caused more than 14,000 deaths by the fall of 2009, along with a massive escalation of human rights violations that have been documented by the Human Rights Watch (Ballinas 2010). The economist and well-known commentator Rolando Cordera Campos, has summed up the current mood on the democratic left: 'But the gravest and most ominous thing is not the lamentable state of the economy, but the ideological and moral collapse in politics and the media. Not even the most pessimistic of our political observers could have imagined the symptoms of decomposition that we have been living these days' (Cordera Campos 2006, *my translation*).

Structural Reproduction and the Contradictions of the Status Quo: The Impasse Thesis

The current basic structure of the migration pattern – if not all of its details – is closely linked to its structural relation to the interests of the dominant economic and political elites of both the US and Mexico, which can be defined in terms of the intersection and mutual reinforcement of two structures of hegemony: the external dominance of the US over Mexico (which has not altered fundamentally with a change of administrations) and the internal hegemony within Mexico of the social classes now represented by the informal alliance between the PRI and PAN.

Bush's shifting stance on immigration reflected a balancing effort to deflect nativist and local pressures from below, as well as respond to the elite interests that recognize the need for a flexible supply of cheap labour. At the same time, while the Mexican administrations have officially promoted open borders with respect to labour in addition to trade, this stance is not only domestically popular, but consistent with using the export of workers as a safety value that distracts attention away from the stagnation of the domestic economy. Given these structural constraints of supply and demand, it is unlikely that a further heightening of controls, even the construction of a wall, would fundamentally alter the current situation.

Two key consequences of these relations of interdependence as a process of social trans-border social reproduction – the border impasse – need to be singled out. These consequences can be summarized as the incoherence of US policy and the impotence of Mexican responses:

First, the conflicting pressures upon US policy have created a contradictory set of policies, despite the widespread suggestion that security and migration control policies are complementary or can be paired. The neoliberal globalization agenda is problematic in the sense that the advocacy of unlimited expansion of markets and free trade is applied inconsistently by rejecting labour mobility and has disruptive social and economic effects that cannot be contained in the long run. Although the primary thrust of US policy is toward a de-bordering of the world in the name of free trade and liberalization, it is increasingly driven by security, drug, and immigration issues toward a re-bordering. Hence, there is 'a constitutive tension between a rebordering national security territoriality and a debordering geography of participation in open markets and trade networks', which suggests that this practice is not 'the coherent product of a properly sovereign center of policy power capable of balancing and managing diverse security and trade agendas' (Coleman 2005).[11] In other words, these contradictions suggest that US policies may not even reflect a realistic assessment of national interests.

Second, the currently dominant US policies are brewing a recipe for chronic crisis, given Mexican weaknesses and the impotence and contradictory effects of the resulting policy responses. For example, some more informed observers in the US, largely on the right, routinely denounce what is called the hypocrisy of the Mexican government in exporting its problems by encouraging illegal migration and in fact depending on it for political stability. From this perspective, the solution would be for Mexico to have the discipline to reform itself along lines necessary for domestic job creation through the full implementation of structural adjustment policies: for example, more flexible labour laws, the further reduction of state controls, and the privatization of the energy and electricity sectors. What these suggestions ignore is that (1) the demand for labour on the US side would not be reduced in the longer run (despite the current slowdown); (2) supply on the Mexican side would likely remain relatively unchanged, given immense levels of underemployment and the low quality of new jobs even if substantial numbers were created; and (3) that such doctrinaire neoliberal policies could not in fact be implemented democratically without major political instabilities that would be very worrisome from the perspective of official US policy. In other words, it can be argued that this militant neoliberal version of the US-sponsored prescription for a cure would likely make the patient sicker and more unstable. Though the reform of the Mexican economy and other institutions is clearly necessary, much of what would be required would involve strategies of social democratic reform that would often be perceived – often wrongly, if viewed as a longer term process – as against American interests.

In summary: given the nature of the border issues and the fragility of the Mexican economy and democratic institutions, the aggressive pursuit of what is perceived to be national interest on the part of vocal minorities in the US would most likely culminate in a massive de-stabilization that would otherwise be of the highest security priority to avoid. Paradoxically, a dogmatic 'realist' pursuit of US dominance may have the opposite of the intended effects, a result inherent in the contradiction of the project of neoliberal transnational elites.

---

11   This incoherence is also reinforced by overlapping bureaucratic jurisdictions, as discussed in Wiarda 2000.

The Transformative Thesis: The Conditions of Possibility for Change

Agency, Dialogue and Transformative Change

With this structural contradiction produced by Mexico–US relations in mind, it is now possible to turn to the longer-run sources of agency that might contribute to transformative potentials. As Linklater has suggested, questions of agency in the context of a critical theory of international relations pose three basic considerations: an ethical universalism that extends political community to all; the necessity of post-sovereign forms of relations that can recognize the needs of the excluded; and how to develop reformist strategies for choosing to construct new forms of relations beyond the anarchy of existing international relations (Linklater 1992). Related formulations have pointed to the role of emergent forms of transnational and global civil society and expressions of cosmopolitan democracy that extent beyond the traditional nation state.[12]

In the short run, the prospect of extending principles of cosmopolitan justice to those affected on both sides of the border appear to be limited, given US dominance in what is defined as a purely bi-lateral relationship between two sovereign states. NAFTA, as primarily an economic agreement, does not provide the kind of framework for the development of transitional institutions of the kind emerging in the European Union. And aside from Mexico, the other two members have not officially expressed an interest in moving beyond economic union. In short, it is very difficult to envision exactly what any extension of cosmopolitan democracy would look like or why it would even take place, given the diverse forms of resistance.

The concluding discussion, however, will briefly take up three themes or working points that illustrate some of the possibilities for initiating and facilitating forms of discourse necessary for creating longer term alternatives: (1) recognizing and facilitating the existing bilateral civil society organizations on both sides of the border that have initiated such process of dialogue; (2) the priority that should be given to constructing more trilateral relations including Canada, as well as global dialogue on the social justice issues involved; and (3) the challenge of constructing an alternative vision of democratic transition for Mexico that is based on autonomous choices about modernization that are not merely a reflection of the narrow demands expressed through US hegemony and an obsession with security issues.

---

12 On cosmopolitan democracy, see Held 1995, Held and Guibernau 2001; for global civil society, Germain and Kenny 2005.

Agency as Transnational Civil Society Networks: Facilitating Cross-Border Democracy

The first theme is that transformative possibilities already have a partial institutional form in the non-state actors in the US and Mexico that are creating new forms of agency as part of a transnational civil society. A central issue here is asking how the resources and possibilities embodied in cross-border forms of voluntary association and civil society can be mobilized to have significant effects on state actions. The broader question here is thus part of the general issue of whether and how non-state actors may draw upon communicative discourse as a form of capability (Holzscheiter 2005). In the case of the US, matters are further complicated by the mobilization of a right-wing coalition that draws upon misinformation, misguided nationalism, and anxiety – from the late Samuel Huntington in the ivory tower of Harvard to Hanson on the frontlines in California – as part of a virulent attack upon what is taken to be the 'open border conspiracy' (Hanson 2003, Huntington 2004).

As recent research has shown, a remarkable combination of bi-national links have emerged in the domains of both state–civil society and civil–civil society in areas such as labour, the environment, trade issue advocacy, democracy and human rights, women's rights, and issues more specific to Chicano and Latino civil and immigrant rights (Fox 2004). Three basic types of links have been identified as having rather different characteristics: transnational networks, transnational coalitions, and transnational movement organizations. The evidence regarding the impact of such activities, however, remains mixed:

> Bi-national networks and coalitions have had significant impact upon official policy discourse, but they have only rarely won tangible increases in public or private accountability ... The NAFTA-origin border environmental institutions are the main exceptions to this generalization, and their impact so far has been quite limited compared to their mandate and such coalitions must be viewed as 'long-term investments with uncertain payoffs' (Fox 2004: 509–510).

Nevertheless, beyond the defensive character of such forms of bi-national communications, in the future they will also contribute to unprecedented forms of cross-cultural dialogue that governments cannot ignore.

Injustice and the Social Costs of Globalization from Below: Globalizing Transnational Dialogue

The second theme suggests that priority should be given to the importance of reconstructing a more trilateral and global dialogue on the undocumented migrant question and related issues. This strategy requires going beyond the existing bi-lateral civil society networks. Under conditions of hegemony and asymmetry, a more global space of debate becomes necessary as a check on the dominant partner, as well as on the governments in power. Otherwise transnational co-operation at the elite level may reflect manipulative skills and access to resources more than broadly-based representation. For example, previous contact between 'transnational' Mexican and US intellectuals has, in its more recent phases, been dominated by elites closely linked with official power stemming from the Salinas government's successful selling of the NAFTA idea to largely conservative intellectuals in the US. In the context of NAFTA, Canada has a potentially constructive mediating role to play as part of a trilateral dialogue.

In some respects, a model for such possibilities already exists in the case of the international attention that was given to the Zapatista movement, thus creating significant constraints upon the options of the Mexican government at crucial turning points (see Johnston 2000). The Zapatista movement is distinctive precisely because of the participation of European civil society networks, including discussions that reached the level of the European Union and Italy in particular. Unlike the Chiapas case, however, the question of undocumented migration does not lend itself to romanticization as a 'postmodern revolution' by indigenous peoples – as was especially the case in Europe – even though ironically Indigenous people from Chiapas and other states are increasingly contributing to the migrant stream. Nevertheless, the border issues provide a dramatic focal point for understanding the contradictions of neoliberal globalization and the human costs of escalating surveillance and enforcing the repatriation of migrants. Constructing a more global debate around these issues, hence highlighting the reality of economic refugees who have been abandoned by both their home and host countries, would require the extensive expansion of complementary efforts by a number of international agencies, NGOs, transnational civil society groups, journalists, and academics. Within this process both governmental and non-governmental relations might suggest agendas that go beyond the current NAFTA agreement.

An important question is also whether such a debate could be constructed without falling into the rhetorical pitfalls of what could be perceived to be an essentializing anti-Americanism, as opposed to a well-grounded critique of policies that have been created by diverse groups and ideological perspectives. What is required is recognizing the social costs on both sides of the border and for those communities that unequally bear the burden of dealing with the social upheavals resulting from 'globalization from below'. As well, such international discussion could force the US to be confronted by the reality of the general effects of its own economic mismanagement and deepening levels of social and economic inequality. In other words, the resentments caused by undocumented migrants are closely linked to these larger problems. The larger interests of the other US of the working poor are ideologically disguised by using internal ethnic and racial divisions as part of the classic divide and rule strategies that deflect attention from the underlying reality: steeply declining rates of mobility, static or declining real incomes for the majority, and the rapid expansion of incomes and accumulation of wealth at the highest levels (Krugman 2004). To be sure, the mortgage debt crisis and stock market collapse of late 2008 was a wake-up call, but it remains to be seen whether the Obama administration can confront these issues adequately.

Though it is easy to frame the ideological underpinnings of immigration debates in terms of a pro-migrant stance as egalitarian and progressive and the anti-immigration one as racist and xenophobic, the issues are more complicated than that. Much of the support for tightened controls derives from confusion resulting from the right's capacity to define the problem through the media and a sense of lack of alternatives. The US has reasonably well-developed institutions for facilitating social inclusion and a strong tradition of pluralism, but these are overburdened and under attack from the right. Perhaps a good indicator of this complexity is the surprisingly high percentage of Americans of Mexican origin who also support tighter immigration controls, largely out of desperation and fear for their own communities (Vila 2000).

Though Octavio Paz late in his career was plagued by an inadequately differentiated attack on the left that impeded dialogue, his overall vision of the contradictions of US–Mexico relations remains prescient. As he noted some time ago, the greatest threats to the US are not external:

> [T] mortal danger comes from within ... from that mixture of arrogance and opportunism, blindness and short-term Machiavellianism, volubility and stubbornness which has characterized its foreign policies during recent years ... To conquer its enemies, the United States must first conquer itself – return to its origins. Not to repeat them but to rectify them: the 'others' – the minorities inside as well as the marginal countries and nations outside – do exist ... each marginal society, poor though it may be, represents a unique and previous version of mankind. If the United States is to recover fortitude and lucidity, it must recover itself, and to recover itself it must recover the 'other' – the outcasts of the Western World. (Paz 1979)

Agency as Autonomous Empowerment: Mexican Modernization as Democratization

As a third alternative theme, as part of a longer term response, it is also necessary to recognize the strategic importance of democratization and economic reform within Mexico as a crucial component of escaping from the current impasse. Genuine partnership cannot be negotiated from a position of weakness. Here the question of agency shifts to the context of a form of collective empowerment as a process of democratization that might allow Mexico to negotiate its global interdependence on terms consistent with its contradictory past and distinctive needs as a society undergoing a complex process of democratic consolidation. Again, Paz's earlier diagnosis of the Mexican crisis remains cogent, even if he lost sight of the necessary political consequences of his own insights toward the end of his life. As he often re-iterated, the challenge to Mexico is to deal with modernization on its own terms, consistent with its past: 'To avoid new disasters, we Mexicans must reconcile ourselves with our past: only in this way shall we succeed in finding a route to modernity' (Paz 1979, 272).

The issue of Mexican reform is not primarily the superficial economic goal of providing a few more low quality jobs through the further Americanization of the economy as imagined by the right in the US and the Salinas regime and its sequels. The continuing failure of Mexico's NAFTA strategy suggests the need for recognizing the strategic importance of a transformation of Mexico that can retain some autonomy from the hegemonic pressures of US dominance and the uncritical application of US models for reform. What is required is a greater diversification of models for change of the kind signalled by a trade agreement with the European Union involving conditions relating to democracy and human rights,[13] and alternative Latin American models, such as Lula in Brazil, that embody the opening up of new spaces of democratic participation and economic autonomy (Avritzer 2002).

This challenge is now widely recognized, despite routine denial on the part of the two dominant parties (PAN and PRI). There now exists an extensive Mexican journalistic and academic literature on the challenges of a democratic consolidation that includes a new vision of democracy and economic development despite the immense obstacles. As the writer and public intellectual Carlos Monsiváis has stressed, the first step in this process is coming to terms with the exhaustion of the older ideology of post-revolutionary 'nationalism' and the infatuation with neoliberal models of 'modernization'. As he notes, the Zapatista rebellion signalled the end to such illusions:

> Before the rebellion in Chiapas, the key word in Mexico was 'modernization,' the illusion of the First World around the corner: 'Happiness is here again for the first time.' Modernization took the place of nationalism, the old-time 'act' that united all sectors through festivity, mythology. And Chiapas, I think was powerful in destroying, first, the mirage of 'modernity' and, second, that kind of nationalist mythology ... We had really lived in a world of make-believe. For the first time we asked: How was it possible that we could live in the Noah's ark of the happy few, and that we could overlook the existence of ten million Indians ... If you have an unequal nation – 80% of the Mexican population lives in either poverty or misery – you can't have modernization and can't trust nationalism. And that's what Chiapas helped us discover. (Monsiváis and Thelen 1999)

The construction of an expanded democratic public sphere that might engage *México profundo* ('deep Mexico') has tentative beginnings: a notable expansion

---

13 Significantly, Mexico's recent trade agreement with the European Union includes conditional clauses relating to democracy and human rights. See Syzmanski and Smith 2005. Similarly, the US Senate has made reducing military abuses of human rights in the drug war a condition of security assistance, though there will likely be no serious follow up.

of civil society networks and indigenous autonomy movements; a credible left-of-centre PRD presidential candidate (López Obrador) in the 2006 election who was narrowly defeated by probable electoral fraud, a well co-ordinated politics of fear and the abusive use of presidential power by the outgoing leader Fox; and the new extra-parliamentary spaces opened up by *la otra campaña* of Marcos (now *Delegado Cero*) and the Zapatistas. Nevertheless, the obstacles cannot be minimized. Above all, the internal divisions in the PRD and the related resurgence of the PRI and the lack of fundamental difference between PRI and PAN have created an electoral political stalemate that ensures the ritualistic maintenance of the status quo for the foreseeable future. What is required is an unprecedented form of social reconstruction and democratization that Mexico cannot undertake without global input and support. This task goes beyond the purely political in order to confront the tasks of creating new forms of 'social density' in local and intermediate groups (most concretely embodied in civil society and social movements) (Olvera 2004, Olvera 1999, Otero 2004). For example, the problem of corruption is not merely a matter of the political will to crack down on individuals or visible mafias in a social order in which family survival has long depended on forms of clientelism that function as the only alternatives to the weak rule of law and the lack of equal opportunities. As a result of a deformed process of what might be called 'patrimonial modernization' and the manipulation of popular fears of disorder, Mexico has been ravaged by a parasitic state, the dominance of patrimonial elites and brutal market forces, and the result is in what sociologist Sergio Zermeño has called '*la desmodernidad mexicana*' (Zermeño 2005). Consequently, transformative change must also address how the forms of subjectivity arising from patrimonial domination are the site, even among the oppressed, of what Norbert Lechner has called the 'interior patios of power' that facilitate the reproduction of autocratic authority and social domination (Lechner 1990).[14] To conclude, as Paz might have put it, both the US and Mexico must recover themselves historically and democratically before they can authentically engage each other, given their deepening misunderstandings as tragically estranged distant neighbours in a new transnational world.

---

14 The Mexican anthropologist Rossana Reguillo has provocatively explored Lechner's notion of the "authoritative appropriation of fear" in relation to the fragmentation experienced by youth cultures in Mexico and Latin America; in English, see Reguillo 2004.

Part VII
Conclusions

Chapter 14
North America: A Trilateral, Bilateral, or Unilateral Space?[1]

Stephen Clarkson

Abstract

Understood as one among a number of world regions, North America is an enigma displaying many diverse realities. Seen in its formal institutionalization by NAFTA, it is considerably less than meets the eye. When examined in such governance spheres as transborder water management or the steel industry, it turns out to have considerably more substance than one might first have suspected. In other cases, such as the regulation of financial services or intellectual property rights, what appears as continental policy harmonization is really a manifestation of globalization. In contrast, antiterrorist border security measures are just what they seem: US-driven inter-governmental policy co-ordination in which the hegemon ends up depending on the periphery's collaboration. As for determining where North America is heading, global market consolidation in the automobile industry suggests that the continent has lost its chance to become a regional regulatory space. The 2005 Security and Prosperity Partnership (SPP) of North America may have renewed the three federal governments' commitment to reconciling the US priority for border security with the periphery's need for prosperity but it did not give any sign that North America was an embryonic EU about to develop along the lines of the European model.

Introduction

When the editor of this volume wrote that 'in January 1994, North America formally entered the club of world regions, launching the project of an integrated economic space' (Castro-Rea 2006), he was engaging in an intellectually tempting, but academically risky venture.

Depicting as part of a global phenomenon the continent that is dominated economically, demographically, culturally, and geopolitically by the US is

---

1   © **not for quotation without permission.** This overview is based on the research incorporated in *Does North America Exist? Governing the Continent after NAFTA and 9/11* (Toronto and Washington: University of Toronto and Woodrow Wilson Presses, 2008).

intellectually intriguing because it connects scholarship on North America with the rich vein of academic research that understands world market integration as a double movement. On the one hand, globalization is seen primarily as an economic and technological phenomenon in which corporations have largely escaped the regulatory reach of nation states while they expand their production and distribution to a regional scale. On the other hand, these states, which used to compete with their neighbours, are responding to globalization's challenge by forming regional groupings in order to compete at the global scale with other regional economies. In this dialectical conception, the evolution of the European Community into the European Union (EU) during the second half of the twentieth century is presented as the prototype of the new 'world region'. In the terminology of the regulation school of analysis, the political economy of this phenomenon is described as a regional regime of capital accumulation being managed by a regional mode of policy regulation.[2] Placing North America within this framework is tempting because the continent is similar to the EU in culture (whether measured by common heritage or linked histories) and in size (whether measured by population or gross national product, as documented by Table 1.2 in the editor's introduction).

But such exercises are academically problematic, because the very act of looking at North America in the context of comparative world regions leads many to assume that the former is an embryonic, institutionally lighter version of the model that evolved on the eastern shores of the Atlantic Ocean. This is a daring assumption given its small membership (three compared to the EU's 27 member-states); given its stark asymmetries (the US is not just overwhelmingly more powerful than its neighbours to the north and south, it is the global hegemon); and given the disparate nature of its two bilateral relationships (rich Canada has long enjoyed a relatively easy, even cosy relationship with Washington, whereas a much poorer Mexico has mostly had to manage a tense, extremely conflictual one with Uncle Sam).

It is well known that the processes forming the European Community after the Second World War constrained the largest power, Germany, from flexing its economic muscles and empowered the smaller members with institutions that offset their low political weight, and with programs that raised the poorer members to the economic level of the richer. The EU's highly complex system, which contained the strong and strengthened the weak, derived from an ideological consensus about the need to guarantee intergovernmental peace and the value of a generous social-policy framework. However, if our interest is understanding the nature of North America's transborder governance, NAFTA did little to create anything in its two bilateral sets of asymmetrical, market-led relationships that resembles the extraordinary model of state-led governance established in Europe by the EU.

---

2 An accumulation regime can be defined by its production processes, market organization, distribution systems, and division of labour (Aglietta 1979).

This chapter argues that the apparently descriptive phrase, 'North America', actually conceals two historically separate realities whose cross-border dynamic is moving the continental model along a path that is divergent from rather than congruent with the one offered by Europe. It makes the case by distinguishing four different realities that constitute North American governance:

- It *is less than meets the eye* as far as its formal trilateral institutions are concerned.
- It *is more than meets the eye* in certain policy areas such as border-region management and some sectors such as the steel industry.
- Its apparent tri-national policy harmonization *is not at all what meets the eye* in other economic sectors such as bank regulation and the three countries' intellectual property rights regimes.
- It *is just what it seems* when we look at the intergovernmental regulatory transformations that have taken place under Washington's insistence since 9/11.

Each section will assess the extent to which transborder governance has created trilateral, bilateral or unilateral spaces and, in the process, has augmented or reduced the continent's power asymmetries and maintained or mitigated the once stark discrepancy between the US–Mexico and US–Canada relationship.

The concluding section will pick up the hazardous challenge of trying to see in what direction continental governance is moving, whether in the market place or in its state structure.

Formal Trilateral Institutionalization: Less than Meets the Eye

If North America, whose principal characteristics this volume has described, is identified as a world region, this is thanks to two economic agreements: the first forged bilaterally between the US and its northern neighbour as the misleadingly-labelled Canada–US Free Trade Agreement (CUFTA, 1 January 1989), the second known as NAFTA, which came into force exactly five years later when CUFTA's provisions were deepened and extended to include Mexico within NAFTA.

The proposition that NAFTA is less than meets the eye does not depend on arguing that its norms, rules, and rights are inconsequential. On the contrary, these three components of what became part of each signatory's 'external constitution'[3] severely disciplined the practices of the two peripheral states, if not those of the hegemon:

---

3 For an elaboration of the argument that continental free trade agreements combined with the World Trade Organization comprise an external constitution for its member-states, see Clarkson 2004.

- The extension of the national treatment (NT) *norm* from applying to goods (as it had under GATT) to including foreign investment required a wholesale change of Canada's industrial-strategy policies that had previously provided incentives to domestic corporations to bolster their capacities to compete with foreign – mainly US – companies. Applying the NT to investment also nailed shut the coffin of Mexico's import substitution industrialization model, which had delivered an annual growth rate of 6 per cent from the Second World War to the early 1980s.
- Dozens of new *rules* obliged Canada, for example, to raise drastically the minimum size of domestic companies whose acquisition by foreign corporations could be vetted by the federal government. For its part, Mexico agreed to open up its banking sector to foreign acquisition according to detailed protocols.
- Important new *rights* were granted to foreign investors who could now directly sue North American host governments from the municipal to the federal level for 'expropriating' their wealth.

These norms, rules, and rights did not meet many eyes, because they were buried in the reader-unfriendly pages of CUFTA's and NAFTA's turgid texts. It was CUFTA's, then NAFTA's, much-ballyhooed institutions that provided little for the eye. To be sure, NAFTA boasts an executive body, the North American Free Trade Commission (NAFTC). But however hard one might look, this commission is nowhere to be found, having no staff, no address, and no budget. Despite the substantial responsibilities for managing NAFTA's implementation conferred on it by the agreement, it consists solely of sporadic meetings by the Canadian trade minister, the Mexican secretary of the economy, and the US trade representative – a threesome which has been loath to make major decisions.

Nor does NAFTA have much in the way of an administrative arm. Buried in each of the three governments' trade departments, there is a small office responsible for documenting NAFTA-related business. NAFTA's remaining bureaucratic sinew consists of some thirty committees and working groups mandated by the agreement's various chapters. These tri-national groupings, which are in theory staffed by middle-level civil servants from each federal government, barely exist in practice (Clarkson et al. 2005).

As for a legislative capacity to abolish, add to, or amend NAFTA's new norms, rules, or rights – a necessary feature of any institution that hopes to retain its relevance as conditions evolve – this 'world region' has none. Changes require trilateral negotiations by the three governments.

NAFTA's only institutional feature with any substance lies in its judicial capacities. But of the half-dozen different dispute settlement mechanisms, two have remained dormant (energy and financial institutions) and two are ineffectual (those of the environmental and labour co-operation commissions). The agreement's two chief conflict resolution processes are specified in Chapter 20 and Chapter 19. Disputes between the parties over the interpretation and implementation of

NAFTA's provisions were to be resolved by panels established under Chapter 20's clauses, but such panel rulings merely take the form of recommendations to the NAFTC which, in turn, can only offer suggestions to the three governments about how to proceed. When, for instance, after long delays caused by US obstructionist tactics, a NAFTA panel ruled that the US government had failed to honour its obligation to allow Mexican truckers access to its market, Washington persisted in its non-compliance.

Putatively binding rulings are made by panels established under Chapter 19, which replace domestic legal appeals of the antidumping or countervailing duty determinations made by individual states' trade-administrative tribunals. While useful in the majority of cases, the US government's refusal to actually comply with these rulings, in such high-profile cases as the long-drawn-out softwood lumber dispute with Canada, underlines the point that NAFTA's institutions enjoy strikingly little clout, as Greg Anderson showed convincingly in his chapter in this volume.

The single arbitral function with definite muscle is the investor-state dispute process established in Chapter 11, which allows NAFTA corporations to initiate an arbitration process governed by World Bank rules in order to rule on the validity of a domestic measure they claim has expropriated their assets. Because these rulings must be implemented by the defendant jurisdiction, they have been the cause of much dismay among nationalists, who protest the derogation of domestic judicial sovereignty, and among environmentalists, who believe the threat of such actions prevents the regulation of corporate environmental misdemeanours. But because the number of Chapter 11 cases remains small and their effects limited, their overall institutional importance must be considered marginal.

In short, the transborder governance established by NAFTA's institutions is considerably less than observers had cause to expect when listening either to proponents or opponents of what President Ronald Reagan had called North America's economic constitution. Compared to Norway which, even though it is not a member of the European Union, must implement European Commission directives – with exceptions in farming, fishing, and oil exportation – NAFTA's institutional impact even on the two peripheral states is low.

Institutionally speaking, NAFTA does not create a trilateral space. Nevertheless, its norms, rules, and rights make the regulatory space in the two peripheral states more similar to that of the hegemon with the result that transnational corporations (TNCs) can operate more easily as continentally structured production and marketing entities in the three economies. Given that NAFTA's norms, rules, and rights were largely defined by the US in defence of its interests in the periphery, they can be seen to have augmented US hegemonic power in the continent. Because Mexico had to make the largest changes to its political order – for instance, inserting an entire trade-remedy arbitral system under Chapter 19 – NAFTA has also reduced the imbalance between US–Canada and US–Mexico relationships.

Transborder Governance that is More than Meets the Eye

Although NAFTA created a new North America that could be analyzed as a 'world region', the old North America had long enjoyed – or suffered from – forms of governance that were often much more than met the eye because their institutionalization was either informal or largely invisible. Out of many possible cases, this section will consider one, water management, which pre-existed NAFTA by a century, and another, the steel industry, for which NAFTA had unanticipated consequences.

Water

Some forms of North American transborder governance developed through processes that took place in a zone of decision-making and consultation that transcended one or other of the two international boundaries. From the nineteenth century on, concerns about the exploitation and oversight of North America's transboundary water resources gave rise to several treaties and corresponding bi-national institutions established to manage the flow, level, and quality of water in the lakes and rivers bisected by the US/Canada and US/Mexico borders. While the International Joint Commission (IJC), which was set up in 1909 thanks to the Boundary Water Treaty of that year, is well known, the actual US–Canada management – often mismanagement – of joint water matters straddling both borders is little understood because it is carried out by hundreds of collaborative arrangements involving agencies, business corporations, scientists, and environmentalist groups concerned about their local or regional eco-systems.

The legal basis for co-operative governance of the Tijuana River Basin lies in the 1944 US–Mexico treaty relating to the Utilization of Waters of Colorado and Tijuana Rivers and of the Rio Grande. The 1944 treaty substantially expanded the powers of the International Boundary Commission and changed its name to the International Boundary and Water Commission (IBWC) / *Comisión Internacional de Límites y Aguas* (CILA). The roles and responsibilities of the IBWC–CILA and the IJC are quite different because of the hydrological and socio-economic features of the respective border regions: the US southern border zone suffers from much greater water scarcity than the northern, and Mexican border infrastructure is much poorer than Canada's.

North America's water governance is a vast and multi-layered regime of national and international institutions, legal frameworks, and interacting social and economic values which, according to circumstance, converge and diverge in an irregular and unpredictable fashion (Buie 2005). Given the high levels of social and economic integration in the zones along the US-Canada and US-Mexico borders, the management of water resources presents a highly complex dynamic between different levels of government and public participation in political processes, which are not necessarily evolving in the direction of transborder integration.

In keeping with the George W. Bush administration's general hostility to international law, the US government resisted recognition of the IJC's mandate for supervision over such major problems as the ecosystem-threatening diversion of Devil's Lake into the Red River watershed and the withdrawal of Great Lakes water through Illinois. Although transborder North America's water governance remains separated into two bilateral spaces, and although their hydraulic geography and their economic character are quite different, the increased environmental pressures engendered by the *maquila* industrialization in the northern Mexican states has caused border governance patterns there to resemble those along the Canadian border because of the cross-border involvement of government, market, and civil society at various levels. Water governance in the north reduces the power asymmetry between hegemon and Canada because the former depends on the latter to implement agreements once they have been negotiated. In contrast, cross-border water governance in the south aggravates the already huge asymmetry between Uncle Sam and its neighbour because the US controls most of the water flows and can continue to act unilaterally to satisfy its citizens' claims.

Steel

With NAFTA's explicit aim to enhance continental economic integration, we should find evidence of continental governance in the marketplace. Beyond the powerful intervention of corporate lobbyists during the negotiation of the free-trade agreements (Lachapelle 2005), a few economic sectors provide evidence of governance with a continent-wide substance. Steel offers a fascinating case in point.

In spite of the fact that, as a traditional heavy industry, steel provides the backbone of the old manufacturing economy, it did not do well under NAFTA, which failed to eliminate the protectionist anti-dumping, safeguard, and countervailing-duty measures with which the US steel industry had long been harassing the exports into its market of their more efficient competitors from the North. When, in their frustration, the Canadian firms invested heavily in the US, they produced a phenomenon similar to the 'Toyotafication' which occurred when US restrictions on Japanese car imports caused firms such as Toyota to set up manufacturing operations within the US.

But instead of retaining their own identity and lobbying for their national sector's interests as did Toyota, the US subsidiaries of Canadian companies became active as US members of such industry associations as the American Iron and Steel Institute. As AISI players in good standing within the US economy, they proceeded to lobby – along with the US steelworkers' labour union, which had fortuitously been run for a decade by Canadian presidents – to exempt Canada and Mexico from the Bush administration's safeguard duties that were imposed in 2002 on foreign steel imports. This collaborative action suggested that, in the steel sector, a single governance space was developing in which Canadian, and later Mexican, firms have partially 'Americanized' themselves within the US economy, rather than create a continent-wide industry containing nationally competitive elements.

A more equitably balanced trilateralism appeared with the creation of an instrument of tri-national governance, the North American Steel Trade Committee. The NASTC involves the three governments with their respective industry associations in efforts to develop common North American policy positions at the OECD, the World Trade Organization (WTO), and the now-defunct negotiations for a Free Trade Area of the Americas.

Although the steel sector in North America became more of a space in which US hegemonic control increased, the skewed quality of the two bilateral relationships also increased because the Canadian industry was so much better positioned to participate in the US economy than was its Mexican counterpart, which – having flourished, but inefficiently, under import substitution industrialization – was seriously shaken by the loss of government protection in the 1980s. Nevertheless, US hegemony has been challenged on its own soil and in its periphery by such foreign investors as the Indian giant Mittal acquiring leading steel companies in all three countries. The acquisition in 2006 of five of Canada's six largest domestically-owned steel corporations by conglomerates from overseas suggests that NASTC's apparently continental regulatory consolidation is being trumped by the steel industry's corporate globalization. As a world region in steel, North America remains a distinct market while its ownership becomes globalized.

Trinational Policy Harmonization: Not at All What Meets the Eye

Although the integrated nature of the North American steel industry is world-regional, other economic sectors where harmonization has increased are not necessarily evidence of continentalization. Take for instance the regulation of two sectors: intellectual property rights for the pharmaceutical industry and rules for financial services.

Intellectual Property Rights for Pharmaceuticals

Because NAFTA was negotiated just before GATT's Uruguay Round reached its successful conclusion, the creation of the WTO in 1995 presents many analytical complications for students of North American governance. The question of intellectual property rights (IPRs) provides an illuminating example, because the IPRs in NAFTA's Chapter 17 are virtually identical to those in the WTO's Trade-Related Aspects of Intellectual Property Rights agreement. The fact that Washington used the WTO's dispute settlement body, rather than NAFTA's, as its legal venue for pressing Canada to make more concessions to US-branded drug companies suggests that weak continental judicial governance has been trumped by the stronger judicial governance established at the global level. This shows how global governance displaced continental governance before the latter could get firmly established.

While the transborder governance for the pharmaceutical industry is different from what we would expect if North America were a genuinely trilateral space, the power implications in this sector are similar to changes in other sectors. New IPRs increase hegemonification through the expanded agency of US pharmaceutical TNCs in the two peripheral economies. At the same time, the transformation of Mexico's property rights regime tends to eliminate its discrepancy with that of Canada and so reduces the skewed quality of the US–Canada and US–Mexico relationship.

Financial Services

Although harmonization of the three banking sectors' regulations has occurred within North America, this is not due to any transborder governance created by NAFTA. Rather, this apparent continentalization actually reflects the three countries' participation in global governance. If banking regulations in the US, Mexico, and Canada are becoming more similar, this is because the three central banks participate in the monthly meetings of the Bank of International Settlements in Basel. It is the multilaterally negotiated norms that are negotiated in Switzerland that are then applied at home. Instead of banking regulations showing that North America is a 'world region', they indicate that the three countries of North America participate in a global mode of regulation on behalf of a globalizing system of accumulation.

Because these norms are negotiated in an international forum in which US power is offset by that of Europe and Asia, the effect in North America is to reduce US hegemonic control over the periphery in financial services. Similarly, because banking regulations are tending to harmonize, the regulatory discrepancy between Canadian and Mexican banking has declined. The implications of this regulatory reality is that North America's banking space is less trilateral, bilateral, or unilateral than it is global.

The Breakdown of a Continental Marketplace

Between the evidence of a continentally integrated economic sector and signs of other sectors participating in global governance regimes lies another reality. The passage of time since the mid-1990s has revealed a number of sectors whose continental integration is breaking down under the pressure of globalizing market forces. Two important sectors illustrate this process of transition. If NAFTA produced winners, these were surely the US auto and textile sectors which had managed to obtain rules of origin which gave them protection – at least for a time – against their Asian and European competitors.

Automobiles

The culmination of many years of US automotive TNCs' lobbying, NAFTA was thought to have set up a fully integrated system of production for those manufacturers, principally the 'Detroit Three', that could meet its protectionist rules-of-origin requirements. However, the trilateral working groups created to negotiate continental safety and emissions standards proved incapable of producing the regulatory harmonization necessary for fully integrated continental production.

Meanwhile, transcontinental corporate consolidation through mergers and equity linkages, which had left but six automotive groups accounting for 80 per cent of world production, was developing a regime of accumulation which was truly global and was generating pressures to create a globally harmonized system of regulation for the automotive industry. Global competition has completely broken down Detroit's oligopolistic dominance in the continent. At the same time, continuing foreign auto and auto-parts investment in both Ontario (which benefits from socializing the cost of medical care and provides an excellent transportation system) and Mexico (which offers well-trained labour power at a small fraction of US wages) has reduced the disparity between the two peripheries' car economies. While this continental industrial space has become largely trilateral, the walls of Fortress America have now fallen.

Textiles

NAFTA's rules of origin also appeared to succeed in connecting the three countries' disparate textile and apparel industries in a common North American production system, in which the interests of US firms combined more intimately with burgeoning Mexican firms than they did with shrinking Canadian companies. Greater asymmetries developed as NAFTA-generated continental market integration was shaken by two exogenous developments: the expiry of the Multi-Fibre Agreement (which had allowed industrialized countries to impose draconian quantitative limitations on apparel imports from the Third World) and China's emergence as the dominant supplier to the North American market.

Continental governance in a severely shaken textile and apparel industry still follows a hub-and-spoke model, with US industry responding unilaterally to its challenges, a battered Mexican industry retreating to the informal economy, and a hollowed-out Canadian sector sitting on the sidelines. Onto this picture of a disintegrating continental economy an opposing design was superimposed after 9/11, when US security concerns wrestled control of the continental agenda away from trade and investment liberalization.

North America as a Security Zone: Just What It Seems

The radical shift in the US provoked by the terrorist coup in New York and Washington on 9/11 instantly affected the nature of North America, as Jimena Jiménez and Janine Brodie have made clear. The economic integration fostered by NAFTA had been reducing the government-made economic barriers along the US's two territorial borders in order to allow the marketplace to accelerate human and economic flows across the continent. Throughout the 1990s, the growth in cross-border traffic in goods and people had generated increased attention to border governance issues as business coalitions, which were concerned about the efficiency of their continent-wide production systems, lobbied their governments to make the increased investments in the transportation infrastructure and security technology needed to create a near-borderless continent. President Clinton had signed agreements with Ottawa to improve border security management, but his administration had not taken significant actions in this direction. The 9/11 attacks led to intergovernmental shifts in both security and defence.

Security

Washington's sudden move to a security paradigm was dramatized for North America on 9/11 by the immediate blockade of its two land borders. This unilateral action demonstrated that, once Washington declared its national security to be at stake, it would simply reassert its control over the policy space it had previously vacated in the name of trade liberalization. Its subsequent demands that Canada and Mexico do what it felt was necessary to make their borders safe for the US showed how much of North American governance was unilaterally driven by Uncle Sam.

In the post-9/11 context, traditional bi-national relations reasserted themselves as Washington dealt with each neighbour separately. In this first phase of the US domestic war on terror, a detailed 30-point US–Canada smart border agreement was signed in Ottawa in December 2001. By March 2002, Washington had negotiated a parallel 22-point smart border agreement with Mexico City.

That this process was driven by US pressure on its neighbours suggests that the result was to increase US control over Mexico and Canada. But because Washington depended on Ottawa and Mexico City to implement the measures that had been agreed upon, the power asymmetry between the centre and its periphery diminished.

The fact that the US–Canada border agreement had provided Washington with a template for its arrangement with Mexico also suggests that this process diminished the disparity between Ottawa's relationship with Washington and Mexico City. Although the narco-traffic and immigration problems were far more intense along its southern then its northern border, Congress pushed the administration to adopt common policies toward biometric identity cards for all persons crossing US borders. For its part, the administration's support for universal technological solutions to the passage of low-risk merchandise across the border and through its ports of entry further reduced the disparity between the two countries' responses to Washington.

If the first securitization phase following 9/11 showed North America as a more bilateral and hegemonic, while more symmetrical, space, the proclamation of the SPP by the three governments' leaders following their tri-national summit in March 2005 appeared to herald a shift to a more trilateral continent. Nationalist critics on the periphery feared the SPP was a manoeuvre through which the executives in Canada and Mexico were stealthily advancing their agenda to integrate their political systems with the hegemon's. Corporate leaders in the three countries, who aspired to operate in a borderless North America, criticized the SPP as a mere wish list of low-profile bureaucratic initiatives whose implementation would do nothing to engage with such major challenges facing the continent as a common currency, a customs union, a security perimeter, or even a fully integrated energy market.[4]

As seen from the Mexican presidency ('*Los Pinos*'), the US's security imperative needed to be accepted as the paradigm within which the continental periphery had to operate. The SPP presented Mexico with an opportunity to resolve many irritating problems in the bilateral economic relationship and so move NAFTA incrementally toward its grander vision of an EU-type regional governance. The trade-off was to exchange full co-operation with US demands on security matters for getting inside the US policy loop in order to negotiate the regulatory corollaries that applied to trade.

Thus, when the US Congress passed a tough bioterrorism law and outraged Mexican legislators called for retaliatory action to block imports of US goods at their northern border, *Los Pinos* decided that the better part of valour was compliance. Faced with the new US requirements, President Vicente Fox's officials worked intensively with Mexican food exporters' associations to help them adapt their members' certification and packaging to conform with Washington's new specifications. This effort climaxed in December 2005 when the bioterrorism law came into effect and no Mexican produce that met the new standards was blocked at the border for non-compliance.

If SPP negotiations could produce certification standards governing Mexican foodstuffs, then such Mexican products as avocados would no longer be vulnerable to unilateral rulings by the US Food and Drug Administration. This would give Mexico's agricultural exporters a vital competitive advantage over their rivals in Latin America, Asia, and even Europe. Facilitating the documentation for transborder flights of private aircraft was a far cry from a Big Idea for North

---

4 This section is based on half a dozen off-the-record meetings held in the Mexican Presidency in February and March 2006 and another half dozen in the US Department of Commerce and National Security Council in Washington, DC in April.

America,[5] but implementing myriad incremental changes would lead implicitly toward that objective.

While the bulk of the SPP's proposed measures dealt with either the US–Canada or the US–Mexico relationship, the informal telephone and e-mail communications among the bureaucrats who had put them together suggested that some significant trilateral space had been created in the process. Although the security side of the SPP reaffirmed Washington's dominance in the continent, the prosperity issues seemed to promise some autonomy for the periphery. 'Regulatory harmonization' might conjure up images of Mexico and Canada simply having to adopt US standards, but the complexities and differences between each country's multi-level governmental system implied that this nightmare was unlikely to be realized within anyone's lifetime. Issues would have to be worked out pragmatically. In some cases, the US officials would still be getting their Mexican counterparts the familiar 'do it our way or your product will not cross our border' message. In others, a practical problem would have to be worked out by all parties having to resolve their problems co-operatively.

Passionate resistance within the US government to creating continental institutions made it unlikely that the SPP's many small measures would lead ineluctably to the implementation of a Big Idea. Even though the three countries' executives were marching in step on this initiative, which merely engaged the upper-middle ranks of their bureaucracies, the three governments pay virtually no attention to each other's interests when negotiating new trade agreements with other countries, and have shown little sign – apart from the one exception of developing a common position on steel policy – of moving toward a common position on international economic policy.

Following the argument so far, the reader will have seen that, as a world region, the North America created by NAFTA has little substance in institutional terms. While border-region water management and the continental steel industry provide examples of significant transborder governance, other domains, such as intellectual property rights and financial services, show that what appears to be regulatory harmonization is often a manifestation of the US, Canada, and Mexico participating individually in global governance. Global market consolidation in the automobile industry and disarray in the textile and apparel sectors suggested that North America had lost its potential to be a regional regime of accumulation for which it needed a counterpart regional mode of regulation.

Therefore, North America is simultaneously *less than meets the eye, more than meets the eye, not at all what meets the eye* and *just what it seems*. A fifth North

---

5 The "Big Idea" for an EU-style institutionalization of a borderless North America in a grand NAFTA Plus vision was suggested in Canada by Wendy Dobson (2002) who leaned on work by Robert Pastor (2001). Pastor had already sold the analysis to the Mexican political scientist Jorge Castañeda who, in turn, had persuaded Vicente Fox to adopt a version of the scheme for his successful 2000 election campaign for the Mexican presidency.

American reality, which became particularly evident after Washington declared its global war on terror, was the largely bilateral intergovernmental US-led relations focusing on border security.

The difficulty in aggregating these diverse realities into an overall portrait of the continent becomes clear if we try to divine in which direction North America is moving. Is the continent becoming a more trilateral space? Is it remaining primarily bilateral? Or is it, deep down, increasingly moulded by US unilateralism? The concluding paragraphs will extrapolate from trends observable in the light of the financial crisis of 2007–10.

Conclusion: In What Direction is Continental Governance Moving?

It is said that crises bring out the best in people. The 2007 sub-prime financial crisis brought out the worst in North America, showing its continental governance to be completely irrelevant in playing a part in its rescue. No trilateral summit convened to work out a North American position prior to the global governance meetings of the G20 or G8. Like all other capitals, Ottawa and Mexico City simply waited to see what Washington would do.

Far from being seen as a helpful crutch, NAFTA had already been identified as a threat to industrial jobs by Barack Obama when he was campaigning for the Democratic nomination. Nor was NAFTA even able to protect existing levels of tri-national integration when its spirit was rejected by the Obama administration endorsing Buy America provisions being attached to the US government's massive stimulus package. As a result of requirements that all the stimulus money dispensed by Congress be spent on projects having 100 per cent American content, US TNCs had to break their cross-border production chains and seek suppliers of all their products' components from within the American market. While walling itself off in commercial terms, the US was also walling itself off territorially by continuing to build an impassable fence along its border with Mexico.

For its part, the ideologically extreme Conservative government of Canada preened itself on its banking system (which had been exempted from NAFTA's liberalizing provisions) being closely regulated enough to have survived intact. Having first denied the seriousness of the crisis, Ottawa then conformed to the international consensus that had veered suddenly from a neoconservative scorn for government regulation to a Keynesian belief that state intervention in the marketplace could once again save capitalism from itself. At the same time, Canada began erecting walls of its own, although in this case they were politically constructed. The Stephen Harper government made it clear that it was no longer interested in supporting North American trilateralism. On the contrary, it aspired to re-establishing the special bilateral relationship with Washington that Canadian political and economic elites were suddenly remembering as characterizing Canada's diplomatic golden age. The federal government pointedly highlighted its rejection of North America's embryonic trilateralism by requiring all Mexicans, including tourists, wanting to come to Canada, to apply for visas.

Humiliated by Canada and walled off by the US, the Mexican government found itself isolated from rather than integrated in the two developed economies to the north with which it had implemented NAFTA sixteen years previously. Battered by destructive storms, shaken by an influenza panic, displaced by China as the US's prime source of low-cost products, destabilized by ever more violent drug cartels, and isolated by the US security wall growing along its northern border, Mexico was left to cope on its own with the disastrous consequences of having hitched its economy to the hegemon's. While other economies in the hemisphere stagnated during the crisis, Mexico's was the only one to suffer decrease (7.5 per cent) in its GDP. It suffered alone.

Since Barack Obama was sworn in, the leaders of Mexico, Canada, and the US did meet at a publicly billed leaders' summit in Guadalajara in 2009. However, by that time the SPP had been buried, and the get-together was so inconsequential that it served more to confirm the absence than the presence of continental governance in North America. There, the federal and provincial/state governments do the governing, business does the complaining to nationally or locally elected politicians, and civil society watches, ever more helpless, from the sidelines within its national boundaries.

As a world region with multiple identities, North America can alternately be seen as a unilateral, bilateral, trilateral, and global space depending on the viewer's point of view. Certainly, it is not an embryonic EU destined to develop along the lines of the European model in which asymmetries diminish and solidarities emerge. Some of the political disparities between Mexico and Canada may be diminishing, but in most governance dimensions the hegemon is becoming more dominant vis-à-vis its periphery. Small signs of tri-national governance have appeared, but, when seen in the broader context of global governance trends, these are not enough for us to conclude that North America has developed into a primary regulatory space or has a potential for launching any grander institutional project.

Chapter 15
Our North America? From the Mexican Standpoint, Not Yet

Lorenzo Meyer

Just a Distant Possibility

From a Mexican perspective, the idea that the three nations that occupy the northern region of the American continent can share something more substantial than a geographical location and economic and demographic exchanges is at best just a mere possibility in a distant future. North America as a common historical enterprise where the national interests of the US, Canada, and Mexico converge in a way that reinforces each other as a result of long term political arrangement is just a theoretical prospect and an almost impossible reality. North America as a common endeavour requires a significant and dramatic redefinition of each national interest, particularly in the case of the US, now an imperial superpower that has no counterpart in the international system.[1] At present there is no sign that such a redefinition is possible. Mexicans in North America cannot call this continent 'our North America' in the sense that many Europeans can call Europe their own common home and enterprise. On the other hand, Mexicans, especially poor Mexicans, are precisely the ones who are moving against the current from south to north as if North America had no borders and could be thought of and lived in as a unit.

A Negative Indicator

On 22 March 1966, President Lyndon Johnson wrote a short letter to his Mexican counterpart, Gustavo Díaz Ordaz, stating 'Our borders, yours and mine, are unguarded because there is no need for soldiers where trust and faith abide'.[2] By the end of 2006, the US/Mexico border was guarded by around 90 per cent of the twelve thousand members of the U.S. Border Patrol. More recently, six thousand national guards were added to this force as a temporary solution to stop a wave of

---

1   The new nature of the US in the international arena is explored by, among others, Lieven 2004; Ferguson 2004.

2   Lyndon B. Johnson Archives, National Security Files, Special Head of State Correspondence, Presidential Correspondence, Part I, Box 38, document 3.

undocumented Mexicans looking for low paying jobs. The guards were a stopgap until Washington could recruit and train more Border Patrol agents and build a physical barrier to separate the two countries. The distance between the ideal picture of a neighbourhood without fences depicted by a president from Texas in 1966 and the call 40 years later by another president from Texas for the National Guard and a high-tech barrier is an indicator of how much the situation between the two countries has changed.

The transformation of the nature of US-Mexico relations is more striking if we take into consideration that during those forty years, the US, Canada, and Mexico created NAFTA (1993), aimed precisely at linking their interests in a historic economic and political new way. It is ironic that precisely one of the main reasons given by the governments of Washington and Mexico City at the time of the NAFTA agreement was that free trade would be the best way to create more and better jobs in Mexico and permanently eliminate the incentives for Mexicans to cross illegally into the land of the rich neighbours to the north. Considering that 400,000 undocumented Mexicans are now entering annually into the US, the least that can be said is that NAFTA is not working as intended, either as a stimulus for job creation in Mexico or as an inhibitor of undocumented migration to the US.[3]

The last time the US had called the National Guard to deal with a Mexican border problem was at the beginning of the Mexican Revolution in 1911. In those days, the deployment of US Army troops and the Texas National Guard along the US/Mexico border was intended to reassure US public opinion that everything was under control (Hall and Coerver 1990: 16–27). In fact it was not. A US army at the Mexican border did not prevent a popular uprising south of the Rio Grande or isolate the border from some of its consequences. Rather, what it did was to help create in Mexico the expectation of the imminent downfall of Porfirio Díaz's government or, even worse, of an impending US invasion. In any case, it helped to precipitate precisely what Washington did not want at the time: the violent end of a friendly and stable dictatorship in Mexico (Ulloa 1976: 25–26).

Of course the present situation is different and the US has every right to call the National Guard,[4] to increase the numbers of the Border Patrol by 50 per cent in

---

3   The calculus of four hundred Mexicans crossing now illegally the US-Mexican border comes from the National Population Council of the Interior Secretary of México (CONAPO, for its Spanish acronym). According to the CONAPO's information, the loss of population had increased considerably in the last 35 years. Taking into account the difference between immigration and emigration, the actual loss of Mexican population tripled, passing from a total average of 26–29,000 persons in the 70s to more than 300,000 per year in the 90s, and around 400,000 in the first four years of this century. This information was consulted in http://www.conapo.gob.mx/mig_int/03.htm, on August 21, 2006.

4   This article on a local newspaper illustrates the scope of the governmental attitude: "The National Guard has more troops along the Mexico border than planned, but that's not stopping a few Utah Guard members from volunteering for duty there. At the beginning of August, there were 6,199 soldiers on the border, according to the Department of Defense. President Bush wanted 6,000 troops along the border by Aug. 1. Utah's 116th Construction

three years, and to build an impenetrable fence along 700 of the 2,000 miles of the US/Mexico border.[5] Obviously, to be effective, such a barrier has to be physically similar to the one that now separates Israelis from their Palestinian neighbours – with all of the same political implications.

A heavily guarded border is one that underlines the key historic and negative characteristic of US-Mexico relations for the last two centuries: asymmetry of power and rejection of the 'other' because, in the terms of Samuel Huntington, it is a demographic menace to the key national values of the American Anglo-Protestant culture and civilization (Huntington 2004: 221–256). For Patrick Buchanan, a flag bearer of US conservatism, what the US is facing now in its southern border is a kind of barbaric invasion, a conspiracy to retake, through sheer demography, that part of the US that was Mexican before 1848. Mexico, in Buchanan's view, is deliberately pushing its poor and unemployed into the US and urging them to take US citizenship to advance Mexico's strategic national interests (Buchanan 2006).

In May 2006, the White House acknowledged the need for a new immigration policy to confront a massive wave of undocumented migrant workers from the south – Mexico and Central America – after the House of Representatives passed in December 2005 a very tough bill against undocumented migrants (H.R.4437). The bill, sponsored by James Sensenbrenner (R), made every undocumented foreign worker a criminal and closed all avenues to their possible legalization.[6] The presidential call for the National Guard also came after hundreds of thousands

---

Support Equipment Company was among the first group of guard members to arrive at the border in Arizona last June, "Guard offer to help out at border", *Desert Morning News*, 21 August 2006.

5   Nevertheless, there are some disadvantages that must be pointed out. For example, it is going to be difficult to establish equilibrium between the simultaneous interest of the American Government to strengthen the security and accelerate the interchange of goods and people in the border (Ramos García 2004). The possible violation to human rights and the weakening of the American sovereignty are other aspects that some observers have considered problematic, (*Los Angeles Times*, 20 August 2006).

6   See http://thomas.loc.gov/cgi-bin/bdquery/D?d109:43:./temp/~bdpgOE, consulted on 21 August 2006. "To end this migration of illegal aliens into the US, we must stop the businesses that hire them. Without employment opportunities, people will be less likely to break the law to enter this country. Moreover, companies that hire legal residents are placed at a disadvantage when compared to those that hire illegal aliens because they have to pay a higher wage to their employees. In order to survive, many of these 'legitimate' businesses have to depress their employees' wages just to remain competitive with the companies that hire illegal aliens. This is bad for all the people involved, and it is bad for our economy. To address this, my bill requires businesses to verify the accuracy of employees' social security numbers, and raises the penalties assessed to corporations that hire undocumented workers from $250 per illegal alien to $5,000 for first-time offenses," said Sensenbrenner in a press release on March 16, 2006, when the Senate was discussing a possible migration reform (http://www.house.gov/sensenbrenner/wc20060329.html, consulted on 21 August 2006.

of those migrants – undocumented but already integrated into the US economy – marched in dozens of US cities asking for a positive, not punitive, solution to their precarious situation in a country that hires them, uses them, pays them low wages, and keeps them in a kind of legal, social, and political limbo.[7]

What to do with Each Other?

Illegal or undocumented migration of Mexican workers to the US is only one of a number of tribulations in the complex bilateral agenda of the US and Mexico. There were in the past periods in which both countries had a more or less coherent strategy and set of policies toward each other. That is not the case at the beginning of the twenty-first century in spite of the existence of such important factors as a free trade agreement, conservative governments in Washington and Mexico City, and the transformation of Mexico's political regime in the year 2000 from authoritarian to democratic.

A clear set of policies in the US and Mexico does not necessarily imply agreement or smooth co-operation; clashes of interests are an integral and unavoidable part of US–Mexico history. However, the most conspicuous aspect of today's bilateral relationship between Mexico and its powerful neighbour to the north is the combination of a notorious increase in economic and demographic integration coupled with the absence on both sides of the border of a guiding set of principles and policies to manage and guide this integration into the future. In a time of war against terrorism, Washington needs above all a very secure border. On the other hand, Mexico has to have a way to expedite goods through customs

---

7 The American mainstream mass media covered the marches intensively, and the leading newspapers gave them the front page. After the marches, the Pew Hispanic Center conducted a survey from June 5 to July 3 that showed that the Hispanics in the United States felt that prejudice against them, during the debates about illegal immigration reforms, intensified, and showed them united in their lack of expectations to improve their situation through the actions and political negotiations carried out by either the Republican or the Democrat parties. "The pro-immigrant marches were notable both because of their size in some cities and because they took place in so many communities across the country. They were also notable because these unprecedented rallies were mainly the result of a grass-roots effort that involved the Spanish-language media, local immigrant rights coalitions, local labor leaders, the Catholic Church, other religious organizations, student groups and many more. Asked to choose which of two statements came closest to their views, almost two thirds (63%) of Latinos said the immigrant marches were the beginning of a new Hispanic/Latino social movement that will go on for a long time. In contrast, about one in four (24%) described the marches as a one-time event that will not necessarily be repeated. Latino Democrats (65%) and independents (64%) were more likely to take this view than Latino Republicans (52%). But overall—and regardless of income, education, language ability and other factors—Hispanics by a sizeable margin agreed that a new movement would emerge from the marches." (Pew Hispanic Center 2006: 8).

as well as to protect and institutionalize the massive presence of Mexican workers in the US. It is high time for both countries to work out a comprehensive and mutually beneficial set of policies in all areas they see as vital to their national interest.

From Mexico's standpoint, a comprehensive agreement with the US could have been the historic achievement of the first government of its new democratic regime. Unfortunately that was not the case because of two factors: First, the internal political polarization in Mexico made impossible an agreement among the main political actors about what policies should be followed toward the US. Second, after 9/11, there was an almost total marginalization in Washington's foreign agenda of anything not related to its global war against terror and the reshaping of the Middle East. In the end, nothing significant was done by either government.

The best way to outline the dilemma of US–Mexico relations at present is to consider that both societies are economically and demographically integrated as never before, but they do not have the internal political agreements on which to build a general framework that would enable them to manage the complex task of negotiating their respective interests.[8] Integration was not in the minds of either US or Mexican leaders as recently as a quarter of a century ago, but today all the indicators point in that direction: 300 million annual crossings of the US/Mexico border (Ramos García 2004: 616), an increase in trade from US$106 billion in 1994 to US$304 billion in 2005, and 27 million Mexicans living in the US and probably half a million US citizens living in Mexico.[9] This is a de facto integration, not a planned one, and the result is an accumulation of problems and dilemmas as a product of the economic and demographic processes connecting US and Mexican societies: illegal migration, drug trafficking, contradictory energy policies, environmental degradation, water disputes, crime increase, and many others. In the end, it seems that as national societies, Mexico and the US are adrift in their integration because they are not yet ready to imagine a real association between partners that are so unequal in power and so different in cultural and historic background.

---

8   For statistical indicators see Layton 2001. In this issue of *Nexos* there are essays of people from both sides of the Mexico–US border that reflect the lack of an integral vision in the management of the relationship. The former US ambassador in Mexico, Jeffrey Davidow (2003) shares this idea up to a point.

9   These numbers comes from the Secretary of the Economy in Mexico, http://www.economia.gob.mx/index.jsp?P=2261#. Neither Mexican nor US authorities have reached a consensus about the exact number of US citizens living in Mexico. The National Population Council estimates that they were more than 385,000 in 2004, but the Consular Service of the US Embassy in Mexico says that they were between 500,000 and 600,000 the same year. In my last consultation with the US Embassy in 2006, the public affairs office of the Embassy confirmed that it was fair to say that more than half a million Americans live in Mexico.

On both sides of the Mexico/US border, governments are just reacting to the circumstances and improvising in trying to cope with the day-to-day complexities of their coexistence. The challenge is to tame the evil of the imbalance of power and devise a mutually acceptable set of rules as a basis for a respectful and constructive long-term bilateral relationship. Such a relationship has to be based on the recognition and acceptance of differences in their respective national interests as they understand them.

To understand the importance as well as the possibilities of formulating an intelligent and solid set of political answers to overcome the different national interests of Mexico and the US, we must go back as far as the 1930s and 1940s. The so-called Good Neighbour Policy proposed by the US to Latin America in those years effectively solved problems as delicate and complex as those that originated with the Mexican Revolution – agrarian reform, oil expropriation and nationalization, and foreign debt, as well as the new ones produced by the Second World War (Wood 1961). Out of this policy came close military co-operation, the first trade agreement and, last but not least, the institutionalization of the presence of Mexican workers in US fields to replace the US workers recruited into the army (Chacón 1996).

Of course, one can point to a more recent 'golden age' of co-operation as is suggested by President Johnson's letter to President Díaz Ordaz in 1966, quoted earlier in this chapter, or the beginning of the 1990s and the inception of NAFTA. However, at the end of the 1960s the US–Mexico bilateral relationship suffered a setback as a result of the unilateral decision of Richard Nixon in 1969 to launch Operation Interception at the border to punish Mexico for not doing enough to intercept illegal drugs entering the US (Craig 1972: 206–207; Torres 2000: 207–212).[10] The 1990s effort was a half-failed 'great policy' because the negotiation did not include some key issues, such as migration, that are haunting us now.[11]

An Agenda and Its Problems

The bilateral US–Mexico agenda at the beginning of twenty-first century is as complex as it is urgent. For two countries that are otherwise at peace with each other and have an ongoing free trade agreement, the outstanding issues make an impressive list.

1. Because of public attention, Mexican undocumented migration into the US is right now at the centre of such an agenda. In the 1960s Mexicans fleeing their country to find a place under the sun of the US economy averaged 29,000 a year. At the beginning of the new century the annual average

---

10   For the American government vision, see Massing 1998.
11   The best background study of NAFTA is Weintraub 1990. NAFTA negotiations are analizad in Bulmer-Thomas, Craske and Serrano 1994 and Globerman 1993.

had jumped to 400,000 and some observers even put the figure at around half a million. According to official data, there are now about 10 million Mexicans living and working in the US. There are 17 million US citizens of Mexican descent. Of those Mexicans now living north of the Rio Grande, about half are there without proper authorization.

Mexico's northern border is the port of entry of illegal migrants from all over the world, but citizens of Third World countries are a minority. In the year 2005, 85 per cent of 1.2 million people apprehended when they were trying to enter the US illegally were Mexican nationals.[12] For the US, Mexico is at the core of its illegal migrants problem.

2. Mexican exports to the US last year amounted US$183 billion (although there was a high level of imports). If we add the remittances sent home by Mexicans working in the US (US$20 billion) then the economic link between Mexico and the US is almost the equivalent to Mexico's total relationship with the rest of the world market. Dependency is the key characteristic of Mexico's economic relationship with its northern neighbour.[13]

3. Mexico is one of the main suppliers of the array of illegal drugs demanded by consumers in the US. Hard data are very difficult to get in this field, but according to the UN in 2003 the total value of illicit drugs at the consumer level in the world amounted to $332 billion. The White House calculates that Mexican drug dealers are getting 4.2 per cent of that amount, or $14 billion.[14]

4. As a result of the importance of drug production, transportation, and commercialization, drug cartels in Mexico are virtually ungovernable and a source of violence along the border. This violence is increasing at an alarming rate. In 2005, there were 1,500 homicides related to drug cartel internal warfare. In Nuevo Laredo, for example, the homicide rate is now three and a half times that of Washington, DC, a very dangerous city in the US.[15] A violent southern border is a menace for a US that has security as its highest priority.

---

12 This information was consulted in http://www.conapo.gob.mx/mig_int/03.htm, on August 21, 2006.

13 The total value of Mexican exports in 2005 was $213.7 billion. Mexican exports to the US are 85 per cent of the total.

14 US Government 2005, p. 36, available at http://www.whitehousedrugpolicy.gov/publications/policy/ndcs06/chap3.pdf, consulted on May 15, 2006.

15 Though Nuevo Laredo is an important place for the drug-related violence, the problem is spreading around the country. According to Mexican newspaper *El Universal*, Mexico is experiencing unprecedented levels of killings related with this problem. Mexico witnessed at least 1,537 drug-related killings from February 28 to December 31, 2005. These homicides continued increasing during 2006. The first semester of 2006, the same source registered, at least, 1,003 deaths ("Violencia del narco deja mil muertos", *El Universal*, July 1, 2006). Also see Freeman 2006.

5. Water pollution and mismanagement of the environment are affecting people on both sides of the Mexico/US border. Water is increasingly a scare resource in the region and its distribution and conservation is another element of tension and open conflict between the two countries. In recent years, the State Department has protested because Mexico has not fulfilled its obligations according to the water treaties to which both countries subscribe. The future requires careful administration of surface and underground water resources along the border and developing alternative sources of supply (Torres 2004: 333–356).[16]

6. Oil has been a key element not only in US–Canada relations but also in US–Mexico relations. In the 1970s, Washington began to develop plans to incorporate Mexican oil into the US strategy to increase its energy security. Part of President Bush's reason for negotiating a free trade agreement with Mexico at the end of the 1980s was to secure access to his southern neighbour's oil. Today the Mexican government is closer than ever to privatizing the oil industry which was expropriated and nationalized in 1938, but which is now falling behind in technology and investment, and deeply in debt because of extremely heavy taxation (two-thirds of PEMEX revenues are taken by the government). Constitutional clauses – remnants of Mexican nationalism – remain as the last defence against privatization and the acceptance of foreign (US) investment in the oil industry. US pressures in the oil industry are constant; the conflict is between the definitions of national interest held by each nation (Puyana Mutis 2006).

7. In this new unipolar international system, Mexico and the US have very different perceptions of what is the proper definition of legal intervention by one country in the affairs of another and the proper role of the United Nations in such interventions. The discussion of sanctions against the government of Iraq in the United Nations Security Council in 2003 at the moment in which Mexico had one of the non-permanent seats brought these differences to the surface in a very dramatic way.[17] For Mexico, any

---

16 For an historical background, see Samaniego López 2006.

17 Mexico's ambassador to the United Nations, Adolfo Aguilar Zínser was due to be relieved of his post on January 1, 2003, because of US displeasure with Aguilar's position about Iraq; but he resigned a month and a half earlier. Before his resignation Aguilar had declared that Washington was acting as if Mexico was "its backyard" and treated it as a subordinated, not as a partner. That assertion sounded true to many Mexicans, but the Secretary of State Colin L. Powell, considered it "outrageous" and President Vicente Fox called it "an offense to Mexico". The most important American newspapers reported the diplomatic tension around Aguilar's resignation. *The New York Times*, (21 November, 2003) reported "He gave no public explanation but told reporters, "It's clear I have to leave the UN" Mexican officials said this week that Mr Aguilar was being dismissed because he refused to retract comments he made in a speech last week in Mexico City in which he said that Washington wanted a "relationship of convenience and subordination" with Mexico and that the political and intellectual classes of the United States regarded

claim made by the US to have a right to unilateral intervention was and continues to be an unacceptable proposition. Unilateralism goes against one of the key elements of Mexico's historical position in defence of the principle of self determination.

Canada and Mexico

The first step in the construction of an economic and political North America was the negotiation of a free trade agreement between Canada and the US. However, Canadian participation in the negotiation of a North American free trade agreement at the beginning of the 1990s was less out of enthusiasm for a new relationship with Mexico and more to protect Canadian interests in the US market from possible Mexican encroachment. Mexican exports to Canada are just a fraction of its exports to the US (1.8 per cent) and Canadian imports from Mexico are also a fraction of its imports from the US (5.2 per cent).[18]

A Canadian economic presence in Mexico dates back to the end of nineteenth century. NAFTA has given a push to trade and investment between the southern

---

their southern neighbor as «a backyard.» At Mr. Aguilar's final Security Council meeting, Secretary General Kofi Annan praised him for his «independent spirit»" *Los Angeles Times*, (November 22, 2003) reported "Aguilar Zinser knows why Washington was irritated. A lawyer and former senator, he took apart resolutions on Iraq paragraph by paragraph to question apparent conflicts with international law. "This became kind of a pattern in the [Security] Council," he said with bemused hindsight. "They all knew they just had to wait and I would throw them the book. " His political skills also came into play in the Security Council. He and the then Chilean ambassador to the UN, Juan Gabriel Valdés, persuaded some of the 10 nonpermanent members to join forces to influence the Iraq debate: Six of them decided to withhold their votes on the resolution seeking the UN's blessing to invade Iraq. Facing a shortfall of support, the U.S. withdrew the resolution and invaded Iraq without the UN's approval. During negotiations in the spring, Powell met with Mexican Foreign Minister Luis Ernesto Derbez and Aguilar Zinser in a small room off the Security Council chamber. Powell leaned over and, shaking his finger at the ambassador, jokingly lectured him on what a problem he had created for the US But Washington's displeasure was not a joke. Privately, Powell reportedly asked Derbez to restrain his ambassador «many times» and Bush twice asked Fox to recall him. [...] After the war began, things changed for Aguilar Zinser. Bush froze out Fox, taking six weeks to return the Mexican president's phone call to explain his position. In Mexico, critics who thought standing on principle had become too costly grew more vocal. After the midterm elections in July, more of those critics gained Fox's ear. Suddenly, Aguilar Zinser seemed to be out of favor. In October, during Fox's first phone conversation with Bush in months, the US president reportedly told Fox that he had a problem with his ambassador."

18 Mexican exports to Canada in 2005 amounted $3,3 billion versus $185.4 billion to the United States. Imports from Canada amounted to $6,2 billion versus $118,4 billion from the United States. The information comes from http://www.economia.gob.mx/index.jsp?P=2261#, consulted on August 30, 2006.

and northern neighbours of the US, but they remain relatively marginal to each other. Mexico and Canada still have miles to go before they can become meaningful partners (Castro Martínez 2001). Mexico has been so preoccupied and overwhelmed with its bilateral relation with the US that it has given very little thought to the Canadian factor.

An Overview

As a result of President George W. Bush's decision to invade Iraq, Mexico as well as many other nations, including Canada, were politically marginalized by Washington. The initiative of the Mexican government to work out with the US an agreement on migration – the main element of Mexican President Vicente Fox's foreign policy agenda – was simply pushed aside by Washington, and so the door opened again to the spirit of 'distant neighbors' that characterized US-Mexico relations before NAFTA and was so well described by Alan Riding in 1985 (Riding 1985).

At the beginning of September 2001, during the state visit of Mexico's president to the White House, George W. Bush did not hesitate to state that the most important foreign relationship of the US was the one with Mexico. However, a few days after that visit Washington's view of the world changed dramatically: world-wide war on terrorism became the new focus of its interest and Mexico and the whole idea of a possible 'Our North America' was forgotten.

In 2005 a group of academics and businessmen with interests in Mexico presented a plan to re-launch NAFTA. The core of the project was a fund to invest heavily in the infrastructure of Mexico so it could compete with China on better terms in the American market. The fund of $20 billion should be made up with contributions by Mexico, the US, and Canada, in that order. In the end, nothing substantial came out of such a positive proposal.[19] It was not until much later that President Bush began again to focus his attention on Mexico, but then only in respect to migration.

In his address on May 15, 2006 dealing with the need of a course of action regarding migration, President Bush said that he was thinking of new comprehensive immigration legislation that would include a guest workers

---

19   The idea of a special fund for Mexico is based on the European model: "The evidence on the diverging effects of integration is mixed but not inconsistent with what was learned from Europe. The strongest economic power in North America experienced the least effect. The weaker countries suffered the most volatility, although this was due also to mistaken macroeconomic policies. The weakest country experienced the widest disparities in income among classes and regions. The Canadian and US system of income transfers among regions mitigate these disparities and lift the countries as a whole, but Mexico does not yet have the fiscal system that could permit such transfers, and there is no regional mechanism." (Pastor 2005: 51).

program, but in the meantime he was calling on the National Guard to help secure the border with Mexico. Behind the president's proposal were two other, very different, proposals: one presented by conservative Republicans – the already mentioned bill by Sensenbrenner in the House of Representatives – and another by liberal Democrats and Republicans in the Senate. The only part of the negotiation between all the interests involved that was clear was that Mexico did not have a part in a negotiation that would affect it deeply as part of North America.

Washington's interest in a reform of migration laws has nothing to do with Mexico's insistence on a general negotiation on the subject. It was a reaction to internal pressures from a divided public opinion that demanded some sort of action in regard to illegal migrants.

Conclusion

Mexico is obviously the weakest link in any attempt to create a real North American partnership. In terms of purchasing power, Mexico's per capita income is only one fourth that of the US and one third of Canada's. The gap between the underdeveloped Latin country in the south and the two Anglo countries of North America is not closing but widening. In per capita terms, Mexico's growth in the at the dawn of the twenty-first century has been less than one percent. This situation alone can explain illegal migration to the US and many other negative phenomena. If there is going to be a legitimate great North America, this trend has to be reversed, because only a prosperous and confident Mexico can be a real partner of the US and Canada.

At the present and from the Mexican standpoint, the idea of US citizens, Canadians, and Mexicans living harmoniously in a space that all three of them can really call their own is still in the realm of Utopia. To be a reality, 'Our North America' requires a dramatic and historical change in the political, economic, and mental framework of the three countries. At the present there are no indicators that such a change is taking place. However, to close the door to the possibility of a more meaningful and harmonious North American region is an abdication of an idea that is full of positive elements, especially for Mexico. Therefore, let us continue the exploration of a path that is full of difficulties and contradictions but that just a quarter of a century ago was just unimaginable.

Bibliography

Ackelson, Jason and Kastner, Justin, 2005. "The Security and Prosperity Partnership of North America." Presented at the biennial meeting of the Association for Canadian Studies in the United States, St. Louis.

Adams, Michael. 2003. *Fire and Ice. The United States, Canada and the Myth of Converging Values*, Toronto: Penguin Canada.

Adelman, Jeremy and Stephen Aron. 1999. "From Borderlands to Borders: Empires, Nation-States, and the Peoples in between in North American History," *The American Historical Review*, 104(3), 814–841.

AFP and Reuters. 2010. "Cayó 41% la inversión extranjera directa en América Latina en 2009," *La Jornada* 20 Jan.

Aglietta, M. 1979. *Theory of Capitalist Regulation*. London: New Left Books.

Aguayo, Sergio. 2008. *El Almanaque de México: 2008*. Aguilar: Mexico City.

Alden, Edward. 2009. *The Closing of the American Border*. New York: Harper Perennial.

Ali, Tariq and David Barsamian. 2005. *Speaking of Empire and Resistance. Conversations with Tariq Ali*. New York: The New Press.

Amador, Roberto González and David Brooks. 2007. "Lenta reducción de la pobreza por alta concentración del ingreso en México," *La Jornada*, 21 Oct.

Anderson, B. 1991. *Imagined Communities*. London: Verso.

Anderson, Greg. 2003. "The Compromise of Embedded Liberalism, American Trade Remedy Law, and Canadian Softwood Lumber: Can't We All Just Get Along," *Canadian Foreign Policy* 10(2) (Winter), 87–108.

Anderson, Greg. 2004. "The Canada-United States Softwood Lumber Dispute: Where Politics and Theory Meet," *Journal of World Trade* 38(4) August: 661–699.

Anderson, Greg. 2005. "The End of the Renaissance? U.S. Trade Policy and the Second Term of George W. Bush," in George Maclean (ed.), *Bison Paper 7, Canada and the United States: A Relationship at a Crossroads?* Winnipeg: Centre for Defense and Security Studies: 79–93.

Anderson, Greg. 2006a. "The Doha Round After Hong Kong: Is The Cup Half-Empty or Half-Full?" *The WTO Ministerial Conference Hong Kong, December 2005*. Information Bulletin No. 89 (Edmonton: Western Centre for Economic Research, February: 3–9.

Anderson, Greg. 2006b. "North American Economic Integration and the Challenges Wrought by 9/11," *Journal of Homeland Security and Emergency Management* 3(2) (Summer).

Anderson, Greg. 2006c. "Can Someone Please Settle this Dispute: Canadian Softwood Lumber and the Dispute Settlement Mechanisms of the NAFTA and the WTO," *The World Economy* 29(5) June: 585–610.

Anderson, Greg. 2006d. "The Parallel Lives of Softwood and Cement," *North American Integration Monitor* 3(3). Washington, DC: Center for Strategic and International Studies.

Anderson, Greg. 2009. "The Reluctance of Hegemons: Comparing the Regionalization Strategies of a Crouching Cowboy and a Hidden Dragon," in Emilian Kavalski (ed.), *China and the Politics of Regionalization*. Farnham: Ashgate Publishing.

Anderson, Greg, and Christopher Sands. 2007. "Negotiating North America: The Security and Prosperity Partnership," *Hudson Institute White Paper*. Washington, DC: Hudson Institute.

Andreas, Peter. 2002. "The Re-Bordering of America After 11 September," *World Affairs* 8:1, 195–202.

Andreas, Peter. 2003. "A Tale of Two Borders: The U.S.-Canada and U.S.-Mexico Lines after 9-11," in Peter Andreas and Thomas J. Biersteker (eds), *The Rebordering of North America*. New York and London: Routledge.

Anonymous, "Mexico: Migration, Remittances, Economy" in *Migration News* 14(4), October 2008; available online at http://migration.ucdavis.edu/mn/more.php?id=3436_0_2_0, accessed November 7, 2008.

Anzaldúa, G. 1991. *Borderlands: The new mestiza = La frontera*. San Francisco, Aunt Lute Books.

Appadurai, A. 1990. "Disjuncture and difference in the global cultural economy," in M. Featherstone (ed.), *Global Culture: Nationalism, Globalization, and Modernity*. London: Sage.

Appadurai, A. 1996. *Modernity at Large*. Minneapolis: University of Minnesota Press.

Associated Press. 2002. "US Criticized on Immunity Demand," at http://www.globalpolicy.org/intljustice/icc/crisis/0710de.htm, July 10.

Audley, John J., Demetrios G. Papademetriou, Sandra Polaski, and Scott Vaughn. 2003. *NAFTA's Promise and Reality: Lessons from Mexico for the Hemisphere*. Washington, DC: Carnegie Endowment for International Peace.

Avritzer, Leonardo. 2002. *Democracy and the Public Space in Latin America*. Princeton, NJ: Princeton University Press.

Axtell, James. 1992. *Beyond 1492: Encounters in Colonial North America*, New York: Oxford University Press.

Ayres, Jeffrey. 1998. *Defying Conventional Wisdom: Political Movements and Popular Contention Against North American Free Trade*. Toronto: University of Toronto Press.

Ayres, Jeffrey and Laura Macdonald. 2006. "Deep Integration and Shallow Governance: The Limits to Civil Society Engagement Across North America," *Policy and Society* 25(3), 23–42.

Bacevich, Andrew J. 2005. *The New American Militarism: How Americans are Seduced by War*. Oxford: Oxford University Press.

Bacon, David. 2008. "The Right to Stay Home," *New America Media*, July 9, 2008. Online http://www.news.newamericamedia.org/news/view_article.html?article_id=66a8eccf43428bfe3542bfc7ddfb19ff.

Ballinas, Víctor. 2010. "Abusos aberrantes de soldados en operativos anticrimen: HRW," *La Jornada*, 21 Jan.

Bandy, Joe and Jackie Smith (eds), *Coalitions across Borders: Transnational Protest and Neoliberal Order.* Lanham: Rowman and Littlefield.

Barman, Jean. 1999. "What a Difference a Border Makes: Aboriginal Racial Intermixture in the Pacific Northwest," *Journal of the West* 38, 14–20.

Barry, Donald. 2003. "Managing Canada-U.S. Relations in the Post 9/11 Era: Do We Need a Big Idea?" *Policy Papers of the Americas*, XIV, No 11. Washington, DC, Center for Strategic and International Studies.

Barry, Tom. "The US Power Complex: What's New" at http://www.fpif.org/fpiftxt/913.

Bartelson, Jens. 1995. *A Genealogy of Sovereignty.* Cambridge: Cambridge University Press.

Bartra, R. 1993. "Introduction," in *Warrior for Gringostroika: Essay, Performance Texts and Poetry*, trans. Coco Fusco. St. Paul, Minnesota: Graywolf Press, 11–12.

Beith, M. 2005. "The beat goes on". *Newsweek*. Nov. 14. Retrievable from: www.msnbc.msn.com/id/9917082/site/newsweek/.

Bergsten, C. Fred and Edward M. Graham. 1992. "Needed: New International Rules for Foreign Direct Investment," *The International Trade Journal* 7, 1 (Fall), 15–44.

Bergsten, C. Fred. Nov./Dec. 2002. "A Renaissance for U.S. Trade Policy?" *Foreign Affairs* 81(6).

Bhabha, Homi. 2004. *The Location of Culture*. London: Routledge.

Bhagwati, Jagdish. 2004. "Don't Cry for Cancun," *Foreign Affairs*, Jan./Feb.

Bipartisan Trade Promotion Authority Act of 2002, technically Division B, Title XXI of the Trade Act of 2002, PL107-210, 6 August 2002.

Blank, Stephen. 2005. "North American Integration: Looking Ahead," *Mimeo*. July.

Boltvinik, Julio. 2001. "Criterios de pobreza para México," *La Jornada*, 18 May.

Bondi, Loretta. 2004. *Beyond the Border and Across the Atlantic: Mexico's Foreign and Security Policy post-September 11th*. Washington, DC: Center for Transantic Relations.

Borden, Anthony. 2002. "Criminal Court Impasse Broken," Institute for War and Peace Reporting, at http://www.globalpolicy.org/intljustice/icc/crisis/0713impasse.htm, July 13.

Bortz, Jeffrey. 1992. "The Effect of Mexico's Post-War Industrialization on the U.S.-Mexico Price and Wage Comparison," in Bustamante, J.A., Reynolds,

C.W. and Hinojosa-Ojeda, R.A. (eds), *US-Mexico Relations: Labour Market Interdependence*. Stanford, CA: Stanford University Press.
Bow, Brian. 2006–2007. "Out of ideas? Models and strategies for Canada-US relations," *International Journal*, Winter, 123–142.
Bow, Brian. 2010. "We can't return to our special relationship with the United States", *Globe and Mail*, April 29.
Bow, Brian and Lennox, Patrick (eds). 2008. *An Independent Foreign Policy for Canada?* Toronto: University of Toronto Press.
Brodie, J. 2006. "North American Deep Integration: Canadian Perspectives," *Asia-Pacific Panorama* 4(1), 1–25.
Brodie, J. 2008. "Performing North America as Community," in Yasmeen Abu-Laban, Radha Jhappan and François Rocher (eds), *Politics in North America: Redefining Continental Relations*. Peterborough, ON: Broadview Press, 441–460.
Brodie, Janine. 2009. "A Public Relations Disaster? The SPP and the Governance of North America," *Revista Mexicana de Estudios Canadienses*, 16, 15–33.
Brodie, Janine. 2012a. "Will North America Survive?" in Jeffrey Ayres and Laura Macdonald (eds), *North America in Question: Regional Integration in an Era of Political and Economic Turbulence*. Toronto: University of Toronto Press.
Brodie, Janine. 2012b. "Mobility Regimes: Reflections on the Short Life and Times of the Security and Prosperity Partnership of North America ," in Suzan Ilcan (ed.), *Mobilities, Knowledge and Social Justice*. Montreal: McGill-Queen's University Press.
Brooks, David. 2005. "Expertos de EU: fracasarán medidas antimigrantes," *La Jornada*, 7 Dec.
Brooks, David. 2007. "Reporta AILF más de 2 mil muertos en la frontera suroeste de EU," *La Jornada*, 10 February.
Brown, Jennifer and Schenck, Theresa. 2002. "Métis, Mestizo and Mixed Blood," in Deloria, Phillips J. and Salisbury, Neal (eds), *Companion to American Indian History*. New York: Blackwell.
Brown, Richard Harvey. 1993. "Cultural representation and ideological domination," *Social Forces* 71(3), 657–676.
Brysk, Alison. 2000. *From Tribal Village to Global Village: Indian Rights and International Relations in Latin America*. Stanford University Press: Stanford.
Buchanan, Patrick. 2006. *State of Emergency: The Third World Invasion and Conquest of America*. New York: Thomas Dunne Books/St. Martin's Press.
Buie, Christiane. 2005. "Does North American Transboundary Water 'Governance' Exist?" Paper presented to the Canadian Political Science Association, June 2.
Bulmer-Thomas, V., Craske, Nikki and Serrano, Mónica. 1994. *México frente al TLC: costos y beneficios*. México: El Colegio de México-Lotería Nacional para la Asistencia Pública.
Burciaga, J.A. 1993. *Drink Cultura: Chicanismo*. Santa Barbara, CA: Joshua Odell Editions.

Bush, George W. 2004. Address to Graduation Exercise of the United States Military Academy, West Point, New York, June 1, 2002, reprinted in Gregory M. Scott, Randall J. Jones, Jr., and Louis S. Furmanski (eds), *21 Debated, Issues in World Politics*, 2nd edition, Upper Saddle River, New Jersey: Pearson/Prentice-Hall, 53.

Bush, George W., Vicente Fox, and Paul Martin. 2005. 'Joint Press Conference', *The Washington Post Online*, March 23, http://www.washingtonpost.com/wp-dyn/articles/A59996-2005Mar23.html.

Burney, Derek H. 2005. "The Perennial Challenge: Managing Canada-US Relations," in Andrew F. Cooper and Dane Rowlands (eds), *Split Image, Canada Among Nations*, Montreal and Kingston: McGill-Queen's University Press.

Burney, Derek. 2009. "Engaging Obama," *Policy Options*, April, 23–4.

Bustamante, Jorge A. 1992. "Interdependence, Undocumented Migration and National Security" in Jorge A. Bustamante et al. (eds), *U.S. Mexico Relations; Labor Market Interdependence*. Stanford, CA: Stanford University Press.

Bustamante, Jorge A. 1983. "Mexican Migration: The political Dynamics of Perceptions," in Clark W. Reynolds and Carlos Tello (eds), *U.S.-Mexico Relations: Economy and Social Aspects*. Stanford, CA: Stanford University Press.

Bustamante, J.A., Reynolds C.W. and Hinojosa-Ojeda R.A. (eds) 1992. *U.S.-Mexico Relations; Labor Market Interdependence*, Stanford, CA: Stanford University Press.

Butcher, Bernadette. 1990. "Al oeste del Edén: la semiótica de la conquista, reconstrucción del ícono y política estructural," in López-Baral, Mercedes (ed.), *Iconografía política del nuevo mundo*. San Juan: Universidad de Puerto Rico.

Calderón Hinojosa, Felipe. 2010. "Speech to Canadian Parliament." http://www.scribd.com/doc/32070392/Felipe-Calderon-s-remarks-to-Parliament-May27-2010.

Cameron, Maxwell A. and Brian W. Tomlin. 2000. *The Making of the NAFTA: How the Deal Was Done*. Ithaca, NY: Cornell University Press.

Campbell, Bruce. 2005. "The Case Against Continental Deep Integration." Ottawa: Canadian Centre for Policy Alternatives, November. www.policyalternatives.ca.

Canada. 1985. *Report of the Royal Commission on the Economic Union and Development Prospects for Canada, Volume One*. Ottawa: Minister of Supply and Services Canada.

Canada. 2002. *Report of the Standing Committee on Foreign Affairs and International Trade. Partners in North America: Advancing Canada's Relations With the United States and Mexico*. Ottawa: Public Works and Government Services Canada.

Canada. Department of Foreign Affairs and International Trade. 2000. *Canada-U.S. Partnership: Building a Border for the 21st Century.* Ottawa, Ontario: Department of Foreign Affairs and International Trade.

Canada, DFAIT. 2001. Canada-U.S. Smart Border Declaration, December 12. http://www.international.gc.ca/anti-terrorism/declaration-en.asp.

Canada. Department of Foreign Affairs and International Trade. 2005. *Canada-Mexico Partnership: Report to Leaders.* http://www.fac-aec.gc.ca/cmp-en.asp#report.

Canada. DFAIT. 2005. *Security and Prosperity Partnership of North America. Report to Leaders.* June. www.fac.gc.ca/spp/sppmenu-en.asp.

Canada. Department of Foreign Affairs and International Trade. n.d. *Welcome to Canada's Human Security Website.* http://www.humansecurity.gc.ca/menu-en.asp.

Canada, Prime Minister's Office. 2006. *The Security and Prosperity Partnership of North America: Next Steps.* http://pm.gc.ca/includes/send_friend_eMail_print.asp?URL=/eng/media.asp&id=1084&1.

Canada, Prime Minister's Office. 2007a. "Prime Minister's statement at closing press conference of SPP meeting," Montebello, Quebec, 21 August.

Canada, Prime Minister's Office. 2007b. "PM raises Canadian concerns on trilateral agenda at North American Leaders' Summit," Montebello, Quebec, 21 August.

Canada, Prime Minister's Office. 2008. "Joint Statement by President Bush, President Calderón, Prime Minister Harper – North American Leaders' Summit," Ottawa, Ontario, 22 April.

Canada, SPP. 2006. Prosperity Priorities. http://www.spp-psp.gc.ca/eic/site/spp-psp.nsf/eng/00052.html.

Canadian Press. 2002. "Mexico would support shift to security perimeter with U.S. and Canada," February 2, www.cp.org/english/hp.htm.

Cardoso, Víctor. 2010a. "Cayeron remesas en noviembre al peor nivel desde febrero de 2005," *La Jornada*, 5 Jan.

Cardoso, Víctor. 2010b. "Crece a 25.7 millones la cifra de mexicanos en la economía informal," *La Jornada*, 25 Jan.

Careless, J.M.S. 1967. *The Union of the Canadas: The Growth of Canadian Institutions, 1841–1857.* Toronto, McClelland and Stewart Limited.

Carleton University. 2009. Canada-US Project, *From Correct to Inspired: A Blueprint for Canada-U.S. Relations under a New Administration*, 19 January.

Carlsen, Laura and Talli Nauman. 2004. "10 Years of NAFTA's Commission on Environmental Cooperation: Has It Made a Difference?", Silver City: International Relations Center, 16 December.

Carreras de Velazco, Mercedes. 1974. *Los Mexicanos que devolvió la crisis 1929–1932*, Mexico, D.F.: Secretaria de Relaciones Exteriores, Dirección General de Archivo.

Castellanos, Antonio. 2006. "Pobres resultados en empleo: economistas; falta avance: Sojo," *La Jornada*, 2 March.

Castillo García, Gustavo, 2006. "Cárteles mexicanos obtienen 13 mil 800 mdd por ventas de drogas en EU," *La Jornada.*
Castro Martínez, Pedro. 2001. "Las relaciones México-Canadá: su evolución reciente", *Foro Internacional*, 41, 761–783.
Castro-Rea, Julián. 1996. "Towards a Single North American Polity? The Effects of NAFTA upon Mexican and Canadian Domestic Politics," in Christos Paraskevopoulos, Ricardo Grinspun and George Eaton, (eds), *Economic Integration in the Americas.* Cheltenham: Edward Elgar, 88–102.
Castro-Rea, Julián. 2006. "Are US business priorities driving continental integration?" *Edmonton Journal*, March 27.
Castro-Rea, Julián. 2009a. "Canada Must Respect Mexico," *Edmonton Journal*, June 3.
Castro-Rea, Julián. 2009b. "Why is the Right Winning in North America? Comparisons and Mutual Influences in Canada, Mexico and the United States," in Galeana, Patricia (ed.), *Historia comparada de las Américas*. Mexico City: Pan American Institute of Geography and History, 535–562.
CCCE. Canadian Council of Chief Executives. 2003. "Security and Prosperity: Toward a New Canada-United States Partnership in North America. www.ceocouncil.ca/publications/pdf/716af13644402901250657d4c418a12e/presentations_2003_01_01.pdf.
CCCE. Canadian Council of Chief Executives. 2004. "New Frontiers: Building a 21st Century Canada-US Partnership in North America." www.ceocoucil.ca/en/view/?document_id=365.
Cellucci, Paul. 2005. *Unquiet Diplomacy*. Toronto: Key Porter.
Certain Softwood Lumber Products from Canada. Final Affirmative Countervailing Duty Determination File USA-CDA-2002-1904-03, Decision of the Panel on the Fourth Remand Determination, 5 October 2005; Decision of the Panel on the Fifth Remand Determination, 17 March 2006.
Chaney, D. 1994. *The Cultural Turn.* London: Routledge.
Chacón, Susana. 1996. "Entre el conflicto y la cooperación: negociación de los acuerdos militar, de comercio y de braceros en la relación bilateral México-E.E.U.U., 1940–1955." Mexico City: Universidad Iberoamericana. PhD thesis.
Chávez, John R. 1989. "Aztlán, Cibola, and Frontier New Spain," in Anaya, Rudolfo A. and Lomelí, Francisco A. (eds), *Aztlán: Essays on the Chicano Homeland*. Albuquerque: Academica-El Norte Publications.
Cheng, Joseph Y.S. 2005. "Latin America in China's Peaceful Rise." Paper presented to the conference *Re-Mapping the Americas: Globalization, Regionalization and the FTAA*, St. Augustine, Trinidad and Tobago, The University of the West Indies, October.
CIEPAC. 2005. "Summary of Toronto Meeting." www.cipac.org/otras%20temas/nafta-plus/index.htm.
Ciuriak, Dan. "Canadian trade policy development: Stakeholder consultations and public policy research," in John M. Curtis and Dan Ciuriak (eds), *Trade Policy*

Research 2004. Ottawa, Department of Foreign Affairs and International Trade, 215.

Clarkson, Stephen. 2002. *Uncle Sam and Us: Globalization, Neoconservatism, and the Canadian State*. Toronto: University of Toronto Press.

Clarkson, Stephen. 2004. "Canada's External Constitution under Global Trade Governance," in Ysolde Gendreau (ed.), *Dessiner la société par le droit/ Mapping Society Through Law*. Les Éditions Thémis, CRDP, Université de Montréal, 1–31.

Clarkson, Stephen, Davidson Ladly, Sarah, Merwart, Megan and Thorne, Carlton. 2005. "The Primitive Realities of Continental Governance in North America," in Edgar Grande and Louis W. Pauly (eds), *Complex Sovereignty: Reconstituting Political Authority in the Twenty-first Century*. Toronto: University of Toronto Press, 168–94.

Cleaver, Henry. 1998. "The Zapatistas and the Electronic Fabric of Struggle," in Holloway, John and Peláez, Eloína (eds), *Zapatista: Reinventing Revolution in Mexico*. London: Pluto Press.

Coalition for Fair Lumber Imports Executive Committee v. United States of America, et al. United States Court of Appeals for the District of Columbia, September 2005.

Coleman, M. 2004. "U.S. Statecraft and the U.S.-Mexico Border as Security/ Economy Nexus," *Political Geography* 24, 189.

Conference Board of Canada. 2001. "Border choices: Balancing the need for trade and security", 3–5. http://www.conferenceboard.ca/pubs/borderchoices.10.01.pdf.

Conference Board of Canada. 2003. "Renewing the Relationship: Canada and the United States in the 21st Century." Ottawa: Conference Board of Canada.

Cordera, R. and Cabrera Adame, C.J. (eds). 2008. *El papel des las ideas y las políticas en el cambio estructural en México*. Mexico City: Universidad Nacional Autónoma de México/Fondo de Cultura Económica.

Cordera Campos, Rolando. 2006. "Cuesta abajo," *La Jornada*, 19 Feb.

Cornejo, Guillermo. 2008. "Latin America and Europe: The Future of EU-CAN Trade Negotiations," 23 July. Retrieved from http://.coha.org/2008/07, August 2008.

Council on Foreign Relations, Canadian Council of Chief Executives and Consejo Mexicano de Asuntos Internacionales. 2005. *Building a North American Community. Report of an Independent Task Force*. New York: CFR.

Cox, Robert. 2005. "A Canadian Dilemma: The United States or the World," *International Journal* 60(3), 667–684.

Craig, Richard B. 1971. *The Bracero Program. Interest Groups and Foreign Policy*, Austin, TX: University of Texas Press.

Craig, Richard. 1972. "Operación intercepción: una política de presión internacional," *Foro Internacional* 21, 206–207.

Croucher, Sheila. 2004. "Homeland Insecurity: Ambivalent Attachments and Hegemonic Narratives of American Nationhood post-9/11." Presented at the International Studies Association meeting, Montreal.

Cunningham, H. 2004. "Nations Rebound? Crossing Borders in a Gated Globe?" *Identities: Global Studies in Culture and Power* II, 337.

d'Aquino, Thomas. 2003. "Coaxing the Elephant: Can Canada Best Support Multilateralism by Cozying Up to the United States," *Policy Options*, May. www.ceocouncil.ca/en/view/?document_id=100&area_id=7.

d'Aquino, Thomas. 2008. "Rethinking the Spirit of 1993: Forging a New Path Forward for North America. Remarks to the North American Forum, Washington, D.C., 2008. www.ceocouncil.ca/publications/pdf/test.../Remarks_by_Thomas_d_Aquino_to_the_North_American_Forum_June_17_2008.pdf.

d'Aquino, Thomas. 2009. 'Enhancing the Canada-United States Partnership." Testimony Before the Standing Committee of Parliament on Foreign Affairs and International Development, February 24. www.ceocouncil.ca/publications/pdf/test_9b81a7ba7ba7b50855be2232023a41d091c/Submission_Standing_Committee_on_Foreign_Affairs_and_Intl_Dev_Feb_25_2009.pdf.

Dark, Michael, Greg Anderson, and Anne McLellan. 2009. "Place A Call to Mexico City," *Ottawa Citizen*, 22 May.

Darwin, C. 1859 [1979]. *The Origin of Species*. New York: Random House.

Davidow, Jeffrey. 2003. *El oso y el puercoespín. Testimonio de un embajador de Estados Unidos en México.* Mexico: Grijalbo.

Davis Hanson, Victor. 2003. *Mexifornia: A State of Becoming*. San Francisco: Encounter Books.

De Genova, Nicholas. 2004. "The Legal Production of Mexican/Migrant 'Illegality'," *Latino Studies* 2(2), 160–185.

Delaney, David. 2002. "The Space That Race Makes," *The Professional Geographer* 54(1), 6–14.

DePalma, Anthony. 2001. *Here: A Biography of the New American Continent*. Toronto: HarperCollins.

Destler, I.M. 1997. *Renewing Fast-Track Legislation*. Washington, DC: Institute for International Economics.

Dobson, Wendy. 2002. "Shaping the Future of the North American Economic Space," *C.D. Howe Commentary No. 162, The Border Papers*. Toronto: CD Howe Institute, April.

Dobson, Wendy. 2003. "The North American Economic Space," *Borderlines* 2(4), 23–29.

Doern, Bruce and Robert Jackson (eds). 2006. *Rules, Rules, Rules, Rules: Multilevel Regulatory Governance in Canada*. Toronto: University of Toronto Press.

Dombois, Rainer, Hornberger, Erhard and Winter, Jens. 2003. "Transnational labor regulation in the NAFTA – a problem of institutional design? The case of the North American Agreement on Labour Co-operation between the USA,

Mexico and Canada," *International Journal of Comparative Labour Law and Industrial Relations* 19(4), 421–40.

Dombois, Rainer and Winter, Jens. 2003. *A Matter of Deficient Design? Observations on Interaction and Co-operation Problems in the NAALC.* Bremen: University of Bremen, Institut Arbeit und Wirtschaft.

Donnelly, Brendan and Anthony Hawes. 2004. "The Beginning or the End of the Beginning? Enhanced Co-operation in the Constitutional Treaty," *The Federal Trust: European Policy Brief.* (November): 7, http://www.fedtrust.co.uk/admin/uploads/PolicyBrief7.pdf.

DPA. 2009. "Asesinan 12 periodistas durante 2009, informa CNDH," *La Jornada,* 25 Dec.

Drache, Daniel. 2005. "'Friends at a Distance': Reframing Canada's Strategic Priorities after the Bush Revolution in Foreign Policy," in Andrew F. Cooper and Dane Rowlands (eds), *Split Image, Canada Among Nations.* Montreal and Kingston: McGill-Queen's University Press.

Dukert, Joseph M. "North American Energy: At Long Last, One Continent" CSIS, October 2005 http://www.asu.edu/clas/nacts/bna/archive/Dukert,%20North%20American%20Energy%202005.pdf.

Eagle Woman, Angelique. 2008. "Fencing Off the Eagle and the Condor, Border Politics, and Indigenous Peoples," *Natural Resources & Environment* 23(2), 33–35.

Earle, R.L. and Wirth, J.D. (eds). 1995. *Identities in North America: The Search for Community.* Stanford, CA: Stanford University Press.

Eastby. John. 1985. *Functionalism and Interdependence: The Credibility of Institutions, Policies and Leadership.* Lanham, MD: University Press of America Inc.

Eckes, Alfred E. 1995. *Opening America's Market: U.S. Foreign Trade Policy Since 1776.* Chapel Hill: University of North Carolina Press.

Edgar, A. and Sedgwick, P. 1999. *Key Concepts in Cultural Theory.* London: Routledge.

Edwards, Steven. 2002. "US Veto Threat 'Frontal Attack' On Law," *National Post,* June 22.

Elliot, Kimberly Ann. 2006. *Delivering on Doha: Farm Trade and the Poor.* Washington, DC: Institute for International Economics.

Enciso, Angélica. 2008. "ONG desmienten a Semarnat sobre avances en reforestatación," *La Jornada,* 24 January.

Enciso, Angélica. 2009. "Sólo 18 por ciento de mexicanos tienen ingresos suficientes para vivir: CONEVAL," *La Jornada,* 11 Dec.

Esteva-Fabregat, Claudio. 1995. *Mestizaje in Ibero-America.* Arizona: University of Arizona Press.

Faux, Jeff. 2003. "How NAFTA Failed Mexico. Immigration is Not a Development Policy," *The American Prospect Online* 14(7), 3 July.

Faux, Jeff, 2006. *The Global Class War: How America's Bipartisan Elite Lost Our Future – and What It Will Take to Win it Back.* Hoboken: John Wiley and Sons.

Feagin, Joe R. 1999. *Racial and Ethnic Relations* (Sixth Edition). Upper Saddle River, New Jersey: Prentice Hall.

Fernández-Vega, Carlos. 2005. "Estabilidad sin crecimiento de la economía," *La Jornada*, 16 Dec.

Florescano, Enrique. 1998. *Etnia, Estado y nación*. Mexico City: Aguilar, p.186.

Foster, John. 2004. "The Trinational Alliance against NAFTA: Sinews of Solidarity," in Joe Bandy and Jackie Smith (eds), *Coalitions Across Borders: Transnational Protest and the Neoliberal Order.* Lanham: Rowman & Littlefield, 209–229.

Foster, John, with Kristof Krudniewicz, 2005. "NAFTA 'Plus' or 'Minus': The Future of the North American Free Trade Agreement," *The USA and Canada 2006*. London: Taylor and Francis.

Foster, John. 2011. 'NAFTA and After: The Triumph of Bilateralism,' in *The USA and Canada 2012*, edited by Neil Higgins. Abingdon: Routledge.

Foster, Michael S. 1986. "The Mesoamerican Connection: A View from the South," in Mathien, Frances and McGuire, Randall (eds), *Ripples in the Chichimec Sea: New Considerations of Southwestern-Mesoamerican Interactions.* Carbondale: Southern Illinois University Press.

Fox, C.F. 1999. *The Fence and the River: Culture and Politics at the US–Mexico Border.* Minneapolis: University of Minnesota Press, 122.

Fox, Jonathan. 2004. "Assessing Binational Civil Society Coalitions: Lessons from the Mexico-U.S Experience," in Kevin J. Middlebrook (ed.), *Dilemmas of Political Change in Mexico.* London: Institute for Latin American Studies, University of London/San Diego Center for US-Mexican Studies, University of California, San Diego.

Fox, Jonathan and Gaspar Rivera-Salgado. 2004. "Building Civil Society Among Indigenous Migrants," *Americas Program*. Silver City: Interhemispheric Resource Center.

Freeman, Laurie. 2006. *State of Siege: Drug-Related Violence and Corruption in Mexico. Unintended Consequences of the War on Drugs*. Washington: WOLA.

Fry, Earl Fry. 1983. *The Politics of International Investment*. New York: McGraw-Hill, Inc.

Fuat Keyman, E. 1997. *Globalization, State, Identity/Difference: Toward a Critical Social Theory of International Relations*. Highlands, NJ: Humanities Press.

Ferguson, Niall. 2004. *Colossus. The Price of America's Empire*. New York: Penguin.

Gabriel, Christina and Laura Macdonald. 2003. "Beyond the Continental/Nationalist Divide: Politics in a North America 'Without Borders'," in Wallace Clement and Leah Vosko (eds), *Changing Canada: Political Economy as Transformation*. Toronto: University of Toronto Press, 213–240.

Gabriel, Christina and Laura Macdonald. 2004a. "Of Borders and Business: Canadian Corporate Proposals for North American 'Deep Integration'," *Studies in Political Economy* 74, 79–100.

Gabriel, Christina and Macdonald, Laura. 2004b. "Chrétien and North America: Between Integration and Autonomy," *Review of Constitutional Studies* 9(1&2), 71–91.

Gabriel, Christina, Jimena Jiménez and Laura Macdonald. 2003. "Toward North American 'Smart Borders': Convergence or Divergence in Border Control Policies"? Paper presented at the annual meeting of the International Studies Association, Portland, Oregon.

Gagné, Gilbert. 2000. "North American Free Trade, Canada, and U.S. Trade Remedies: An Assessment After Ten Years," *The World Economy* 23(1), 77–91.

Gagné, Gilbert. 2003. "The Canada-U.S. Softwood Lumber Dispute," *The World Economy* Summer, 335–368.

Galarza, Ernesto. 1970. *Spiders in the House and Workers in the Fields.* Notre Dame, IN: University of Notre Dame Press.

Galloway, Gloria. 2004. "US-Canada Poll Finds Some Similar Views," *Globe and Mail*, December 2, A10.

Garcia, Juan Ramón. 1980. *Operation Wetback: The Mass Deportation of Mexican Undocumented Workers in 1954.* Westport: Greenwood Press.

García Canclini, N. 1989. *Culturas híbridas: estrategias para entrar y salir de la modernidad.* Mexico City: Grijalbo.

García Canclini, N. 1995. *Hybrid Cultures: Strategies for Entering and Leaving Modernity*, trans. Christopher L. Chiappari and Silvia L. López. Minneapolis: University of Minnesota Press.

García-Cantú, Gastón. 1978. "Política Exterior y Braceros 1838–1946," in *Utopías Mexicanas.* Mexico City: Fondo de Cultura Económica.

Germain, Randall D. and Kenny, Michael (eds). 2005. *The Idea of Global Civil Society: Politics and Ethics in a Globalizing Era.* London and New York: Routledge.

Giddens, A. 1990. *The Consequences of Modernity.* Stanford, CA: Stanford University Press.

Gilbert, Emily. 2005. "The Inevitability of Integration? Neoliberal Discourse and the Proposals for a New North American Economic Space in the Aftermath of 9-11," *Annals of the Association of American Geographers* 95(1), 202–222.

Glick Schiller, Nina. 2005. "Transborder Citizenship: an Outcome of Legal Pluralism within Transnational Social Fields," in Bender Beckman, Franz and Keebit Bender Beckman (eds) *Mobile People, Mobile Law: Expanding Legal Relations in a Contracting World.* Aldershot: Ashgate.

Goar, Carol. 2004. "Odd Way to Build Consensus," *Toronto Star*, April 13, A3.

Goldfarb, Danielle. 2003a. "The Road to a Canada-U.S. Customs Union," *CD Howe Commentary No. 184, The Border Papers.* Toronto: C.D. Howe Institute.

Goldfarb, Danielle. 2003b. "Beyond Label: Comparing Proposals for Closer Canada-US Economic Relations," *The Border Papers*, No. 76, October. Toronto: C.D. Howe Institute.

Goldfarb, Danielle. 2007. "Is Just-In-Case Replacing Just-In-Time," *Conference Board of Canada, Briefing.* Ottawa: Conference Board of Canada, June.

Golob, Stephanie. 2002. "North American Beyond NAFTA? Sovereignty, Identity, and Security in Canada-US Relations," *Canadian American Public Policy*, 52, 1–50.

Gómez Mena, C. 2004. "Es muy poco lo que se destina al gasto en salud, admite Julio Frenk," *La Jornada*, 21 April.

Gómez-Peña, G. 1993. *Warrior for Gringostroika: Essays, Performance Texts and Poetry*. St. Paul, Minnesota: Graywolf Press.

Gómez-Peña, G. 1994a. *New World Border: Prophesies, Poems and Loqueras for the End of the Century*. San Francisco: City Lights.

Gómez-Peña, G. 1994b. "The Multicultural Paradigm: An Open Letter to the National Arts Community," in Diana Taylor and Juan Villegas (eds), *Negotiating Performance: Gender, Sexuality and Theatricality in Latin/o America*. Durham: Duke University Press.

González, Henry Gedges. 1999. "Icon, Conquest, Trasnationalism: the Visual Politics of Contructing Difference in the Americas," *Passages: A Journal of Transnational and Transcultural Studies* 1(1), 33–52.

González, Susana G. 2009. "Caída de 15% en el turismo en 2009, pronostica el titular del Sectur," *La Jornada*, 10 Oct.

González Amador, Roberto, Rodríguez, Israel and González, Susana. 2005. "Se dispara el ingreso petrolero, pero también la salida de divisas," *La Jornada*, 25 Feb.

González Amador, Roberto. 2010. "Contracción económica 6.8% en 2009," *La Jornada*, 30 Jan.

Gotlieb, Allan. 1998. "Negotiating the Canada-U.S. Free Trade Agreement," *International Journal* 53(3), 522–538.

Gould, Eliga H. 2007. "Entangled Histories. Entangled World: The English Speaking Atlantic as a Spanish Periphery," *Contemporary Review* 289 (1684), 764–786.

Globerman, Steven. 1993. *Assessing NAFTA: A Trinational Analysis*. Vancouver: Fraser Institute.

Grady, Patrick. 2009. "A More Open and Secure Border for Trade, Investment and People," in Carleton University, *Canada-US Project. Background Papers. From Correct to Inspired: A Blueprint for Canada-US Engagement*, 41–48. www.ctpl.ca.

Granatstein, Jack. 2003. "The Importance of Being Less Earnest: Promoting Canada's National Interest through Tighter Ties with the US," Toronto: C.D. Howe Institute, Benefactors Lecture, at http://www.cdhowe.org/pdf/benefactors_lecture_2003.pdf.

Greenpeace México. 2008. *Admite Semarnat fracaso de Proárbol*, 17 Feb 2008, Available: http://www.greenpeace.org/mexico/news/admite-semarnat-fracaso-de-pro,

Gutstein, Donald. 2009. *Not a Conspiracy Theory: How Business Propaganda Hijacks Democracy*. Toronto: Key Porter Books.

Haas, Ernst. 1961. "International Integration: The European and the Universal Process," *International Organization* 15(3), 366–392.

Hale, Geoffrey and Christina Marcotte. 2010. "Border Security, Trade, and Travel Facilitation," in Monica Gattinger and Geoffrey Hale (eds), *Borders and Bridges: Canada's Foreign Policy Relations in North America*. Toronto: Oxford University Press, 100–119.

Hale, Geoffrey and Stephen Blank. 2010. "North American Integration and Comparative Responses to Globalization – Overview," in Monica Gattinger and Geoffrey Hale (eds), *Borders and Bridges: Canada's Foreign Policy Relations in North America*. Toronto: Oxford University Press, 21–40.

Hall, Linda B. and Coerver, Don M. 1990. *Revolution on the Border. The United States and Mexico, 1910–1920*. Albuquerque, NM: University of New Mexico Press, 16–27.

Hannerz, U. 1990. "Cosmopolitans and locals in world culture," in M. Featherstone (ed.), *Global Culture: Nationalism, Globalization and Modernity*. London: Sage.

Hansen-Kuhn, Karen. 2003. *Lessons from NAFTA: The High Cost of Free Trade*. Ottawa: Canadian Centre for Policy Alternatives.

Harris, C. 2004. "How did Colonialism Disposses? Comments from an Edge of Empire," *Annals of the Association of American Geographers* 94(1), 165–182.

Hart, Michael, Bill Dymond, and Colin Robertson. 1994. *Decision at Midnight: Inside the Canada-U.S. Free-Trade Negotiations*. Vancouver: UBC Press.

Harvey, Frank. 2005. "Canada's Addiction to American Security: The Illusion of Choice in the War on Terrorism," *American Review of Canadian Studies* 35(2), 265–294.

Harvey, Frank. 2006. "Canada and the New American Empire: Implications for Security Policy," Paper presented at the Canada and the New American Empire Conference," at http://www.globalcentres.org/can-us/security_harvey.pdf. Accessed on May 25 2006.

Haynal, George. 2004. "The Next Plateau in North America: What's the Big Idea?" *IRPP Working Paper Series* 2004-09b. Montreal: Institute for Research in Public Policy.

Healy, Teresa. 2007. "North American Competitiveness Council and the SPP: Les Agents Provocateurs at the Montebello Leaders' Summit." Research Paper #44. Ottawa: Canadian Labour Congress. www.canadianlabour.ca/index.php/thealy_en/1282.

Heine, Jamie. 2008. "China's Claim in Latin America: So Far, a Partner, not a Threat," July 25, 2008. Retrieved from http://.coha.org/2008/07, August 2008.

Held, David 1995. *Democracy and the Global Order: From the Modern State to Cosmopolitan Governance*. Stanford, CA: Stanford University Press.

Held, David and Guibernau, Montserrat. 2001. "Globalization, Cosmopolitanism, and Democracy: An Interview with David Held," *Constellations: An International Journal of Critical & Democratic Theory*, 8.4.

Helliwell, John 1998. *How Much Do Borders Matter?* Washington: Brookings Institution Press.

Hettne, Björn. 2005. "Beyond the New Regionalism," *New Political Economy*, 10(4), 543–571.

Hoberg, George. 2002. "Introduction: Economic, Cultural and Political Dimensions of North American Integration," in George Hoberg (ed.), *Capacity for Choice: Canada in the New North America*. Toronto: University of Toronto Press, 3–13.

Hoberg, George, Banting, Keith and Richard Simeon. 2002. "The Scope for Domestic Choice: Policy Autonomy in a Globalizing World," in Hoberg, George (ed.), *Capacity for Choice: Canada in a New North America*. Toronto: University of Toronto Press.

Hocking, Brian. 2004. "Changing the terms of trade policy making: from the 'club' to the 'multistakeholder' model," *World Trade Review* 3(1), 3.

Hoffman, Abraham. 1974. *Unwanted Mexican-Americans in the Great Depression: Repatriation Pressures, 1929–1939.* Tucson, Arizona: University of Arizona Press.

Holzscheiter, Anna 2005. "Discourse as Capability: Non-State Actors' Capital in Global Governance," *Millennium: Journal of International Studies* 33.3.

Hudson, Charles. 1982. *The Southeastern Indians*. Tennessee: Tennessee Press.

Hufbauer, Gary Clyde and Jeffrey J. Schott. 2005. *NAFTA Revisited: Achievements and Challenges*. Washington, DC: Institute for International Economics.

Huntington, Samuel P. 2004. *Who Are We? The Challenges to America's National Identity.* New York: Simon & Schuster.

Ibbitson, John. 2007. "America: Say goodbye to North America's special partnership," *The Globe and Mail*, November 10.

Inglehart, Ronald, Neil Nevitte and Miguel Basáñez. 1996. *The North American Trajectory: Cultural, Economic, and Political Ties among the United States, Canada, and Mexico*. New York: Aldine de Gruyter.

Inside U.S. Trade. 2002a. "Administration Proposes Higher Thresholds for Investor Suits," 27 September.

Inside U.S. Trade. 2002b. "Administration Kills Judicial Exhaustion Plan for Investment Disputes," 27 September.

International Bank for Reconstruction and Development (World Bank). 2003 *Lessons from NAFTA for Latin America and Caribbean Countries*. Washington, DC: The World Bank, December.

Inwood, Gregory. 2005. *Continentalizing Canada: The Politics and Legacy of the Macdonald Royal Commission*. Toronto: University of Toronto.

Jackson, Andrew. 2003. "Why the 'Big Idea' is a Bad Idea: A Critical Perspective on Deeper Economic Integration with the United States." Ottawa: Canadian Centre for Policy Alternatives, June. www.policyalternatives.ca.

Jackson, Andrew. 2005. "Canadian workers, the Canadian Corporate Elite and the American Empire: Contradictions of Deep Integration, and a Note on Alternatives," paper presented to the CCPA 25th anniversary conference,

"Living with Uncle: Canada-US Relations in a Time of Empire," May 27, accessed at www.canadianlabour.ca.

James, Deborah. 2005. "Summit of the Americas, Argentina: Tomb of the FTAA," www.Commondreams.org, November 23,

Jessop, Bob. 2002. *The Future of the Capitalist State*. Cambridge: Polity Press.

Jockel, Joseph T. and Sokolsky, Joel J. 2005. "A New Continental Consensus? The Bush Doctrine, the War on Terrorism and the Future of US-Canada Security Relations," in Andrew F. Cooper and Dane Rowlands (eds), *Split Image, Canada Among Nations*. Montreal and Kingston: McGill-Queen's University Press.

Johnston, Josée. 2000. "Pedagogical Guerrillas, Armed Democrats, and Revolutionary Counterpublics: Examining Paradox in the Zapatista Uprising in Chiapas Mexico," *Theory and Society* 29.4.

Judt, Tony. 2003. "The Way We Live Now," *New York Review of Books*. March 27.

Katzenstein, Peter J. 2005. *A World of Regions. Asia and Europe in the American Imperium*. Ithaca: Cornell University Press.

Keil, Roger and Rianne Mahon (eds). 2009. *Leviathan Undone? Towards a Political Economy of Scale*. Vancouver: UBC Press.

Keohane, Robert. 1984. *After Hegemony: Cooperation and Discord in the World Political Economy*. Princeton, New Jersey: Princeton University Press.

Kirtz, Mary K. and Carol L. Beran. 2006. "My Heart Will Go on Living *La Vida Loca:* The Cultural Impact on the United States of Canada and Mexico," in Kirtz, M.K. (ed.), *The Elections of 2000: Politics, Culture and Economics in North America*. Akron: University of Akron Press, 119–135.

Klepak, Hal (ed.). 1996. *Natural Allies? Canadian and Mexican Perspectives on International Security*. Ottawa: FOCAL and Carleton University Press.

Kobayashi, Audrey. 1994. "Unnatural Discourse. 'Race' and Gender in Geography," *Gender, Place & Culture: A Journal of Feminist Geography* 1(2), 225–44.

Kotschwar, Barbara. 2009. "Trade Rift Deepens With Mexico," *Peterson Perspectives*. Washington, DC: Peterson Institute for International Economics, 19 March.

Kottak, C. 1990. *Prime-Time Society: An Anthropological Analysis of Television and Culture*. Belmont: Wadsworth.

Krauthammer, Charles. 2001. "The New Unilateralism," *The Washington Post*, June 8.

Krauze, Enrique. 2009. "The Mexican Evolution," *New York Times*, 24 Mar. http://www.jornada.unam.mx/.

Krickeberg, Walter. 1971. *Mitos y leyendas de los aztecas, incas, mayas y muiscas*. Mexico City: Fondo de Cultura Económica.

Krugman, Paul. 2004. "The Death of Horatio Alger," *The Nation*, 5 January.

Kukucha, Christopher J. 2008. *The Provinces and Canadian Foreign Trade Policy*, Vancouver: University of British Columbia Press.

La Jornada de Oriente. 2003. "Xóchitl Gálvez: etnias enviaron a nuestro país en 2000 más de 6000 millones de dólares," *La Jornada*, 26 Jan.

Lachapelle, Erick. 2005. "Business' Role in North American Governance: Free Trade, 'Smart Borders' and other 'Big Ideas'," Paper presented to the annual meeting of the Canadian Political Science Association, June 2.
LaDuke, Winnona. 1995. "An Indigenous View of North America," Speech presented at North Carolina State University, Raleigh, November 13.
Laghi, Brian. 2006. "Canadians turn more sour on US," *Globe and Mail*, March 20, A1, A7.
Lake, Jennifer and M. Angeles Villareal. 2009. "Security and Prosperity Partnership of North America: An Overview and Selected Issues," Congressional Research Service.
Larner, Wendy and William Walters. 2002. "The Political Rationality of 'New Regionalism:' Toward a Genealogy of Region," *Theory and Society* 31, 391–432.
Larsen, N. 1995. *Reading North by South. On Latin American Literature, Culture and Politics.* Minneapolis: University of Minnesota Press, 124.
Laurell, Asa Cristina. 2010. "Coneval. Baile de los números de acceso a la salud y seguridad social," *La Jornada*, 13 Jan.
Layton, Michael D. 2001. "La fuerza de los hechos", *Nexos* 23(286), October.
Lechner, Norbert. 1990 [2006]. "Los patios interiores de la democracia," in Paulina Gutiérrez and Tomás Moulian (eds), *Obras escogidas: 1*, vol. 1. Santiago, Chile: Editorial LOM: Colección pensadores latinoamericanos.
León-Portilla, Miguel. 1961. *Los antiguos mexicanos a través de sus crónicas y cantares*. Mexico City: Fondo de Cultura Económica.
Ley, David and Audrey Kobayashi. 2002. "Back to Hong Kong: Return Migration or "Transnational" Sojourn?" *Global Networks* 5, 111–127.
Lieven, Anatol. 2004. *America Right or Wrong: An Anatomy of American Nationalism*. New York: Oxford University Press.
Linklater, Andrew. 1990. *Beyond Realism and Marxism: Critical Theory and International Relations*. London: Macmillan.
Linklater, Andrew. 1992 [2000]. "The Question of the Next Stage in International Relations Theory: A Critical-Theoretical Point of View," in Andrew Linklater (ed.), *International Relations, vol. IV Critical Concepts in Political Science*, vol. IV. London and New York: Routledge, 1646–1651.
Livingstone, David. 1993. *The Geographical Tradition: Episodes in the History of a Contested Enterprise*. New York: Blackwell.
Lowenthal, Abraham. 2003. "Security for all of North America," Pacific Council on International Policy.
Lower, Arthur. R.M. 1964. *Colony to Nation: A History of Canada*. Longmans Canada Limited, Fourth Edition.
Lull, J. 2000. *Media, Communication, Culture: A Global Approach*. Cambridge: Polity Press.
Lull, J. 2001. "Superculture for the Communication Age," in James Lull (ed.), *Culture in the Communication Age.* London: Routledge, 134.

Luna-Firebaugh, Eileen M. 2002. "The Border Crossed Us: Border Crossing Issues of the Indigenous Peoples of the Americas," *Wicazo Sa Review* 17(1), 159–181.

Lyon, Eugene. 1990. "The Enterprise of Florida," in Thomas, D.H. (ed.) Columbian Consequences Volume 2, *Archaeological Perspectives on the Spanish Borderlands East*. Washington DC: Smithsonian Institution Press.

Macdonald, Laura. 2002. "Governance and State-Society Relations: The Challenges," in George Hoberg (ed.), *Capacity for Choice: Canada in a New North America*. Toronto: University of Toronto Press, 202–03.

Macdonald, Laura and Jeffrey Ayres (eds). 2009. *Contentious Politics in North America: National Protest and Transnational Collaboration under Continental Integration*. London: Palgrave Macmillan.

MacDonald, Laura and Rounce, Andrea. 2003. "Federalism and Transborder Integration in North America," *Horizons* 6(2), 50–51.

Macrory, Patrick. 2003. "NAFTA Chapter 19: A Successful Experiment in International Dispute Resolution," *Commentary* No. 168. Toronto: C.D. Howe Institute.

Madsen, Kenneth D. and Ton van Naerssen. 2003. "Migration, Identity, and Belonging," *Journal of Borderlands Studies* 18(1), 61–75.

Malkin, Elizabeth. 2007. "Mexico Moves to Cut Back Tax Loopholes for Businesses," *New York Times*, 21 June.

Martín-Barbero, J. 1993. *Communication, Culture and Hegemony*. Newbury Park: Sage.

Martin, Philip. 2003. "Economic Integration and Migration: The Mexico/US Case," Discussion Paper no. 2003/35, United Nations University, April.

Massey, Doreen. 1999. "Imagining Globalization: Power-Geometries of Time-Space," in Autar Brah, Mary Hickman, and Mairtin Mac an Ghaill (eds), *Global Futures: Migration, Environment and Globalization*. London: Macmillan, 27–44.

Massing, Michael. 1998. *The Fix. Under the Nixon Administration, America Had an Effective Drug Policy. We Should Restore It. (Nixon Was Right)*. New York: Simon & Schuster.

McDougall, John. 2004. "The Long-Run Determinants of Deep/Political Canada-US Integration," in Thomas Courchene (ed.), *Thinking North America: The Art of the State II*. Montreal: Institute for Research on Public Policy, http://www.irpp.org/indexe.htm.

McDougall, John. 2006. *Drifting Together, The Political Economy of Canada-US Integration*. Toronto: Broadview.

McKinney, Joseph. 2000. *Created from NAFTA: The Structure, Function and Significance of the Treaty's Related Institutions*. Armork, NY: M.E. Sharpe, Inc.

Meeks, Erik. V. 2008. *Border Citizens: The Making of Indians, Mexicans and Anglos in Arizona*. Texas: University of Texas Press.

Méndez, Enrique and Garduño, Roberto. 2007. "Reforma fiscal, aprobada con IETU y gasolinazo," *La Jornada*, 14 Sept.
Methanex Corporation v. United States, Notice of Claim, December 3, 1999.
Mexico. Secretaría del Trabajo y Previsión Social (STPS). 1964. *Los braceros*. Mexico City: STPS.
Meyer, Lorenzo. 2001. "The United States and Mexico: The Historical Structure of their Conflict," *Journal of International Affairs* 43.1.
Mikkelson, Jeppe. 1991. "Obstinate or Obsolete? A Reappraisal in the Light of the New Dynamism of the EC," *Millenium: Journal of International Studies* 20: 1–22.
Mize, Ronald L. and Alicia C.S. Swords. 2011. *Consuming Mexican Labour. From the Bracero Program to NAFTA*. Toronto: University of Toronto Press.
Monsiváis, Carlos and Thelen, Davi. 1999. "Mexico's Cultural Landscapes: A Conversation with Carlos Monsiváis," *The Journal of American History* 86(2), 61-3-4.
Montpetit, E. 2003. "Public consultations in policy network environments: The case of assisted reproductive technology policy in Canada," *Canadian Public Poilcy* 29(1), 95–110.
Morton, Adam David. 2003. "Structural Change and Neoliberalism in Mexico: 'Passive Revolution' in the Global Political Economy," *Third World Quarterly* 24.4.
Morrow, R.A. 1994. *Critical Theory and Methodology*. Newbury Park and London: Sage.
Mraz, John and Vélez Storey, Jaime. 1996. *Uprooted : Braceros in the Hermanos Mayo Lens*. Houston, TX: University of Houston, Arte Publico Press, 47–49.
Muller, Benjamin J. 2009. "Borders, Risks, Exclusions," *Studies in Social Justice* 3(1), 67–78, 80.
NACC, North American Competitiveness Council. 2007a. "Enhancing Competitiveness in Canada, Mexico and the United States: Private Sector Priorities for the Security and Prosperity Partnership of North America (SPP)," February. www.ceocouncil.ca/en/publications.
NACC, North American Competitiveness Council. 2007b. Building a Secure and Competitive North America. 2007 Report to Leaders. August. www.ceocouncil.ca/en/publications.
Nadal, Alejandro, Aguayo, Francisco and Chávez, Marcos. 2003. "Los siete mitos del TLC," *La Jornada*, 30 Nov.
NAFTA. 2001. Free Trade Commission Clarifications Related to NAFTA Chapter 11, 31 July.
NAFTA. 2002. Challenge of Final USITC Injury Threat Determination, USA-CDA-2002-1904-07, 22 May.
NAFTA. 2005. Challenge of DOC Final CVC Determination, USA-CDA-2002-1904-03, 5 October.
NASCO. n.d. http://www.nascocorridor.com/default.asp.

Nelson, Jay. 2003. "A Strange Revolution in the Manners of the Country: Aboriginal-Settler Intermarriage in Nineteenth-Century British Columbia," in McLaren, John et al. (eds), *Regulating Lives*. Vancouver: UBC Press.

Neufeld, Mark. 2001. "Theorising Globalisation: Towards a Political of Resistance – A Neo-Gramscian Response to Mathias Albert," *Global Society* 15.1.

Neumann, Iver. 2003. "A Region-Building Approach," in Fredrik Soderbaum and Timothy Shaw, eds. *Theories of Regionalisms: A Palgrave Reader*. Basingstoke: Palgrave Macmillan, 160–178.

Newsweek. 3 March 2008. "The Facts About NAFTA-Gate".

Nye, Joseph. 1968. "Comparative Regional Integration: Concept and Measurement," *International Organization* 22(4): 855–880.

O'Brien, Robert. 1995. "North American Integration and International Relations Theory," *Canadian Journal of Political Science* XXVIII (4): 693–728.

OECD, *OECD Economic Survey: Mexico 2007 – Addenum*. Available: http://www.oecd.org/dataoecd/17/8/39431351.pdf.

Office of the Press Secretary. 2005. Fact Sheet; Security and Prosperity Partnership of North America. http://www.whitehouse.gov/news/releases/2005/03/print/2005/03/print/20050323-4.html.

Office of Press Secretary. 2005. "Joint Statement by Pres. Bush, Pres. Fox and Prime Minister Martin on the Security and Prosperity Partnership, March 23, 2005." www.whitehouse.gov/news/releases/2005/03/20050323-2.html.

Ojeda-Gomez, Mario. 1971. "Estudio de un caso de decisión política: el programa norteamericano de importación de braceros," in *Extremos de México*. Mexico City: El Colegio de México.

Olloqui, Juan José (ed.). 2001. *Estudios en torno a la migración*. Mexico City: UNAM, 7–19.

Olson, Eric. 2008. "Six key issues in United States-Mexico Security Co-operation," Woodrow Wilson Center, July.

Olvera, Alberto J. (ed.). 1999. *La sociedad civil: De la teoría a la realidad*. Mexico City: Colegio de México.

Olvera, Alberto J. 2004. "Civil Society in Mexico at Century's End," in Kevin J. Middlebrook (ed.), *Dilemmas of Political Change in Mexico*. London: Institute for Latin American Studies, University of London/San Diego: Center for US.-Mexican Studies, University of California, San Diego.

Ortiz, Alfonso. 1983. *Handbook of North American Indians* Vol. 10. Washington: Smithsonian Institute.

Ostry, Sylvia. 1999. "Foggy in Seattle," *The National Post* (November 26), p. 21, cited in William A. Dymond and Laura Ritchie Dawson, "The consultative process in the formulation of Canadian trade policy," Memorandum for Inter-American Development Bank/Inter-American Dialogue, 2002 (Ottawa: Centre for Trade Policy and Law, September 2002), p. 17.

Otero, Gerardo. 2004. *Mexico in Transition: Neoliberal Globalism, the State and Civil Society*. Halifax, Nova Scotia/London: Fernwood Publishing/Zed Books.

Oxford Analytica. 2004. "North America: Security fears spur cooperation".

Paz, Octavio 1979 [1985] "Mexico and the United States ," trans. Lysander Kemp, Yara Milos and Rachel Phillips Belash, *The Labyrinth of Solitude*, expanded edn. New York: Grove Press.

Pew Hispanic Center. 2006. "2006 National Survey of Latinos: The Immigration Debate," New York: The Pew Charitable Trust, June 13, p. 8. Available at www.pewhispanic.org.

Polaski, Sandra. 2004. *Mexican Employment, Productivity and Income a Decade After NAFTA: Brief Submitted to the Standing Canadian Senate Committee on Foreign Affairs.* Washington, DC: Carnegie Endowment for International Peace.

Pastor, Robert. 2001. *Toward a North American Community: Lessons from the Old World for the New.* Washington, DC: Institute for International Economics.

Pastor, Robert A. (ed.). 2005. *The Paramount Challenge for North America: Closing the Development Gap.* Washington: North American Development Bank/American University.

Pastor, Robert. 2008. "The Future of North America: Replacing a Bad Neighbour Policy," *Foreign Affairs* 87(4): 84–98.

Patterson, Kelly. 2007. "Continental Divide: All Eyes are on Montebello," *Ottawa Citizen*, August 18, B1.

Pickard, Miguel. 2005. "Trinational Elites Map North American Future," August 24, www.americanspolicy.org.

Pollard, Robert. 1985. *Economic Security and the Origins of the Cold War, 1945–1950.* New York: Columbia University Press.

Porter, Robert B., Sauvé, Pierre, Subramanian, Arvind and Zampetti, Americo Beviglia eds. 2001. *Efficiency, Equity and Legitimacy: The Multilateral Trading System at the Millennium.* Washington DC: Brookings.

Portes, Alejandro. 2003. "Theoretical Convergencies and Empirical Evidence in the Study of Immigrant Transnationalism," *International Migration Review* 37, 814–892.

Pratt, M.L. 1992. *Imperial Eyes: Travel Writing and Transculturation.* London: Routledge.

Pries, Ludger. 2001. *New Transnational Social Spaces: International Migration and Transnational Companies in the Early Twenty-first Century.* New York: Routledge.

Prime Minister's statement at closing press conference of SPP meeting. 2007. http://news.gc.ca/web/view/en/index.jsp?articleid=346219.

Public Citizen, *The Ten Year Track Record of the North American Free Trade Agreement. US, Mexican and Canadian Farmers and Agriculture,* available at www.tradewatch.org.

Puyana Mutis, Alicia. 2006. "Las fuerzas que moldean la política energética mexicana: entre la constitución y el TLCAN," in Isabelle Rousseau (ed.), *Hacia la integración de los mercados petroleros en América.* Mexico City: El Colegio de México, 237–298.

Ramos, Alcita. 1998. *Indigenism: Ethnic Politics in Brazil*. University of Wisconsin: London.

Ramos García, José María. "La política de seguridad fronteriza de Estados Unidos: estrategias e impactos binacionales", in *Foro Internacional*, 44(4), 613–634.

Reguillo, Rossana. 2004. "The Oracle in the City: Beliefs, Practices, and Symbolic Geographies," *Social Text* 22.4.

Riding, Alan. 1985. *Distant Neighbors: A Portrait of the Mexicans*. New York: Alfred A. Knopff.

Ríos Cázares, Alexandra and Shirk, David A. (eds). 2007. *Evaluating Accountability and Transparency in Mexico: National, Local and Comparative Perspectives*. New York and London: Routledge/University Readers.

Robinson, William I. 1996. *Promoting Polyarchy: Globalization, US Intervention, and Hegemony*. Cambridge: Cambridge University Press.

Robson, William B.P. and David Laidler. 2002. "No Small Change: The Awkward Economics and Politics of North American Monetary Integration," *C.D. Howe Commentary No. 167, The Border Papers*. Toronto: C.D. Howe Institute.

Rodríguez, Israel. 2010. "Desplome de 40.7 por ciento en el valor de las exportaciones petroleras," *La Jornada*, 23 Jan.

Román, José Antonio. 2007. "Han muerto este año 437 mexicanos tratando de cruzar hacia EU: SRE," *La Jornada*, 18 Dec. Available: http://www.news.harvard.edu/gazette/2008/02.14/05-calderon.html.

Rosamond, Ben. 2000. *Theories of European Integration*. New York, New York: St. Martin's Press.

Rowe, W. and Schelling, V. 1991. *Memory and Modernity: Popular Culture in Latin America*. London: Verso.

Salacuse, Jeswald. 1990. "BIT by BIT: The Growth of Bilateral Investment Treaties and their Impact on Foreign Investment in Developing Countries," *International Lawyer* 24, 664–673.

Salacuse, Jeswald. 2002. "Toward a Global Treaty on Foreign Investment: The Search for a Grand Bargain," unpublished manuscript.

Salas, Carlos. 2001. "The Impacts of NAFTA on Wages and Incomes in Mexico," *NAFTA at Seven. Its Impact on Workers in All Three Nations*, Briefing Paper, Washington: Economic Policy Institute.

Salinas de Gortari, Carlos. 2002. *Mexico: The Policy and Politics of Modernization*. Barcelona: Plaza & Janes Editores.

Samaniego López, Marco Antonio. 2006. *Ríos internacionales entre México y Estados Unidos. Los tratados de 1906 y 1944*. Mexico City: El Colegio de México/Universidad Autónoma de Baja California.

Sancak, Cemile and Someshwar Rao. 2000. *Trends in Canada's Inward FDI*. Strategic Investment Analysis Directorate, Micro-economic Analysis Branch, Industry Canada, 18 October.

Sands, Christopher. 2003. "Canada-US Relations: What can we do to improve them," Excerpts from a presentation at the 2003 Canadian Crude Oil Conference, at http://www.sfu.ca/casr/ft-csands2-2.htm.

Sands, Christopher. 2005. "The Changing of the Guard," *International Journal*, 60, 2, 483–96.
Sands, Christopher. 2006. "Different Paths Leading from Cancún," *North American Integration Monitor* 3(2). Washington, DC: Center for Strategic and International Studies.
Sands, Philippe. 2005. *Lawless World*. London: Penguin/Allen Lane.
Sassen, Saskia. 1998. "The Transnationalization of Immigration Policy," in Frank Bonilla, Edwin Meléndez, Rebecca Morales, and María de los Ángeles (eds), *Borderless Borders*. Philadelphia: Temple Press, 53–67.
Schwartz, Jeremy. 2007. "U.S. Plan for Drug War Has Some in Mexico Worried," October 14, www.coxwashington.com.
Security and Prosperity Partnership. 2005a. www.spp.gov/2005_launch.asp.
Security and Prosperity Partnership. 2005b. Leaders' Communique. www.spp.gov/pdf/security-and-prosperity_partnership_of_north_America_statement.pdf.
Security and Prosperity Partnership. 2005c. Report to Leaders. http://www.spp.gov/report_to_leaders/Trilingual_Report_to_Leaders.pdf?dName=report_to_leaders.
Security and Prosperity Partnership. 2005d. Report to Leaders Annex. http://www.aec-fac.gc.ca/spp/spp-en.pdf.
Security and Prosperity Partnership. 2007a. Consultations. http://www.psp-spp.gc.ca/progress/consultations-en.aspx.
Security and Prosperity Partnership. 2007b. The Prosperity Agenda. http://www.psp-spp.gc.ca/overview/prosperity-en.aspx.
Security and Prosperity Partnership. 2007c. "Common Regulatory Principles and Inventory of Best Practices." http://www.spp.gov/docs/RCF_Common_Regulatory_Principles_Inventory_Best_Practices_FINAL.doc.
Security and Prosperity Partnership. 2010. US Government Website. http://www.spp.gov/.
Seed, Patricia. 2001. *American Pentimento. The Invention of Indians and the Pursuit of Riches*. Minneapolis, MN: University of Minnesota Press.
Selee, Andrew. 2008. "Overview of the Merida Initiative," Woodrow Wilson Center, May.
Serrano, Mónica. 2003. "Bordering on the Impossible: U.S.-Mexico Security Relations after September 11," in Andreas, Peter and Thomas J. Biersteker (ed.), *The Rebordering of North America: Integration and Exclusion in a New Security Context*. New York and London: Routledge.
Shah, Anup. 2007. "World Military Spending", February 25, at http://www.globalissues.org/Geopolitics/ArmsTrade/Spending.asp.
Sharp, Mitchell. 1972. "Canada-US Relations: Options for the Future," *International Perspectives*. Special Issue. Ottawa: Department of External Affairs, Autumn, 1–24.
Shirk, David. 2003. 'Law Enforcement and Security Challenges in the US-Mexican Border Region,' *Journal of Borderlands Studies* 18(1), Fall: 1–24.

Silliman, Stephen W. 2006. "Struggling with Labor, Working with Identities," in Martin Hall and Stephen Silliman, *Historical Archeology.* Oxford: Blackwell, 147–165, 153.

Slater, David. 2004. *Geopolitics and the Post-Colonial: Rethinking North-South Relations.* Oxford: Blackwell.

Smith, A. 1990. "Towards a global culture?" in M. Featherstone (ed.), *Global Culture: Nationalism, Globalization, and Modernity.* London: Sage.

Softwood Lumber Agreement. 2006. http://www.international.gc.ca/controls-controles/softwood-bois_oeuvre/other-autres/agreement-accord.aspx.

Spieldoch, Alexandra. 2004. "NAFTA through a Gender Lens: What 'Free Trade' Pacts Mean for Women," in *CounterPunch*, 30 December.

Staples, Steve. 2004. "Paul Martin, George W. Bush and Fortress North America." http://www.polarisinstitute.org.

Stewart, Patrick. 2002. "Multilateralism and Its Discontents," in Patrick Stewart and Shepard Forman (eds), *Multilateralism and United States Foreign Policy*, Boulder: Lynne Rienner, 12.

Stewart-Patterson, David. 2007. "North American Competitiveness Council Seeks to Strengthen Continental Prosperity," Fraser Forum, December 2006/January 2007, 12–13. www.ceocouncil.ca.

Stoler, Ann. 1989. "Rethinking Colonial Categories: European Communities and the Boundaries of Rule," *Comparative Studies in Society and History* 31, 134–61, 134–135.

Struever, Stuart. 1972. "The Hopewell Interaction Sphere in Riverine-Western Great Lakes Culture History," in Leone, Mark P. (ed.), *Contemporary Archaeology*. Carbondale: Southern Illinois University Press.

Studer, Isabel. 2007. "Obstacles to Integration: NAFTA's Institutional Weakness," in Isabel Studer and Carol Wise (eds), *Requiem or Revival: The Promise of North American Integration.* Washington, DC: Brookings Institution Press: 53–75.

Swyngedouw, E. 1997. "Neither global nor local: Glocalization and the Politics of Scale," in K.R. Cox (ed.), *Spaces of Globalization: Reasserting the Power of the Local*. New York: Guilford, 137–166.

Syzmanski, Marcela and Smith, Michael E. 2005. "Coherence and Conditionality in European Foreign Policy: Negotiating the EU-Mexico Global Agreement," *Journal of Common Market Studies* 43.1.

Taylor, Paul Schuster. 1981. *Labor on the Land: Collected Writings, 1930–1970.* New York, NY: Arno Press.

TEMBEC, INC. et al. v. United States of America, United States Court of International Trade, Consol. Court No. 05-00028, Slip Op. 06-152.

The Loewen Group and Raymond L. Loewen v. United States of America, Statement of Claim, October 30, 1998.

Thompson, John, and Stephen Randall. 1994. *Canada and the United States: Ambivalent Allies.* 2nd edn. Athens, Georgia: The University of Georgia Press.

Tomlinson, J. 1997. "'And besides, the wench is dead': Media Scandals and the Globalization of Communication," in J. Lull and S. Hinerman (eds), *Media Scandals: Morality and Desire in the Popular Culture Marketplace.* Cambridge: Polity Press; New York: Columbia University Press.

Tomlinson, J. 1999. *Globalization and Culture.* Cambridge: Polity Press.

Torres, Blanca. 1979. *Historia de la Revolución Mexicana VII. México en la Segunda Guerra mundial. Período 1940–1952*, Vol. 19. Mexico City: El Colegio de México.

Torres, Blanca. 2000. *México y el mundo, historia de sus relaciones exteriores. De la guerra fría al mundo bipolar, t. VII.* Mexico: Senado de la República, 207–212.

Torres, Blanca. 2004. "A diez años de las firma de los acuerdos ambientales vinculados al Tratado de Libre Comercio de América del Norte", *Foro Internacional* 44, 333–356.

Torres, Blanca 2009. "North American Transnational Actors and Mexico: Labor and Environmental Coalitions and Networks," in Jeffrey Ayres and Laura Macdonald (eds), *Contentious Politics in North America: National Protest and Transnational Collaboration Under Continental Integration.* Houndmills Basingstoke, Hampshire and New York: Palgrave Macmillan, 195–210.

Trew, Stuart. 2009. "The SPP is Dead, so Where's the Champagne?" http://www.rabble.ca/news/2009/08/spp-dead-so-wheres-champagne.

Tyler, Patrick E. 2003. "A deepening Fissure," *New York Times*, March 6.

US–Central American Free Trade Agreement. Available at http://www.ustr.gov/trade-agreements/free-trade-agreements.

US–Chile Free Trade Agreement. Available at http://www.ustr.gov/trade-agreements/free-trade-agreements.

US Government. 2005. *National Drug Control Strategy.* Washington: Office of National Drug Control Policy/Executive Office of the President of the United States.

US–Singapore Free Trade Agreement. Available at http://www.ustr.gov/trade-agreements/free-trade-agreements.

Ulloa, Berta. 1976. *La revolución intervenida.* Mexcio City: El Colegio de México, 25–26

United States Chamber of Commerce. 2007. "North American Competitiveness Council" http://www.uschamber.com/issues/index/international/nacc.htm.

United States of America v. Canada, Request for Arbitration, January 18, 2008, pursuant to Article XIV of the 2006 Softwood Lumber Agreement, accessed at www.ustr.gov, February 4, 2010.

US Congress. 2002. *Trade Act of 2002. Division B, Bipartisan Trade Promotion Authority, PL 107-201, Sec. 2102 (b)(3).* August 6.

US Department of Labor. 1994. *Migrant Farmworkers: Pursuing Security in an Unstable Market.* Research Report No. 5, Office of Program Economics. May.

United States Trade Representative. 2009. Press Release, "Tribunal Finds Canada Failed to Cure Breach of Softwood Lumber Agreement," September.

United States. White House. 2002. Security and Opportunity at the U.S.-Canada Border, June 28. http://www.whitehouse.gov/news/releases/2002/06/20020628.html.

United States. White House. 2006. News Release: "The Security and Prosperity Partnership of North America: Next Steps," March 31.

United States. White House. 2007. President Bush Participates in Joint Press Availability with Prime Minister Harper of Canada, and President Calderon of Mexico. http://www.whitehouse.gov/news/releases/2007/08/20070821-3.html.

United States. White House. 2008. Joint Statement by President Bush, President Calderon, Prime Minister Harper. http://georgewbush-whitehouse.archives.gov/news/releases/2008/04/20080422-4.html.

United States. White House. 2009. Joint Statement by North American Leaders: Guadalajara, August 10. http://www.whitehouse.gov/the_press_office/Joint-statement-by-North-American-leaders/.

United States. White House. 2010. The Security and Prosperity Partnership of North America. http://www.spp.gov/.

United States. White House. 2011. http://www.whitehouse.gov/the-press-office/2011/02/04/declaration-president-obama-and-prime-minister-harper-canada-beyond-bord.

United Steelworkers of America, AFL-CIO, CLC, et al Petitioners v. The United States of America, February 2001.

Urry, John. 2003. *Global Complexity*. Cambridge: Polity Press.

Valdez, Luz María. 1995. *Los indios en los censos de población*. Mexico: UNAM.

Valenzuela Arce, José Manuel. 1997. *El color de las sombras*. Mexico City: Plaza y Valdéz-Universidad Iberoamericana.

Van Kirk, Sylvia. 2002. "From 'Marrying-In' to 'Marrying-Out': Changing Patterns of Aboriginal/Non-Aboriginal Marriage in Colonial Canada," *Frontiers: A Journal of Women Studies* 23(3), 1–11.

Vargas Suárez, Rosío, Gómez Arnau, Remedios and Castro Rea, Julián (eds). 2001. *Las relaciones de México con Estados Unidos y Canadá: Una mirada al nuevo milenio*. Mexico City: Universidad Nacional Autónoma de México/Centro de Investigaciones sobre América del Norte.

Velasco C., Elizabeth. 2009. "Seguro Popular incumple fines: Cristina Laurell," *La Jornada*, 24 Nov.

Veraccini, Lorenzo. 2011. "Introducing Settler Colonial Studies," *Settler Colonial Studies* 1, 1–12, 6.

Vila, Pablo. 2000. *Crossing Borders, Reinforcing borders: Social Categories, Metaphors, and Narrative Identities on the U.S.-Mexico Frontier*. Austin TX: University of Texas Press.

Walker, Ruth. 2008. "Calderón Cites Nation's Progress," *Harvard University Gazette Online*, 14 Feb.

Wallace, William. 1999. "PM seeks freer trade in Americas," *Toronto Star*, June 30.

Waters, M. 1995. *Globalization.* London: Routledge, 4–5.
Weber, David J. 1992. "The Spanish Legacy in North America and the Historical Imagination," *The Western Historical Quarterly* 23(1), 4–24.
Weintraub, Sydney. 1990. *A Marriage of Convenience: Relations between Mexico and the United States.* New York: Oxford University Press.
Weintraub, Sidney. 2004a. "Trade, Investment, and Economic Growth," in Sidney Weintraub (ed.), *NAFTA's Impact on North America: The First Decade.* Washington, DC: Center for Strategic and International Studies, 3–20.
Weintraub, Sidney. 2004b. "Free Trade Area of the Americas: How to Screw Up A Perfectly Good Proposal," Center for Strategic and International Studies. *Issues in International Political Economy* 53, May.
Welsh, Jennifer. 2004. "North American Citizenship: Possibilities and Limits," *The Art of the State, Volume II: Thinking North America,* vol. 2(7): 33–50. Toronto, Ontario: The Institute for Research on Public Policy, http://www.irpp.org/books/archive/AOTS2/folio_7.pdf.
Weston, Ann. 2005. "The Canadian 'model' for public participation in trade policy formulation," Ottawa: North-South Institute, August.
Wiarda, Howard J. 2000. "Beyond the Pale: The Bureaucratic Politics of United States Policy in Mexico," *World Politics* 162, 4.
Wimmer, Andreas. 2002. *Nationalist Exclusion and Ethnic Conflict. Shadows of Modernity.* Cambridge: Cambridge University Press.
Winograd, B. 2004. "Follow the Stat," *American Journalism Review,* 27(1), February/March: 114–15.
Wolfe, Patrick. 2006. "Settler Colonialism and the Elimination of the Native," *Journal of Genocide Research* 8(4), 387–409, 387–88.
Wolfe, Robert. 2006. "Transparency and public participation in the Canadian trade policy process," unpublished paper accessed at http://post.queensu.ca/~wolfer/Papers/Consultations.pdf on June 16, p. 2.
Wood, Bryce. 1961. *The Making of the Good Neighbor Policy.* New York: W.W. Norton.
World Bank. 2008. http://siteresources.worldbank.org/NEWSSPANISH/Resources/remittances-LAC-SP.pdf.
World Trade Organization. n.d. DS308, Mexico—Tax Measures on Soft Drinks and Other Beverages, http://www.wto.org/english/tratop_e/dispu_e/cases_e/ds308_e.htm.
Young, Robert J.C. 1995. *Colonial Desire: Hybridity in Theory, Culture and Race.* London: Routledge.
Zabin, Carol, Michael Kearney, Anna Garcia, David Runsten, and Carole Nagengast. 1993. *Mixtec Migrants in California Agriculture: A New Cycle of Poverty.* Davis: California Institute for Rural Studies.
Zermeño, Sergio. 2005. *La desmodernidad mexicana y las alternativas a la violencia y la exclusión en nuestros días.* Mexico City: Oceano.
Zoellick, Robert. 2001. "Countering Terror with Trade," *Washington Post,* 20 September.

Zúñiga, David. 2000. "90% de trabajadores del país ganan menos de cinco minisalarios," *La Jornada*, 13 Oct.

Index

Note: Page references in bold relate to Tables and Figures.

American Federation of Labor (AFL-CIO) 117–18
Anti-globalization movement 49, 143
Asemblea Popular de los Pueblos de Oaxaca 39
Aspe, Pedro 99
Association of Southeast Asian Nations (ASEAN) 7,8
Aztecs
  myth of origin 28
Aztlán 28

Battle of Seattle 63
Beyond the Border *see* Canada-US joint declaration Beyond the Border
Big Idea 97
  debates about 65
Bilateral investment treaty (BITs) 59
Binational Organisations Indigenous Front *see* FIOB
Black Legend 1, 30, 33, 34
Bolivarian Alternative for the Americas (ALBA) 159
Bonior, David
  proposals 166
Border Brujo
  symbols 171
Border Citizens 36
Bow, Brian
  bilateral relations, on 204
Bracero Program 38, 111, 112, 115, 116, 117, 125
Brazil
  role of diplomacy 159
Building a North American Community ITF final report 99
Bush administration
  influence of 8

Bush, George, Sr 98, 126, 144
Bush, George W.
  Canadian public opinion, and 223
  continental strategies, on 95
  foreign policy 199, 206–208
  immigration policies, on 122, 181, 245, 280
  international law, and 261
  invasion of Iraq 280
  leaders' summit 74
  NAFTA, and 160
  oil, and 278
  prosperity and security, on 218
  re-election 89
  Secure Fence Act, and 40
  SPP, and 85, 98, 220
  trade policy 50, 61–4
Business Council on National Issues (BCNI) 88, 143
Business Roundtable 47, 98

Canada
  Anthony DePalma on 45–6
  dependence on foreign trade 9
  International Policy Statement 2005 217
  Liberal Party 8
Canada and North American integration 139–50
  Canadian model for public participation in trade policy formulation 141
  Canadian proposal to WTO on transparency 141
  consultation, and 140–42, 143
  deepening NAFTA 146–9
  exclusionary model of decision-making 149
  ITAC 142
  SAGITS 142

Security and Prosperity Partnership
  146–9
  lack of consultation 147–8
  opposition to 148–9
  policy style 147
9/11, effect of 146
Canada-Mexico relations 22, 279–80
Canada-US joint declaration Beyond the
  Border 13
Canada-US Partnership 1999 (CUSP)75, 77
Canada-US relations 21–2, 199–215
  accumulation of power by US 205–7
  Afghanistan 201
  bilateral trade relationship 200
  border security 201
  Canadian economic interests 215
  Canadian foreign policy, and 209, 212
  Canadian politics, and 199
  Canadian security 200–201
  Canadian support of US foreign policy
    objectives 211–13
  challenges 214
  changed policy-making environment
    205
  changes in US 202
  changes in US foreign policy 205
  co-operation, policy of 210
  contemporary imbalance 199–215
  developments in US politics 204
  domestic setting 202–205
  foreign policy 201
  incidents of co-operation 211
  Iraq, invasion of 212–13
  models for managing bilateral relations
    204
  multilateral conditions 207
  PDD 25 207
  policy shifts 202
  sources of change in domestic policy
    203
  unilateral action by US 207–8
  US challenges to international
    institutions and agreements 208
  US sense of moral conviction 208–9
  US use of military force 208
Canada-US Shared Border Accord 1995 75
Canada-US Smart Border Declaration 67, 73

Canada-US softwood lumber dispute 16,
  51–9
  agreement 58–9
  April 2006 truce 58
  bonds 57–8
  Canadian attitude to NAFTA, and 55
  Canadian environmental regulation, and
    55
  challenge to constitutionality of Chapter
    19 process 56–7
  Chapter 16 59–60
  Chapter 19, NAFTA, and 51–5
  issues left over from Lumber IV 56–9
  land management, and 52
  Lumber IV 51–9
  Uruguay Round Agreements
    Implementation Act, and 57
Canadian Council of Chief Executives
  (CCCE) 47 see also Business
  Council on National Issues (BCNI)
  argument for strategic bargain between
    Canada and US 164, 165
  New Frontiers 98
  strategy for new Canada-US partnership
    97–8
Cancun WTO Ministerial Conference 2003
  158
Caribbean Community (CARICOM)8
C.D. Howe Institute 96
Cellucci, Paul 99
Centro de Investigación y Seguridad
  Nacional (CISEN) 228
Chávez, Hugo
  Mar del Plata, on 159
Circular migration 193
Civil society
  international trade agreements, and
    139–43
    Brian Hocking on 141,142
  North American integration, and 143–6
    CUFTA, and 144
    NAAEC 146
    NAALC 145
    NAFTA side accords 144–5,146
    Pro-Canada Network 144
    Red Book 144
  periods of engagement 152

Civil society organizations
   cross-border collaborations, and 9
   essential issues 168
Clarkson, Stephen
   Uncle Sam and US: Globalization, Neoconservatism and the Canadian State 163
Clinton, Hillary 50
Coalition for Secure Trade and Efficient Borders 95–6
Colonialism
   access to wealth, and 30
   altepetl 31
   assymetric relationship between Spain and Great Britain 33–4
   Black Legend 30, 34
   competition in trade, and 34–5
   Creoles 31–2
   English 29
   exterminatory slavery, and 30
   extractive 30–31
   intermarriages, and 34
   knowledge production, and 32
   legal uniformity of citizens 32
   Leyes de Indias 31
   'logic of elimination' 29–30
   miscegenation, and 34, 35
   post-colonial theory 33
   repartimiento de afectos 31
   República de Españoles 31
   República de Indios 31
   rivalry between Spain and England 33
   settler and extractive distinguished 27
   Spanish 30
   tequio 31
Commission for Environmental Cooperation (CEC) 71
Competition Policy Review Panel 103
Conservative governments 9
Conservative/right wing traditions
   government, and 8
Co-operation
   meaning 75
Corporate sector
   continentalization of 89–90
Council of Foreign Relations (CFR) 99, 102
Creolisation 21

Critical social theory
   globalization, of 23
CUFTA
   Chapter 16 59
   corporate privileges, and 162–3
   debates over 46
   movement against 151
   origins 86
   shallow integration, and 87
Cultural change 183–96
   cultural melding and mediation 189
   cultural shores of North America 195–6
   Mexican immigrants to US 193–5
      communications technology 194–5
Cultural globalization 187
Curnoe, Greg
   America 176–8

Daddy Yankee
   Barrio Fino 183–5
   Gasolina 183–5
d'Aquino, Thomas
   strategy for new Canada-US partnership 97–8
Darwin, Charles 195
Declaration of San Xavier 41
Deep integration (DI) 14, 16, 17, 52, 80, 85, 89, 93, 96, 97, 99, 103, 105, 147, 148, 152, 162, 164, 219, 230
   meaning 85
   policy recommendations for 14, 16
   projects as political artefacts 92
Deeper integration
   predictions of inevitability of 88
Democracy
   economic integration agenda, and 19
Democratic deficit 19–20
DePalma, Anthony
   Canada, on 45–6
   Mexico, on 45–6
Department of Foreign Affairs and International Trade (DFAIT) 70, 212
Department of Homeland Security (DHS) 98, 102
Deterritorialization 188–9
   migration, and 188–9

DI *see* Deep integration
Diasporas 191, 192
   questions raised by 39
Dobbin, Murray
   deep integration,on 165
Dobson,Wendy
   'Big Idea' 97
Doha Development Round 63,64, 65
DR-CAFTA 63–4,65
Dual bilateralism 78

Economic development strategies 90–92
   struggles over space and scale 90
Economic growth
   unevenly distributed benefits 10
European Union (EU)
   model established by 256
   NAFTA, and 70–71

FIOB 27, 37, 38, 39, 42
   electoral policies in Oaxaca, and 39
   functions of 39
Foreign Direct Investment (FDI) 49
Foreign policy
   Canada 199, 201, 202, 206, 210, 212, 215, 217, 222, 224
   Canada-US relations, and 22
   integration, and 70, 87
   Mexico 280
   US 64, 202, 203, 205–215
Fox, Claire
Fox, Vicente 85, 95, 120–128
   globalized border, on 179,180
Free idea zone
   nature of 20
Free Trade Area of the Americas (FTAA) 49, 95,155–60
   challenge to agenda 155–6
   continuity of opposition to 156
Fulbright, Senator William
   power, on 209

Gabriel, Juan
   songs 194
Gadsen Purchase 1853 40
Galarza, Ernesto
   bracero program, on 111–12

Canclini, Néstor García
   cultural imperialism, on 187–8
General Agreement on Tariffs and Trade (GATT) 50, 51, 140, 141, 143, 258
Gini index
   Canada 11
   Mexico 6, 11
   US 6
Global cultural mix 185–8
   cultural borrowing 186
   cultural stresses 187
   Latin inflection 185–6
   linguistic hybridity 86
   nation state, and 187
   Quebec separatist movement 187
Globalization
   anti-globalization movement 49, 143
   continental policy harmonization, and 255
   'cosmopolitan democracy', and 239
   cultural 187
   cultural competency, and 193
   democratic redesign 166
   destructive effects 37
   deterritorialization, and 191
   DI projects, and 92
   Doreen Massey on 91
   economic and technological phenomenon, as 256
   economic growth, and 110
   effect 186
   ethno-national conflict, and 36
   frictions within 104
   human migration, and 37
   hybrid identities, and 172, 181
   international markets, of 128
   international relations, and 129, 130, 131, 134, 135, 136, 237
   James Lull on 21
   John Urry on 91–2
   Juan Gabriel on 194
   NAFTA debates, and 51
   neoliberal agenda 245, 249
   neoliberal theories 236
   North American integration, and 88
   Raymond A. Morrow on 22–3
   social costs 248

social upheavals, and 249
steel industry 262
Stephen Clarkson on 163
suffering, and 240
Gómez-Peña, Guillermo
  America, on 180
  Border Brujo 171–2
  identity and culture, on 180
  Taller de Arte Fronterizo 179
  The Great Mojado Invasion, Part 2 182
  theorization of borders 20
Guanajuato Agreement 95

Hemispheric Social Alliance (HAS-ASC) 19, 151, 152,155–60
  alternative proposal for regional integration 156
  civil society committee 157
  contribution of 167
  mobilization of public opinion 158
  strategic leadership 157
  transfer to Brazil 158
Heredia, Carlos
  proposals 166
Hicks, Emily
  Border Writing 179
Hispanic
  use of term 40
Hocking, Brian
  trade issues,on 141,142
Homo nullius 29
House of Commons (Canada)
  Standing Committee on Foreign Affairs and International Trade 96
'Hub and spokes' model 22
Human rights
  immigration, and 136, 179
Hybrid identities
  use of term 20
Hybridization
  cultural 21
  transculturation, and 189–90
Hybridity 172–4
  biological and botanical origins 172
  colonialism, and 173
  meaning 172–4
  origin, idea of 172–3

transnationalism, and 37
Identities
  threat to 20
Identities in flux 20–21
Immigration 18
  US agenda 65
  apparent illegal status 114
  Canadian laws 230
  Canadian officials 45
  CCCE, and 164
  control of borders, and 135
  CUSP, and 77
  effect 194
  emergency in US/Mexico borderlands 41
  George W. Bush, and 122, 181, 245, 280
  globalizing agreements, and 175
  harmonization of policy 219, 221
  human rights, and 136, 179
  ideological underpinnings of debates 250
  Latino vote, and 127
  Mexican 220
  Mexican peasants to US 18
  Mexicans to US 110, 114, 119
  new policy, need for 273
  officials 45
  Proposition 187, and 126
  restrictive 36
  Samuel Huntington on 14
  undocumented 113, 120
  US labour policy, and 112
  US legislation 38
  US-made policy 223
Independent Task Force on the Future of North America (ITF) 99
Indigeneity 27–42
  articulation, and 27
  colonialism, and *see* Colonialism
  exchanges between Meso-American and northern Indigenous societies 28
  FIOB *see* FIOB
  migration and border-crossing rights 36
  oral history 28
  transnationalism, and *see* Transnationalism

Treaty of Guadalupe Hidalgo (1848) 35–6
Treaty of Oregon (1846) 35
US/Mexico border policies 36
Indigenization 190–91
  McDonald's, and 190–91
  mutual transformation of cultures, and 190
  national boundaries, within 191
Indigenous Border Summit of the Americas 41
Indigenous communities 15
Indigenous migration
  effect 38
Indigenous populations
  founding human reality, as 15
Immigration and Naturalization Service (INS) 114, 118
Independent Task Force on the Future of North America (ITF) 99, 100, 102
  composition 99
  final report 99–100
  Toronto meeting 99
Informal economy
  growth of 11
INSETS 225
Institute for Public Policy 96
Integrated Border Enforcement Teams (IBETS) 225, 227
Integration
  concept difficult to define 70
  definition 70
  federalism, and 70
  meaning 75
  NAFTA, and 70
  power asymmetries, and 71–2
  public opinion, and 89
  Smart Border policies 70
Intergovernmental relations 21–23
International Criminal Court (ICC) 212
International Joint Commission (IJC) 260, 261
International Labour Organisation (ILO) 156
International migrants 109–36
  asymmetry of power 132–3
  California economy 132
  Constitution, and 131
  dialectical understanding of vulnerability 109–36
  dialectics 129–31
  human rights, and 128
  integration, and 130
  law and sociology 135
  Schengen Agreement 133
  social process 128
  sovereignty, exercise of 134–5
  theoretical framework 128–36
  US/Mexico border 109–10
  virtual contradiction between immigration and human rights 133–4
International Workers Day 2006 181

Jay Treaty 1794 35

Krauze, Enrique
  Mexico, on 231–2

LaDuke, Winona
  Indigenous North America, idea of 27
Landrum-Griffin Act 1959 111
Latin America
  failure of economic growth 151
Latino
  use of term 40
Logic of elimination
  colonialism, and 29

Manley, John 99
Martí, José
  Our America 3
Massey, Doreen
  globalization, on 91
McDougall, John
  Canadian military action, on 210–11
Mercado Común del Sur (Mercosur) 7, 8, 159
Mérida Initiative (MI) 229, 230
Mestizos 34
Métissage 34
Mexican migration to US 110–28
  AFL-CIO, and 117–18
  Águila Azteca 123
  anti-Mexican ideology 114
  bilateral agreement, need for 110–11

bilateral *de facto* labour market 127
bracero agreements 111–12, 116
Brown v Texas Board of Education 123
citizenship 124
criminalization of illegal aliens by ethnic profile 114
end of *bracero* programs 117–18
escape valve 114–18
Fox, Vicente 120–24
General Leonard Chapman, and 118–19
George W. Bush, and 122
Governor Pete Wilson, and 113
Guanajuato 121–2
historical perspective 110–14
human rights violations 120
indifference of Mexican civil society 116–17
indifference of Mexican government 115–16
INS statistics 114
Latino vote in US 124, 126, 127
Mexican American organizations in US 123
'Mexican illegal question' 119
Mexican racism, and 116–17
nationality 124
Operation Gatekeeper 119–20
options for agreement on migrant workers 125
peasants 115
positive impact on US economy 127
Proposition 187 113, 126–7
racism, and 112–13
racist ideologies of White supremacy 121
recessions, and 118
reinforcement of consular protection 123–4
'silent invasion' issue 118–20
temporary visa programs 125
US ambivalence about 112–13
voting rights 124–5
Wagner Labour Act 1935 111
Zedillo, President Ernesto 119–20
Mexican racism 116–17
Mexico
  Anglo-American war against 35
  Anthony DePalma on 45–6
  average individual income 11
  circular from Secretariat of Foreign Affairs 116
  dependence on foreign trade 9
  development process of North America, and 2
  household Gini index 11
  regional security bubble, and 217
Mexico-US relations 22–3, 231–52
  agency argument 240
  agency as autonomous empowerment 250–52
  agency as transnational civil society networks 248
  agency, dialogue and transformative change 247
  anti-Americanism 249–50
  anti-realists 238
  Calderón, Felipe 234–5
  conditions of possibility for change 247–52
  constructivist theories of international relations 239
  contradictions of status quo 245–6
  critical social theory, implications of 238–40
  debates in international relations theory 237–8
  disputes 236
  facilitating cross-border democracy 248
  fragility of democratic consolidation in Mexico 244
  globalism 237–8
  globalizing transnational dialogue 248–50
  hegemony, systems of 236
  illegal migration 233
  impasse thesis 240–46
  injustice and social costs of globalization from below 248–50
  interpretive perspectives 236–7
  intersecting hegemonies 240–46
  Mexican economy 243–4
  Mexican modernization as democratization 250–52
  Mexican public health system 235
  Mexican reform 251
  Mexico as failed state 232

Mexico, status of 231
migration pattern, structure of 245–6
Minutemen 233–4
myths of modernization 242–5
NAFTA, myth of 242–3
neo-Gramscian approach 239
North-South frontier: beyond official discourses 231–6
OECD indicators of modernization 244
options for integration 238
persistence of internal hegemony in Mexico 242
potential alternatives 237
poverty in Mexico 234–5
realism 237
'realist' theories 236
structural argument 240
structural reproduction 245–6
tension 233
transformative thesis 247–52
tree planting in Mexico 234
two theses on structure and agency 240
US hegemony 241–2
Zapatista movement 249, 251
Migration 17–18
deterritorialization, and 188–9
dialectic of migrants' vulnerability **129**
disadvantages of Indigenous migrants in US 38
economic globalization, and 37–8
intense movements of people 13
Mexican migration to US 38
Miscegenation 34, 35
differing perspectives 34, 35
Mitrany, David
neo-functionalism, and 69
Mixtecs 38
Montebello Summit 74
Montreal
mob attack on Parliament 1849 162
Multi-level governance
concept of 76

NAFTA
administration 258
Canada-US softwood lumber dispute 51–9 *see also* Canada-US softwood lumber dispute

Chapter 11 46, 51, 59–62
  Loewen Group 60
  Methanex corporation 60–61
  perceived weaknesses 61–2
  process transparency 62
Chapter 19 46, 51–5
Clinton administration, and 63
cornerstone of continental co-operation, as 72
corporate privileges, and 162–3
criticism of 50
degrees of integration and separation 53–5
debates over 46
dispute settlement mechanisms 51
EU, and 70–71
impact of 47–8
implementation 8
inventor-state dispute process 259
judicial capacities 258–9
legislative capacity 258
limitations 46
movement against 151
myth of 242–3
plan to re-launch 280
proposals for reform 94–5
shallow integration, and 87
shallow PTA, as 53
shortcomings 257–8
statistics 48–9
  foreign direct investment 49
  trade 48–9
trade liberalization, and 49–50
trade politics, and 49–50
transborder governance 259
US hegemonic power, and 259
weaknesses of 66
NAFTA engagement 153–5
cross-border working relationships 155
social agenda 154
tri-national alliance of coalitions 153–4
NAFTA Free Trade Commission 71
NAFTA Plus 95, 152
NAFTA Plus or minus 160–61
Neo-functionalism 69–72
central theoretical postulations 68
David Mitrany 69
integration, and 70

political spill-over 69–70
'spill-over' 69
New Frontiers 98
New regionalism 91, 92
9/11
   crossing procedures, and 36
   effect on North American agenda 73
North America
   accelerated market integration 9
   asymmetry 4
   'Black Legend' 1, 30, 33, 34
   breakdown of continental marketplace 263–4
      automobiles 264
      textiles 264
   common historical enterprise as theoretical prospect 271
   comparative world regions, and 256
   competition with other blocs and major economies 8
   conservative governments 8–9
   consolidating as security community **94**
   convergence of values 14
   co-operation for security and military purposes 13
   cultural mix 14
   current ideological landscape 8
   deep integration 14
   direction of continental governance 268–9
   economic outlook **10**
   economic performance 9
   enigma, as 255
   facts and trends defining 3–14
   formal trilateral institutionalization 257–9
   geographic and demographic facts **5**
   informal economy 11–12
   intense movements of people 13
   land area 4
   linguistic borders 14
   market integration **11**
   pervasive social problems 13–14
   population 4
   population movements 3
   real nature of 23–4
   realities constituting governance 257
   regional market integration 9–11
   security zone, as 265–8
      post-9/11 context 265–6
      SPP 266–7
   societal realities 2–3
   standing relative to other blocs and leading economies 4, 8
   sub-prime financial crisis 2007 268
   sustainability 12
   three sovereign states 1
   trade within **48**
   transborder governance 260
      steel 261–2
      water 260–61
   transnational crime 12
   transnational political networks 9
   transportation systems 12
   trinational policy harmonization 262–3
      financial services 263
      intellectual property rights for pharmaceuticals 262–3
   world regions, as 7
   world region with multiple identities 269
   world's leading region 4
North America's Super Corridor Coalition (NASCO)
   aim of 12
North American Aerospace Defence Command (NORAD) 13, 66, 211, 214, 225
North American Agreement on Environmental Co-operation (NAAEC) 12–13, 145, 146
North American Agreement on Labour Co-operation (NAALC) 145, 146
North American Competitiveness Council (NACC) 65, 74, 80, 102, 165
   creation of 102
   three priorities 102
North American economic integration 45
   see also Integration
   Bush administration, and 62–3
   Clinton administration, and 63
   mature trade agreement, as 66
   salience of the border 45–7
   security, and 47

US malaise over trade liberalization 65
North American Energy Security Initiative 74
North American hybrid identities 171–182
  cultural studies, and 178
  deportation of illegal workers 181
  hybridity as fusion 181–2
  Latin American reactions to US hegemony 178
  US/Mexico border 174–6 see also US/Mexico border
North American integration
  saying no to 221–2
    Canada and Mexico as natural allies 221
    contention between Canadian and Mexican decision makers 222
North American Leaders' Summit Cancun 102
North American Leaders' Summit Guadalajara 67, 68
North American Regulatory Framework 102
North American Security and Prosperity Initiative (NASPI) 96, 98, 100
North American security co-operation 217–30
  Canadian perspective 222–6
    Chrétien, Jean 223
    foreign policy 224
    Harper government 224–5
    IBETS 225
    INSETS 225
    Mexican participation in perimeter, and 224
    NORAD 225
    NORTHCOM 225
    perimeter, concept of 223, 224
    sovereignty 222–3
  common security perimeter 218
  Mexican perspective 226–30
    Adolfo Aguílar Zínser 228
    border security 226
    corruption 227–8
    lack of security confidence along border 229
    Mérida initiative 229
    migration 226–7
    national security strategy after 2000 general election 228
    political infighting 228
    sovereignty 229
    "whole enchilada" 229–30
  smart border agreements 230
North American Union
  secret scheme for, whether 16
  SPP, and 80
NORTHCOM (Northern Command) 13, 103, 225

Oaxacalifornia 37
Obama, Barack 50
López Obrador, Andrés Manuel
  imaginary citizens, on 163
Organization of American States (OAS) 120, 157, 159
Our North America 3
  Mexican standpoint 271–81

Paradigms of regionalism 8
Paradox of integration 89
Partido Acción Nacional (PAN) 234, 235, 245, 251, 252
Partido de la Revolución Democrática (PRD) 244, 252
Partido Revolucionario Institucional (PRI) 116, 120, 121, 147, 153
Partnership
  rhetoric 164
Paz, Octavio
  US-Mexico relations, on 250
Peoples' Summit of the Americas
  declaration 159–60
Performance
  meaning 90
Perle, Richard 98
Popular music 184, 186, 187, 191, 193, 194, 195
Population movements/migration 3
Post-9/11 North American security context 219–21
  border agreements with US 220
  Conference Board of Canada 221
  free flow of goods, business and travel 219

pressures for cooperation, and 16
security threats from Canada and
    Mexico 219–20
SPP 220
terrorists, and 219
Poverty
recent economic restructuring, and 17
Preferential Trading Agreement (PTA) 53
Proposition 200 114
Public opinion
integration, and 89

Quebec
separatist movement 187

Racism
internal geopolitics of 32
Mexican immigrants, about 38, 112,
    116, 117, 126
Reggaetón 21, 183–5
República de Españoles 31
República de Indios 31
Réseau québécois sur l'integration
    continentale (RQIC) 144, 154
Reterritorialization 191–3
Chilean popular culture 192
consumer communication technologies
    192
diasporas, and 191–3
ethnic shopping malls 192–3
media and culture industries 191
nostalgia 192
Rozental, Andrés 99

Sectoral Advisory Group on International
    Trade (SAGIT) 142, 143
Secure Fence Act 2006 40–41
Securitization
operation of 40
Security
impact of 17
Security agenda
implications 17
Security and Prosperity Partnership of North
    America (SPP) 1, 16, 65, 67–83,
    85–105
agenda setting 92–7

agendas 73
bilateral nature of 78
building consensus **93**
'bureaucratic integration' 68
challenges and implications for
    governance in North America 79–82
complex, bureaucratic-led policymaking
    75–6
consensus-building 97–100
consolidation and performance of
    security agenda 102–3
cooperation, and 67–8, 74–5
cooperation between business and
    political elites 81
criticisms of 79
CUSP, and 77
deep integration project 103–4
demise of 104
framework for cooperation, as 75
further political integration, as 68
goals 73
implementation 67
incrementalism 76–7
Montebello Summit 74
multi-level governance 76
NAFTA, and 77
NAFTA plus or minus, and 160–61
nature of transnational regionalization,
    and 104
official launch 100
origins 85–6
political realities, and 76
prelude to North American
    union, whether 80
private sector, and 80–81
prosperity agenda 101–2
security, and 81–2
security agenda 103
socio-political variables, and 82
Smart Border policies, and 78
supposed death of 67
targeted initiatives 101
two speed co-operation 78
working groups 74
Seed, Patricia
colonialism, on 29
Shallow integration 87–8

Silent invasion 118
Smart Border
 plans, call for 73
Smart Border policies
 cooperation, and 74–5
Smith, Anthony D.
 culture, on 186
Softwood Lumber Agreement *see* Canada-US softwood lumber dispute
Strategic partners
 Canada and Mexico 22

Taft-Hartley Labor Act 1947 111
Terra nullius 29, 33
Tohono O'odham 37, 40–42
 challenge to conceptions of state sovereignty and borders 42
 lack of protection 36
 movement across borders 40
 occupation of land of 40
 struggle of 27
 territorially and legally based in US
Trade promotion agreements 64
Trans-border Indigenous peoples
 vulnerability 35
Transculturation 189–90
 hybridization, and 189–90
 modern technology, and 189
Transnational corporation 81, 259, 263, 264, 268
Transnational crime
 growth of 12
Transnational governance agreements
 network of 23
Transnational political action
 usefulness of 39
Transnationalism 36–42
 border controls, and 40
 category, as 36
 challenge to Eurocentric conceptions of borders 42
 economic globalization, and 37
 meaning 36–7
 security policies, and 39
Treaty of Amity 1794 35
Treaty of Guadalupe Hidalgo 35
Treaty of Oregon (1846) 35

Truman, President
 one-armed economist, on 47
Turtle Island 3, 27, 28, 37, 42
 diversity of 27–8

Unauthorized migration
 main factor propelling 13
Undocumented migrants 12, 13
Undocumented workers 12, 13
Urry, John
 globalization, on 91
US Borders
 closure of, effect 17, 95–6
US Business Round Table 47, 98
US Immigration and Naturalization Service (INS) 114
US/Mexico Border 109–10, 174–6
 arts projects 179–80
 border brujo, and 175
 nature of 174
 9/11, and 109
 Secure Fence Act 175
 US/Canada border, and 176
US-Mexico Border Partnership 67, 73
 migrant labour, and 175
 vital needs at borderlands 110
US/Mexico relations 271–81
 agenda 276–9
 asymmetry 111
 clashes of interests 274
 Good Neighbour Policy 276
 heavily guarded border 272–3
 illegal drugs 277
 integration, and 275
 Mexican exports to US 277
 Mexican Revolution 272
 NAFTA, and 272
 National Guard 271–2
 oil 278
 Operation Interception 276
 undocumented migration 276
 unilateral intervention, and 278–9
 water 278

Wagner Labour Act 1935 111
Western Hemisphere Travel Initiative 103
World Bank 11, 47, 49

World Social Forum 158
World Trade Organization (WTO) 8, 49

Zapatista movement 249, 251
Zapotecs 38

THE INTERNATIONAL POLITICAL ECONOMY OF NEW REGIONALISMS SERIES

Other titles in the series

Global and Regional Problems
Towards an Interdisciplinary Study
*Edited by Pami Aalto, Vilho Harle
and Sami Moisio*

The Ashgate Research Companion to
Regionalisms
*Edited by Timothy M. Shaw, J. Andrew Grant
and Scarlett Cornelissen*

Asymmetric Trade Negotiations
*Sanoussi Bilal, Philippe De Lombaerde
and Diana Tussie*

The Rise of the Networking Region
The Challenges of Regional Collaboration
in a Globalized World
*Edited by Harald Baldersheim, Are Vegard
Haug and Morten Øgård*

Shifting Geo-Economic Power of the Gulf
Oil, Finance and Institutions
*Edited by Matteo Legrenzi
and Bessma Momani*

Building Regions
The Regionalization of the World Order
Luk Van Langenhove

National Solutions to Trans-Border
Problems?
The Governance of Security and Risk
in a Post-NAFTA North America
Edited by Isidro Morales

The Euro in the 21st Century
Economic Crisis and Financial Uproar
María Lorca-Susino

Crafting an African Security Architecture
Addressing Regional Peace and Conflict
in the 21st Century
Edited by Hany Besada

Comparative Regional Integration
Europe and Beyond
Edited by Finn Laursen

The Rise of China
and the Capitalist World Order
Edited by Li Xing

The EU and World Regionalism
The Makability of Regions in the 21st
Century
*Edited by Philippe De Lombaerde
and Michael Schultz*

The Role of the European Union in Asia
China and India as Strategic Partners
*Edited by Bart Gaens, Juha Jokela
and Eija Limnell*

China and the Global Politics
of Regionalization
Edited by Emilian Kavalski

Clash or Cooperation of Civilizations?
Overlapping Integration and Identities
Edited by Wolfgang Zank

New Perspectives on Globalization and
Antiglobalization: Prospects for a New
World Order?
Edited by Henry Veltmeyer

Governing Regional Integration for
Development: Monitoring Experiences,
Methods and Prospects
*Edited by Philippe De Lombaerde,
Antoni Estevadeordal and Kati Suominen*

Europe-Asia Interregional Relations
A Decade of ASEM
Edited by Bart Gaens

Cruising in the Global Economy
Profits, Pleasure and Work at Sea
Christine B.N. Chin

Beyond Regionalism?
Regional Cooperation, Regionalism and
Regionalization in the Middle East
*Edited by Cilja Harders
and Matteo Legrenzi*

The EU-Russian Energy Dialogue
Europe's Future Energy Security
Edited by Pami Aalto

Regionalism, Globalisation
and International Order
Europe and Southeast Asia
Jens-Uwe Wunderlich

EU Development Policy
and Poverty Reduction
Enhancing Effectiveness
Edited by Wil Hout

An East Asian Model for Latin
American Success
The New Path
Anil Hira

European Union and New Regionalism
Regional Actors and Global Governance
in a Post-Hegemonic Era.
Second Edition
Edited by Mario Telò

Regional Integration and Poverty
*Edited by Dirk Willem te Velde
and the Overseas Development Institute*

Redefining the Pacific?
Regionalism Past, Present and Future
*Edited by Jenny Bryant-Tokalau
and Ian Frazer*

The Limits of Regionalism
NAFTA's Labour Accord
Robert G. Finbow

Latin America's Quest for Globalization
The Role of Spanish Firms
*Edited by Félix E. Martín
and Pablo Toral*

Exchange Rate Crises
in Developing Countries
The Political Role of the Banking Sector
Michael G. Hall

Globalization and Antiglobalization
Dynamics of Change in the New
World Order
Edited by Henry Veltmeyer

Twisting Arms and Flexing Muscles
Humanitarian Intervention and
Peacebuilding in Perspective
*Edited by Natalie Mychajlyszyn
and Timothy M. Shaw*

Asia Pacific and Human Rights
A Global Political Economy Perspective
Paul Close and David Askew

Demilitarisation and Peace-Building
in Southern Africa
Volume II – National and
Regional Experiences
*Edited by Peter Batchelor
and Kees Kingma*

Demilitarisation and Peace-Building
in Southern Africa
Volume I – Concepts and Processes
*Edited by Peter Batchelor
and Kees Kingma*

Reforging the Weakest Link
Global Political Economy and Post-Soviet
Change in Russia, Ukraine and Belarus
Edited by Neil Robinson

Persistent Permeability?
Regionalism, Localism, and Globalization
in the Middle East
*Edited by Bassel F. Salloukh
and Rex Brynen*

The New Political Economy of United
States-Caribbean Relations
The Apparel Industry and the Politics
of NAFTA Parity
Tony Heron

The Nordic Regions and the European Union
*Edited by Søren Dosenrode
and Henrik Halkier*